FOSTERING NATION?

i

Studies in
Childhood and Family
in Canada

A broad-ranging series that publishes scholarship from various disciplines, approaches and perspectives relevant to the concepts and relations of childhood and family in Canada. Our interests also include, but are not limited to, interdisciplinary approaches and theoretical investigations of gender, race, sexuality, geography, language and culture within these categories of experience, historical and contemporary.

Series Editor:
Cynthia Comacchio
History Department
Wilfrid Laurier University

For literature and media related projects, send proposals to:
Lisa Quinn, Acquisitions Editor
Wilfrid Laurier University Press
75 University Avenue West
Waterloo, ON
Canada N2L 3C5
Phone: 519-884-0710 ext. 2843
Fax: 519-725-1399
Email: quinn@press.wlu.ca

For all other disciplines, send proposals to:
Ryan Chynces, Acquisitions Editor
Wilfrid Laurier University Press
75 University Avenue West
Waterloo, ON
Canada N2L 3C5
Phone: 519-884-0710 ext. 2034
Fax: 519-725-1399
Email: rchynces@wlu.ca

FOSTERING NATION?

Canada Confronts Its History
of Childhood Disadvantage

Veronica Strong-Boag

Wilfrid Laurier University Press

[WLU]

This book has been published with the help of a grant from the Canadian Federation for the Humanities and Social Sciences, through the Aid to Scholarly Publications Programme, using funds provided by the Social Sciences and Humanities Research Council of Canada. We acknowledge the financial support of the Government of Canada through the Canada Book Fund for our publishing activities.

Library and Archives Canada Cataloguing in Publication

Strong-Boag, Veronica Jane, 1947–
    Fostering nation? Canada confronts its history of childhood disadvantage / Veronica Strong-Boag.

(Studies in childhood and family in Canada series)
Includes bibliographical references and index.
Also available in electronic format.
ISBN 978-1-55458-337-9 (paper)

    1. Child welfare—Canada—History. I. Title. II. Series: Studies in childhood and family in Canada

HV745.A6S774 2011   362.70971   C2010-905158-0

ISBN 978-1-55458-319-5
Electronic format.

    1. Child welfare—Canada—History. I. Title. II. Series: Studies in childhood and family in Canada (Online)

HV745.A6S774 2011a   362.70971   C2010-905159-9

Cover design by Angela Booth Malleau. Cover photograph courtesy of the Malleau family. Text design by Catharine Bonas-Taylor.

© 2011 Wilfrid Laurier University Press
Waterloo, Ontario, Canada
www.wlupress.wlu.ca
This printing 2015

This book is printed on FSC® recycled paper and is certified Ecologo. It is made from 100% post-consumer fibre, processed chlorine free, and manufactured using biogas energy.

Printed in Canada

*For the feminist students, staff, faculty, and activists who
have made me a better historian and scholar*

CONTENTS

ACKNOWLEDGEMENTS

A generation of children and young people whose courage and need deserve our close attention has inspired *Fostering Nation?*. I have always thought of them as I composed this volume. I am also very grateful for the assistance and friendship along the way of Nora Angeles, Wynn Archibald, Bettina Bradbury, Jane Charles, Cynthia Comacchio, Gillian Creese, Karen Dubinsky, Tara Fenwick, Wendy Frisby, Sneja Gunew, Tineke Hellwig, Ellen Herman, Franca Iacovetta, Mona Gleason, Jan Hare, Vinit Khosla, Andrée Léveque, Kristina Llewellyn, Angus McLaren, Arlene McLaren, Kathy Mezei, Suzanne Morton, Tamara Myers, Bryan Palmer, Leslie Paris, Nancy Roberts, Joan Sangster, Mary Lynn Stewart, Jennifer Stoddart, Richard Sullivan, and Susan Walsh. They have made life easier and more fun and made me think harder about my arguments. Ruppa Bagga, Patricia Barkaskas, Bjorg Hjartardottir, Sally Mennill, Michele Murphy, Laurie Parsons, and Gabriel Ross have provided indispensable research assistance. Canada's librarians and archivists have everywhere made research more possible. I especially appreciate their efforts to make records of every kind electronically available. This is especially important for those of us who live on the periphery of an enormous country. I am also tremendously grateful to the University of British Columbia's Women's and Gender Studies Programme in the Faculty of Arts, the Centre for Women's and Gender Studies in the School for Interdisciplinary Studies, and the Department of Educational Studies in the Faculty of Education for their generous support of scholarship on disadvantaged youngsters. I tested many of the ideas for this book on my undergraduate students in women's and gender studies. Their enthusiasm and insights helped me in ways they could not have imagined. Like many other fortunate Canadian scholars, I owe a great deal to the financial support of the Social Science and Humanities Research Council of Canada and of my own institution, the University of British Columbia. Cynthia Comacchio, who is the general editor of the series in which this volume appears, has been indispensable in her encouragement and persistence. My editor at Wilfrid Laurier University Press, Lisa Quinn, juggles many manuscripts, and I was glad that mine got her attention. I am also grateful to the anonymous readers who gave a close reading to an earlier draft. Finally, I would like to recognize my sons, Christopher, Dominic, and Gabriel, my new daughter-in-law, Jude Russell, and my ever-present canine companion, Emma, for their constant reminders of life beyond the sad tales I encountered in writing *Fostering Nation?* My thanks to all of you.

INTRODUCTION

Fostering Nation? is not a happy book. It struggled throughout its creation to escape submersion in the tide of human tragedies that threads throughout the history of child welfare in Canada. Many girls and boys have not found kindness and assistance in their dealings with adults. Too frequently, they in turn have become women and men with compromised capacities to care for others. No one should be indifferent to this suffering. Children's pain and failure to reach potential through many generations disgrace all of us and most notably those Canadians in charge of public affairs. Sadness and anger in this volume flow from its investigations of both the recurring anguish of youngsters and the apparently profound indifference of so many adults.

Recent public reports readily feed such sentiments. In 1991, Canada signed the 1989 United Nations *Convention on the Rights of the Child.*[1] Although signature encouraged official support for such worthy causes as a ban on land mines and improvements in education and health for the world's children, the convention has at best "unevenly" informed "federal and provincial legislation, policy, program support and investment."[2] Reports from the UN Children's Fund (UNICEF) in 2007 and 2009 highlighted the gap between the goals of the international convention and the reality facing many Canadian girls and boys. After several decades of neo-conservatism's zealous attack on social security, one in six children live in poverty, and large numbers reside in state care and detention. Aboriginal youngsters are among the most terribly disadvantaged. Their mortality, morbidity, and educational and employment prospects provide an object lesson in the costs of prejudice and structurally induced inequalities.[3] Even the

Canadian Senate, an institution established by Sir John A. Macdonald in 1867 to protect the interests of the rich, has been compelled to speak out on behalf of the nation's youngest "silenced citizens."[4] Once again, Canada has been condemned as a poor parent, promising much and delivering significantly less.

Such damning assessments merely update the conclusions of diverse inquiries and commissions over many decades. Like the 1889 report of the Royal Commission on the Relations of Labour and Capital, Dr. Peter Bryce's 1907 observations on residential schools, the Canadian Welfare Council's denunciations of child welfare programs in provinces such as New Brunswick and Alberta between the Great Wars, David Croll's 1971 *Report of the Special Senate Committee on Poverty*, and the 2000 report on child abuse by the Law Reform Commission of Canada, they detail truncated lives and broken hearts and illuminate conditions that should unsettle consciences and produce redress.[5]

Yet for all the many moments of despair encountered in the course of researching and writing *Fostering Nation?*, I have also found many occasions for inspiration. These occurred first and foremost as a result of the courage and generosity of ordinary citizens, both youngsters and adults, who regularly surmounted the constraints of both disadvantage and privilege to demand a fair deal and dream of equality. Particularly inspirational were courageous young clients of child protection efforts who somewhere found the capacity to reject messages that called into question their fundamental humanity. Some women and men have also proved worthy stewards of the future in both private and public life. Remarkable souls such as United Nations' representative Stephen Lewis and British Columbia's Advocate for Children and Youth, Mary Ellen Turpel-Lafond, who motivate everyone to do better at the beginning of the twenty-first century, form part of an inspiring lineup of both the anonymous and the exalted who have always committed themselves to best outcomes for children. The voices of youngsters themselves and the encouragement offered by all kinds of parents, community activists, Native rights champions, feminists, and child welfare workers—which are often overlapping categories—have always suggested ways to move beyond despair, and they do so today. Their efforts sustain the hopes of this study's last chapter in particular.

Fostering Nation? was preceded in 2006 by my *Finding Families, Finding Ourselves: English Canada Confronts Adoption from the Nineteenth Century to the 1990s.*[6] That volume advanced the argument that adoption should properly be understood as embodying shifting national values. Policies and practices negotiated at the most official and the most intimate level capture questions raised in the meeting of diverse populations in the course of colonialism and nation building. Private choices about whom to include in families have always had public implications. In fostering, as in adoption, these are not always pretty.

Adoption has been, however, arguably very often a good news story. Even granted the selfishness and the blinkered vision that have often been involved, it has meant significantly improved lives for many children and adults. In some cases, it has also enhanced the ability and willingness of mainstream Canadians to look beyond their own narrow self-interest. Both domestic and international adoption has been at their best an expression of growing capacity for empathy and world-mindedness. These capabilities ultimately promise to contribute to a more egalitarian world.

In its attention to how a nation has understood and treated its youngest members and what this suggests about Canada itself, this second volume is very much in the spirit of *Finding Families*. It is, however, also ultimately broader in scope and less sanguine. The youngsters who have encountered domestic foster care and its various alternatives have been no less deserving of the embrace that has commonly greeted girls and boys who are adopted. Comparable enthusiasm for fosterlings has been, however, far less common. While the two groups have never been entirely distinct, fostered youngsters have been far more likely to encounter hard times and hard hearts. Indeed, they have frequently been in far worse shape than their adopted contemporaries when they first met the gaze of strangers. From the nineteenth century to the present, most have been beyond, often well beyond, infancy and members of sibling groups, more often boys or teenagers, suffering obvious psychological or physical injury or disability and victims of racism and other prejudices. They have been youngsters with whom mainstream adults, in particular, have had generally little sympathy and some have proved especially taxing even for birth parents and kin.

As I composed my thoughts on adoption some years ago, I became increasingly conscious that I was leaving out a far larger group of girls and boys who commonly stood significantly lower in the hierarchy of care that is allocated to the nation's youngest citizens. *Fostering Nation?*—with its essential question mark—results from my resolve that this especially vulnerable group deserved the historical attention that I had given their more glamorous counterparts. In other words, I wanted myself and others to pay serious attention to the commonly darker side of Canada's response to childhood disadvantage.

Fostering Nation? explores the missteps and the detours of a century and more of child protection efforts by Canadians and their governments as they confronted the specter of children judged neglected, abused, deficient, and delinquent. Although its special interest lies in the evolution and character of state fostering initiatives, this assessment is located in the broader context of diverse arrangements for youngsters. Substitute households for disadvantaged children occur as part of a continuum of possible alternatives, from social assistance shoring up original families to kin care and institutional provision.

Options for girls and boys have always been highly contingent. Much depends on the relative value assigned to particular groups. Gender, class, race, and ability always provide important qualifiers on access to resources. No level playing field has ever existed. In the hierarchy of power and status accessed by families and communities, children most distant from the mainstream ideals of their day have been the most likely to suffer, and this suffering is likely to continue into adulthood and into subsequent parenthood as well. This trajectory is never, however, inevitable. Human beings are infinitely resourceful and often stronger than the structures that seek to contain their spirits and bodies. As this volume suggests, contingency, constraints, resistance, and resilience have all shaped Canadians' continued engagement with childhood disadvantage.

This account has benefited substantially from a generation and more of Canadian and other scholars asking hard questions about the treatment of girls and boys, the value of caring labour, and the evolution of social policy. Feminist and anti-racist perspectives that tackle the underlying logic of social arrangements have been especially persuasive when it came to understanding why our youngest citizens and disadvantaged families in general so often get a rough ride. In particular, this study is obliged to critical scholars in the social sciences and humanities who have offered insights on the limits of caregiving in a society dominated by capitalist, colonial, and patriarchal power. As Canadian political scientist Olena Hankivsky has observed, feminist theorists in particular have brought "an ethic of care" increasingly to public notice. Such attention requires us to consider "a set of distinct values for guiding our social lives and understanding the entire spectrum of human experiences and human needs."[7] For the purposes of Fostering Nation? such an ethic insists that children's welfare cannot be divorced from that of their parents and communities and that women bear disproportionate responsibility for caregiving. A "free ride on female care underpins," as another Canadian scholar, Paul Kershaw, has cogently argued, "men's patriarchal dividend."[8] Until this connection is broken, children, as well as women, will be denied the full benefits of democratic citizenship.

As my citations confirm, Fostering Nation? also depends very much on the self-critical reflections and field work experience of generations of Canadian social work practitioners and scholars. Assigned to clean up society's casualties, they risk becoming complicit or scapegoated. Many have suffered burnout and despair. Such observers have also frequently been clear about how good intentions can go awry and why community development and anti-poverty initiatives promise far more than conventional orientations fixated on individual casework and risk management. They were ultimately hard put, however, to escape the limitations of political masters who rarely kept children, or the disadvantaged in general, at the forefront of pragmatic calculation.

International comparisons in this volume, notably with Australian, British, and American practices and ideas, offer reminders that issues rarely arise in a single jurisdiction. Canadians have always had their eye on other places and sometimes the reverse has been true as well. The nation's French and English communities have occasionally had each other in their sights, but they were more likely to compare themselves with their linguistic counterparts elsewhere. Once First Nations' groups began to gain control of child welfare in the last decades of the twentieth century, they too generated responses that drew on diverse traditions and practices, however much they might have wished to honour peculiarly indigenous traditions. In Canada, where migration has been commonplace and the media increasingly strong, every public and private decision with respect to girls and boys, as with much else, evolved through a network of influences. Tracking particular inspirations and comparisons has not, however, been the major aim of *Fostering Nation?*. Ultimately, it remains preoccupied with one nation's encounter with disadvantaged youngsters. This account has proved sufficiently complicated and, sometimes, contradictory to require my full attention.

Although scholars and official voices often loom large in *Fostering Nation?*, I have tried hard to recover and to listen to accounts by girls and boys, women and men who have been at the centre of private and public child protection initiatives. I directed my interest in the first instance to youngsters, from infants to teens, who may often have been victims but who have also rarely been merely ciphers in adult calculations. Wherever possible, I have given them opportunities to present their side of the story. Too often, unfortunately, access to their experience and feelings has occurred through the veil of human memory as veterans of child protection endeavour to recall events many years past. Young people, commonly adolescents, living in the midst of state arrangements have, however, offered invaluable reflections on what has been done to them. These first-hand observations have been fewer than I would have liked. Much work needs to be done to ensure that girls and boys are better heard in our homes, our schools, our courts, in child protection generally, and in our academic practice.

The second group to whom I have attempted to grant a fair hearing is birth or natural or, as I sometimes term them, "first" parents and their kin. Over the centuries, their various predicaments have been pivotal in casting offspring adrift and into the hands of others. Their viewpoints too have often been obscured. Assessments have regularly summed them up as either victims or demons, individuals who have ultimately failed to measure up to the supposedly legitimate and attainable demands of mainstream parenting standards. While I have not ignored the personal shortcomings of individual parents, which so often preoccupy child protection accounts, I have been most interested in the social structures and group histories that inhibit effective caregiving. Like their progeny, birth parents have frequently been handicapped in making history as they might wish. Many apparently delinquent adults did not themselves get a good start in life. Horrific beginnings help explain, although never justify, many later failings as mothers and fathers.

The third group who figure largely in these pages are foster or surrogate parents, those adults who have assumed responsibilities for girls and boys who are not their sons and daughters by birth. Their contribution similarly cannot be reduced to a single inspiration or outcome—duty, status, love, labour, and money all mattered at one time or another. Foster mothers and, to a lesser degree, fathers functioned as key players in Canada's engagement with disadvantage from the nineteenth century to the present. They have been expected to honour the obligation of caring for girls and boys that properly belongs to the entire nation and regularly denounced when their efforts proved inadequate to that gargantuan task.

As *Fostering Nation?* examines the interactions of adults and girls and boys from infancy to late adolescence, it never forgets that adults are only children grown up and that children are adults in germ. What happens to one will necessarily impact the other—a lesson that First Nations people have identified in the long-term consequences of residential schools for family life over several generations. In particular, *Fostering Nation?* resists all suggestion that the well-being of the young can be disassociated from the liberation of women to make real choices about their lives, how to support themselves, with whom to partner, and whether or not to have children and how many. As Paul Kershaw, Jane Pulkingham, and Sylvia Fuller have convincingly concluded, men's more limited obligation to care and their too common resort to violence sustain a broad pattern of inequities that injures the entire social fabric.[9] While some have done better than others, none of Canada's diverse communities has entirely escaped patriarchal structures and assumptions that especially jeopardize the welfare of women and children. The recurring allocation of often poorly remunerated duties of care overwhelmingly to women and men's persisting assumption of their right to determine outcomes for both women and youngsters provide, in addition, a model for disfranchizing the less powerful in general. The recurring failure of communities and governments everywhere to hold fathers to the same standards as mothers lies close to the heart of many tragedies for children and nations in both past and present. The eradication of patriarchy is the critical step to full democracy and equality.

Fostering Nation? tells this story in seven major chapters. The first chapter turns its attention to the role of family and kin in the safeguarding of offspring.

It points to the power of mythology, both for good and for ill, as well as the efforts of diverse communities, from the Aboriginal to the newly arrived, to weave a fabric of obligation. At its best, it provides that famed village to which youngsters can be safely entrusted and the basis for agreement about collective responsibility that sees ultimate fruition in a fully formed social commonwealth, something that Canadians have as yet only glimpsed. Nurture is nevertheless a far-from-certain outcome. Much depends on who wields power. In general, those closest to cultural ideals and economic resources have reaped the greatest rewards of collective life. Gender, class, race, rank, and ability everywhere matter when it comes to the allocation of resources.

Chapter 2 concerns itself with the institutional provision for youngsters, from poor houses to infant homes, orphanages, reformatories, asylums, and group homes. It examines the various possibilities embodied in inclusive and segregated settings and shifting and diverse responses to institutional provision for children. Many institutions deserved a bad press. Others offered welcome respite to hard-pressed families and opportunities for specialized treatment unavailable in private homes. Enthusiastic critics of oppression and conformity have often rang their death knell, but institutions have remained a significant feature of Canada's child protection landscape from the nineteenth century to the present.

Chapters 3 and 4 describe in broad strokes the evolution of Canadian policies and programs in child protection with special attention to fostering. Despite recent calls for a federal ombudsperson responsible for the nation's youngsters, Ottawa's intermittent attention to girls and boys with Indian status, and early federal initiatives such as the *Little Blue Books* directed to Canadian mothers after the First World War, the provinces, territories, and municipalities have remained the key players when considering child protection. The third chapter explores the first two periods of initiatives in Canadian child welfare. The first, running generally from the last half of the nineteenth century to the 1920s, saw the contest between champions of institutions and those of fostering. Although they did not differ as much from later state initiatives as has often been claimed, institutions sometimes appeared more sympathetic to original kin, especially mothers, while model foster families under (male) state supervision focused on the restoration of patriarchal governance. The second period covers the 1920s to the 1960s. Although the Great Depression of the 1930s slowed momentum, important advances were occurring in both social security and legal adoption. These provided the main rivals for fostering. While still ahead of institutions, which were ever-present but far less visible as solutions to childhood disadvantage, this now came a clear third in the child protection Olympics.

Chapter 4 takes the policy and programmatic story from the 1960s up to the new millennium. The fate of Aboriginal youngsters looms most large, although their predicament is not so much an aberration as an extension of long-standing prejudice against impoverished and otherwise vulnerable populations. Initial decades brought enhanced, often unprecedented, attention to structural disadvantages as various "isms"—sexism, racism, classism, heterosexism, ableism—named old problems. More than ever before, Canadians were offered useful vocabularies and models of regeneration, resistance, and redress. Some youngsters and the adults who cared for them clearly benefitted. Despite invitations to despair and much policy inertia and retreat, important anti-poverty, feminist, First Nations, and disability rights champions mapped a more generous future for those who would listen. In the last part of this period, their resolve was especially hard tested. A long-standing pessimism deeply rooted in notions of the biological and cultural inferiority of certain groups of human beings came increasingly to the fore in various versions of a so-called "common sense revolution" that targeted the poor for discipline.[10] Canada's younger citizens were inevitable casualties.

Chapter 5 turns to the experience of surrendering adults, those mothers and fathers who did not, for one reason or another, retain youngsters. Regularly depicted as victims, monsters, or some combination of the two, many can be better understood as a product of structural inequities that made many Canadians uncertain custodians of the young. It has been too easy to be preoccupied with individual personal failings. These matter, but systems of inequality routinely set the conditions for much failure. The special vulnerability of groups such as the poor in general, single mothers, racialized communities, those with disabilities, and the incarcerated has been especially significant in determining who cannot successfully mother or father. Just like wealth, disadvantage is readily heritable.

Chapter 6 concentrates on the recipients of the offspring of others. Early hopes focused on free care and cost saving for governments. At the beginning, in particular, fostering was regularly confused with legal adoption or earlier traditions of apprenticeship. When its distinctions became clear, few middle-class applicants applied. Most resisted the appeal of youngsters that they regularly interpreted as damaged or otherwise inferior and effectively irredeemable. Governments and others increasingly counted on respectable working-class households to resocialize the offspring of the dangerous classes into their proper station. When unrelated children entered their midst and were expected to go to school rather than to work, their domestic economies still needed cash to survive. State support was always meagre. Right from the beginning, foster mothers were expected to subsidize the remaking of poor children into acceptable citizens. Youngsters' salvation depended on female commitment to nurture and the absence of many viable economic options for married women. Breadwinning dads were part of this economic calculation. They were first and foremost to support women's efforts to mother; few men were expected to meet the daily demands of caregiving itself. Such idealized heterosexual households remained, however, like their natural predecessors who had lost progeny, ultimately hard put to offer long-term stability to girls and boys. Single women and widows, and, over time, same-sex partners, had roles to play, although their contributions were rarely preferred. By the last decades of the twentieth century, efforts to professionalize foster care struggled to resolve contradictions invoked in the meeting of money and caregiving.

Chapter 7 focuses on youngsters themselves, the most important players in fostering's multiple dramas. While very many began life in straitened circumstances and with early disabilities, they have been a diverse crew. Although observers in every period declared the numbers of disadvantaged and injured youngsters to be unprecedented, shifting diagnoses and sensibilities made it impossible to chart precise trends. Many girls and boys have been highly transient, entering and leaving institutions, group homes, adoption, and fostering as original families strove, sometimes to falter and sometimes to succeed, to gain a secure footing for raising progeny. Foster care released some youngsters from difficult, sometimes dangerous, beginnings and provided otherwise unavailable opportunities for security and accomplishment. Early injuries also sometimes multiplied in the course of drift among different caregivers. By the end of the twentieth century, growing numbers of kids in care were dealing with substantial, sometimes newly identified, physical and emotional problems. While such clients of the state regularly tried to make their desires known, by running away, by complaining to social workers and friends, by stubborn disobedience, and even by suicide, for a long time they lacked any collective voice. At the end of the twentieth century, a rights movement emerged among youngsters in care. Alongside First Nations challengers to colonial relations, they offered convincing testimony about the gulf between what Canada promised its most disadvantaged young and what it actually delivered.

Given the findings of these pages, closing with uniformly negative conclusions would have been easy. It would not, however, have honoured many Canadians' persisting determination to nurture and the rising demand for a better deal for girls and boys that characterize not only this nation but also much of today's world. *Fostering Nation?* chooses to find hope in human rights campaigns that increasingly tackle the unequal allocation of resources among Canadians and the caring gap that impoverishes so many young citizens and helps create mothers and fathers ill equipped to offer their best. Happy outcomes, like the unhappy so often chronicled here, are ultimately the product of human will. Governments and Canadians can choose to do better. It is possible for fostering to live up to its dictionary definition and not so often to reflect and confirm lives of pain.

I

CLAIMING KINSHIP

CHILDREARING IS UNCERTAIN. CANADIANS KNOW THAT THIS is true. When contemplating domestic complication or disaster, many parents have dreamed of having caregivers on hand to help. Most adults place hopes for vulnerable offspring first with family members, but Canadians have turned as well to a wider circle of friends, neighbours, and members of shared cultural communities to act as substitute grandparents, aunts, and uncles—in other words, fictive kin or what have been termed "familiar strangers."[1] Unfortunately, "no Canadian agency" today or in the past has tracked "the number of children in the care of grandparents and/or other relatives."[2] Vulnerable parents, such as Stompin' Tom Connors' teenage mum Isabel, who hitchhiked and couch-surfed around the Maritimes in the 1940s when the deaths of her mother and stepfather left her homeless, always preferred shelter from those they knew.[3]

As they tendered claims for assistance, such Canadians often assumed a customary culture of mutual benefit that would extend over lifetimes as individual fortunes ebbed and flowed. Such exchanges form part of what historians have elsewhere dubbed "calculative reciprocity," in which communities of shared interest, including not only kin but also friends, neighbours, and cultural groups, pool resources. Children in need of care, supervision, and training could shift about as needed among households, most often but not always from poorer to richer. Economic and settlement patterns often required flexible arrangements. Offspring's opportunities for schooling or training, or even contacts that might generate prospects of inheritance, often depended on moving away. As historical sociologist, Gordon Darroch has suggested, "leaving home to board and to work became even more common among youth and young adults over the last three decades of the [nineteenth] century in both urban and rural areas and was especially common in the recently populated and economically unsettled regions of the West in 1901."[4] Traditional apprenticeship was one such long-standing arrangement that had clear connections to subsequent state foster care programs. Such strategies maximized opportunity and addressed the limitations of nuclear families. Affection was one possible return but so too were labour, loyalty, and respect.[5] When benefits were unforeseen or unrealizable, houseroom was far less likely.

Becoming modern has often been associated with leaving ascriptive relationships and entering earned relations. Distinctions, however, are never clearcut. Traditional societies commonly offer various earned statuses, while those that believe themselves to be right up to date have practised ascription based on kinship as well as on class, race, gender, sexuality, age, and (dis)ability. Sociology's preoccupation with the nuclear family has, until very recently, often obscured modernity's continued investment in the emotional and material benefits of both real and fictive kinship. In Canada, as elsewhere, this predilection has nonetheless always found substantive expression in the oversight of girls and boys, as much as in eldercare, employment, inheritance, and life in general.

Collaborative child rearing has been a sensible response to the domestic insecurity that stalks households of every sort. In particular, as one thoughtful American scholar, John Gillis, has observed, "for most of its history ... the Western family system has functioned with an imaginary that has enabled individuals to form familial relations with strangers and to feel at home away from home."[6] Many of the diverse cultures that contribute to modern Canada have similarly embraced outsiders as needs dictate and occasions allow. External linkages offer insurance in case of shortfall or catastrophe. Charities and governments have been presumed to be at most second best and, sometimes, dangerous substitutes for what parents commonly have trusted should come naturally and best from blood ties and shared identities. Authorities have shared such conclusions, often to the detriment of possible recipients of aid. The pervasive and persisting ideology of residualism has regularly required that public solutions to domestic needs appear less attractive than what private effort, whether of families or markets, can supposedly achieve.

The work of making and keeping kin has been in most circumstances profoundly gendered. Women and men are often expected and often wish to assume different tasks. Even when they perform the same duties, their perception and performance, as well as the perspective of others, commonly differ. Persisting structural considerations, such as relative wages, job options, inheritance patterns, and economic security in general, further influence who takes up duties and the nature of their performance. Like other relations, gender is never set in stone. Individual temperaments and capacities always matter as Lucy Maud Montgomery conveyed so effectively in her characterization of the stern Marilla Cuthbert and her loving brother Mathew in *Anne of Green Gables*.[7] Ultimately, such uncertainties keep kinship highly contingent.

This chapter examines the role of kinship, both real and fabricated—in other words, supposedly natural relations—in arrangements for Canadian girls and boys from the mid-nineteenth to the beginning of the twenty-first century. It begins with a cautionary reminder of the prevalence of nostalgia for ideal relations in both indigenous and newcomer communities. Even though utopian fantasies often prove to be a misleading guide to what life has been or is really like on families' front lines as well as sometimes a battleground for conflicting versions of the good life, they do sometimes have merit. They help construct duties of care as part of what it means to be responsible, caring, and admirable members of communities. The chapter turns next to the demographic, cultural, and institutional conditions shaping Canadians' dependence on kith and kin over the years and then to options provided by relatives, notably grandmothers and aunts, as well as by friends, neighbours, and cultural groups. The task of assuming responsibilities has involved both short- and long-term commitments and has brought both pleasure and pain. Youngsters have benefitted and suffered at the hands of those reckoned near and dear enough to raise them, and the implications for adults are equally diverse. Recurring complications help explain why institutions supply the subject of the next chapter.

Idealized Worlds and the Promise of Care

Family and community memory likes to flatter. Selective pasts conjure up reassuring, often didactic, stories that are meant to mobilize as well as to inform. "Bad" bits are readily written over or completely dismissed in self-justifying narratives that are tended by custodians of precious memory. Since the modern world views the treatment of children as a central measure of human worth, adult–child relations are especially vulnerable to air-brushing. Domestic myth-making regularly conjures up responsible loving elders and cared for and caring youngsters. Power and its handmaiden, abuse, easily disappear.

Over the course of Canadian history, French and English authorities have frequently taken deliberate aim at the parenting traditions of those they have designated inferior. As Australian scholar of child welfare Shurlee Swain has correctly concluded in her assessment of Britain and its former colonies of settlement, "parental failure, rather than poverty or social inequality, was identified as the key enemy of childhood."[8] By connecting disadvantage and problems for children firmly to supposedly bad mothers and fathers, those in power, from philanthropists to policy makers, priests, ministers, teachers, and social workers, could claim the high road and, not so incidentally, sidestep responsibility for inequalities.

Subordinated groups have never, however, readily accepted full blame. In confronting the costs of colonization, immigration, or modernization, disadvantaged Natives and newcomers have sought assistance and autonomy and resisted control in child rearing. To counter calumnies, they have resorted to self-justifying genealogies, faith in preceding domestic utopias, and hopes for better outcomes. When the present and the future so often have appeared uncertain and intimidating, familial mythologies have offered compelling solace and indeed inspiration for resistance.

Indigenous and immigrant communities have prized autobiographies centred on solidarity, homogeneity, and mutual benefit. Commonplace stories, including various creation myths, have suggested that elders, a term that was more popular than patriarchs by the end of the twentieth century, formerly ruled in the interests of all. In sepia memory, everyone benefitted from roles assigned by gender, birth order, clan, caste, clan, and age. The resulting Edens hold, so it seems, little abuse or pain but, instead, only happy acceptance of conditions determined by god(s) or nature. As generations recede from view, collective memories readily ignore contradictions. The unequal distribution of resources is rarely taken into account nor is, for that matter, the past's high mortality and generally limited options. Recurring violence against women and girls and the favouring of men and boys in inheritance, employment, and education typically vanish in homogenized accounts of domestic worthiness with which groups position themselves for modern contests of authority. The monolithic families of sentimental memory leave little room for understanding how youngsters and adults have varied in their capacity to inspire and give care.

Rejecting imperial slurs that stripped them of humanity, Aboriginal peoples have proffered rosy portraits of historic harmony and respect.[9] Scholars have also sometimes documented pasts that often seem preferable to presents in their levels of violence.[10] "Pristine, utopian Indian societies" loom distant in time, commonly before there was even a rumour of European strangers. None living can readily contradict the dream.[11] One former foster child, Ojibwa writer Richard Wagamese, typically conjured up a splendid vista where ancestors "trapped, hunted and fished and pretty much lived off the land like our people had for centuries, and according to everyone we were a pretty happy clan."[12] In their struggle for equality within both Native communities and Canada, some Aboriginal women have similarly referenced a golden age: "Before Christianity got in here ... men and women lived together equally ... It was the women who chose their leader traditionally, because they were the ones raising the children; they knew who was strong."[13] Such inspiration continues:

> It is widely believed by Aboriginal peoples throughout North America that family violence rarely existed prior to the breakdown of traditional societies caused by colonization. We know this because it has been passed down from generation to generation via oral teachings by our Elders. Family violence did not exist because of the values connected to women and children and because of the strong collective setup of communities.[14]

Fierce debates about exactly what familial "traditions—what cultures and identities—were considered authentically Indian" have divided Aboriginal dreamers, but many share faith in the innate virtue of domestic prehistories, if only as a resource for countering the pervasive racism of others and promoting resilience.[15]

Newcomers to the continent similarly conjure up contented forebears raising youngsters with few problems and fine results. They too tend to homogenize history along ethnic or racial lines. Even scholarly commentators can succumb to filiopiety. Sentimental memory courses through the wide-ranging *Encyclopedia of Canada's Peoples*.[16] The Filipino family "pattern" takes typically lyrical form:

> Children are valued for the joy and happiness that they bring, as economic assets, and for providing security to parents in their old age. Parents transmit to them the traditional values of love and respect for elders, good interpersonal relations with relatives, friends, and neighbours, honesty and hard work, and the fear of God. Relations between siblings are characterized by mutual love, respect, and protection. The older children, male or female, assume responsibility for the younger ones. In fact, the eldest child may even punish younger siblings if they misbehave. In return, the younger children are taught to show respect for their older brothers and sisters ... Traditionally, the elderly are treated with love and respect.[17]

Coming from the other side of the globe, Greeks offer comparable domestic settings where "children are the centre of attention and interest ... Early life involves a high degree of interaction (hugging, kissing, and playing) with parents and relatives. Such contacts extend even into adult life as expressions of solidarity and warmth."[18] Canadian Gujaratis emerge as equally fortunate with "filial bonding between parents and children ... highly cherished."[19]

French and English-speaking elites likewise embrace domestic virtue. Their domination of Canada's social hierarchy is justified, so their story commonly goes, by a heritage of independent, industrious, and respectable households where youngsters have been properly raised. In the late nineteenth century, a middle-class version of northern European-Canadian normalcy informed philanthropic endeavours and provincial child welfare programs that aimed to transform the domestic relations of others. The post–Second World War "gatekeepers" described by Franca Iacovetta had a long history of idealizing their own families.[20] What such planners largely failed to honour was the determination of target populations to harbour their own versions of admirable kin relations.

All domestic myths feature mothers or maternal substitutes looming large, both for good and for ill. As community kin keepers, they ensured cultural survival. The recurring presence of unpleasant mothers-in-law in much story telling nevertheless offers reminders of unhappy and unequal relations.[21] Their highly individualized grotesquery also diverts attention from male power that commonly limits female choice and distorts relations of every kind. Individual crones, rather than patriarchal systems, appear as serpents in systems of domestic relations that go otherwise unexamined. While frequently problematic as in-laws, grandmothers have acquired a better press in their relations with youngsters. Their transformation in the Western imagination over the course of the nineteenth and twentieth centuries from worrisome old biddy and sometimes threatening witch to endearing granny and even powerful matriarch has underscored our reliance on them for caregiving. No longer "wilful" and "sexual," they stand as "loving" and often undemanding companions to benign patriarchs. In the context of an emerging public endorsement of conjugal equality in modern Canada, the latter figures increasingly occupy the background of family stories. The fact that men of all ages are far less present when it comes to dependable childcare is hardly incidental.[22]

As nostalgic narratives construct agreeable pasts and Native and newcomers position themselves in the hierarchy of domestic virtue, injustice, pain, and diversity, the bedrock of so much intergenerational life, go largely unmarked. Indigenous accounts omit enslaved or captured wives and polygamy. Highland Scots forget their common lack of interest in educating girls and women. Somalis sidestep female genital mutilation, while Chinese, Mormons, and others ignore the costs of marriages arranged in childhood. Domestic violence, not to mention unequal rewards of inheritance, employment, and status, which carry in their wake explicit consequences for both material and emotional well-being, get little or no mention. Nostalgia requires much forgetting.[23] It can also get in the way of the realistic calculation of nurturing capacities. At the end of the twentieth century, First Nations' desires to retrieve youngsters were too often informed by politics rather than by reality, as demonstrated by the fair assessment of Native scholar and veteran of the foster care system Cheryl Marlene Swidrovich.[24] Although she does not say so specifically, looking backward beyond colonialism with rose-coloured spectacles contributes to the ahistoricism that she documents as central to contemporary problems in Native child protection.

Yet, for all of their self-serving distortions, assertions of pasts characterized by collective care and respect for young and old have value. Idealized relations call on parents and communities to account and to do better. The reiteration of supposedly common traditions of responsible caregiving helps future generations resist demoralization and improve behaviour. Given the recurring difficulties between the generations and the gap between the needs and the realities of many youngsters, encouragement may help adults, children, and communities escape destructive patterns. The question remains, however, can they shed legacies of domestic inequalities while embracing an ethic of collective obligation.

Shaping Kith and Kin Care

Whatever the familial ideals, "the exigencies of life" have always prompted unpredictable arrangements, as American sociologist Karen Hansen so effectively demonstrates in *Not-So-Nuclear Families*.[25] Choices are contextual. Life expectancy sets obvious conditions for caregiving. High morbidity and mortality rates for much of the past have constrained possibilities for linking youngsters and adults. Only one-half of every thousand Canadians born in 1831 survived until the age of forty-five and less than one-third reached sixty-five. Only some two-thirds of the generation born in 1901 saw age forty-five. Survival rates for Canadians born in the 1980s, in contrast, are infinitely better: more than 93 percent could expect to see their mid-forties and some three-quarters would live to be sixty-five, with unprecedented numbers approaching the century mark.[26] When it comes to potential caregivers, extended life expectancy helps compensate for falling fertility and fewer siblings.

In the days before antibiotics (essentially before the Second World War, at least in mainstream Canada), widows, widowers, half orphans (those who had lost one parent), and full orphans (those who had lost two parents) were commonplace. While deaths associated with the automobile kept differences smaller than they might have been, premature mortality figured less and less in the lives of most Canadians over the course of the twentieth century. While the entire population could anticipate longer lives, the discrepancy between Native and non-Native populations persisted, with the former suffering a persisting life gap of up to ten years. This difference added significantly to the need for non-parental care.

Gender always mattered in shaping options. The consequences of losing a mother or a father might well have differed sharply. Widowed fathers were more likely than mothers to remarry as a solution to single parenting. Stepmothers could improve or diminish relations. On the other hand, widows (or deserted wives) often found fewer new partners. Many also remained in closer contact with their offspring. This intimacy, whether a product of greater mutual dependence in the face of special economic vulnerability or the greater value placed on maternal-child ties, has fuelled a recurring popular fascination with widow sacrifice and filial love. Paternal affections may well be diverted, but maternal care is widely reckoned not so fickle. When the latter fails, however, it looms as somehow unnatural and inexplicable. It would frequently seem that proper women live to mother.

After the Second Great War and especially in the 1960s and beyond, divorce and remarriage produced their own versions of fragmented and blended households.[27] Once again, fathers found it easier to find new spouses, while mothers repartnered less often. In 2001, stepfamilies made up almost 12 percent of all couples with children. By 2006, Statistics Canada reckoned that 2.4 percent, or 231,000, Canadian families were "blended."[28] In response to such developments, experts forecast the revival of the extended family.[29] In fact, it had never disappeared—its form now simply embraced the consequences of divorce.

The shifting age of marriage, birth rates, and family formations have further diversified caregiving. Lisa Dillon's provocative assessment of grandparenting in late Victorian Canada and the United States describes how a low age of marriage and high fertility caused many eighteenth-century Quebecers to become grandparents even as they nurtured their own young offspring. Grandparenting was both a more pervasive and less distinctive relationship to youngsters than it would become. Over the course of the nineteenth and twentieth centuries, Canadians and Quebecers reduced their fertility as well as the maternal age at last childbirth. As a result, grandparenting slowly emerged as a separate stage of life with "enhanced opportunities for meaningful connections."[30] Since they were less likely to have young progeny at home, the doting Victorian and Edwardian granny, or, more rarely, grandpa, emerged to benefit another generation.

Other changes also affected childcare options. Unfortunately, no scholar has yet to consider the implications of the reduced number and age range of siblings. As family size fell, sisters and brothers, and, later, aunts and uncles and sometimes great aunts and uncles, may not as often have parented younger siblings but, alongside older and frailer grandparents, they could become more significant.[31] Individual populations could offer variations on overall trends. After the Second World War, Aboriginal-Canadian families were, comparatively speaking, awash in extra hands to help as well as mouths to feed. For many, parenting and grandparenting still overlapped. In contrast, those born at the beginning of the twenty-first century during a time of falling and condensed fertility had fewer sisters and brothers as prospective helpers, and grandparenting was more clearly separated from parenting. Other communities, in turn, produced their own opportunities. Canadian Mennonites and Hutterites traditionally offered better prospects for sisters and brothers, and thus aunts and uncles, than Jews or Seventh Day Adventists. Such Canadian variations ensured unpredictability in parental surrogates.

Ethnic intermarriage, a phenomenon that has increased since the nineteenth century, has further complicated assistance. Significant out-marriage often had a major impact on who was on call. Among Japanese Canadians born during or immediately after the Second World War, 78 percent of men and 61 percent of women married outside of their communities, and this continuing trend undermined conventional obligations.[32] By the 1970s, nearly half of marriages in Ontario's Six Nations territory involved non-band members. This choice was not new. By the mid-nineteenth century, no "pure-blooded" Mohawk was believed to exist. By 2006, 41.4 percent of Canadians reported multiple ethnic origins, which was an increase from 38.2 percent in 2001 and 35.8 percent in 1996.[33] In such situations, the duties of kinship were necessarily fluid.

While ethnic and racialized groups regularly fancy themselves unusual, even unique, in meaningful relationships with kin, this idea is nonsense. As their mythologies suggest and particular customs allow, however, cultures support varied expressions of care.[34] Despite the diversity in communities that have ranged from the egalitarian to the hierarchical, and from the matrilineal to the bilateral and patrilineal, children have always been generally prized. In more egalitarian societies such as the Dakota and the Nakota tribes of the prairies, complex kinship patterns helped link "large numbers of people into a network of responsibilities and rights which extended beyond the local community or residential group." Children used the "same words for their birth mothers, their sisters, and the wives of fathers' brothers and for their birth fathers, their brothers, and the husbands of their mother's sisters' husbands."[35] As in the case of the Ojibwa, those "whose fathers had brothers, or whose mothers had sisters, had extra fathers or mothers."[36] In more hierarchical societies such as the Haida, rank also mattered in claims for support. "Noble" youngsters, like those everywhere, found more would-be caregivers than did commoners or slaves.[37]

Many newcomers drew similarly on particular tribal histories. Catholic Irish and Scottish Highlanders were notorious for clannishness and so too in later decades were Sikhs and Ukrainians. Down-on-their-luck migrants regularly turned to their fellows and sisters for food, work, clothes, and childcare, and many were reckoned "ready to assist should the need arise."[38] As Donald Akenson has noted, sibling migrant groups from Ireland typically reaffirmed ties of obligation.[39] Scotland's "difficult terrain and marginality to European culture" in turn "nurtured a very intense and permanent feeling for kinship" that included "extensive fosterage" as a "feature of highland society."[40] Such kinship found obvious expression not only in ethnic settlements such as Glengarry, Ontario, but also among the Scots who were more integrated into the new world. Early Black refugees from American slavery similarly asserted mutuality in hosting orphaned youngsters who could offer labour as well as companionship and affection.[41] Long-standing practices of both agricultural and industrial apprenticeships, sometimes sanctified by legal contracts, drew on such shared identities. Later, Italian and Somali migrants once again relied on kin and clan ties as they too sought houseroom, board, and training.

Kin and community understanding of respectability and honour everywhere informed a willingness to care. Unless the group was matrilineal as in many First Nations, but sometimes then as well, youngsters born outside of marital relations or as a result of recognized unions with non-community members tested obligations. While many such girls and boys were folded more or less discretely into maternal households, they and their mothers could also reap hostility and shame. The numbers to be integrated have overwhelmed some First Nations. The late twentieth-century crisis over claims for band membership by so-called "C-31ers" and their descendants reveals just this problem.[42] When resources have been limited, households have been more likely to reject altogether, or to shuttle among family members, more marginalized youngsters as well as to send them into institutional and state custody. This fate was far less likely for offspring whose birth had been more unreservedly welcomed and who were linked to multiple paternal and maternal networks.

Rank and class always matter in the distribution of youngsters. Some girls and boys, born outside of or even within marriage, are always regarded as more important. Offspring of the powerful have had far better chances of nourishment and protection. Fewer adults care about the well-being of the poor and those with little status. Child slaves among the Kwakiutl were not candidates for potlatches, and young paupers in European settlements similarly missed out when it came to affirmations of value. The introduction of Canada's Registered Education Savings Plan and the Registered Disability Savings Plan at the end of the twentieth century, which were both subsidized by the federal government, stand in a long line of particular benefits that have included tuition for special education and counselling for psychological and emotional difficulties for privileged offspring. The generation of inequalities has, after all, been one of kinship's lasting legacies.

The nature of state and public support for children supplies another critical context for considering kith and kin care. Universal protection for girls and boys stands near the heart of the emergence of social security in the mid-twentieth century. Yet, as one commentator has correctly observed, "minimal adequacy, selectivity, localism, and tests of needs" has kept the social safety net as a last stop resource for many citizens.[43] Despite the recurring enthusiasm for social insurance for all, the older doctrine of residualism that stigmatized parents as failures has never disappeared and, indeed, was revived in the late twentieth century. The neo-conservative shift to the increased targeting of aid meant that public help in parenting has remained frequently stigmatizing. Services to preserve households and protect children have too often confirmed pathology and social control and more rarely appeared as a right of citizenship or a stepping stone to significant social mobility. This mean-spirited sensibility has undermined supports for preventive, as well as protective, programs.

Not surprisingly, parents at the beginning of the twenty-first century have sought to avoid child welfare authorities much as their predecessors did in the nineteenth century when Ontario's early child welfare legislation made little distinction among delinquent, dependent, and neglected youngsters. The persisting stigmatization of involvement with state welfare and more particularly with child protection has directed parents to kith and kin, even when these are inadequate and even dangerous. The most obvious example is women who are reluctant to leave violent partners lest they and their children attract dangerous attention. As a 2004 report from BC's Ministry of Children and Family Development matter-of-factly acknowledged, "abused women are often judged harshly and characterized inaccurately ... as dysfunctional, unstable, weak and passive ... These beliefs can influence the way women are assessed as mothers and lead to inappropriate interventions."[44]

First Responders: Grandmothers, Aunts, and Male Relatives

Canadian parents have looked first of all to their own mothers and sisters for help in child rearing. Maternal female kin commonly prove to be the best bet, with those in the paternal line ranking second best. Reliance on male kin has been much less evident. Some men, nonetheless—notably maternal grandfathers and uncles and then their paternal counterparts—have supplemented women's efforts and, more occasionally, supplied the lynchpin of assistance. Even as gender supplies the key to kin work, its implications are often taken for granted. Studies of every kind regularly mention relatives as the first responders, but they regularly fail to specify who does the actual work. Just beneath the surface, however, is the ubiquitous presence of grandmothers and aunts. Their near invisibility, except when matters go wrong or when they invoke cultural symbols of survival and sacrifice, once again obscures the extent of women's unpaid labour and implies that sacrifice is, or should properly be, its own reward.

Since the nineteenth century, grandmothers have stood at the symbolic and practical centre of the network of part- and full-time aid. Children's very survival has sometimes depended on their supplementing parental capacity.[45] The more disadvantaged the population, the greater the need for grandmothers. While the majority of three-generation and skipped-generation households (those in which no middle generation is present) in both Canada and the United States has been European in origin, Black, Asian, and Aboriginal families have often found fewer substitutes when it comes to mobilizing resources.[46] In 2006, 9 percent of Canadian-Aboriginal, as compared to 5 percent of other, youngsters lived with grandparents, especially grandmothers.[47]

Parents have been freed to take up paid work, whether in hop fields, on factory lines, or in the homes of others, because their own mothers tended hearths and hearts in their absence. Many families, such as those employed in the Paris, Ontario, woollen mills from the 1880s on, counted on such collaboration to gain economic security.[48] Women's much-celebrated employment during the 1914–18 and 1939–45 wars frequently depended on similar cooperation. In the 1950s, the Women's Bureau of the Canadian Department of Labour highlighted kin care's continuing importance in its study of forty Halifax offspring of "working mothers." It matter-of-factly revealed that fifteen of these youngsters were in the daily care of their grandmothers, including two who "boarded" full-time.[49] In 1981, an investigation of eighty-seven single teen mothers in Ottawa, Toronto, Windsor, and Sault Ste. Marie reconfirmed these patterns. Approximately one-half of them lived with their parents, another 10.6 percent lived with other relatives, and a scant 3.1 percent lived with the father of their child. More than 25 percent of maternal grandmothers babysat daily, and almost half of the young mothers had applied to their own parents or other kin for money at least once during the year.[50]

In later decades, as Canadian mothers with young offspring flocked into the labour market and promises of a national daycare system were repeatedly broken, senior women became all the more visible as the bedrock of kin care. In 1990, 36 percent of female Canadians aged forty-five to fifty-four, 42 percent aged fifty-five to sixty-four, and 22 percent aged sixty-five and older reported supplying unpaid assistance with childcare. Male rates at the same ages were 17 percent, 28 percent, and 14 percent respectively. Maternal grandmothers also stood out for their practical and emotional help to adult grandchildren. Paternal grandfathers remained the least likely of their generational cohort to provide aid of any kind.[51] Even as it failed to specify the predominance of maternal grand-mothers in kin care, the finding of a 1991 report that "close to 80 per cent of all unmarried mothers in Nova Scotia received and continued to receive child-care help from relatives" told a familiar story of public invisibility and private necessity.[52]

Part-time assistance was only one part of the evolving story. In the decade 1991–2001, Canadian adults raising grandchildren under the age of eighteen increased 20 percent. In 1996, 59 percent of them were grandmothers without male partners. Of this number, 17 percent were First Nations, although the latter made up only 2.8 percent of the total population. Some one-third of all such grandmothers reported disabilities, while the same proportion survived on annual household incomes of less than $15,000. In 2001, more than 56,700 grand-parents raised children on their own in skipped-generation families, and more than 473,000 lived with both children and grandchildren. One in six such adults was an immigrant.[53] Slightly more than a quarter of skipped-generation house-holds possessed "comfortable middle class incomes," while a "similar propor-tion has a trade diploma, or a college or a university degree." Others encountered "substantial economic problems" and were possibly "living in extreme poverty."[54] One in five households included two or more youngsters, and two racial groups—Blacks and Natives—were "substantially over-represented."[55] Despite their sig-nificance, such numbers are generally regarded as under-estimates, failing to capture the extent of what social workers term "the underground child welfare system."[56]

In relations with the next generations, many grandparents have prized oppor-tunities for intimacy and service.[57] In the face of prejudices that regularly cast older people as burdens, they can often take pride in their continuing value. This situation is not new. As historian Lisa Dillon has suggested of the Victorian period, a swath of diaries and letters has testified to "the genuine pleasure grandmothers took in relating to their grandchildren, the support they exchanged with grand-children, the sense of continuity these relationships provided, as well as the desir-able status conferred by grandmotherhood."[58] My own mother, who lived in a separate flat in my house for close to twenty years, found her co-resident grand-sons a source of continuing interest. She ensured their affection, and an indispen-sable place in the household, by providing a haven from parental oversight, help with homework, a second opinion on problems, and an unending supply of good-ies, not to mention occasionally sharp reminders of the virtues of their parents. She also appreciated that she could retreat behind her door when she was too tired to cope or unsympathetic. Her grandsons had active parents and nanny-house-keepers who allowed her the liberty to choose her level of engagement.

Some grandmothers have also been aware of the larger impact of their contributions. In particular, many Native women have treasured a "second chance to be parents of a healthy Aboriginal community." Their labour, which is often in the most difficult of circumstances, has promised critical "pockets of resilience and improvement" for their nations.[59] The reflections of one such woman on her choices in the 1950s and 1960s pointed to the connection between family obligations and community well-being:

> Another important decision was to come to Toronto and live with my grand-daughters. I was very concerned for them. They had finished High School and wanted to go to Business College. So I decided to come with them just for a year. That's all I intended. But then I became involved in the Indian community here in Toronto, and realized the bad image Indians have ... and so I felt I just couldn't leave ... It never occurred to me that I would run a boarding house for other students. I was only thinking of my relatives.[60]

In such instances, the personal readily becomes the political.

Situations have not, however, always been positive. Even part-time duties have sometimes been more endured than welcomed. One mid-twentieth-century Halifax mother had hoped to rely on her mother while she worked outside the home but soon changed her mind. Finding her two oldest locked out "whenever company came over," she shifted her four youngsters to an orphanage that promised better oversight.[61] Family daycare operators have also had the potential to disappoint. In the 1970s, one report discovered a significant number of caregivers rejecting "children from outside their families because they don't really like children, and are only looking after some for their relatives because of feelings of family obligation." The same investigators also concluded that parents were exploiting their "daily sitters" because neither regarded family childcare as "real and serious work."[62] Little wonder no one was happy. Studies of middle-class Australian grandmothers also suggest that there is resentment when anticipated retirement freedom is curtailed by expectations of free babysitting.[63] Since women may often be reluctant not to defend, at least publicly, the pervasive code of maternal sacrifice, such dissenters remind us to question silences, whether they are eloquent or poignant.

International research shows that grandparents rarely "choose to take on full-time care of their grandchildren."[64] This is true of both the poor and the rich. In particular, however, women who have experienced "early childbearing, single parenthood, economic hardship, or a combination thereof" can harbour strong and unfulfilled desires for "personal autonomy." Not surprisingly, when called upon to nurture another generation, such survivors are vulnerable to burnout and distress.[65]

Grandparents of all origins assume primary duties in the face of little choice. A 2005 Canadian study pointed to "incarceration rates, chemical dependency and child welfare placements" that generated the need for rescue.[66] Children's parents might be regarded as blameless or hapless victims, but they have regularly broken the hearts of those who have borne them as well as those they have borne. As one study of Ontario grandparents caring for youngsters revealed, "the adult child" is often seen "as intrusive and disruptive."[67] Not surprisingly, even potent symbols of community endurance, such as African-American grandmothers, have sometimes resisted engulfment in family tragedies by distancing themselves from their grandchildren.[68] Their response would have been understood by an Albertan raising her two grandchildren, aged thirteen and nine years old, early in the twenty-first century. Voicing sentiments that others might be shyer in sharing, she concluded: "It's really difficult. My advice to people has been: 'Don't do it.' That sounds terrible, [but] there's no support."[69]

Studies of Canada's Native grandmothers suggest predicaments similar to those of disadvantaged African Americans. Even as many endure the consequences of lifelong poverty, they face inordinate pressure to rescue youngsters injured by parental drug abuse and neglect.[70] The case of an Ojibwa widow and tuberculosis survivor, who found herself simultaneously coping with the disintegration of her second marriage, the loss of a daughter in a house fire, and the raising of orphaned grandchildren, captured the enormous degree of disadvantage that marks so many skipped-generation homes.[71] In the 1990s, the emergence of a Canadian group known as Cangrands signalled these pervasive struggles for survival. Although most leaders and members seemed to be women of European origin, its outspoken 2008 campaign against Ontario's cuts to temporary care child allowances offered ample evidence of widespread distress.[72]

While grandmothers receive the greatest attention by social policy and scholarly commentators, aunts regularly substitute for parents. Older children have often routinely cared for younger siblings, and such patterns readily persist into subsequent generations. In the 1930s, seven Saskatchewan orphans typically rallied to care for one another. The older girls who had already left home for paid employment rescued their sisters, and their brothers found refuge with the parents of best friends, but all of the siblings stayed in touch.[73] Sisters have also struggled to help parents keep families together. In the 1920s, such a case gained public attention when a married woman pushed her teamster father to go to court to regain the younger daughter whom he had deposited in Vancouver's Alexandra Orphanage after the death of her mother.[74]

Many sisters have grown up only to extend their interest to the next generation. The significance of their involvement was confirmed years ago by a Victorian panic. Canadians, like others elsewhere, have loudly debated in the

House of Commons and in the press the right of widowers to marry their sisters-in-law.[75] This overblown controversy testifies to the intimate networks in which sisters have often moved as well as to the ties that they have had to the children they might "step-mother-aunt," although these have gone largely unnoticed. Whatever the law, communities have understood that sisters are very often invaluable.

The commitment of genteel pioneers Mary O'Brien and Anne Langton to nieces and nephews in mid-nineteenth-century Ontario and of Margaret Wymss to her niece and step-daughter, namesake, and future writer Margaret Laurence in early twentieth-century Manitoba has contributed to the accepted fabric of life. As Langton explained to family members, "the life I seemed destined to lead in England appears to me objectless, while the Canadian one I proposed to myself had a distinct purpose of usefulness ... if I had a career in England it would be different; I should not feel that I was frittering my life away."[76] Lisa Dillon has also noted that nineteenth-century Quebec women "did not tend to take apparently orphaned grandchildren into their own homes," suggesting that "higher fertility rates among French-Canadians created greater opportunities" for them "to live with aunts and uncles."[77] The 1901 census reported that 48 percent of youngsters under five who lived with kin resided with aunts and uncles.[78] All across the country, an older generation might be absent, dead, or frail, making aunts the hard-working backbone of complex households.

Denyse Baillargeon's study of working-class Montreal housewives during the 1930s reveals commonplace initiatives. One woman kept a niece until she left to be married. Another sheltered eleven nieces and nephews as well their parents who were facing an especially rough patch. Yet another maintained a nephew from infancy until he was six, retrieved him again at puberty to keep him until he was an adult, all the while contributing to grocery bills and clothing for her other nieces and nephews.[79] Such doughty kin would have appreciated the choices of a post–Second World War Ontario farm woman who returned to parenting "treasured" orphans—her niece and nephew—after her own children had left home. She refused to let them go to strangers.[80]

Many parents have counted on sororal loyalties. The Micmac poet Rita Joe, who had her own unhappy experiences being passed among relatives as child, turned to her sister when a new partner proved hostile to one son. She believed that "he found a home where he was loved until he died."[81] In the 1950s, the St. John's, Newfoundland, parents of Canadian comedian Mary Walsh dealt with their daughter's pneumonia at eight months by sending her next door. She stayed there with her aunt and uncle even as her other family with her six siblings remained neighbours.[82] In the next decade, a widowed program supervisor from the Canadian Broadcasting Corporation (CBC) turned with similar relief to his sister-in-law to care for a daughter after her older siblings had married and left home.[83] Public and private welfare authorities have often counted on such solutions. At the end of the twentieth century, Manitoba's Awasis Pimicikamak Cree Native Kinship Care program reported that "female relatives, specifically aunts" were playing a "major role," accounting for almost 75 percent of foster parents.[84]

Male kin have never been as visible as grandmothers and aunts. When they appear, they have usually been partners of women willing to mother. Research on male caregiving is, however, just beginning. The work of anthropologists on mothers' brothers and fathers suggests that this group deserves special attention.[85] Occasional anecdotal and popular evidence makes the same point. Farley Mowat's bestseller *Lost in the Barrens* presents a fascinating portrait of stoic Uncle Angus who takes in his nephew Jamie after his parents die in a car crash.[86] A sixteen-year-old Armenian refugee, later a famous photographer, Yousuf Karsh had his mother's brother, Uncle Nakash, to thank for sponsoring him as an immigrant and for arranging for him to apprentice in photography.[87] More than a century of judicial decisions about disputed inheritances reported in the *Dominion Law Reports* and its predecessors similarly disclose grandfathers and uncles involved with, and sometimes attempting to direct, younger kin, much like Uncle Scrooge in Charles Dickens's *A Christmas Carol*.[88] Such relations appear especially likely if uncles and aunts were childless. As noted in the *Cambridge Handbook of Age and Ageing*, adults without partners or offspring "may have been higher priorities throughout their lives as both recipients of and providers of support."[89] Such conclusions provide ample reminders that fathering, or its absence, always reflects material as well as ideological influences.

Relations among adults are rarely simple. They always constitute works in progress that face the challenge of both intergenerational memories and current exigencies. Interactions may be cool or even hostile. As Dorothy Scott and Shurlee Swain have observed of experiences in Australia, kith and kin have struggled about "what childhood should be about."[90] Communities and families have their own notions of proper behaviour, and they have not spared members advice and censure. Legal contests over custody and guardianship from the nineteenth century to the present regularly pit relatives, notably grandparents and aunts, against parents in disputes about best interests. At the end of the twentieth century, one nineteen-year-old young woman represented a familiar predicament in electing to surrender her two-year-old daughter for adoption. After leaving a problematic marriage and "having a very hard time coping, both financially and emotionally," she judged her family only "marginally supportive." They had concluded that she had made her bed and "must sleep in it."[91] The

Native child welfare agencies that emerged at the end of the twentieth century confronted similarly unsettled relations. Scenarios could include an aunt
who felt rejected by a brother whose child she had fostered, another whose relatives challenged her child-rearing practices, and still another who angrily confronted drunken kin demanding access to their offspring.[92] Such complaints
were by no means unusual.

The situation of unwed mothers was especially difficult. Supportive kin
could be the key to survival. One poverty-stricken father of a dozen and widower who sheltered his pregnant sixteen-year-old in 1945 explained his action
very simply—it was a "family problem and adoption was undesirable." The suggestion of the putative father that his unwelcome offspring be given up to
strangers was greeted by outright refusal: "We don't give up our own children."[93]
Yet, if some people proved stalwart, many families from all stations of society
broke ranks in the face of unwed pregnancies, fearing a loss of respectability
and a drain on resources.[94] Even supposed bastions of domestic ties such as
Newfoundland's outports proved to be reluctant hosts to those offspring whom
critics considered dishonoured.[95] From the 1880s until the 1970s, Catholic and
Protestant maternity homes all across the nation demonstrated the material
and emotional limits of kin support.[96] Social and legal discrimination against so-
called "bastards" and their mothers survived well into the twentieth century, as
even the confident journalist Doris Anderson, whose birth parents later married, remembered.[97]

Illegitimate girls and boys were not the only young kin to test relations.
Those with disabilities received especially uncertain receptions when parents died
or became overwhelmed. A study of asylum care in Alberta in the twentieth century tells the common story of siblings and other relatives unwilling to replace
mothers and fathers. Like other jurisdictions, this province was forced to accept
rejected children in adult institutions.[98] Their fate resembled in turn that of
young relatives judged to be otherwise difficult or demanding—a group that
was especially likely to include teenagers. When kin confronted orphaned or
abandoned siblings, some were simply more in demand than others.

Families resisted duties that threatened to consume resources even as they
yoked them to relatives that they might consider uncongenial or worse. Youngsters left behind in orphanages and victims of infanticide, such as a baby who
died soon after birth in the home of her mother's aunt in Toronto in 1900, surfaced throughout the decades, leaving ample evidence of the limits of kinship.[99]
One BC five-year-old, who was a daughter of a young unwed mother and
"handed around between relatives and neighbours so frequently" that she understandably felt and acted as if she "belonged nowhere" and was a "confirmed
run-away," supplied another casualty in the 1940s.[100] So, too, a few decades

later did a twenty-nine-year-old who spent much of her teenage years and young adulthood in prison and on the street. After her parents died, she went to residential school. Nuns denied her Aboriginal culture, but memories of holidays with an abusive grandmother and uncle supplied another version of hell.[101]

Children themselves frequently have had something to say about proposed arrangements with kin. One pre–First World War teenager adamantly refused to leave her maternal aunt and grandmother to return to the custody of her father and his new wife. According to the judge who determined her future, she displayed "almost abject terror" at the prospect.[102] Even seemingly amicable arrangements could leave scars. Comedian Mary Walsh, best known as a satirist on CBC television's *This Hour Has 22 Minutes*, moved in with her aunt and uncle soon after birth. She recalls many years learning to cope with being "given away," concluding that "that is the piece of sand that has made me the ... pearl that I am today."[103] For children, as for adults, kinship was a complicated mix of dreams and realities.

The Second Line: Friends, Neighbours, and Community

When kin were unavailable or unsuitable, parents broadened their search. Well into the nineteenth century, as Susan Houston has noted with regard to public school children, distinctions between friends and relatives were not hard and fast.[104] The "term 'friend' was commonly used for relatives, neighbours, and members of the same religious faith ... [and] the familial idiom was extended to guilds, confraternities, monasteries, and the military—groups that today we would not call families."[105] Domestic vocabulary implied protection and obligation. Boarders, friends, and neighbours became aunts and uncles in expressions of respect and intimacy. Native elders were similarly hailed as aunties by those who were younger and often only distantly, if at all, related. In the 1920s, the noted folklorist Helen Creighton drew on widespread practice in assuming the comforting title of "Aunt Helen" when she ran a children's radio show in Halifax.[106] In the next decade, Canadian historian Hilda Neatby became an "honorary member" of the family of her University of Minnesota doctoral advisor, and his offspring addressed her as aunt.[107] At the onset of the twenty-first century, a plethora of honorary aunts, uncles, grandparents, and cousins surfaced on the World Wide Web, suggesting the hardiness of traditions of making kin out of strangers. Whatever the state of social security programs, an expansive net of potential caregivers has always promised comfort.

Communities could spring up in even the most problematic locations.[108] Prostitutes with little option but to keep their offspring in bawdy houses might have only those around them for support. Not surprisingly, Mary Anne Poutanen's study of nineteenth-century Montreal suggests that "brothel residents more than likely shared child-care responsibilities."[109] Adult employment has often supplied the basis for a domestic safety net. After the First World War, the predicament of four orphaned siblings in the coal-mining town of Blairmore, Alberta, generated a collective solution that many communities would have understood. The local Masonic Lodge hired a housekeeper to keep them in their own home.[110] Fraternal organizations, including the Independent Order of Foresters and the Loyal Order of the Moose, also stood at the forefront of institutions that established homes for orphaned and half-orphaned offspring of their members. The children of their "brothers and sisters" were in this way symbolically and practically "uncled" and, not so incidentally, supported by fundraising by their honorary aunts in the women's auxiliaries and related associations, such as the Masonic Order of the Eastern Star and the Daughters of the Nile.

Compact settlement increased the prospect of help from those who shared ethnic and racial identities. In the 1960s, over half of Montreal's Italians, much like previous immigrants, purchased homes "in neighbourhoods with relatives or other compatriots, and almost the same proportion worked with other Italians."[111] Arrangements were especially important as migration and genocide disrupted old networks. As with the Armenians, "everyone in the neighbourhood was 'aunt' or 'uncle,' every Armenian house was a second home, and every Armenian peer was a 'cousin.'"[112] After the Second World War, Lithuanian survivors of Europe's displaced persons' camps "often extended virtual kinship ties to co-nationals" in similar efforts to defy compromised futures.[113] Encounters with mainstream prejudice could encourage bonding. Since the Halifax Infants' Home, which was run by the city's philanthropic elite, refused their infants, African-Canadian households knew that homeless youngsters depended on them.[114] Solidarity promised survival.

Godparenting supplied another common expression of mutuality. It routinely drew on friends, neighbours, and community members as well as on formal kin.[115] Life's uncertainties, spiritual and otherwise, underpinned Catholic practices, and Confucian and Buddhist Canadians employed comparable relations. North America's nineteenth-century newcomers typically used godparenting to reinforce ties that were compromised by migration.[116] In the next century, Italians made much the same choice as they constructed "an elaborate system of rights and obligations [that] had as their aim the provision of security through mutual aid."[117] Filipino immigrants drew, in turn, on their "ritual or ceremonial kin" to help parents cope in new worlds. Chosen godmothers and godfathers were themselves rarely isolated figures. They were often expected to bring their own kin into the networks, enlarging a critical "co-parenthood" that was rooted in visions of practices cherished in former homelands.[118]

Various other arrangements, many of which were largely informal and with little public notice, kept families afloat.[119] New technologies could encourage keeping in touch. In post–Second World War Ontario, those young couples in Hamilton who were in possession of cars, which the husbands generally controlled, kept in closer touch with the men's families, establishing what one sociologist interpreted as a "patrifocal" extended family.[120] Telephones and computers could prompt more diverse networks. Relationships could unfold rather casually, with religious or legal recognition coming later, if at all. Such was the experience of a childless widow from the Second World War who mothered the offspring of desperate neighbours after they immigrated to Canada in 1949. By 1955, the wife had left the husband with six children, and the long-time standby agreed to take one youngster "on a temporary basis." Eventually, she became the legal guardian of the child who later hailed her as "a loving, caring, supportive mother to me." The bestowal of the Queen's Golden Jubilee Medal on that modest saviour supplied all too rare public recognition.[121] One Ontario spinster saleswoman, who was already responsible for an elderly father, found herself similarly positioned in regard to a young stranger in the 1950s. She could not resist a badly neglected girl who turned to her for help. Since she was deemed to be a volunteer, she was refused state assistance even as she assumed the duties and costs of legal guardianship.[122] Such accounts, with their commonplace tale of female sacrifice, underpin much kith involvement.

When men appear in the public record, they have been more often positioned as beneficiaries of caregiving. In the 1960s, the *Star Weekly*, Canada's leading newspaper supplement, described the survival strategies of single fathers. The profile included a part-time student, bartender, and widower in Lethbridge, Alberta, with five children. His was the uplifting story of close friends who took in his three-year-old during the week, while he saw her on weekends. In Prince Rupert, a widowed hospital orderly was depicted as desperate to find care for his seven-year-old. He advertised for help but received replies that seemed, to his considerable surprise, "more interested in the money than helping out in a difficult situation." Eventually, he counted himself fortunate to find "neighbors who took her right into their own family. She stays with me on the weekend and I take her out at every opportunity. She has adjusted well to her new life and is having a ball. When my wife died, I had the choice of leaving her with relatives or bringing her up on my own. My family doctor recommended the latter and I've never regretted it." His comments convey the nature of much fathering. Although his daughter's daily care rested elsewhere, he congratulated himself for "bringing her up on my own."[123] Such sentiments contrast starkly with the observations made by his single mother contemporaries in the same magazine. When asked how they coped as single parents, they pondered finances and

feelings rather than substitutes. All of them parented full time and were responsible for earning income as well.[124] Like their communities, they were accustomed
to taking maternal care largely for granted.

Unpredictable racial as well as kin loyalties sometimes surfaced to complicate kith care. The question of who could properly foster Catholic children in
the care of Ontario Children's Aid Societies triggered many post–Second World
War battles among citizens still invested in the customary battles between the
Orange (Protestants) and the Green (Catholics). When White adopters showed
unprecedented interest in Black youngsters in the same period, African Canadians also sometimes worried about threats to identity and culture. By the closing decades of the twentieth century, however, most Canadian conflicts centred
on threats to Aboriginality. Provinces slowly recognized opposition to placing
Aboriginal youngsters with non-community members. While, ironically enough,
the descendants of "C-31ers" received an uncertain welcome across the nation,
bands increasingly worried about the loss of other youngsters. The creation of
indigenous child welfare authorities was one result. Interventions could pit band
claims for cultural survival against parental rights. Some Aboriginal mothers
rejected tribal claims for sons and daughters, determined to place them outside
of traditions and situations that they judged to be dangerous.[125]

Interracial marriages produced particular opportunities for controversy.
Such was the situation in 2004 when an Ojibwa woman, married to a White man
but settled on her reserve, died and left two children. As her husband fought
her family for custody, the band protection agency investigated and then removed
the youngsters. The father could not take them off the reserve to his parents and
sister. From his perspective, his paternal rights had been violated "in an abuse
of power," but opponents insisted that "the best interests of native children—
even half-native—are inextricably bound to aboriginal culture and can never
be trumped by the rights of a parent."[126] Just whose rights should take precedence
remains unsettled. In 2006, the Saskatchewan Children's Advocate concluded
that "placing children in their home communities and meeting their cultural
needs is best, but their cultural needs don't trump their need for protection."[127]
As he put it, "we can't have a sliding scale, a sliding protection bar for different groups of children."[128] Ironically, child protection in Canada, like kith and
kin care as well, has always had a "sliding scale" when it comes to arranging for
youngsters. More marginal groups have often been its particular victims.

Like Black American kin, who have been repeatedly identified as highly
stressed, Canada's poorest populations, often but not only Native, have frequently been set up to fail.[129] The consequences can be disastrous. In January
1950, one overwhelmed Montreal grandmother "dressed her daughter's two
illegitimate children in their best clothes, put them in a baby carriage, and took

them to the waterfront where she pushed the carriage into the ice-choked St. Lawrence river." As she explained to police when she gave herself up, the tots were headed to an orphanage, and she could not bear it. At her wit's end, she had intended to kill herself and them, confessing: "I have just murdered the only two things in this world I love."[130] The 2008 death of seven-year-old Katelynn Sampson in Toronto at the hands of her mother's supposed "best friend," who had been appointed as her guardian without ever being investigated about her ability to parent or her police record, served as another reminder of what could go dreadfully wrong.[131] Such tragedies echo down through the years.

For all of the hopes that it has generated, kith and kin care is uncertain, and it can often be short term as in the case of the well-intentioned neighbours who sheltered four boys and two girls who were deserted by their widowed father in pre–First World War Manitoba. When he failed to return, they became state wards.[132] A leading Canadian psychiatrist who battled for extra support for youngsters and their families in the late twentieth century supplied an appropriately balanced reflection:

> Some parents leave their children in the care of grandparents or other extended-family members, either repeatedly or for a prolonged period of months or even years. The effect on the child will depend on a number of factors, including the age of the child, the nature of the continuing relationship and contact between parent and child during the placement, the quality of the care supplied by the substitute caretaker, and how well the substitute parent was known to the child prior to the placement. The reason for the placement may also be significant: it may signify rejection ... or it might be temporary and occasioned by financial, health, or other short-term family stresses.[133]

Its recurring uncertainty means that kith and kin care has necessarily remained only the first stop in making provision for youngsters who cannot reside with their birth parents. As the next chapter suggests, institutions have regularly supplied the next stop for the needy.

2

"IT WAS AN EVIL PLACE.
IT WAS A BEAUTIFUL PLACE"
Institutions for Children[1]

TOTAL INSTITUTIONS—IN OTHER WORDS, THOSE THAT ARE aimed at regulating lives each and every day—often get a bad press. This is especially so when it comes to the nurture of children. Revelations of mistreatment in orphanages, reformatories, and special needs sites in the twentieth and twenty-first centuries, much like exposure of sexual abuse at the hands of relatives, justify extreme caution when it comes to listening to advocates. Yet, despite their recurring danger, institutions persist as one of the regular, even normal, options for girls and boys who do not reside with their birth parents. Over the entire period considered by this volume, institutions served variously as replacements for, and extensions of, families as well as precursors and alternatives to fostering. Many existed, as Alvin Finkel has pointedly reminded us, because Canadians and their governments were most often deeply suspicious of outdoor relief that might seemingly reward the poor by allowing them to sustain families at home. Only the slow introduction of usually meager supports, including mothers' allowances beginning during the First World War, unemployment insurance in the 1930s and 1940s, and family allowances in 1945 started to acknowledge the uncertainty and insufficiency of employment income and the special vulnerability of women.[2] A national daycare program, the institutional response that makes best sense for children and their parents, has remained a dream, however, despite the steady recommendations of government reports and expert assessment into the twenty-first century. Given the shortcomings of social support for family life, total institutions retained a clear role. The fact that they offered abuse as well does not distinguish them from kith and kin.

Many foster kids have passed through group residences in the course of their lives in child protection. Some institutions have loomed as foreign sites of restraint, discipline, and, sometimes, opportunity, while others have functioned to reinforce the messages of parents and community. Some custodians, such as the offenders among the Christian Brothers in St. John's Mount Cashel Orphanage in the twentieth century, clearly delighted in tormenting young charges. Others such as the nuns who taught female students at BC's All Hallows' Anglican school sometimes offered inspiration.[3] As Carol T. Baines reminds us in her study of Earlscourt Children's Home in Toronto, it is important to "re-examine the premise that children who do not grow up in two-parent families are somehow victims."[4] This outcome has been far from inevitable.

The first part of this chapter reviews hopes for the redemption, restraint, and punishment of children for whom kin care was not available or deemed insufficient. Like the domestic mythologies considered in the first chapter, high expectations of these institutions were inextricably linked to community, sometimes even national, dreams and were shaped in very large part by the social origins of the target clientele. While this volume focuses on the poor, the offspring of elite have also been significantly represented in residential care, such as that provided by private schools and summer camps. Such privileged sites aimed quite explicitly to consolidate familial power into the next generation. Such a goal, however, was not the prospect facing the majority of youngsters under 24/7 supervision. The second section of the chapter considers this disadvantaged group. It begins with a consideration of omnibus institutions, or those with diverse populations, and then turns respectively to orphanages and infant homes, industrial and reform schools, Native residential schools, and finally to total institutions for youngsters with presumed physical and mental disabilities. Despite their very real differences, all these enterprises promised (re)socialization that was superior to that provided by their families, although this might mean little more in reality than long-term warehousing. The final part of this chapter traces the evolution of institutions and their continuation into the twenty-first century as one element in Canada's panoply of provisions for children. Right from the beginning, their presence has informed and shaped the foster care that is the special concern of subsequent chapters.

Redemption, Restraint, and Punishment

Individual institutions emerged for various purposes, evolved for better or worse over time, and offered overseers and youngsters unpredictable opportunities. Just as with kith and kin care, gender, class, race, religion, age, sexuality, and (dis)ability, as well as the time period, shaped the possibilities and outcomes. What has distinguished all these institutions is the basic rationale for their existence. They have been created and have survived because kith and kin and foster care parents have not been able, were not willing, or were not considered suitable to raise certain children and young people. The assessment of the parents and kin of residents by administrators, staff, and sometimes the public at large has been critical in influencing reception and outcomes.

Although Native societies occasionally practised age and residential segregation for ceremonial purposes, European newcomers introduced and developed institutional practices that became a major feature of Canadian childhood by the close of the nineteenth century. Residential schools for both French and Native pupils appeared in New France in order to shape an orderly and industrious society at its roots. In face of the perceived disorder of new lands and diverse populations, British settlement turned to institutions to (re)socialize and assist (which was often regarded as one and same) the young. Small boarding schools, such as the one managed by Anglican minister John Strachan in Upper Canada, emerged to redeem the offspring of the elite from colonial contamination. More vulnerable youngsters, when they were not handed over to the lowest bidder under the *Poor Laws* introduced in the Maritimes or simply fostered out in versions of apprenticeship for similarly pitiful sums by local municipalities and parishes in Upper and Lower Canada, could well find themselves in hospitals, prisons, and poorhouses alongside unfortunate adults. In these establishments, the tools of salvation might well include physical chastisement and psychological humiliation. Ideas of discipline given intellectual rationale by Jeremy Bentham's hopes for the panopticon, the intensification of racism (increasingly in its scientific version), the emergence of a varied population lacking common customs of discipline and hierarchy, a determination to control social development for the benefit of elites, religious enthusiasm for good works, and, not to be forgotten, undeniable sympathy for the impoverished and the untaught combined to inspire institutional experiments over the centuries. As time went on, especially as social science experts grew more powerful, a broad spectrum of Canadian youngsters were deemed to be in need of specialized service delivered in total environments. Rather ironically, given their repeatedly bad press, space was commonly in high demand and overcrowding was almost a matter of course.

Most institutions have involved girls and boys at opposite ends of the social spectrum. Much like their mutual reliance on kinship to facilitate life's journey, elite and working class or disadvantaged parents have been more likely to encounter collective care. While the phenomenon is little studied, more powerful Canadians have frequently imbedded offspring in recreational, learning, and rehabilitative sites that affirm and develop networks of power.[5] Better than other citizens, they have been able to afford training and therapies for exploring competencies and addressing maladies. While abuses have occurred, elite youngsters have not faced the recurring denigration of families and communities that have poisoned so many institutions for the disadvantaged. Unlike their class superiors, bourgeois households have in contrast regularly counted on domestically minded mothers to keep offspring in line. They have also been prone to suspect (sometimes envy) the transmission of privilege in elite residential sites and to condemn their implication that domestic morality was insufficient for the raising of progeny. On the other hand, they were apt to regard the incarceration of the offspring of social inferiors as an unfortunate, if unsurprising, cost of individual failure to attain middle-class standards. From this perspective, 24/7 institutions were effectively unnecessary for normal middle-class offspring and far more the preserve of suspect others. Only in the case of clinically therapeutic settings would Canada's middle-ranking youngsters have a significant presence.

Plans for the redemption of Native, racialized, or working-class kids from the condition of their forebears, which was frequently considered uncivilized and morally dangerous, were modest at best. Total institutions and many others as well, including public schools, in large measure endeavoured to direct suspect others to an obedient and industrious maturity subordinated to their class, racial, gender, and other betters. To ensure such results, girls and boys faced levels of control and punishment unneeded by their better-placed contemporaries. The great majority of Native, working-class, and racialized families ultimately stood most often at the sharp end of what institutions had to offer.

The explanation of social control is not, however, sufficient. Supporters and staff of institutions were frequently committed to benefiting their young charges. Charlotte Neff's important assessment of Ontario's Protestant children's homes demonstrates persisting recognition that parental poverty, rather than misconduct, drove many admissions.[6] A highly gendered ethic of care was also often visible in children's homes and orphanages in particular. Many female champions identified with parents, especially mothers, and endeavoured to make residences as much like home as possible. A few men seem to have made the same commitment. The Methodist deaconess Hattie Inkman, who maintained the Earlscourt Children's Home as a beacon of hope, was one such figure. So too was public health activist Dr. Peter Bryce, who both condemned Native residential schools and helped found the Earlscourt initiative before the First World War.[7] Such advocates could be deeply sympathetic to girls and boys who went unschooled and unprotected and who encountered adults as brutal taskmasters and seducers.

Inclusion in a shared residential community, whether this included the orphaned offspring of fraternal lodge brothers, youngsters with hearing loss, or Natives from impoverished reserves, was justified as an efficient and even humane way to confer concrete benefits in terms of food, accommodation, and instruction and more intangible advantages such as spiritual and moral train-ing. Institutions won support from authorities and from the general public not only because they promised to discipline the troublesome but also because they appeared to embody the collective concern for youngsters and families that was increasingly embraced as the mark of modern Canada. Optimism flourished in the context of confidence in religious founders and staff as well as in the train-ing and therapy increasingly offered by social work, medical, and educational professionals. This dream never died.

For all the power of their creators, managers, and workers, institutions were never entirely divorced from kith and kin. Parents regularly used them to cope with crisis. As Sara Posen concludes in her study of the Toronto Boys' Home, "while economic survival was the first reason for which many parents sought to gain entry for their sons into the home escaping family violence was the sec-ond … mothers often placed sons in the home as part of their escape from abu-sive spouses."[8] Even when poverty and the law compelled the attendance of girls and boys, interested observers lingered on the sidelines and, at times, directly intervened. Parents and others often took for granted their right to evaluate and, if necessary, condemn treatment. Connections were all the closer because boundaries between insiders and outsiders could be relatively perme-able. Siblings and previous generations might well be prior alumnae. They could share intimate knowledge of schools, orphanages, and reformatories, and they could propose strategies of accommodation and resistance. Occasionally, as with housemothers and cleaning and grounds staff, they might also work on the premises.

The mothers and fathers who have stood before Canadian courts arguing for sterner or easier sentencing for their progeny, like those who have moved their youngsters in and out of asylums as domestic resources allowed, have been active, although never omnipotent, interveners. Claims by managers, directors, and staff in general to act in *loco parentis* have reinforced links between per-sonal and public agendas and provided grounds for involvement. Reference to members of religious orders as mothers, fathers, sisters, and brothers have made the same point. Kith and kin have regularly retained a moral touchstone by which to judge institutions.

Although for the most part the generalization holds that social condition dictates opportunity, institutions have sometimes supplied the best possible alternative and blessed relief for the disadvantaged. For instance, when communities such as Winnipeg's Jews collaborated in the design and oversight of an orphanage or when compassionate and dedicated founders and staff committed themselves to their charges as seems to have occurred with the Montreal Protestant Orphans' Home, good things sometimes happened. Collective efforts can mobilize otherwise unavailable resources and offer protection. Children may benefit from instructors, libraries, technologies, therapies, and each other— assets that might well be unavailable on their home turf.

It is also a hard fact of life that some youngsters are so damaged before birth or by the course of life that it is difficult to meet their needs outside of group settings. They may constitute threats to themselves and to others, and they may require levels of attention and commitment that no one family or even a single community can readily provide. Ontario's Orillia Asylum, British Columbia's Woodlands School, and Quebec's Rivière-des-Prairies Hospital have often failed profoundly, but they have also supplied critical respite, and sometimes hope, to parents overwhelmed by youngsters with intellectual and other disabilities. Early juvenile and family court judges such as Anna Jamieson of Calgary, Emily Murphy of Edmonton, and Helen Gregory McGill of Vancouver intended that reform and industrial schools be used to rescue girls and boys from violent and abusive relations, and this sometimes occurred. Orphanages have given some residents a chance to survive and restore their families. In short, the persistence of institutions has reflected not only the desire to control clients but also the reality that kin have regularly been unable to meet the needs of all members.

Diverse in Origins and Purpose

Institutions have had many sizes, shapes, and goals. They have ranged from enormous edifices that testify to the power of founders and dominate their landscapes to houses and farms that differ little from their neighbours. Staff has included lady managers, semi-skilled labourers, the religious and secularly motivated, the highly credentialed, the transient, and the lifelong. They also have had a wide range of relations with surrounding communities. Some have had deep roots in ethnic, religious, and familial custom, while others have been foreign transplants. Most have had some suspicions about the parents of the children in their custody, but many have also been at least occasionally sympathetic to the predicament and yearnings of their residents and those who loved them. In short, institutions are not readily summed up in a single image or statement.

Omnibus Solutions

Specialized institutions were commonly preceded, and indeed sometimes accompanied, in Canadian colonies, provinces, and territories by the inclusion of girls and boys in settings that were intended for adults. For many years, jails, hospitals, and poorhouses crowded together young and old, sick and healthy, the criminal and the merely unfortunate. Such facilities, while far from adequate, sometimes also equalled, or even surpassed, what inmates might otherwise have experienced. Early inclusiveness was symbolized most dramatically by the provision for abused children in the legislative mandate of Nova Scotia's Society for the Prevention of Cruelty to Animals in 1880. In 1888, two-thirds of its cases involved injury to human young.[9] Only in the mid-nineteenth century did sectarian orphanages and state-run reform and industrial schools slowly challenge custom and embrace childhood as a stage meriting segregated provision, and this shift remained far from complete into the twentieth century. Their inclusion alongside adults reflected the persisting, although never ubiquitous, belief that poverty was largely a moral failing. As Toronto's *Globe* newspaper argued in 1877,

> a very large proportion of both men and women who are the recipients of public bounty are notoriously dissipated. Though they are so, we do not advocate a system which would leave them to starve, but we do say that if they are ever to be taught economical and saving habits they must understand the public have no idea of making them entirely comfortable in the midst of their improvidence and dissipation.[10]

In Nova Scotia, an unusually early orphan home initially housed needy girls and boys, but after 1785 these children joined adults, often kith and kin, in the colonial workhouse. If they survived, they would be apprenticed as cheaply as possible to strangers, commonly as domestic and agricultural labourers in a manner not dissimilar to many early and even later initiatives in foster care.[11] While officially rejecting poor laws, Upper Canada experimented with revealingly titled "houses of industry" to accommodate the distressed poor. While the preference was to save funds by channelling youngsters to toil in other households, Toronto's House of Industry, founded in 1837, and its counterparts quickly accommodated children, both with and without parents.[12] Early in its history, the Kingston federal penitentiary, like local gaols everywhere in British North America, similarly barracked youngsters alongside their elders. All ages were regarded as properly paying the piper for insobriety, sloth, immorality, and stupidity.

The frequent economic disadvantage and sometime social conservatism of Maritime Canada long kept integration familiar. In 1900, the matron of Nova Scotia's Yarmouth County Asylum still sought suitable residents to nurse "infant waifs and strays." Hardly surprisingly, modern advocates of child protection reckoned such remedies unsatisfactory—all the more so since "the staff is a small one and it has been necessary to place these helpless little ones in the care and under the charge of insane women inmates of the house!" In 1900, this poorhouse sheltered twenty-one inmates: seven sane men, two sane women, four insane male paupers, four insane female paupers, one boy, and four girls.[13] By the First World War, Nova Scotia still reared children "under the same roofs as the poor (mostly old and decrepit), the defective and insane." At the time, one critic concluded that,

> while they are doubtless kindly treated, and while the effort is generally made to have them attend school, it is manifestly impossible for these children to have the care and attention which is to develop the traits necessary to good citizenship. Moreover one cannot but feel that the environment of the County Asylum or Alms House is most prejudicial to children, physically, intellectually and morally.[14]

Despite recurring condemnation, such inclusion persisted. By the Second World War, the Halifax poorhouse counted, in a clear violation of child protection legislation, eighteen young among its 353 residents.[15] It nevertheless survived into the 1950s, housing "mentally challenged or chronically ill, as well as unmarried mothers, prostitutes, juvenile delinquents, and the elderly poor."[16]

Such programs persisted longest in Maritime Canada because specialized institutions and outdoor relief were deemed beyond the region's means, but indiscriminate mingling survived elsewhere as well. Among the most infamous examples was the inclusion of girls and boys, known colloquially as the "Duplessis orphans" after the provincial premier of the day, in Quebec's mental hospitals from the 1940s to the 1960s, as part of a provincial ploy to obtain federal subsidies.[17] The placement of mentally ill youngsters everywhere in adult psychiatric wards at the beginning of the twenty-first century demonstrated a comparable unwillingness to finance targeted programs. Debates in 2007–8 as to whether jailed BC mothers should be allowed to have newborns stay in their rooms suggests also the difficulty of hard-and-fast rules. Separation of adults and youngsters sometimes ignored the best interests of both.

Nineteenth-century religious and reform sensibilities slowly made inroads into presumptions that parental, especial paternal, guardianship was sacrosanct and that the young properly shared the fate of their elders. In the 1880s, Nova Scotia and Ontario legislated the possibility of state wardship for dependent children. In the next decade, the Ontario *Children's Protection Act* endeavoured to keep youngsters out of adult institutions. The cautious emergence of the "best interest" of the child doctrine testified to determination to break histories of abuse and despair. New institutions never, however, entirely shed long-standing assumptions of blame. Nor were they intended to address the social inequalities that caused so much of the damage to young charges. In their frequent affirmation of the status quo, they were not as different from the earlier poorhouses and houses of industry as their advocates had hoped.

Orphanages and Children's and Infant Homes

The creation of orphanage, children's, and infant homes in the mid-nineteenth century nevertheless signalled a major shift in the public perception of how best to address children in distress. As historians have suggested, the appearance of such specialized sites reflects in part the principles of dependence, protection, delayed responsibilities, and segregation associated with modern childhood.[18] Distinct provision for boys, girls, and infants who lacked one parent (commonly described in error as orphans) or both parents demonstrated new optimism about both the possibility of redemption and their potential as citizens of modern states.

Some early initiatives set out to isolate inmates from prior associates, but many acknowledged continuing ties and the value of respite to desperate widows in particular. They hoped to safeguard children, aid respectable families, and, in general, enhance social stability. Infant homes, which were frequently a somewhat later phenomenon, similarly often endeavoured to maintain kin ties, notably with nursing mothers. Only as artificial feeding improved and illegitimacy became less associated with inherited immorality did such residences turn increasingly to adoption, at least of the healthy, and the deliberate breaking of blood ties.

The early hopes of orphanages depended to a significant degree on selective admissions. The offspring of the respectable dead and hard-up but worthy widowers and widows supplied the ideal clientele. With reputable, albeit economically inadequate, ancestry, these children could properly be redeemed as the pitiful but essentially moral youngsters described by Charles Dickens and Lucy Maud Montgomery. Well into the twentieth century, those presumed to be illegitimate and delinquent, as well as those who were Native, Black, and otherwise racialized, were regularly refused entry. Their inclusion was resisted lest it appear to reward disreputable parents and contaminate the deserving.

Although first appearing in the late eighteenth century, the heyday of Canadian orphanages stretched from the mid-nineteenth century to the early twentieth century. Some, like New Westminster's True Blue and Orange Home, Toronto's Neil McNeill Home, and Halifax's Guardian Angel Home survived until after the Second World War. Serving as substantial landmarks in many towns and cities, some operated for only brief periods while others lasted many decades. A few eventually transitioned into modern social services for young-sters. Admissions focused on those who were leaving toddlerhood or those who had just passed the age of most demanding care to those who were entering puberty, after which they were considered to be variously less vulnerable to exploitation, old enough to work for others, or able to contribute more than they cost to their families. On rare occasions, orphanages kept exceptionally tal-ented teenagers in attendance at local high schools. Sibling groups were com-mon, but boys and girls were regularly segregated on the premises. Relatively few were complete orphans. In 1946, Arthur Saint-Pierre's survey of veterans of Quebec's Catholic orphanages found that only 13.4 percent of his group had lost both parents. In comparison, 30.3 had lost fathers, 33.8 percent had lost moth-ers, and 21.8 percent had both living parents. Even with the fully orphaned, many had kin who demonstrated interest by visiting, making occasional payments for care, and sending notes and parcels.[19] Since many such institutions were private initiatives, their exact number and that of their residents remain unknown, but many hundreds existed and many thousands of children moved through them in the period covered by this volume.

Over time, many orphanages and homes received grants from provincial governments that hoped to avoid direct responsibility for child protection. Philanthropic donations, religious funding, and payments from kith and kin were critical in paying bills. Most also required household and farm labour from res-idents—a contribution that was viewed as possessing both vocational and moral merit and corresponding to the practice of the poorest households. It is important, however, not to draw too sharp a distinction between the operations of children's institutions and the advocates of fostering such as Ontario's chil-dren's aid societies. As Charlotte Neff has documented, nineteenth-century homes were active, in a continuation of long-standing state and private efforts that favoured pauper apprenticeships, in placing youngsters in individual house-holds. Nor did the foster care system, which was implemented officially by Ontario in 1893, represent a major shift. It merely shifted the responsibility for placement from institutions to the children's aid societies.[20] Despite their much prized independence and continuity with other child-saving initiatives, orphan-ages became increasingly subordinated to state authorities, which generally regarded them as rivals or inferiors to official programs of fostering and adop-tion.[21] By the 1960s, the vast majority had disappeared or transitioned into specialized treatment centres.

The best establishments strove to become second homes. This was the intent of the female directors of Montreal's Protestant Orphan Asylum, which was founded in 1822. As Janice Harvey has emphasized, "institutions were not alien to them as places to raise children—many of their own children had probably spent time in a boarding school—and they were not fearful of creating an institutional child."[22] Indeed nineteenth-century children's homes can be understood as one expression of the expansion of education to destitute youngsters.[23] Collective supervision also promised some protection. After witnessing abuse when they placed young charges in private households, Montreal's lady directors preferred to retain them for retrieval by kin in better times or until they could be more safely apprenticed as teenagers. Such concerns were not unusual. In 1914, the lady managers of Toronto's Boy's Home defended their operation by explaining that fostering undermined the opportunity of "re-uniting the family."[24] On Prince Edward Island, the Catholic Sisters of Martha operated a home that closed in summers, a strategy that saved money and offered time to reconnect youngsters with families and communities, just as happened with private boarding schools.[25] The similarities were clear to one Quebec champion who characterized the orphanage as "le pensionnat des enfants pauvres."[26]

In Toronto, the female founders, volunteers, and staff of Earlscourt Children's Home endeavoured to strengthen families in the anticipation that offspring would return. Middle-class and upper-class women supporters established rules, such as specified visiting days, requirements for clothing to be marked, and notices for removal upon misbehaviour, that were "not unlike those for upper- and middle-class boarding schools."[27] Many beneficiaries appreciated the intended atmosphere of such disciplined respectability: "The women who placed their children at Earlscourt did so with the understanding that they were sharing the caregiving, not relinquishing it."[28] Such Canadian children's homes offered educational opportunities that destitute families might desire but would have found difficult to supply.

Much like many Canadian households, orphanage populations were often relatively transient. In Montreal, St. Alexis typically accommodated "children [who were] continually arriving and leaving. Ten per cent of the girls stayed one month or less, half for under one year. Between 1860 and 1885 the length of the girls' stays grew shorter. Increasingly, parents seem to have used the orphanage to solve short-term rather than long-term family crises."[29] Established in 1892 and described as more an "adequate temporary familial substitute" than a "grim Dickensian image," Vancouver's Alexandra Orphanage was similarly busy. Between 1892 and 1938, it admitted 1,500 to 2,000 youngsters, who flowed back and forth as need and opportunity demanded among various institutions, kith, and kin.[30] As soon as they could clean house, mind others, go on errands, tend livestock, clear fields, or find wages, boys and girls were often sent out by managers or retrieved by parents. In many ways, their lives mixed the domestic and the institutional, in ways familiar to many poorer families across the country.

For residents, their experiences might well have seemed "normal and without stigma" and "discipline, training, and emphasis on school achievement" were sometimes valued.[31] Such seems the case for example with Frank Berton, later the father of the popular journalist and historian Pierre. His widowed mother could keep only her younger son, and so she placed Frank in the very respectable Wiggins Male Orphan Institution of St John, New Brunswick, from which he left to enter the provincial university. In 1946, Quebec's Arthur Saint-Pierre defended educational opportunities, declaring "c'est que les anciens qui ont eu la chance de poursuivre leurs études à la sortie ont pu entrer ... dans les collèges classiques, sur un pied d'égalité avec les élèves de leur âge venant des autres institutions d'enseignment." He pointed in particular to girls' orphanages, arguing that it often happened that particularly brilliant students "ont bénéficié de l'appui financier de l'institution afin de poursuivre des études académiques ou meme un cours de garde-malade."[32] Such sentiments could also inspire Catholics in other Canadian communities. In his preface to the English translation of Reverend Charles Bourgeois' thesis on child welfare in Quebec, James C. Cardinal McGuigan, archbishop of Toronto, praised the author for escaping the fashionable tenets of "North American sociological circles" and defending "institutional homes" for youngsters.[33]

Mutual benefit societies created many children's homes as one expression of group respectability and solidarity, and their establishments stressed misfortune as the singular distinguishing mark of residents and their families. In Ontario, the Independent Order of Foresters dedicated itself to preserving "the children's self-respect, to make them feel that they are natural, normal citizens." They dressed like others of their rank and attended local schools. Individual courts of Foresters committed themselves to the well-being of particular girls and boys.[34] Beginning in 1913, other Canadians, and sometimes their mothers, went south to Mooseheart, the Illinois complex maintained by voluntary contributions and taxes from members of the Loyal Order of the Moose. Once again, families supplied a key part of the calculation, with some widows acting as housemothers.[35] Shared identities could also humanize religious foundations. One former resident of a twentieth-century Winnipeg initiative summed up possible outcomes: "The orphanage was the jewel of the Jewish citizenry, the visible proof of a compassionate community."[36]

For many girls and boys, however, such settings held a far bleaker story. Even short-term separation from kin could be traumatic, and abuse was reported even in institutions judged to be successful. Zeal and sensitivity frequently dropped precipitously over time as staff became hardened to domestic tragedy and pessimistic about unending applications for admission. A recent study of American, Canadian, and Australian residents tells just such a sad tale. Despite differences of gender and location, they remembered

> discipline and corporal punishment, though this was tempered in recent times. Household chores dominated daily routines. There was little possibility of love and affection, and children retreated into solitary pursuits. Many of the respondents found difficulty in developing close personal relationships after leaving care and had to work through anger or confusion.[37]

Like the "home children" who were parcelled off to Canada by British philanthropies during the Second World War, many of these children lost connection with kin. Since training too frequently consisted of little more than the primary grades, inmates were hard pressed not to repeat their parents' lifetime of poverty.

The frequent shift from cavernous buildings to "family cottages" in the twentieth century endeavoured to mitigate isolation and alienation identified by critics.[38] Toronto's Sacred Heart Orphanage clearly hoped for better outcomes when it turned to small buildings grouped in a Children's Village in 1949.[39] A British study has nonetheless noted problematic intentions and results:

> They had similarly strict daily schedules and their primary goal was to produce good citizens and qualified, deferential labourers. The main difference was that the recreated "family" in the cottage homes served to naturalise and legitimize this process, while at the same time further delegitimising the children's biological family structures.[40]

Ultimately, although they promised relief for many parents as well as protection for the residents, children's homes remained spaces over which both had little control. In a case of hopes gone dreadfully awry, the superintendent and his wife from the Catholic Boys' Home in Burnaby, British Columbia, were dismissed for abuse in 1930. Despite this and other warnings, children nevertheless stayed put because the province preferred to pay a pittance for institutional care and avoid the greater costs associated with fostering.[41] On the other side of the country, Stompin' Tom Connors experienced similar meanness. After apprehension from his young mum, he was sent eventually to New Brunswick's St. Patrick's Orphanage where he recalled "drab overalls and a shirt," hunger, hard agricultural labour, and nuns who ruled with an "iron fist-iron rod." As he remembered, the Second World War "was coming to an end, but in some sectors the atrocities were still going on. As children with weak kidneys we could no more help wetting the bed than a Jewish kid could help being Semitic." Like other unfortunates, he had "neither family nor friends to turn to."[42] It took many complaints and investigations to close offenders such as St. Patrick's or Mount Cashel in St. John's, Newfoundland. Their inmates, like those in Native residential schools, only intermittently provoked public concern.

In contrast, infanticide, foundlings, and illegitimacy sparked recurring outrage. Infant and foundling homes appeared across the country from the mid-nineteenth century onward. Discovered in back alleys, farm fields, and lodgings, dead babies had long been a fact of Canadian life, but they and their generally unwed mothers elicited moral panics.[43] In the 1860s, respectable citizens responded to what was believed to be an increase in abandonment with the Halifax Foundlings' Home.[44] The tragedy of vulnerable newborns in Canadian cities caused religious leaders, such as St. Boniface's Archbishop Langevin in the 1890s, to advocate infant homes, challenging critics who feared that their very existence might encourage promiscuity and immorality.[45] As Suzanne Morton has observed of Halifax's Infants' Home (founded in 1875), such institutions largely assisted "a minority of women who did not use or have access to family or community support for their child-care needs."[46] Across the country, in cities such as Montreal, St. Boniface, and Edmonton, the Sisters of Misericordia served unwed Catholic mothers who could not or would not return to parents and communities. Infants' special vulnerability, as well as desires to punish moral trespassers, explains why orphanages and poorhouses admitted foundlings with considerable reluctance and why homes for the unmarried frequently required mothers to nurse their own and sometimes others' offspring.

By admitting mothers with newborns, the infant homes in Halifax and Toronto (established in 1876) lowered otherwise high rates of mortality.[47] Admissions were also intended to inspire individual improvement and hopes for salvation. As Andrée Lévesque has observed in the case of Montreal's Misericordia Hospital, such sites might well be punitive, designed to remind the unwed of their transgressions and deter further offences.[48] Even when mothers and families contributed to their upkeep, infants remained extremely susceptible to respiratory and other infections. Death tolls lingered well above 50 percent and often beyond 80 percent in many residences until the 1930s.

Surviving offspring sometimes departed with mothers who might subsequently wed or struggle with single parenthood. Many, however, were fostered, adopted, or moved into the orphanages that were often associated with the infant homes. Some were later retrieved by kin. Since most such babies were illegitimate, a condition that was frequently assumed to connote inherited immorality until at least the Second World War, few people were willing to take them. The stigma of bastardry not only deterred the morally sensitive, but it also meant that a smaller pool of relatives, commonly in the maternal line, were likely to know and to care about their existence.

As mothers' allowances, widows' pensions, and other social security programs were introduced during the twentieth century, the clientele of orphanages and infant homes slowly shifted. More youngsters could remain with kin. Expanding provision for state foster care provided another alternative. By the 1960s, orphanages had become the preserve of the most desperate and the most unwanted of children, as the sad gathering of little victims in Toronto's Neil McNeill Home demonstrated. When it finally closed its doors in the 1960s, most of the children headed into fostering households.[49] By the last decades of the twentieth century, familial solutions triumphed as orphanages, like infant homes, which had little purpose once healthy babies could readily be adopted straight from hospitals, gradually disappeared from the Canadian institutional landscape.

Industrial and Reform Schools

Even as orphanages and infant homes emerged in the nineteenth century to assist those who were judged to be for the most part more respectable and innocent, other locations set their sights on girls and boys evaluated as more problematic. Reformers condemned prisons and gaols for incarcerating youngsters with adults and for imposing brutal regimes that often included corporal punishment. Even as public schools appeared to meet the needs of middle-range or so-called "normal" youngsters, state-boarding institutions, referred to variously as industrial and reform schools and sometimes as training schools and reformatories, emerged to deal with others. Industrial schools initially targeted children and youth believed to be in danger of unsuitable conduct and criminal activity, while reform schools attended to those who had already crossed the line.[50] Distinctions were never, however, hard and fast, and youngsters might well be almost indistinguishable from the residents of orphanages. Industrial and reform schools shared a common inspiration. They existed because authorities and some parents concluded that some families could not ensure that girls and boys behaved properly. Non-kin were assigned the task of (re-)educating potential and actual delinquents from ages five or six to sixteen or eighteen. When inmates became too old for the system, most disappeared into poorer populations or transferred soon enough into adult prisons.

In 1869, Quebec led in proposing industrial and reform schools to save youngsters from immorality and the public from their depredations. Other provinces, notably Ontario, soon came on board.[51] In 1875, Ottawa amended the *Criminal Code* to allow sentencing to provincial reformatories instead of federal penitentiaries for those aged sixteen and under.[52] Ontario's 1879 legislation providing for industrial schools typically encompassed poor, abandoned, neglected, and delinquent youngsters. In 1880, the province permitted the incarceration of children aged ten to thirteen who were deemed pre-delinquent upon a complaint by their guardian.[53] Over subsequent decades, the province developed a complex network of reform and training programs for both girls and boys. By the First World War, Nova Scotia, British Columbia, and Manitoba had industrial schools. Such sites often housed diverse residents. In 1889, Ontario's Penetanguishene reformatory included a seven-year-old, five nine-year-olds, six ten-year-olds, six eleven-year-olds, seventeen twelve-year-olds, and twelve thirteen-year-olds. The province's Industrial Refuge for Girls admitted one four-year-old, two eight-year-olds, two nine-year-olds, three ten-year-olds, two eleven-year-olds, three twelve-year-olds, and two thirteen-year-olds in the same year.[54] Boundaries among categories of inmates were often uncertain. Manitoba's Knowles Home for Boys was not unusual in evolving to admit a heterogeneous assortment of kids committed by child protection and criminal justice authorities as well as by their own parents. During the Second World War, sons of Canadian servicemen and working mothers constituted some 30 percent of its population, while others included British evacuees and those who still entered through the judicial system.[55]

In 1908, in response to growing concern with abuse and recidivism, Ottawa introduced the federal *Juvenile Delinquents Act*.[56] This legislation encouraged provinces to set up special courts, which provided for probation and stressed treatment and redirection rather than punishment for those under the age of sixteen. In 1921, age was extended to eighteen. Despite some improvement, results proved far less than anticipated. Hopes for redemption frequently battled recurring eugenic and therapeutic pessimism. By the 1960s, progressive concern encompassed fears about the loss of children's civil rights, but the 1982 *Young Offenders Act* returned to an older emphasis on youth responsibility.[57] Twenty years later, the federal *Youth Criminal Justice Act* endeavoured to balance both rehabilitation and punishment. Whatever their precise orientation, such initiatives shared recurring underfunding and only episodic public attention. In both respects, they matched foster care programs, which, ironically enough, were regularly embraced as part of the efforts at redirection from the criminal justice system.

Despite persisting problems, industrial and reform schools set out to be life-changing for disadvantaged and delinquent youngsters. Their target group, which was overwhelmingly the sons and daughters of the poor, was assumed to lack discipline, morality, and proper protection and to pose dangers to themselves and others. At their best, and much like elite boarding schools, they hoped to inspire, as one champion of the latter explained:

Esprit de corps, cooperation, discipline during and after school hours, deport-
ment, influence, environment, inspiration, ideals, the right attitude toward work,
a sense of justice and fairness, honor and mastery over self: a sort of communis-
tic centre which recognizes that every individual owes a certain duty to the home,
the church, the neighborhood and the state.[58]

Even though they were imbued with similar qualities, the graduates of private schools were directed towards leadership, while those of industrial and
reform schools were readied to be a loyal, industrious, and subordinate class
of citizens.

In stark contrast to upper-class Canadians who have regularly depended on
institutions to supplement, and sometimes even replace, their hands-on care,
the parents of inmates of correctional facilities have been commonly judged to
be inadequate.[59] Fathers in working-class and racialized populations were regularly evaluated as deficient when they lacked the employment necessary to
anchor respectable households. Mothers demonstrated inadequacy by not pro-
ducing domestic harmony and obedient and industrious offspring. The choice
of farm or remote sites, such as Ontario's Penetanguishene reformatory, aimed
to separate inmates from such unfortunate or corrupt domestic influences.

Officialdom, however, did not supply the only adults unhappy with youth.
Courts heard from parents seeking help to discipline offspring who refused to
keep curfew, stay away from certain friends, or remit their wages. Many parents
asked magistrates to threaten their children into obedience.[60] Families also wanted
girls and boys returned when they were deemed suitably repentant or when the
needs of kin dictated. Just as some people used orphanages to negotiate the per-
ils of poverty, some parents in difficult circumstances took for granted their right
to use industrial and reform schools to solve domestic problems.

From the beginning, gender and ethnic origin or race mattered along side
class when it came to attracting attention from the courts and the police. Gender codes powerfully determined what was acceptable. Boys offending against
property and person readily found themselves before judges. Girls most often ran
into trouble when they were sexually vulnerable or active, conditions that were
often confused. Families and courts expected both sexes to obey house rules,
which normally included labour and waged contributions. Such duties were
usually interpreted more liberally for boys.[61] In the twentieth century, fostering
emerged as a way to divert youngsters from incarceration, but reformatories
always housed a significant population of boys who were deemed to be the most
resistant to domestic discipline.

Racialized youngsters were especially vulnerable to both the poverty and the
surveillance that increased prospects of apprehension. In 1921, the proportion of

"Negro" youngsters in reformatories, aged ten to twenty years, was the second highest of all ethnic groups.[62] In 1969, Manitoba's Home for Boys in Portage La Prairie reported an increasingly familiar profile: "*Over 50% are of Indian and Metis extraction.*"[63] By the beginning of the twenty-first century, incarcerated Aboriginal and African-Canadian girls and boys far outstripped their communities' share of the national population.[64] Their overrepresentation reflected some combination of racial profiling and original economic and social disadvantage.

Industrial and reform schools set out with high hopes. In many ways, they were superior to the prisons and gaols that had earlier admitted youngsters. Over the course of more than a century and half, they experimented with strategies to redeem inmates. Just as with orphanages, enormous urban edifices gave way to smaller, more personal, and more therapeutic environments. Farm operations and wilderness camps set out across the country to inspire natural improvement. Provisions for parole, alternate residential programs, and fostering tried to redirect vulnerable youngsters.

Despite good intentions, these initiatives could not easily escape the propensity for brutal adult staff, the influence of long-term stigmatization, and destructive peer cultures. Criminal justice programs were too often part of the problem. Training was often not designed and largely unable to deal with previous deprivation. It was generally ill prepared to address learning disabilities or other handicaps. Treatment for prior abuse has been rare or inadequate. Regularly overworked, undertrained, and sometimes predatory employees found themselves in charge of girls and boys about whom the public could only be intermittently persuaded to care and from whom politicians sometimes reaped political advantage in panics about youth crime or in budget-cutting performances.

Outcomes for the graduates of industrial and reform schools have been generally dreary. Most youngsters start out with limited kin resources and are often so damaged that they can make little use of available opportunities. Few secure educations that make them competitive with non-incarcerated contemporaries and many gain habits and networks that reinforce marginalization and criminal behaviour. Many boys and girls moved back and forth between juvenile justice and child protection systems, reaping poor results in both. The potential for reoffence, with eventual transfer to adult jails and prisons, was considerable. Not surprisingly, the first major Canadian post–Second World War scholarly assessment of the incarceration of youth was generally gloomy.[65]

Native Residential Schools

Indigenous youngsters were immediately eyed with interest by European authorities from New France. In the seventeenth century, Marie de L'Incarnation and the Ursuline Sisters hoped to civilize "petits sauvages" in order to transform them into good Christian and French wives and mothers. Residential schools appeared after the War of 1812 when the survival of the British colonies no longer clearly depended on Native support. Any provision for relative equality of outcome had largely disappeared by Confederation in 1867. A major federal report, entitled "Industrial Schools for Indians and Halfbreeds" (1879) by MP Nicholas Davin, proposed industrial schools as a solution to the "problem" of the indigenous population and led to funding for residential institutions run by Christian churches.[66] In 1884, attendance became compulsory for many status Indian girls and boys and remained so until 1948. From the nineteenth century to the 1990s, some 130 residential schools operated in Canada, with a peak of eighty in 1931. Students from all of the provinces and territories, ranging in age from five or so to their late teens, were vulnerable to compulsion, but attendance varied widely depending on local educational alternatives, community resilience, and parental resources and opposition. After the 1970s, bands increasingly set up their own programs, and most youngsters attended provincial public schools. The last residential institution closed at the end of the twentieth century. The damage to families and Native nations proved more long lasting.[67]

Like other total institutions, residential schools had mixed relations with parents. Initially, many leaders such as Shingwauk (1773–1854), an Ontario Anishnaabe chief, had high hopes for a "teaching wigwam lodge," which would mix Native and European knowledges and ensure future equality. Rising racism and newcomer conclusions that Aboriginal peoples were properly dying out or only suitable for menial employments soon dashed such hopes. Residential schools emerged as one part of an overall politics of dispossession from lands and resources. Native parents and customs were singled out as naturally inferior in ways that were reminiscent of the brutal assessment of poorer families in general. Like African Canadians and Irish Catholics during much of the nineteenth century, indigenous mothers and fathers were assumed to embody primitive promiscuity, indolence, and irresponsibility. Salvation, when possible, was believed to depend on assimilation, forced and otherwise, to respectable European practices. Even then, integration overwhelmingly occurred at the lowest level of the nation. For all of the similarities to institutions that housed other disadvantaged populations, the assault was more insidious because Native cultures and families stood in the way of White dominion.

Enthusiasm for residential schooling was always profitably hamstrung by the determination of Native communities to rear their own young on their own terms. As the frontier of colonization advanced, their ability to determine outcomes for their offspring nevertheless deteriorated. Newcomers took for granted that Native girls and boys should be directed to options that became increasingly inferior to those that were offered to other pupils. Residents were prepared for low-waged employment and social and economic subordination, and their well-being was frequently compromised by abysmal food and accommodation.[68] In 1909, Dr. Peter Bryce uncovered residential school mortality rates ranging from 35 percent to 60 percent, a toll regularly superseded only by nineteenth-century infant homes.[69] The systematic undermining of cultural traditions and practices, including language and religion, left children and parents ill equipped to cope with the overall assault.

Not all indigenous Canadians were equally affected. Experience varied tremendously over time depending on the particular institution, the resources of the targeted communities, and the gender and rank of the residents. The range of observations seems very similar to that coming from survivors of other institutions. When times were especially hard or kin were in particularly dire straits or brutal, schools might well provide better food, accommodation, and protection. Female alumnae of the Lejac Residential School in northern British Columbia who talked with anthropologist Jo Fiske sometimes reported a better time than their brothers, completing more grades, developing close friendships, acquiring useful skills, and acquiring mentors among their teachers. In many respects, they sounded like the girls who lived in the Earlscourt Children's Home in Toronto.[70] Native boys seem to have been more vulnerable to physical abuse and less likely to accommodate demands or to benefit from available opportunities. This gendered pattern also recalls what happened elsewhere.

Status within Native societies was also important. High rank seems to have protected some pupils—the good opinion of elite fathers and mothers was valuable in ensuring recruitment and church loyalty. By the mid-twentieth century, schools such as Ontario's Mohawk Institute and Mount Elgin Indian Residential School, like many others, dealt increasingly with "the problem of orphans and needy children," those in other words with fewer adults capable of intervening on their behalf.[71] The growing poverty of most reserves kept admissions high. The Great Depression of the 1930s hit many Native families particularly hard, and children entered the schools "grateful for three meals a day and clothes."[72]

Since times were often so tough on reserves and elsewhere, some survivors have concluded that residential life "stood them in good stead for the rest of their lives."[73] One former student from British Columbia's St. Mary's Residential

School, who was eventually the manager of the Mission Indian Friendship Centre, was typically positive: "There really is no healing for me, because there is nothing to heal, I've come out of there with more than I had."[74] Still another alumna remembered kind nuns whom she idolized and tried to imitate. For her, the fostering that later removed her sister was far more damaging.[75]

The recent assessment of residential schooling has nevertheless been overwhelmingly harsh. Frequent deaths and commonplace abuse destroyed many families and contributed to the disintegration of entire communities. The five-volume report of the Royal Commission on Aboriginal Peoples in 1996 described a tragic history. The 2008 apology for residential schools by Canada's prime minister was long overdue. The voice of one survivor of the Anglican Elhorn School in Manitoba, who declared that he returned home "a total stranger" and a "bitter enemy" to all Whites, told the truth for many.[76] While residential schools resembled other custodial institutions, historian Jim Miller is correct to conclude that such similarities offer "little consolation." "The problems of harsh treatment, emotional deprivation, and inadequate food" were intensified by the overall assault on Native collective life to which there is no clear equivalent.[77]

As residential schools lost mainstream and Native support, child welfare authorities faced growing caseloads of indigenous youngsters. This intake of new provincial wards increased the demands on a foster care system originally envisioned to empty institutions of "normal" youngsters. Youngsters quickly struggled with racism and despair. The fact that Native girls and boys were generally harder to place and that many drifted among foster placements, confirmed the bad news. For too many, foster families supplied only one stop on a road that led back to institutions, whether group homes or facilities for youthful offenders.

Curing and Warehousing

Youngsters with disabilities of every sort, whether deafness, harelips, Down's syndrome, blindness, schizophrenia, epilepsy, or paralysis, presented special challenges to societies and families.[78] The label of disability covered many conditions. Some of these afflictions, such as club foot, can be addressed by modern surgery, while others, such as bipolar disorder, may respond to drug regimes. Some are present at birth, while others occur in the course of maturation. Some impairments make living difficult, while others can be encompassed in the course of daily life. Functional difficulties have always been affected by social and economic conditions. Some families have fewer material resources to aid their offspring. The poor are also likely to suffer worse health. They live with conditions that better-off Canadians can avoid or treat. Home-based therapies might well be beyond their pocketbook. Costs have driven many people to resort to state residential care.

The capacity and the willingness to assist and include youngsters with handicaps have varied dramatically over time and place in Canada. As one thoughtful commentator on Ontario's Orillia Asylum and its successors, which housed children and adults with developmental difficulties from the nineteenth to the twenty-first century, has suggested, "severity of disability and social class" shaped families' abilities to retain, to surrender, and to retrieve.[79] Some combination of affection, fear of public shame, acceptance of disabilities as a fact of life, and children's usefulness in many, perhaps especially rural, settings has kept many Canadians with disabilities at home. As a more modern Canada heightened standards for education, appearance, and performance, domestic incorporation sometimes became more difficult. In 1928, British Columbia's Royal Commission on Mental Hygiene explained that the care of severely disabled members—in this instance, "idiots" and "imbeciles"—in "the average home is too great a burden and often results in break-down of other members of the family."[80]

Later social scientists have acknowledged that offspring with handicaps stress marital and sibling relations.[81] In a revelation of who commonly assumed the additional labour, the loss or incapacity of mothers often spurred institutional admissions.[82] Such was the case of a forty-two-year-old blind and "childish" Alberta woman who had lived all of her life with her parents. Upon her mother's death, her sister requested her entry into the provincial asylum.[83] The patchwork evolution of federal and provincial allowances and tax benefits for rearing youngsters with disabilities rarely met material and emotional costs. In such a context, institutionalization was a choice that many families had to accept.[84]

When kin could not manage, youngsters were sometimes consigned to facilities designed for adults. Jails, hospitals, and provincial poorhouses admitted those with disabilities well into the twentieth century. British Columbia's Provincial Asylum for the Insane was founded in 1878 to deal with mature inmates but rapidly had to admit younger residents suffering developmental delays and mental disorders. In Alberta, the Ponoka Asylum, which was established for adults in 1903, almost immediately found "boundaries pushed" to admit younger Albertans.[85]

Boys and girls who were later designated as having special needs also appeared as particularly unwanted residents of orphanages and reform, industrial, and Native residential schools. In 1929, a staff member of the Canadian Council for Child Welfare observed that provincial institutions of every sort were overloaded with inmates defined by contemporaries as disabled and thus largely untransferable to foster or adoptive parents: "Children with bow legs, cross eyes, ugly brick red hair, jug-handle ears, near-sighted children, half-caste children, the child who stutters, the child with the frowning countenance, the bad complexion, the birth mark or those whose hair stands straight on end, the child who, through physical weakness or lack of training, has not acquired clean personal habits and, perhaps the most pitiful of all, the child with the bad heritage."[86] Such broad interpretations of abnormality stigmatized countless children and helped ensure that they would be hard put to find supporters or function with confidence.

Treatment through greater classification was part of the promise of modernization. Youngsters who were hard of hearing or visually impaired were among the first to be offered segregated regimes, often shared with one another. Montreal led the way with specialized schools for Catholic boys in 1848 and girls in 1851, followed by Halifax in 1856. By the 1870s and 1880s, more residential programs had appeared in Quebec, Ontario, and Manitoba. In 1922, British Columbia established its school for the deaf and the blind in Vancouver.[87] Graduates were prepared for the most part to enter manual employments, which, like those envisioned by the residential schools, promised minimal livelihoods. Epidemics and commonplace diseases produced other specialized sites. In 1926, the Queen Alexandra Solarium for crippled and tubercular youngsters was built in Mill Bay on Vancouver Island. Five years later, a Vancouver Preventorium was established for children with tuberculosis.[88]

Girls and boys with serious mental impairments, whether of development or illness, were especially likely to face warehousing. While public schools made various provision for pupils with minor learning difficulties early in the twentieth century, they did not regard those facing serious mental, or even physical, challenges as their proper preserve, a rejection that was made clear by their inadequate response to youngsters with autism spectrum disorder at the beginning of the twenty-first century. Parents were often advised to send children away and forget them. As one observer reported in 1932, "mentally defective" youngsters "are booked to go to institutions as soon as there are enough institutions—if ever there are."[89] The logic of institutionalizing Canadians defined as abnormal or less than normal remained largely in place until the latter half of the twentieth century.[90] In 1970, Manitoba's Department of Health and Social Development described a common fate for such youngsters who were "transferred to the Manitoba School for Retardates "whenever space is available" after the age of six.[91] While day programs were the common preference of many parents, provincial funding was in short supply everywhere.

The recurring limits of public programs kept private arrangements ever-present. Canadian families explored residential and medicinal remedies at home and abroad from the nineteenth to the twenty-first century. The so-called "baby farmers," who took in charges from desperate parents for a pittance, had long made a living out of such misery.[92] In the 1950s, Ontario's notorious "Mom" Whyte was typical in housing the otherwise unwanted. One critical observer matter-of-factly linked her operation to the failure of public alternatives: "It is no accident … that Mrs. Whyte is caring for a number of mentally retarded children. This is because many institutions are over-crowded and won't accept children until they are five years old."[93]

In the second half of the twentieth century, hopes for therapeutic remedies, often associated with pharmaceuticals and new medical procedures, sparked new initiatives for youngsters diagnosed with mental disorders.[94] The Ottawa Welfare Council, the Community Chest, and the Children's Aid held out high hopes for "children's villages" to assist the "emotionally disturbed, whose parents and foster parents had given up, whom no one wanted." Up-to-date settings promised to make troubled children "constructive, respectful, trustful, and … worthy and loved."[95] In 1957, Ontario introduced the nation's first mental hospital specifically for children (later the Thistletown Regional Centre). One year later, Montreal Children's Hospital set up a special psychiatric wing.

In the 1960s, the introduction of publicly funded hospital care expanded facilities and inspired optimism. The commitment of post–Second World War reformers to behaviour modification, normalization, and comprehensive community services was inspired by "anti-dehumanization" and "prodignity" philosophies. Many also shared a strong human rights orientation. Youngsters and adults with disabilities were to be treated with respect and integrated into local communities.[96] In the 1960s, Saskatchewan, under the leadership of its social democratic government, led in closing institutions and decentralizing social services. An active "parent association movement" emerged across Canada to lobby "for better living conditions for their sons and daughters" with mental disabilities.[97]

The group homes that emerged from many such campaigns promised various therapies, training, and accommodation for youngsters who were seen to be too demanding for private homes. Some were staffed by resident housemothers and fathers; others had staff cycling in and out over days and weeks. Children and youth stayed briefly or for lifetimes, often moving back and forth among birth and foster families and other treatment facilities. Provincial child protection departments managed some settings, but many such services have been contracted out to non-profit agencies and for-profit companies.

Early optimism often dissolved in the face of overwhelming demand and inadequate funding.[98] Like those in other provinces, Quebec's psychiatric wards "not only failed to provide adequate placements for referrals from the child-welfare network, but themselves sought placements in child-welfare institutions for their discharged clients."[99] Some sites presented old problems. One suicidal survivor of an Ontario group home remembered "a lot of kids from the ages of thirteen to eighteen" and "hired staff that weren't trained to deal with the kind of kids they had to deal with … The owner was a farmer and his wife was a hairdresser."[100]

In the last half of the twentieth century, orphanages and children's homes lost so-called normal children to their own families who were better, if for the most part meagerly, supported by the welfare state and to fostering and adoption. As their original clientele diminished, some of these institutions turned themselves into treatment centres for specific disorders. Toronto's Earlscourt Children's Home made just this transition. Founded in 1913, it ended up as the Earlscourt Child and Family Centre with a specialization in anti-social children in the 1970s.[101] In Victoria, the BC Protestant Orphans' Home transformed itself from a nineteenth-century orphanage into the Cridge Centre for the Family in the 1960s with a mission to support households in crisis. Montreal's Mackay Institution for Protestant Deaf Mutes, founded in 1869, eventually shut down in 1997 and emerged as the Mackay Rehabilitation Centre in 2004.[102] Other institutions were replaced, at least in theory, by smaller establishments. In 1964, the Weyburn Mental Hospital closed as part of Saskatchewan's overall decentralization of services.

The diversity of the clientele makes it virtually impossible to sum up the outcomes of residential programs for children with physical and mental difficulties. The story, however, often appears to be one of general inadequacy and frequent tragedy. The BC ombudsman has been damning. In 1993, she condemned the Jericho Hill School for the Deaf and, in 2000, she laid blame on New Westminster's Woodlands School that housed those with developmental delays.[103] The Law Commission of Canada's 2001 report on abuse in children's institutions did not spare residences for the blind and deaf nor for those with mental difficulties.[104] Communication from youngsters in residential treatment, notably when their participation was involuntary, confirms that many "perceive themselves to be controlled" rather than assisted and they often recall bitterness and despair.[105]

The story is nevertheless once again far from simple. Some Canadians with hearing impediments remember

> wonderful years. In spite of having to work hard and to put up with restrictions, they felt that much of their success in adulthood could be traced to the early childhood discipline, the encouragement and interaction with their deaf peers and deaf adults, and their struggles and eventual success establishing their own identities in such a residential and academic environment.[106]

Other citizens diagnosed with mental retardation who spent years in the Hurontario Hospital, which was the successor to the Orillia Asylum, have similarly recollected a "shared history" that involved much more than being "simply victims." As one thoughtful champion of survivors concluded, "they formed supportive and emotionally rewarding relationships which provided a foundation for building their own sense of community."[107]

The emergence of the community living movement and other campaigns for integration by parents and those living with disabilities brought significant advances in public acceptance in the last decades of the twentieth century. Children who were designated with special needs nevertheless remained overwhelmingly overrepresented in provincial child protection systems. Life continued frequently to be very difficult even when social supports, including state respite programs, existed. Many parents, especially if they were poor, were hard put to reconfigure living arrangements and supply special therapies. Young Canadians with disabilities remain, as in the past, the most likely to be institutionalized. Despite deliberate efforts at recruitment and special instruction, foster families that are equipped to meet their needs have proved hard to find. This shortfall, with its reduction of options, presents a continuing tragedy.

On the Defensive, but Surviving

In the nineteenth century and beyond, total institutions became a major feature of the lives of many Canadians. While inclusion with adults never entirely disappeared, expert opinion became largely successful in advocating age-specific locations. Youngsters who were disadvantaged by poverty, race, and presumed disability were especially likely to be sequestered in group settings. Ontario's first superintendent of neglected and dependent children, J.J. Kelso, who served from 1893 to 1934, typically linked institutions to care for damaged children and foster care to responsibilities for the healthy and wholesome. His distinction between Canadians who could meet social expectations for normalcy and those who could not remained the key to determining who was most likely to spend time in institutional care.

Traditions of corporatism, from Catholicism to the Masons, sustained support for institutions, as was evident in the reports of the Quebec Social Insurance Commission in 1933, but they faced growing skepticism. During the Second World War, critics from the Service familial de Québec found a platform before the provincial Garneau Commission investigating health insurance. While they had to battle accusations of secularism, they won strong endorsement in the commission's modernist indictment of institutions for "le débordement, l'exiguïté, l'insuffisance du personnel, le manque criant de ressources, les mélanges néfastes de populations, comme par exemple celui des enfants normaux et des enfants ayant un retard intellectuel, la présence d'une discipline beaucoup trop stricte et le placement d'enfants comme domestiques dès l'âge de dix ans."[108] Contemporary investigations into wartime nursery care by influential British psychologist John Bowlby, which affirmed dangers, especially for infants, proved especially influential.[109] The Cold War celebration of domesticity as the solution to personal and national problems furthered disaffection with collective solutions. Proper mothers could solve, so it was assumed, many of the problems of youth.

By the late 1970s, child and youth care experts were optimistic about the deinstitutionalization of even long-standing clientele. As one important study suggests, progressive programming set about to "move out of its residential homestead into schools, community, and homes" and to reconnect with families.[110] New initiatives, including an emphasis on family therapy, promised help. Late twentieth-century scandals such as those surrounding St. John's Mount Cashel Orphanage, British Columbia's Jericho Hill School for the Deaf, and Native residential schools further undermined credibility. Institutions became ready targets for governments that wished to appear humanitarian while simultaneously cutting social service costs.[111] Enthusiasm for closure was nevertheless everywhere accompanied by insufficient provision for alternative strategies to ensure children's well-being.

Not surprisingly, institutions always retained champions. Some observers believed that they offered real help to birth parents. In 1933, a representative of Toronto's Local Council of Women made a typical case in insisting that "there was something to be said for the argument that a natural mother, instead of being forced to give up her child, might have it kept in an institution where she could have access to it and have hope of later reclaiming it."[112] In the next decade, Quebec's Garneau Commission heard Catholic authorities arguing that faith, the nation, and youngsters were best protected in collective settings.[113]

Teenagers were a particular group for whom family life was deemed sometimes especially difficult, but all offspring who frustrated families and communities were candidates for residential treatment. As one social work student from the University of British Columbia argued in 1950,

> experience had shown that some children received more benefit from a group living experience than from foster home care where closer contact with adults was inevitable. An institution offered more routine than a foster home, relationships with staff were warm but less personal and gave a child an opportunity to become more aware of his feelings and later to be able to adjust to a home environment.[114]

One 1983 Ontario critic explained, "emergency homes, receiving homes, assessment homes, extension homes, treatment homes, mental-health centres" were picking up children whom foster care was not equipped to assist.[115] A decade later, a BC observer summed up "the harsh reality ... that the residential setting is the only alternative for individuals, who, for one reason or another, can or will not function within the established norms of social and family environments."[116]

At the dawn of the third millennium, a few youngsters everywhere remained in institutions intended for adults. Hospital psychiatric wards supply the most obvious examples of such settings.[117] Non-solutions have been identified as an assault on "the tolerance and understanding of families and communities" that leaves youngsters readily "caught up in escalating patterns of rejection and alienation."[118] When traditional foster parents have proven hard put to cope with the realities of modern caseloads, some commentators have concluded that institutions supply the only realistic option for specialized care.[119] A persisting shortage of foster homes kept so-called normal kids in residential treatment long after authorities had hoped for their removal.[120]

Choices and outcomes have ultimately depended both on the status of children committed to care and on institutions' relationship to their communities. At the end of the twentieth century, it was unhappily recognized that "we continue to use residential treatment based upon the level of disturbance that a child is creating for a community rather than on the value of the residential environment."[121] Too often, ethnic background has been the key inspiration for placement. Racial disadvantage has particularly correlated with identification as "special needs" within the modern child welfare system.[122] Many adults have in turn regularly classified boys and girls with deemed disabilities at the bottom of the "hierarchy of preference." Even when accompanied by adoption subsidies and higher foster care payments, they are more often only "placeable" in 24/7 institutions.[123]

Like their predecessors, modern parents have remained divided. While segregation has produced obvious tragedies, deinstitutionalization has offered its own betrayals. Growing numbers of homeless citizens and inadequate supports for community living have been far from the dream of integration and community living.[124] Recent scholarship has also pointed to comradeship among those who have lived collectively.[125] Opposition to closures, such as that of of Ontario's Huronia Centre, was one result. Such observations suggest that certain kinds of institutions might, under proper conditions, support the relationships and development that single households might find difficult to supply. Consider, for example, the collective solution offered by L'Arche Canada, which has worked to offer persons with disabilities respect and meaning. Its first North America foothold, revealingly titled Daybreak, appeared just outside of Toronto in 1969. Bill Van Buren, an early member who was born with muscular dystrophy to terribly overwhelmed parents in the 1950s, found a haven there at the age of sixteen. He remained at the centre and provided leadership to the disability rights movement across North America until his death in 2009.[126] Clearly, some group settings could act as a real home to their residents.

When institutions have represented external impositions by those who were presumed to be class, ethnic, and racial superiors of those admitted, they have regularly brought pain and truncated development. When they have embodied a sense of shared community and worked with kith and kin to find solutions, they have sometimes proven to be helpful. Efforts to maintain relationships with client families have been critical in ensuring better outcomes. At the end of the twentieth century, the SOS Children Village in Surrey, British Columbia, a member of an international movement to align foster with institutional care, suggested that solutions could be found. Part of the Vancouver Aboriginal Child and Family Services Society network of foster parents, this revealing titled 'village' has five homes on one site, and each provides family care for three to six children aged from infancy to nineteen. It is committed to maintaining sibling ties and original cultures.[127] Its connections to communities and families, and its greater resources, recalled the strength of some of the earlier institutional options that strove to retain critical relations. The Surrey initiative came, as we shall see in the next two chapters, after decades of policy and practice that had had limited success in helping the most disadvantaged of Canada's progeny.

3

BEGINNING THE SEARCH FOR BEST INTEREST
Child Protection Considers Fostering from the Late Nineteenth Century to the 1960s

IN THE LATE NINETEENTH CENTURY, CANADIAN CHILD WELFARE authorities set out on a century and more experiment with formal arrangements for domestic care by non-kin and, in time, by kin. This chapter and the next describe how foster care developed in the context of competing and complementary responses to disadvantaged youngsters. Preferred policy and practice always supposed the benefits (and the cost-saving) of original kinship, but effective supports remained in short supply. The backup for problematic original parents set out by modern policy makers and practitioners, which was initially very similar to the long-standing provision of pauper apprenticeships, was the construction of domestic alternatives, notably fostering and official adoption. The third response, described in detail in Chapter 2, was total institutions that, despite their oft-heralded demise, never disappeared. The persisting practical and symbolic power of blood ties ensured that the question of linkages between old and new worlds, whether domestic or institutional, troubled all choices. Breaking up, like staying together, was always hard to do.

These two chapters do not provide a detailed description of governments' response to needy youngsters over more than 100 years. That history is too large for any single volume. What they offer is a broad historical perspective on child protection policies and efforts that identifies significant concerns and approaches and suggests their evolution over time. While the chronology varies among provincial and civic jurisdictions, and overlap always occurred with few solutions ever disappearing entirely, Canadian developments unfolded in roughly three stages. The first two concern this chapter and the third preoccupies the next.

In the first stage, roughly from the 1880s to the 1920s, advocates of state initiatives in child welfare attempted to affirm male leadership and to present foster care as the domestic, voluntary, and patriotic solution to the disarray of modern life. The designated foes for this generation were twofold. On the one hand, obviously, there were the deficient original families, which male bread-winners had not sustained. Then there were the orphanages and shelters, which were the rival remedies to domestic disaster, where women were noteworthy as founders, supporters, and staff. While these institutions were deemed unsuitable for the production of proper citizens by fostering's advocates, such 24/7 sites were to be quietly retained for youngsters designated abnormal or excess to the national imaginary. Fostering's new homes, unlike many institutions, intended for the most part to disrupt problematic pasts and to return to a patriarchal governance that could not be guaranteed in institutions, especially those where women might sometimes rule.

By the 1920s, a second stage in child protection was visible. State assis-tance to worthy families and legal adoption slowly emerged everywhere as the "gold" and "silver" standards respectively of care. In this scenario, fostering, which was now increasingly distinguished from adoption, stepped forward with a bronze in the child-saving competition. Except in Catholic Quebec, institu-tions, while remaining the workhorses of much child protection, were out of the running and largely out of public sight as worthy contenders for the nurture of promising young Canadians. Early experiments in social security concen-trated on enabling respectable citizens, especially mothers, to retain their off-spring. When these experiments proved inadequate, legal adoption emerged as the preferred means to create normal families and citizens.

Foster homes evolved as more complicated options. Girls and boys might eventually return to their birth families, stay in supposedly temporary arrange-ments until maturity, or eventually be consigned to institutions. There was lit-tle attention paid to preserving kin ties and, in fact, considerable confidence in the merits of breaking links to disreputable pasts. By the end of this period, roughly in the 1960s, First Nations girls and boys began to move into view as test subjects for Canadian child protection. In some ways, provision for this group caught up with what had been earlier deemed to be best for others. Res-idential schools were increasingly condemned, just as orphanages had been in the previous stage. The so-called "sixties scoop" of Native youngsters repre-sented the high point of an optimistic and often inclusive environmentalism on the part of mainstream child protection authorities.[1] What it did not change, however, was the essentially colonial relationship between Aboriginal families and the state. First Nations communities were still to be transformed along lines that imperious authorities judged acceptable.

The Beginning: Beyond Original Families and Institutions

Paternal failure lay close to the heart of early panics over child protection. While the duties and characteristics of Canadian citizens, as well as the political prerogatives of men, concerned legislators across the country from the 1860s on, evidence of parental, especially but not only paternal, inadequacy abounded. Just as the medical inspection of potential recruits for the South African and 1914–18 conflicts unsettled assumptions of masculine prowess, abused and neglected youngsters made obvious mockery of claims of fatherly responsibility. Increasing awareness of child labour, at least in its industrial manifestations, school absenteeism, and child abandonment and infanticide offered other occasions for disillusionment. Where paternal shortcomings had previously been considered largely private, properly hidden away, and of limited consequence for governments, they now loomed ever larger in the calculations of modernizing states. While women's limitations as mothers never escaped harsh scrutiny, they were often assumed to be derived from, or deepened by, male shortcomings. In the view of both gods (speaking through religious authorities) and the law, men were still presumed to be the appropriately dominant and superior partner. Only very gradually, ironically encouraged by mounting faith in women's moral superiority, were mothers to become the objects of criticism. Their redemption required re-dedication to approved gender roles, whether in marriage or in collaboration with the male-run state.[2]

By the late nineteenth century, unprecedented attention to poverty and childhood vulnerability offered plentiful acknowledgement that the patriarchal family was inadequate to the challenge of a new age. Canadians, like other populations in the Western world, grew increasingly sensitive to the national costs of malnourished, ill-housed, abused, and delinquent youngsters. Waifs and strays crowding urban thoroughfares challenged the promise of progress, compromised national claims to future greatness, and visibly testified to the limitations of fathers and the unmet needs of mothers for male leadership and support.

The revolutionary implications of an external assessment of familial regimes were nevertheless quickly constrained in at least two ways. On the one hand, the state was determined not to provide adequate support in situ to distressed original families, whether they were led by a mother alone or by a father whose income or other contributions proved insufficient, and this refusal accompanied the introduction of fostering programs. On the other hand, foster families, which were the designated domestic replacements, were intended to reaffirm the male breadwinner principle. Although children's residential institutions invoked the potential of real challenges to male authority and presumptions of familial self-sufficiency, foster programs ultimately set out to re-inscribe the ideal of the autonomous patriarchal family in which both women and men fulfilled their proper roles.

Early municipal and philanthropic solutions frequently focused on aid in kind or on outdoor relief when families faltered. This response was always insufficient to succour the needy and was often criticized as contributing to further dependency. Scientific charity or the charity organization movement that appeared in the nineteenth century endeavoured to put support on a rational and non-pauperizing basis, but the demands of domestic recuperation proved beyond its capacity. Only governments had the potential to address the extent of disarray, whether to offer material resources or to discipline the recalcitrant or ignorant. A significant imaginative embrace of social security, which was a form of outdoor relief, not to mention the enhancement of state coffers through personal and corporate taxation, would not appear until after the First World War and the Great Depression. Governments never entirely surrendered fears that acknowledgement of the vulnerability of wage labour and patriarchal families might reward intemperance, idleness, and viciousness.

Not surprisingly then, provision for the removal of offspring from seemingly failed families appeared earlier than any significant effort to supplement resources. Parents who could not make it on their own were to lose sons and daughters to more respectable householders. As Australian scholar Shurlee Swain has rightly concluded, "by constituting inadequate parents as the enemy ... child rescuers created a discursive environment in which removal could be justified as being in the best interest of the child."[3] The offspring of the poor—those children, by definition, whose male breadwinner had failed—were likely to be deemed by middle-class standards, and could well be, neglected, abused, and delinquent. These categories of assessment began and continued fluid throughout all of the stages considered in this chapter and the next. However, what above all characterized the vast majority of youngsters eyed for official apprehension was the economic desperation of first families.

In the nineteenth and much of the twentieth century, shelters and orphanages in towns and cities across the Dominion supplied hard-to-miss monuments to recurring domestic inadequacy. Housing anywhere from a handful to hundreds of residents, they mobilized supporters in tangible expressions of Canadians' potential for collective care. Ethnic and religious groups, unions, fraternal societies, and female, sometimes feminist, activists all supplied at least tentative dissenters from the faith that all was well with Canada's hearths. As they founded, fundraised, and managed many such settings, middle-class women found ample occasion to observe the absence, intemperance, and violence of would-be patriarchs and the liability and competence of the female sex in general and of themselves in particular. They could well be excused for asking where were the male protectors so celebrated by the anti-feminists who opposed enfranchisement and women's entry into public life.

Non-mainstream households among poor and racialized populations were always vulnerable to especially negative appraisal by middle-class reformers. Adult men in such communities were rarely judged the equals of their better-off counterparts. Non-mainstream women might be similarly assessed, but they were more likely to elicit greater sympathy for their seeming subordination to, and abuse by, inferior men. Their "mother hearts" would, if allowed free rein and aided and abetted by their "sisters under the skin," beat in unison with those of middle-class women. At least, such was the hope of progressives such as Nellie Letitia McClung, Canada's leading suffragist.[4]

The initiative of Vancouver's Women's Christian Temperance Union in founding the Alexandra Non-Sectarian Orphanage and Home for Children in 1892–93 illustrated the close links that could be made between demands for women's rights and institutional remedies for domestic breakdown.[5] As studies by Kathryn Harvey and Carol T. Baines have also demonstrated, women-run shelters might criticize individual mothers, but they also frequently understood their vulnerability in a male-run world. Many such institutions grew accustomed to supplying both short- and long-term support to worthy clients who had been betrayed and battered by men.[6] Where mothers were recognized as unworthy or desperate, solutions were more likely to emphasize children's retention in the 24/7 institutional setting or, sometimes, their removal to more deserving families where they might work for their keep and be better trained for a law-abiding adulthood. Canadian institutions employed both retention and dispersal, depending on how many residents they could manage and their confidence in suitable substitute households for their charges. The abuse by foster parents of both British immigrant and Canadian children gave responsible advocates of institutions considerable pause. This caution, together with their own pride and investment in bricks and mortar and faith in the commitment of particular collectivities to children's well-being, whether of women, fraternal orders, or churches, kept institutions regularly at capacity and offering versions of what we might understand as respite care.

Such collective remedies were nevertheless increasingly viewed as suspect. In the 1880s and 1890s, momentum in child protection slowly began to shift from institutions to fostering programs that were linked to governments. Orphanages and shelters, in general, which had responded to some of the abuses identified with pauper apprenticeships for the impoverished young, increasingly found their operations suspect for maintaining ties with inadequate parents. This negative verdict frequently targeted female managers and patrons. Unlike businesslike and rational men, they were deemed susceptible to sentimentality and inefficiency. The fact that institutions, like many families, were regularly in need of funds, often overwhelmed by the duties of care, and still productive of sad stories only confirmed the limits of women-run enterprises. In the course of critiques of collectivist alternatives, attention readily drifted from the faults of patriarchal rule. In some ways, this dismissal served to foreshadow the lack of respect that female social workers and Catholic sisterhoods would later endure.[7]

Governments considered other remedies. These began in Halifax. The Nova Scotia Society for the Prevention of Cruelty, led by John Naylor, inspired 1880 and 1882 provincial legislation that allowed offspring to be removed from brutal parents. Ontario followed with its 1883 *Children's Protection Act* and its 1893 *Act for the Prevention of Cruelty to and the Better Protection of Children*. The first permitted the state to move neglected children from parental authority to the custody of children's homes, and the second provided for children's aid societies and fostering in non-kin homes as the preferred remedy for parental dereliction. In 2008, Trent University scholar Michael Reid persuasively argued that Ontario's legislation set about to shore up paternal power. Its provision for local societies to act as semi-public/semi-voluntary agents saw the state, which at this point and until the First World War was the vehicle of an entirely male electorate, asserting respectable masculine oversight.

Whereas orphanages supplied landscapes where female founders, staff, and fundraisers operated as key decision makers and regularly recognized the uncertainties of life for mother-led families, state initiatives ensured ultimate male political governance. Canadian parents could now be condemned for severe neglect and abuse, and the state could assume guardianship of their offspring. Arbitrary and inadequate men were to be supplanted by their superiors, a possibility that ironically enough was underpinned by contemporary feminist campaigns for married women's property laws and maternal rights to child custody. They too implicated fathers as a major cause of child suffering and delinquency.[8]

The nineteenth century's growing sentimentalization of childhood might have celebrated motherhood, but women still needed male leadership and supervision. As Reid has argued, "by defining the problem of neglected and dependent children as a 'public' problem, criticizing the feminine solution of the orphanages, and offering government a less expensive, more effective solution, children's aid society advocates could argue for the acquisition of new state powers."[9] The rights of those who were judged to be inadequate family men were to be limited by male-led governments that would better protect the nation's human resources. This substitution was in keeping with the imperial spirit of the age. As Michael Reid has further explained,

> colonial, racializing metaphors of manly conquest appealed to them, and they saw themselves as bringing moral progress to the darkest Africa of their own urban slums. Their colonial dreams served to strengthen their sense of a moral distinction between the savers and those who needed to be saved, and they often drew stark contrasts between the horrors in which the children of worthless families were trapped, and the foster homes to which they could be rescued.[10]

Such optimistic environmentalism fired enthusiastic early child protection regimes in many Canadian jurisdictions. Degeneracy was associated with mother-led families and redemption with external male authority, even if its strictures might have been delivered at the hands of volunteers and then of poorly paid local investigators who might well have been female. The long-term Ontario superintendent of neglected and dependent children, John Joseph Kelso signalled this assertion of moral and practical leadership by the nation's male middle and professional class. As a superior *pater familias*, he loomed over the first half-century of government efforts to redeem domestic patriarchy. He himself tried to reform Toronto children's shelter by reducing the matron to housekeeper and hiring heterosexual couples as superintendents and lady superintendents, thereby reinstalling the correct hierarchy.[11]

Ultimately, as social work scholar Karen Swift has effectively argued, Canada's legislative initiatives in child protection have repeatedly demonstrated that "the first responsibility of the state is not that of supplying care for children but of enforcing needed care through the medium of the family," an institution properly supervised by men.[12] The muscular Christian ideal embodied by men such as Naylor and Kelso incorporated women into new arrangements as handmaidens to male ministers, deputy ministers, and directors. The transition was also visible in British Columbia. The Vancouver Children's Aid Society began in 1901 with only male directors and the women's committee assuming most of the daily work. While female leadership appeared locally, Victoria's male bureaucrats and politicians ultimately held the purse strings and dictated priorities.[13] Despite some degree of autonomy, women on the Pacific Coast, as elsewhere, generally lacked final authority.

State-run, sanctioned, and subsidized fostering spread across Canada in the first decades of the twentieth century in order to replace parents who could not meet the standards for respectable child rearing, which more than ever became the *sine non qua* of modern citizenship. In the process, institutions that offered, at least potentially, a bridge over troubled times to mothers and fathers who wanted to retain contact and even custody but could not support progeny were to be bypassed. Orphanages and other shelters increasingly served short-term clients en route to foster homes or received more permanently the most unwanted of girls and boys—those who were not credited with qualities that would make them good citizens. In the process of being selected for adoption, fostering, or institutional care, children were variously screened as natural resources and potential citizens.

The domestic ideals embraced by the early state child protection move-ment took for granted the unpaid tasks of mothers and the central, if far less visible, contributions of stalwart male breadwinners whose service, like that of their social superiors in the child protection movement, would redeem the nation's masculinity. The original fathers who proved unable to discipline them-selves so as to provide support in life and death for their households, or to guide their offspring away from sloth, intemperance, and criminality, were judged unworthy. Community champions such as Toronto's Kelso and Ottawa's W.L. Scott offered, in contrast, as Xiaobei Chen has usefully noted, male lead-ership and even heroism, even as they cast shadows over the nation's default-ing fathers.[14] Such inferior specimens were presumed to be anomalous and not to be confused with legitimate patriarchs who met obligations and merited entitlements.

Initial plans to recruit unpaid foster families, headed by male breadwinners and secured by nurturing and homemaking women, supplied Canada's cutting-edge solution to maltreatment and potential delinquency prior to the First World War. Reflecting the fact that they assumed the vast majority of tasks associated with introducing new members into their households, substitute mothers have received the most attention from both contemporaries and scholars. Although the free fostering preferred by Kelso's generation was predicated on worthy patriarchs subsidizing child protection and providing models of paternal respon-sibility, foster fathers, like the presumed failures that preceded them, largely escaped close scrutiny. Like other respectable citizens, such men were not to be regulated in their private lives. As citizens who met their domestic obligations and, indeed, subsidized those of the less worthy, they were to receive more moral than material rewards. Ideally, the service of such men, like that of their wifely acolytes, was altruistic.

Official hopes that fosterlings would be welcomed into respectable house-holds, treated fairly, and not exploited quickly ran aground of custom and the shortfalls of domestic economies. As they struggled to close the gap between inputs and outputs, rural and urban householders were long used to using unre-lated youngsters especially hard. From the beginning, state protection services everywhere fielded recurring demands for young female domestics and male agricultural labourers who, like the pauper apprentices of old, were expected to earn their keep and generally to subordinate themselves, their needs, and their futures to the blood members of the household. The steady out-migration of twentieth-century sons and daughters to cities typically left farmers scrambling for young substitutes as "help or companionship."[15] Government efforts to restrict child labour and demand education so that healthy young citizens could mature in ways that would honour the nation quickly discovered a shortage of worthy homes.

In the beginning, authorities sometimes dreamed of middle-class applicants for their youthful charges. Such prospects were always rare. Such householders were most likely to be interested in infants who might masquerade as biological offspring or in older girls and boys who might serve as domestic and agricultural servants to their betters. The first was a desirable outcome, but in an era of high infant mortality babies were rare among the state children who were on offer. The second raised the possibility of abuse and contradicted the promise of democratic inclusion. In any case, few middle-class Canadians were ever eager to demonstrate altruism in the care of disadvantaged older youngsters. Child protection agencies learned to place more hope on placements where youngsters would be incorporated into respectable working-class households. State wards were ideally to move from the irresponsible to the responsible, albeit still lower, stratum of society. In their new homes provided by wage earners, they would learn behaviours expected of ordinary citizens or what Shurlee Swain has identified as "preparation for a dutiful and subservient adulthood."[16]

A major obstacle to official plans surfaced almost immediately. Few working-class families could afford new members without additional revenue. Most dwelled only a mouth, a pay package, or a healthy body away from disaster. By these measures, they were not always distinguishable from the children's first families. The vast majority of Canadians required material support, either in the form of direct transfers of significant labour by children—a remedy made increasingly difficult by provincial requirements for schooling—or by cash for room and board. Even when accompanied by funding, youngsters were expected to contribute to survival. As one scholar observed about Scotland, this fact of life typically required that "boarded children in foster homes worked in patterns similar to those of their working class contemporaries."[17]

By the First World War and especially in the 1920s and 1930s, Kelso and his counterparts across the Dominion slowly and regretfully turned to the payment of what they treated as subsidies rather than salaries. Government payments covered only the bare minimum cost of essentials. Mothering labour remained taken for granted as a natural offering, freely available to shore up essentially male-run enterprises. As one history of the Vancouver Children's Aid Society revealingly observed, "the per capita contribution *per week* paid by provincial and municipal governments in 1919 was $1.50," while "the actual cost of maintenance (lower than it should have been because of the children's unpaid labour) was $14.45."[18] Financial compensation that matched women's material and other contributions remained anathema. A journalist summed up the commonplace reservations: "The woman who boards babies for money may or may not be a good person to have them, but the woman who takes a baby out of sympathy and love is a pretty safe risk."[19] In other words, any hint of pecuniary advantage tainted female service.

Since keeping expenses low supplied a central justification for preferring fostering to institutions, early state supervision tended to be slight. Exploitation and abuse, like that in many original families, frequently went undetected. Indeed, limited contact was one way that foster families were treated as near-equivalents of their natural predecessors. It also affirmed the principle of male rule. When visitors to the Ontario Children's Aid Society were instructed not to "over-regulate" foster parents, they were effectively being directed to allow them to manage like respectable householders.[20] Such preferences meant that fostering families and the fate of youngsters consigned to them readily slipped out of sight. As late as the 1920s and 1930s, British Columbia's Children's Aid Societies were far from unusual in finding it "impossible to do more than guess at the actual numbers in foster homes."[21]

Whether they contemplated institutions or fostering households, the Canadian pioneers of state child protection, like British child emigration societies such as Dr. Barnardo's Homes, which were active in the same period, employed the threat or the reality of a complete break from inadequate origins. Just as contemporary special courts and detention centres for juvenile offenders set out to separate girls and boys from problematic adults in their lives, new homes were intended to disrupt the cycle of contagion. While fostering invoked the attractive prospect of treating children as individuals rather than as undifferentiated inmates, as might institutions, it also frequently entailed their dispersal often well beyond their original homes as well as the loss of contact with friends and kin. By breaking the cake of inferior domestic custom, children might be retrieved as suitable citizens for the modern state.

By the 1920s, the initial experiment with fostering presented some significant lessons. On the one hand, many institutions continued to be preferred by parents who wished youngsters to be potentially retrievable and often relatively close at hand. Orphanages, in particular, produced their own loyalists, especially but not only from the Catholic Church. In this case, faith-based institutions were believed to offer a preferable religious upbringing. Such advantages were not, however, readily apparent to First Nations parents who faced the growing sequestration of their offspring in far-off residential schools. Advocates of fostering also learned that few middle-class households willingly nurtured unrelated youngsters and that restrictions on child labour and demands for education meant that working-class households would require additional income. Initial anticipation of the free fostering of unrelated girls and boys proved clearly unworkable. Such a system could neither redeem patriarchal governance nor rescue disadvantaged children. Paid fostering had to be pursued, but penny-conscious governments resisted its true costs. They soon sought other options.

From the 1920s to the 1960s: Social Security and Adoption Trump Fostering

After the First World War, social assistance to worthy families and legal adoption slowly emerged everywhere as professional social workers' best and better hope for care. Great expectations rested with these favoured solutions to childhood disadvantage. During these decades, the public spotlight rarely focused on fostering or, for that matter, on institutions. Early experiments in social security, including workmen's compensation, mothers' allowances, unemployment insurance, and family allowances, promised to enable respectable Canadians to retain their offspring. However, when some families still faltered and failed despite these pioneering state supplements, especially during hard times such as the 1930s, legal adoption of the best and the brightest, which was often interpreted to mean the youngest and the most mainstream of girls and boys, was deemed the next most effective route to normal citizenry.

Foster homes served a narrowed clientele—those youngsters who could not readily, for whatever reason, be extracted from their original kin and/or those who were older, part of sibling groups, or otherwise deemed unattractive by potential adopters. In some respects, as the problems of their charges and the difficulty of attracting worthy parents proved to be too often intractable, foster homes slowly assumed the invidious reputation in child welfare circles that had been previously occupied by institutions—they too were likely to be singled out as failing to meet fundamental needs for affection and stimulation. Near-complete disillusion would come in the last decades of the twentieth century discussed in the next chapter.

For some time, the most obvious exception to such evolution in child protection was Catholic Quebec. In 1945, Catholic leaders were still able to find significant support for the view that "nos institutions religieuses ont rendu un irremplaçable service à l'enfance totalement ou partiellement déclassée." From this perspective, they provided essential protection "contre le sécularisme moderne et l'étatisme."[22] Such sentiments, while shared to some degree in all Catholic communities, were, however, on the wane. Residential sites, while remaining the workhorses of much child protection, largely slipped from public view, not to surface again until the disclosures of abuse in the 1960s and beyond. Their inmates were likely either to be in transit over the short term, some to return to birth kin while others moved on to fostering and adoption, or to be warehoused semi-permanently or permanently as being irrelevant or even threatening the national project of citizen building.

Social Security

Long, albeit intermittent and paltry, traditions of outdoor relief had repeatedly demonstrated since the days of New France that even respectable households could not always cope with the costs of survival. Real social security initiatives, however, awaited the twentieth century. Provincial provision for workmen's compensation and mothers' pensions or allowances, both slowly and unevenly appearing before the First World War, unemployment insurance from 1941 (with a brief introduction in 1935), family allowances from 1945, and various pension schemes for the elderly and those with disabilities aimed to shore up domestic heterosexuality and recognize social citizenship. Adults received the funds, but the nation's youngsters were always among the expected beneficiaries.

Modern state security programs, with their acknowledgement of the shortfall of breadwinner wages, addressed what many advocates for girls and boys regularly understood to be the key causes of childhood vulnerability. As one social work authority explained in surveying Ottawa's child and family services in 1953, "the underlying problems have many facets—low wages and limited earning capacities, loss of income through unemployment, disability and sickness, limitations in coverage and benefits in our public assistance and social insurance systems, inadequate supply of low rental housing, inability to budget effectively and to maintain a reserve for crises, [and] the high costs of medical services."[23] This enumeration, which could have been assembled by progressive observers in any generation, laid bare the pitfalls that made parenting so uncertain. While a few fathers and mothers could never muster the wherewithal for the safety and developmental needs of their offspring, chances for success were everywhere greatly enhanced by access to the fundamentals of human security—what the Great Depression social security activists, described by historian James Struthers, interpreted as the satisfaction of "minimum need."[24] Without it, parenting was readily compromised.

Ever conscious of the ubiquitous shortage of effective foster parents from the nineteenth century to the present as well as of the limitations of so many substitutes, many child protection advocates campaigned ardently for state supports for original parents. Hard experience taught them that youngsters were generally, although never always, better served by imperfect blood kin and that the vast majority of parents wanted to meet their obligations. Their insights, aided and abetted by psychological and psychiatric preoccupation with birth families in the period, helped inspire social security programs that aimed to support mothers and fathers who were deemed able to meet the minimum standards for domestic normalcy.[25] It is also clear that best intentions were often marred by prejudices of class, race, and gender that readily judged behaviour to be inferior when it differed from mainstream preferences.

While social workers have been commonly more progressive than other middle-class Canadians, they never escaped the stigmata of their age. As Gale Wills has convincingly argued of Toronto from 1918 to 1957, male experts became the dominant force in community-based social work. Women largely became the subordinated custodians of casework, which in turn largely lost "its community perspective and focused on the traditional family as it was constructed by the patriarchal assumptions and practices of corporate and state power."[26] Her case study suggests the "ideals of cooperation and democracy" were the loser.[27] While individuals were always better than their times, self-consciousness about prejudice won few recruits until the civil rights awakening of the 1950s and 1960s.

The emerging social welfare state repeatedly took for granted a gendered mandate that located women first of all in the home as mothers and men primarily in the waged labour force. As Mona Gleason has demonstrated, this was the standard by which normalcy and entitlement were judged.[28] Early mothers' allowances and mothers' pension programs acknowledged women's special duties as citizens, not to mention their recent enfranchisement. Ultimately, however, better male access to social security always assumed that paid employment stood at the heart of good citizenship and fathering and, thus, successful family life.[29] Pensions and allowances were designed to shore up men's commitment to paid labour and women's to unpaid domestic duties. Since assistance very rarely surpassed the least that could be earned by the most unskilled labourer, poverty regularly compromised child rearing. Crusaders in the cause of child welfare could only intermittently interrupt this brutal calculation.[30]

Recipients of mothers' allowances, like the military wives and families supported during the First World War by the Canadian Patriotic Fund, were expected to behave as model custodians of maternal duties. This presumption, however, never included equally all groups of women.[31] The unwed, in general, and those who were Native, Black, or Asian, whose moral capacity to raise good citizens was routinely questioned, were rarely offered funding until after the Second World War. For a long time, parents of southern and eastern European origin faced similar suspicion. They and their offspring were not presumed to be the citizens whom the state wished to encourage. The same assessment of inadequacy also meant generally fewer interventions into the child-rearing regimes of such groups. Before the last half of the twentieth century, they were not obvious candidates for domestic reconstruction.

The evolution of protection services for unwed mothers demonstrated the commonplace resistance to levelling parenting's playing field. As Lori Chambers has movingly demonstrated of Ontario's 1921 *Children of Unmarried Parents Act*, men and women were never held to the same moral standard. Persisting determination to punish women who did not measure up to the ideals of motherhood to a far greater degree than men who failed at normative masculinity ensured that economic vulnerability scarred the modern landscape.[32] The nature of this punishment, however, did shift. In the first instance, it entailed a maternal retention of offspring as a permanent badge of shame. By the 1940s, however, surrender was far more in favour, at least if babies were presumed to be White. Infants, and increasingly unwed mothers themselves, were re-evaluated as suitable for integration into the national imaginary. In exchange, both were to surrender all memory of relations and commit to the secrecy that bedevilled adoption into the twenty-first century.

The Great Depression and the Second World War deepened concerns that normal gender relations and duties were under siege. Jobless or brutalized men and women, who had learned to rely on their own capacities, could not sustain normal families, especially in the context of poor and limited housing.[33] One 1945 observer captured the agitation regularly associated with non-conforming women:

> The number of children who need short-term mothers has been greatly increased by the war; by crowded housing conditions; by emotional upsets caused by the separation of husbands and wives; by the increase in unmarried mothers; and by the number of women who have turned down homemaking for paid jobs, without providing proper care for their small children.[34]

Potential options for female citizens that did not entail around-the-clock maternal devotion raised unsettling questions about the future of the heterosexual nuclear family and men's roles as husbands and fathers. A preference for womanly self-sacrifice undercut recurring calls by progressive Canadians for supplementary services, notably visiting homemakers and daycare.[35] Such investments were ultimately feared lest they decouple women's commitment to men (and sometimes the reverse) and the supremacy of the breadwinner marriage.

The introduction of family allowances, to be paid to all Canadian mothers, in 1944 was a calculated effort to supplement male wages and increase consumption as well as benefit children. Once again, women were the homebound subjects of the patriotic project. As Nancy Christie has argued, assumptions of maternal entitlement associated with early mothers' pensions and allowances were largely over-written by a deepened commitment to breadwinner families that observers believed had been nearly capsized by the Great Depression. Even as they relieved poverty, family allowances aimed to shore up husbands and fathers whose wage earning could not, on its own, guarantee family survival or the maintenance of patriarchal authority.[36] Ultimately, like unemployment insurance and most state job creation schemes, family allowances took for granted women's lesser claim on wages in the marketplace. For all their limitations, the universal payments campaigned for by progressive Canadians embodied an important promise—the inclusion of diverse communities into the national imaginary. Unlike previous state supplements, it made little formal distinction among different groups of women. While access remained a commonplace problem, Aboriginal, Asian, Black, and unwed mothers received unprecedented theoretical entitlement. Gender regularly trumped race as a determinant of right to state resources.

The gradual provision of increased social supports from the 1920s to the 1960s kept many children at home and in school far longer. However modest, they could spell the difference between survival and disaster. Some youngsters who otherwise would have been apprehended remained with kin. In 1951, Nova Scotia's child welfare officials signalled their faith in new programs:

> Today the Elizabethan system of poor relief has been partially hacked away. Public and private social agencies, Mothers' Allowances and Family Allowances, Workmen's Compensation, and Unemployment Insurance are active forces in keeping children in their own homes and improving their lot and care. Today, children out of wedlock are born in hospitals or infants' homes and homeless or neglected children find a new life with adopted or foster parents. The mentally backward and the delinquent receive sympathetic training in special institutions. Today is a better day for the children of adversity.[37]

The year 1966 proved the apotheosis of hope for social security. The Canada Assistance Plan promised greater commitment to children's well-being through its support for universal provincial education and health programs that required no tests of morality. Families were to be the outstanding beneficiaries.

Unfortunately, the promise of a new dawn quickly proved to be greater than the reality. In Saskatchewan, a leading social worker remembered that she and her post–Second World War colleagues were "firmly committed to the belief that the family was the basic unit of society and that every effort should be made to preserve the family and to assist parents to take responsibility for their children" but that escalating workloads presented "an impossible task" of ensuring benefits.[38] This was not the only problem. The assessment of the Child Welfare League of Canada in 2007 that the orientation of child welfare had shifted ·by the 1950s from protection to "a more pathological philosophy" that stressed abuse and thus apprehension also suggested that other considerations could over-ride the official commitment to family preservation.[39]

Even as it slowly expanded, social security never operated as much more than a stopgap in many unravelling lives. It never adequately addressed chronic shortages of affordable housing, economic volatility, low average wages, and women's persisting inequality in all aspects of life. The latter disability always encouraged women to invest in male breadwinners rather than to maximize their own educational and employment opportunities. When the prospect or the reality of husbands failed, mothers were regularly hard put to support offspring on their own. Social assistance programs could tide them over bad times, and perhaps bad partners, but it could never provide a respectable survival, especially for women who refused to conform to social expectations.

Legal Adoption

A persisting security shortfall meant that state welfare initiatives confronted expanding numbers of youngsters in care onwards from the 1920s. This fundamental reality, driven also by raising expectations about child-rearing standards, drove the search for other solutions for the child victims of domestic breakdown. The drawn-out experiment with legal adoption, with its debates about obligations and protections, promised that unremunerated duties would be assumed by would-be parents, the respectable substitutes for damaged original families. Chosen girls and boys, especially infants, were to gain a fresh start, largely unencumbered by bad beginnings. In these years, as my earlier text *Finding Families, Finding Ourselves* describes in detail, adoption appeared in public overwhelmingly as a good news story. New fathers and mothers were able to invest in the future, while child welfare experts and even birth parents avoided the limits of both state (and community) support and of households for hire.

Legislated adoption tapped the desires of middle-class Canadians to remake youngsters in their own image without regard to previous attachments. Recruitment relied on the early separation of potentially acceptable youngsters from their birth families. As Cynthia Comacchio has demonstrated, poor parents were pathologized as "dirty and negligent" and "as the source of ill health."[40] While public health efforts promised improvements, adoption offered to remove the problem itself. Girls and boys, the younger the better, could escape natal failure and contamination. Far more than fostering, tainted as it was by financial considerations and time-limited obligations, the permanent legal transfer of boys and girls "as if born to" new parents promised to restore the supposedly natural equation of nature and nurture.

Only at the end of the second period would the real complications of adoption's relations with the past histories of youngsters and adopters loom as requiring resolution. Sociologist H. David Kirk's *Shared Fate: A Theory of Adoption and Mental Health* signalled this shift.[41] He argues that acceptance, even celebration, of difference from biological reproduction rather than a mimicry or masking was the foundation of healthy adoption. Adults, like himself and his wife, who demonstrated a particular independence of convention by adopting Native, Black, or mixed-race youngsters were most likely to heed his advice.[42] The much-discussed difficulty of telling the truth to adoptees suggests that many others preferred to pretend a re-enactment of biological scripts. In the context of the expanding rights revolution of the last half of the twentieth century, this pretence would be increasingly difficult to sustain. The appearance of the searching movement of adoptees and birth mothers from the 1960s on in Canada upset calculations that relied on erasing the past.

Canada's increased regulation of adoption initially promised happy transitions for acceptable children who were assessed as good citizenship material. Judgment of acceptability was never entirely fixed, although preferences for younger, White, able-bodied, and often female candidates proved hard to shake. The persisting demand for such infants encouraged a reconsideration of illegitimacy. While "at no time has a majority" been surrendered and some child protection workers honoured unwed mothers' common desire to keep their babies, progeny who had long borne the epithet of "bastards" gradually lost the stigma of immorality.[43] Although their mothers suffered far longer, adoptees' histories could in the context of modern sentiments, most readily disappear or be incorporated into good news stories, as with the "chosen child." Rising numbers of illegitimate births until 1970 (their peak year before the late twentieth century's acceptance of common-law unions changed the calculation) offered would-be adopters the supposedly unencumbered and, most commonly, White infants who would, it was trusted, blend seamlessly into new lives through adoption.

After the Second World War, progressive social workers sought to build on new sensitivity to human rights and growing signs of unmet demand for new offspring. Many worked with parent activists, in groups such as the Open Door Society, to encourage sympathies.[44] Would-be adopters were asked to consider a wider range of candidates, namely sibling groups, older youngsters, those with disabilities, and those from previously suspect donor populations—namely those who had been previously considered most suitable for fostering. Children with African, Asian, and First Nations origins were cautiously presented as worthy additions to Canada's middle-class households. While only a tiny minority of adults took up this challenge and even fewer considered youngsters diagnosed with mental or physical disabilities, adoption provided child welfare authorities with some of their greatest hopes for redeeming domestic life.

As adoption became increasingly acceptable and demand for babies grew faster than supply, would-be parents, who for many years had relied on informal connections and economic advantage, were increasingly required to demonstrate worthiness. After the Second World War, provincial officials took unprecedented steps to require adults who were not in receipt of public assistance to open their doors to external assessment. Much evaluation focused on would-be mothers: their age, the quality of their marriage, their housekeeping standards, their satisfaction with gendered marital duties, and the probability of their seeking waged work once children arrived.[45] Not surprisingly, many middle-class candidates were deeply offended by treatment that resembled the interrogations meted out to recipients of state aid. Some resisted, providing ready customers for adoption's black marketers.[46] Only slowly did middle-class claimants begin to accept a certain loss of dignity as the cost for legally acquiring offspring. Like less economically privileged citizens seeking social assistance in hard times, they learned to give required performances of domestic normalcy.

Just as in the early experiments with fostering, adoption's solutions to childhood disadvantage assumed that good families survived on male incomes. To attain authenticity as mothers and fathers, applicants had to possess sufficient funds to support children without any recourse to state assistance. Breadwinning father-husbands had to be able to keep mother-wives concentrating on home-based duties. Although they regularly slipped under the radar of much officialdom in the years before they won legislative approval at the end of the twentieth century, single parent households and those with wage-earning mothers were never encouraged to adopt. Adopters who were able and willing to accommodate gendered expectations were always preferred.

The faith that breadwinner income was sufficient in the one case and not in the other drew an apparently firm line between adoption and fostering. Adults who required monetary rewards and recompense were automatically deemed inferior representatives of gendered normalcy. In the same spirit, formal adoption required would-be parents to forgo any external aid until late in the twentieth century, even when they faced substantial expenses for the medical, therapeutic, and educational support of new sons and daughters.

At its best, legal adoption improved on traditional fostering, offering inclusion that was on equal terms with blood kin and promising stability. As permanency planning and placement drift became recognized as major problems for child protection, the prospect of security, with all that it meant for human development, was tremendously appealing. Nevertheless, even as provincial adoption regimes aimed to distinguish sharply among potential custodians of youngsters, practice often proved far more complicated. In relations between adults and children, legal differences were not always the dominant influence. In some instances, authorities hoped for natural transitions from temporary to permanent residence, making long-term fostering an effectively disguised means of adoption. One journalist, who was critical of paid mothering and hopeful of the strength of natural instincts, voiced commonplace hope in 1919:

> It frequently happens that when a child has been in a home it so attaches itself that the family feel they cannot give it up and they either adopt it outright or the visit goes on indefinitely. In many ways these free adoptions are the more satisfactory. No one is under any obligation, the authorities can keep a closer jurisdiction over the child, and it seems probable that this plan will get more children out of institutions and into good homes, if even for a few months at them, than the system of regular adoptions alone would do.[47]

Vancouver's Catholic Children's Aid Society likewise trusted that "if a child was kept by the foster parents, he was considered by the Society to be 'adopted.'"[48]

Desires for cost saving were fundamental to the calculations of authorities. Whatever their loss of security and attachment, youngsters in Nova Scotia in the 1930s and 1940s were typically routinely moved from "boarding" to "free" homes whenever the opportunity offered. The province also readily labelled children who did not measure up to rigid tests and requirements as "unplaceable or unadoptable." They were immediate candidates for institutions where costs could be minimized.[49] As such preferences suggested, governments preferred solutions that spared expense, even if they potentially compromised their wards' ultimate well-being.

Challenges for Fostering

At the beginning of the twentieth century, foster care started out looking little different than adoption. In terms of day-to-day treatment of youngsters and even their long-term acceptance, especially in households where there was little material to inherit, distinctions in relations sometimes remained slight. In the case of long-term fostering that sometimes morphed into effective kin-hood, knowledge of different origins could even disappear over a generation. Increasingly, however, as adoption law spelled out the nature of connections, if any, to blood and legal kin, fostering stood apart. When the Great Depression effectively eliminated poorer families taking in unrelated youngsters without reimbursement, and the tiny pool of middle-class applicants for foster children dwindled even further, except among more evangelical Christians, adoption's superior prospects were affirmed.

As adoption skimmed off the youngsters who could generally be most read-ily integrated into new households, fostering in turn frequently became more demanding. In a pattern that became increasingly familiar, it dealt with girls and boys who could not be readily extracted permanently from birth parents and who were more likely to be older, more troubled, and rule-breaking kids and sib-ling groups. Fostering householders were expected to supply temporary, although effectively sometimes near-permanent, shelter to those whose birth relatives needed respite or re-education but who resisted complete loss of contact. By the 1960s, there was also growing recognition that foster parents had to manage prior attachments. This slow acceptance of continuing connections, which involved assumptions of culpability and unrespectability or worse, challenged authorities, both sets of parents, and the children themselves.

Budget-sensitive governments resisted the implications of the daunting shift in the makeup of children in care. One 1944 report on New Brunswick offered a devastating assessment:

> It would seem to be the policy of the Provincial Child Welfare Department to press Societies to remove children as soon as possible from temporary homes (where payment is made at the expense of the municipality and the Province) to free homes where no payment whatsoever is involved. The general principle is laid down that children should not generally be kept in "pay care" for a period longer than six to nine months, after which the Director of Child Welfare may exempt the municipality and the provincial treasury from further payments to the soci-ety ... this policy is based upon monetary considerations rather than upon con-sideration of the best interests of children. It is clearly the experience of other Provinces that free homes on the whole offer less suitable care to children than those where the Society, by virtue of the fact that it is making some payment, can exercise an effective degree of supervision and control.[50]

While this province was eventually shamed into payments, these were reck-oned as being scandalous as late as 1965: "The foster parent receives $7.28 per week to feed and shelter the ward. There is no possibility that this amount of money will cover the indirect costs of a child in the home and certainly no financial regard at all for the 24-hour, seven-day-a-week care and supervision of the child."[51] In short, women were to continue to demonstrate good mater-nal citizenship by subsidizing state care.[52]

In face of the mounting cost of living, greater opportunities for women's waged employment, and more challenging state wards, suitable foster parents became increasingly reluctant recruits. The shortfall sparked recurring panics from child protection agencies from the 1920s to the 1960s. While paid substitutes might be regarded as far from ideal from the point of view of moralists who wished to disassociate parenting from financial considerations, they formed the persisting lifeline of state child protection. As an observer put it in 1967, "nearly all Canadian children in public care *are* in foster homes, and whatever our doubts about them, we can't do away with them entirely."[53]

Early official responses focused on upgrading public perception of the job and, one might add, soft-soaping and guilting foster parents. Their contribution was repeatedly hailed, very much in keeping with Kelso's early campaigns, as the fullest expression of community service and good citizenship. In 1949, Ontario officials offered typical recognition: "Much credit is due to those socially minded citizens who provide such good care at a minimum of expense to the Society and to the taxpayer. Such foster parents need the encouragement and co-operation of every citizen in the community."[54] As Chapter 6 discusses in greater detail, women who dedicated themselves to full-time mothering and men who supported them were increasingly likely to be rewarded with titles and medals. These symbols confirmed patriotic service and sacrifice and ignored the material costs. Such plaudits never, however, proved sufficient, and organized recruitment drives by societies, churches, and governments were a constant necessity. In 1965, Montreal's Protestant, Catholic, and Jewish Anglophone child welfare groups collectively campaigned for 1,500 new homes, and, once more, as with so many others, the response proved insufficient.[55] Across the country, home-hunting social workers regularly returned empty-handed.

The continuing shortfall put unrelenting pressure on available households. Even as government policies glacially evolved to restrict the number of placements in any single residence, foster homes took on extra members. Like many other agencies, Vancouver Children's Aid Society found itself effectively abusing homes that it trusted. Emergencies produced too many calls that foster parents were hard put to resist. This recurring situation contributed to the ongoing failure at recruitment and the high turnover rates among foster parents and social workers alike. As one of British Columbia's advocates for children lamented,

> for over fifty years the Agency's main resource for placing children has been the regular foster homes. This resource has been misused through inappropriate placements, as well as greatly abused through overloading. The foster home resource is declining (August 31st, 1967 we had 764 foster homes as compared to the August 31st, 1972 figure of 649) and will continue to do so in spite of our efforts to recruit new ones.[56]

This story echoed across Canada throughout the twentieth century. Shortage of specialized institutions and long waiting lists also meant that children with serious problems remained in foster homes that were ill equipped to cope.[57]

By the 1960s, an already difficult situation took a turn for the worse as First Nations girls and boys began to move to the forefront as candidates for Canadian child protection. This clientele had been building since the Second World War as Natives, like other North Americans, increasingly chose urban over country life and as mainstream society became more willing to extend the promise of modern childhood—protection, dependence, segregation, and delayed responsibilities—to those who many had previously believed were permanently set apart by a heritage of savagery. This extension was never, however, even-handed. In these years, Aboriginal communities were rarely credited with the capacity to sustain modern domestic arrangements. Apprehension commonly continued the strategies of cultural erasure that were long familiar in residential schools. The inclusion of Native youngsters nevertheless reflected more liberal opinions on race relations. The nation's advocates for vulnerable youngsters, notably the Canadian Welfare Council and the Canadian Association of Social Workers, both of which inveighed against residential schools before the House of Commons Committee charged with making changes to the Indian Act in 1947, once again identified institutions as the enemy. In 1951, amendments to the act permitted the intervention of provincial welfare services. Most significantly, however, there was no provision for additional funding for the provinces.[58] Gradually, often unwillingly and always cost-consciously, they apprehended Native youngsters who were believed to be at risk of, or who were experiencing, abuse or neglect. Like the earlier campaign against orphanages, the aim was to replace abuse and institutionalization by parental affection and domestic inclusion. What happened was often in fact a colonial tragedy in another form.

Conclusion

Following the 1920s, a recurring hierarchy of child placement drew key distinctions among girls and boys. The result was sadly conveyed by the story of a boy born in 1961. His parents requested his apprehension even before he was born. As an infant, he was quickly adopted but just as quickly cast off, "apparently due to an unsightly birthmark and small moles all over his body." At eight months, assessed with a subnormal IQ of eighty-four, he entered his first foster home, one repeatedly reckoned inadequate by social workers. By age ten, he was "acting out in the foster home, the school, and in the community."[59] A group home was judged to be his future. In short order, he had passed through all of the stages, in descending order, of Canada's child protection offerings. He appeared in fact to be one of many forerunners of the youngsters known as "crossover kids" reported by Saskatchewan's Children's Advocate in 2009—namely those

> who move from placements in State care in family-based residential settings like foster homes, to mental health institutions or young offender custody. Crossover kids' histories are marked by multiple placements in the child welfare system, poor academic achievements and increased probability of involvement in the youth justice system.[60]

Indeed, the continuing foster care crisis helped keep institutions going throughout these decades. In English Canada, this persisting solution remained, however, largely invisible. After the Second World War, Quebec presented a different picture. As it became more secular, it increasingly looked askance at institutions, the vast majority of which were run by the Catholic Church. More than ever, this province shared the disillusionment that had been more regularly voiced earlier in more Protestant jurisdictions. Whereas in 1930 Arthur Saint-Pierre in *Nos Orphelinats* had praised Catholic orphanages for their protective (and frugal) embrace, the years leading up to the Quiet Revolution in the 1960s saw a seismic reappraisal of the proper provision for disadvantaged youngsters. In 1950, the journalist Gérard Pelletier's *Histoire des Enfants Tristes* told an entirely different story. His sad youngsters were in need, as he suggested, of the attention of good fathers, respectable, self-sacrificing men seemingly much like himself.[61] The administration of the Jean Lesage Liberals in the 1960s secularized education, health, and social services, eventually ending any distinction between "natural" and legitimate offspring and making adopted children fully members of new families.[62] Adoption and fostering now became the preferred solutions of the modern state, just as they had long been among progressive Quebecers. In the process, the province, like other jurisdictions earlier, lost many child protection institutions that had been run by women, such as the religious sisterhoods. The "Quiet Revolution" in child welfare, as in much else, once again asserted public patriarchal dominance.[63] Postwar discussions of Catholic fatherhood in Quebec might not have emphasized "authoritarian concepts of patriarchy," but they offered a powerful reinforcement of fathers' "headship" at home and, ultimately, elsewhere as well.[64]

Nowhere in 1960s Canada, however, would adoption or fostering be sufficient for the needs of youngsters in state care. It proved hard to convince adopters of the merits of older non-mainstream youngsters. They overwhelmingly preferred babies who were presumed to come with little original baggage. When it became increasingly hard to find such treasures at home, they began to turn abroad. Foster families were similarly too few in number. In 1965, the shortage was so severe that Montreal's traditional Anglophone children's institutions were unable to serve even "so-called normal clients, particularly adolescents," and new residential initiatives, such as Summerhill, set up additional sites to cope with demand.[65] Group homes of various types slowly emerged in many provinces "as an acceptable—but expensive—compromise between foster homes and child-welfare institutions."[66] While they sometimes offered practical alternatives for adolescents, they were never judged suitable for younger girls and boys. They became, however, a significant feature of Canada's child protection landscape—a response both to foster home shortages and to youngsters who were regarded as challenging.

The original promise of social security did not keep pace with population growth, the continuing fragility of many Canadian households, and the promise of democracy. As Bridget Moran, an outspoken post–Second World War British Columbia social worker struggling to assist a desperate clientele put it,

> in practice we had no resources that might conceivably have helped to keep families together, and children in their natural homes. We had no mental health facilities, no family support workers, no treatment centres of any kind ... The result was that when we discovered a child at risk in his own home, we had no recourse but to move him into a foster home. This often meant putting children in any home that would take them, whether or not that home had been approved or even investigated.[67]

Rising expectations and standards for childcare made it all the harder to address needs. A leading social work progressive in Saskatchewan described the complicated situation that faced her profession in the last half of the twentieth century: "Before 1944, old records reveal children were found with scabies, lice, and syphilis—much of the neglect was physical. As services changed, the emotional neglect of children became highlighted. This was a much more difficult form of neglect to prove."[68] In short, Canada from 1920 to 1960 experimented with various solutions to the problems presented by disadvantaged children. Advances in social security and preventive programs clearly helped many citizens. Ultimately, however, they were profoundly inadequate. In 1967, one muckraking journalist and future parliamentarian, Simma Holt, summed up the pervasive sense of a system under siege:

> Social workers admit they feel total despair as they see children already terribly hurt by illegitimate birth, broken homes, illness, accident, abandonment, and other rejections being further destroyed by community neglect and apathy. Some say they want to run and hide as the problem snowballs around them.[69]

No wonder British Columbia's remarkable Ruby Mackay resigned in 1960, concluding that "it was no longer possible in the face of the government's restrictive policies to fulfill the responsibilities of Superintendent of Child Welfare."[70] As we shall see, the experience of subsequent decades only continued this story.

4

STILL SEARCHING FOR BEST INTEREST
Child Protection and Fostering from the 1960s to the Present

A S THE THIRD MILLENNIUM APPROACHED AND THEN BEGAN, Canadian child protection policy and practice clearly entered changing terrain. Even as familiar alternatives of recuperated domestic originals or familial or institutional replacements persisted, certainties were scarce. Since fostering dealt with more wards of the crown than any other child protection service, its problems loomed at the centre of debates about what exactly constituted "the best interest of the child." How this might be understood and secured disturbed the national imaginary in ways unknown since early in the twentieth century. In this context, the maintenance of links between first families and subsequent caregivers was publicly considered as never before.

Sustaining original households had proven to be hard when social security programs were generally, if intermittently, expanding after the Second World War. It became substantially more difficult as the old century faded and the next began. From the 1970s on, oil crises, deficit reduction panics, global insecurity, and surging neo-conservatism served to compromise state commitment to the well-being of citizens and shifted "citizenship regimes" from an emphasis on rights to obligations. Families and women in particular were expected increasingly to shoulder the burdens of Canada's caregiving deficit.[1] The well-being of the child was one victim. The nearly simultaneous rediscovery and frequent sensationalization of violence and addiction in the same period—from battered babies to child sexual abuse and fetal alcohol spectrum disorders—added to and tested crowded child protection agendas. Official reports on child deaths confirmed generally bad news and continued the familiar tendency to demonize women, both mothers and social workers, as the causes of, or the contributors to, tragedy. The test of the era was best captured by the recurring conclusion that children coming into care were more challenging than ever: "Prevalence estimates of emotional and behavioural problems of children in foster care" rose "from 30%–40% in the 1970s–80s, to 47%–80% in the mid-1990s."[2]

Canada's child welfare policy makers, researchers, and practitioners were persistently on the defensive. Many shared the feminist, First Nations, disability rights, and community development perspectives that increasingly informed debates over social security, but the political climate was increasingly unfriendly. Torn between commitment to helping disadvantaged households and desires to salvage vulnerable youngsters, they grasped for solutions. The Canadian Child Welfare League summed up the difficult situation in 2007:

> The history of child protection is about understanding that children's rights must trump family rights. But for child welfare as a whole, one of the key themes in children's rights is that the family is the central institution in child development. Reconciling these two truths can be difficult; child welfare has seen the pendulum swing from one extreme to the other ... the delicate line is about how to support the family, whenever that is in the child's best interests.[3]

In this tumultuous environment of often-competing priorities, fostering, like institutions and adoption, struggled for reinvention.

This chapter considers the difficulties and the opportunities—often one and the same—of policy and practice from the 1960s to the twenty-first century. It begins with a review of the central dilemma for child protection—the limits of social security for families. It next describes key issues in modern Canadian child protection: the rediscovery of violence and abuse supplied by both clinical and feminist investigations, the special vulnerability of the First Nations and their resistance to marginalization and despair, and the deinstitutionalization and community inclusion movement.[4] Their demanding presence supplied the critical landscape in which Canadians sought answers to the challenge of disadvantaged children and youth. The period's efforts to secure the "best interest" for children preoccupy the last section of this chapter.

The Continuing Fragility of Social Security and First Families

In Canada, as elsewhere, poverty in these decades provided the staging ground for most suffering. In life and in death, the clients of child protection were defined by their economic circumstances. Whereas problematic patriarchs had preoccupied an earlier generation of Canadians, it was overwhelmingly women who now appeared to have failed in their primary duties. Native mothers, as Marlee Kline reminds us, were especially vulnerable to opprobrium.[5] At the beginning of this period, some administrations, such as those of the New Democratic Party (NDP) in British Columbia (1972–75) and the Parti Québécois in Quebec (1976–85), made a greater commitment to preventive services, and these remained the aim of many Canadians who worked in child protection. In 1989, the Canadian Parliament passed a resolution to end child poverty by 2000. Economic uncertainties and mounting conservatism soon proved, however, powerful deterrents. Any serious tackling of inequality required some redistribution in wealth, which few in power or sufficient numbers of voters were willing to consider.

Even as progressive advocates of child protection preferred to shore up original families, their efforts faced stiffened opposition. The spirit and demands of the 1980s and beyond often seemed more unpromising than they had been for many decades. As governments of various stripes set about dismantling the social safety net and favouring the morality of the marketplace, acknowledgement of social inequities and common risk faded from many policy agendas. As a result, the numbers of children living below the official low-income cut-off grew. By 2008, despite almost two decades of economic growth, 760,000, or one in every nine, Canadian youngsters lived in poverty.[6] Hopes for a national daycare program embraced by the report of the Royal Commission on the Status of Women in 1970 and many other investigations floundered. Only in Quebec, where sovereigntist sympathies kept governments more attentive, did universal daycare cross an important threshold of official acceptance.[7] The shift of most state policies away from earlier tentative consideration of a guaranteed annual income similarly "marked the transition from the welfare state consensus of the postwar period to the gradual triumph of neo-liberalism after 1975."[8] Governments, with the occasional exception of those led by the NDP and the Parti Québécois, generally resisted connecting neglect and abuse to growing social inequities. Many preferred managerial solutions that stressed technocratic and privatized remedies.[9]

Canadian jurisdictions gradually, if unevenly, withdrew from the post–Second World War promise of addressing the nation's social deficits in child welfare as much else. Much of this retreat was stealthy, as with the 1996 termination of the Canada Assistance Plan that cost-shared public and social services between the federal and the provincial and territorial governments. Sometimes, it occurred with great fanfare as with Ontario's so-called "common sense revolution" in the 1990s. Its Conservative government slashed assistance programs, citing "social responsibility, fiscal responsibility, and fiscal flexibility."[10]

In a manner reminiscent of an earlier age, politicians of every persuasion suggested that the marketplace and private partners, not public initiatives, were the best guarantors of progress. Reduction in eligibility and funding for (un)employment insurance, assaults on gender equity, the inauguration of workfare, and reductions to social assistance and continuing education for single parents and those with disabilities, combined with opposition to accessible childcare programs and attacks on unions and public sector employments, to sideswipe countless families. So-called "trickle down" economics steadily widened the gap between Canada's rich and poor.

Ontario under the government of Mike Harris (1995–2002) and British Columbia under various Liberal and NDP leaders in the 1990s and 2000s, like other jurisdictions, paid the cost of a massive disinvestment from justice. Upon election, Ontario's Conservatives savaged social assistance rates by 22 percent and cut far and wide, including the nutritional allowance for pregnant women on welfare. Between 2002 and 2004, the budget of British Columbia's Ministry of Children and Family Development dropped 11 percent as services, such as shelter allowances, income assistance, and childcare, were reduced. In 2006, the United Nations singled out the Pacific province for significantly worsening the plight of women and children.[11] Elimination of funding for contraception for women on welfare typified the mean-spirited and shortsighted response in the new millennium's first decade. Not surprisingly, British Columbia recorded some of the highest rates of kids in care, notably but not only of Aboriginal youngsters, in Canada.[12]

The official message was clear: individuals were responsible for the conditions of themselves, their children, and their community. The pervasive poverty and violence that darkened the lives of marginalized citizens often got forgotten in panics over the apparent failures of individuals and particular communities. Mothers were likely to be singled out as deficient. Investigations rarely spent much time on fathers who everywhere remained nearly invisible. The social work profession also came off as incompetent, unable to determine exactly when children should be apprehended, either doing it prematurely or tragically late. Administrations overwhelmingly run by male legislators and ministers, in contrast, largely got off scot-free. As Andrew Armitage emphasizes in his hard-hitting indictment of British Columbia's 1996 Gove inquiry into the death of young Matthew Vaudreuil, continuing preoccupation with managerial and professional solutions ignored structural disadvantage.[13] Original causes in economic inequities and the prejudices of class, race, gender, and disability were largely invisible.

A recurring fondness for psychological explanations that emphasized personal pathologies rather than social conditions was fuelled by the avalanche of university graduates in psychology in Canadian universities in these years. Many entered the "helping" professions, frequently bringing with them, wittingly or not, a deeply conservative ideology focused on individual therapies. The structure of much social work practice fed the fixation with private shortcomings. As one critic noted,

> a consequence of the unrelenting focus on personal troubles is that child welfare practice has become an individualistic enterprise; individual social workers see parents and children on an individual basis, usually in the agency office. Parents there have little or no opportunity to learn that their situation is shared by others or to come together to identify ways of coming to grips with their problems. At the same time, office-based practice renders invisible the housing and neighbourhood conditions facing families.[14]

Such perspectives allowed some practitioners and the public alike to pay insufficient attention to the slow collapse of Canada's investment in social security.

Mounting assaults on originally universal programs such as the federal family allowances diminished the fragile social contract that had tentatively evolved over the twentieth century. As one social scientist concluded, "recent changes in social policy for children are more concerned with governments acting to promote economic growth and helping their citizens participate in the market economy than with governments acting as a protector of children."[15] Results were devastating. Youngsters entered "care older and more damaged as the result of failures of preventive efforts; some are turned away on the basis of age or fear of the deleterious effects of placement and end up on the streets."[16] Ultimately, as other researchers put it, "current funding does not encourage reunification with adequate supports, or permanency with adequate supports, or prevention of child welfare placement in the first place. In fact, current funding frameworks create an incentive to bring children into care."[17] In sum, as the year 2000 came into sight, Canadian efforts to protect vulnerable youngsters everywhere confronted the specter of governments' withdrawal from duties of care and what often appeared as nothing less than a "war against the poor," particularly against women.[18]

Key Issues in Modern Canadian Child Protection

Tragedies of childhood disadvantage often seem remarkably unchanged over the years—specifics shift, but the consequences in violence and reduced opportunity appear much the same. What has evolved, however, has been the understanding of the dilemmas. In some ways, this era has been a period of significant discovery in child welfare. Canadians have confronted a wealth of new information and enhanced interpretation about injured lives. This information could, if it finds enough listeners, provide a powerful inducement to reconsider old ways of handling child protection.

The outpouring of research from these decades has provided clear indications of previous shortcomings and dangers to avoid. In 1998, the first Canadian Round Table on Child Welfare Outcomes, like the National Longitudinal Survey of Children, the Canadian Incidence Study of Reported Child Abuse and Neglect, and the Youth and National Children's Agenda, mobilized interdisciplinary expertise that permitted the first sustained comparisons among different child populations and demonstrated how a lack of access to key social and economic resources can damage lives.[19] Groups such as the Canadian Council on Social Development, the Vanier Institute of the Family, Campaign 2000, the Children at Risk Program of the Laidlaw Foundation, the Canadian Council on Children and Youth, the Canadian Child Welfare Association, British Columbia's Society for Children and Youth, and the Ontario Association of Children's Aid Societies "kept child poverty on the social policy agenda by issuing reports, holding conferences, and meeting with the Ministers of Finance and Health and Welfare." Despite the retreat from social justice by many federal, provincial, and territorial governments, new initiatives "documented the impact of poverty on the lives of children in a detailed and graphic fashion and have articulated the case for universal programs."[20] Reports from the Canadian Panel on Violence against Women in 1993 and a generation of feminist anti-violence and pro-universal childcare activists similarly confirmed that male power and female disadvantage stood behind the need for many child protection services.[21] This mounting evidence ultimately offered a powerful corrective to old ideologies of blame and shame.

The Rediscovery of Violence and Abuse

Even as governments floundered and prevaricated over social security, Canadians received hard lessons about the extent of distress in their midst. From the 1960s onward, violence and abuse returned to the child welfare agenda in ways unknown since the decades before the First World War. Feminist activists and scholars established indisputable linkages between children's plight and the nation's pervasive violence and discrimination against women, and a range of clinicians supplied influential evidence on the extent of injury inflicted by adults on children.

Child protection policy and practice were initially slow in reacting to these findings. As social work scholar Marilyn Callahan has observed, many feminist activists deliberately chose to work outside of traditional channels. They established "alternative social service organizations such as transition houses and sexual assault centres" and "maintained a clear distance between themselves and mainstream child welfare services to underline the distinction ... [and] to avoid becoming tarred with the same brush as government workers." While her own career and that of other female and male feminists in social work suggested a more promising story, she concludes that "activist women and their reforms have had little influence on child welfare services."[22] At least as important as the activists' choice of where to apply their energies was their commonly hostile reception in many official circles, especially after the 1980s when conservatism took a firmer hold and hopefully pronounced feminism to be dead. Most government departments, with the rare exception of anomalies such as British Columbia's Ministry of Women's Equality in the 1990s, had little interest in self-conscious equality-seeking employees and still less in promoting them to positions of influence. An awareness of the extent of violence nevertheless grew exponentially to inform the overall perspective on child welfare.

Clinical findings reinforced this message. Although medical research on violence against infants had existed since at least the 1940s, the organization of a symposium on child abuse for the American Academy of Pediatricians by Dr. C. Henry Kempe in 1960 popularized the term, the "battered child syndrome." Its conclusions were quickly taken up north of the border. In the 1970s, shaken baby syndrome (SBS), which is a condition similarly made more easily diagnosable with new technologies, also alerted increasing numbers of citizens to the extent of the mistreatment.[23] Canadians learned that SBS occurred in all cultures but that "biological fathers, stepfathers and male partners of biological mothers are more likely to shake an infant."[24]

These findings prompted Canadian governments to enact legislation requiring the mandatory reporting of child abuse, including British Columbia in 1967, Nova Scotia in 1968, Newfoundland and Labrador in 1969, and Alberta in 1970. By the end of the 1970s, most jurisdictions had some such provision. Related initiatives, such as the Child Protection Committees of the Montreal Children's Hospital in 1962 and of the Winnipeg Children's Hospital in 1968 and the Calgary Child Abuse Advisory Committee in 1972, took up the same challenge. Provinces also sponsored unprecedented investigations. In 1972, Cyril Greenland produced his groundbreaking report *Child Abuse in Ontario*, which was followed a year later by a report by Murray Fraser, J.P. Anderson, and K. Burns entitled *Child Abuse in Nova Scotia*.[25] The House of Commons' Standing Committee on Health, Welfare and Social Affairs produced unprecedented assessments of child abuse and neglect in 1974, 1975, and 1976. In 1977, two leading social work scholars captured this new awareness: Ralph Garber with the Ontario Task Force on Child Abuse and Benjamin Schlesinger with his report *Child Abuse in Canada*.[26] Such professional discoveries found popular counterparts such as the 1972 best-selling publication *The Battered Child in Canada* by feminist muckraker Mary Van Stolk.[27]

Battered and shaken babies supplied only the leading edge of public education. In 1984, the federal government published Canada's most extensive study of child sexual abuse, the report of the Committee on Sexual Offences against Children and Youth. Its author, Calgary social worker Christopher Bagley, concluded that 53 percent of adult Canadian women and 31 percent of men had been sexually abused in childhood.[28] The unlocked floodgates of memory produced a stream of Canadian victim-survivor narratives.[29] Crusading feminist journalist, Judy Steed, captured public attention with a riveting popular account, *Our Little Secret: Confronting Child Sexual Abuse in Canada*.[30] Equally unusual on the public stage were Aboriginal feminists such as Emma Laroque who questioned cultural defences of sexual violence. As she emphasized,

> We know that keeping child molesters and rapists in the same vicinity as victims puts victims at greater risk, and studies on sexual abuse also strongly indicate it is psychologically destructive for victims to be subjected to their attacker's presence. This is exacerbated in small communities and, it must be emphasized, most Native communities are small.[31]

While advocates of "false memory syndrome" questioned its prevalence, clinicians joined feminist frontline activists and theorists to greatly expand the understanding of sexual assault and point to the special vulnerability of negatively racialized groups and those with physical and mental impairments. In short, as one legal scholar has concluded, the "relationships between institutionalized power and disempowerment and sexual violence" were broadly exposed.[32]

The third discovery associated with child protection agendas agitating this period and prompting greater levels of apprehension was the recognition of fetal alcohol spectrum disorder (FASD). In the context of a general panic associated with drug-addicted mothers, which seeped in from Reaganite United States, alarm in Canada focused on the impact of alcohol.[33] Canada's larger Native population, the extent of its distress and despair, and the continuing prejudices that emphasized its particular association with alcoholism helped generate special attention.[34] Beginning in the 1980s, the Parliamentary Standing Committee on Health and the Royal Commission on New Reproductive Technologies took alcohol abuse seriously in a manner unseen since the pre–First World War ban-the-bar campaigns. By 1996, sixteen "national health and allied associations identified the use of alcohol during pregnancy as a national health concern." Three years later, Canada created the National FASD Initiative and supported various prevention programs in the new millennium, many directed at First Nations citizens.[35] In 1997, Métis film director Gil Cardinal movingly demonstrated in his film *David with F.A.S.* the terrible consequences for one young adoptee and his family. Clinical discoveries also prompted responses by feminist researchers and community activists who concluded "that prevention of FAS requires that we begin in early childhood to prevent the traumas that drain young women of their ability to define themselves and avoid later mental health problems."[36] The apprehension of damaged youngsters was regarded as far too tardy an intervention that failed to acknowledge the origin of the trauma in the oppression of women.

While findings of abuse and addiction have been horrific, it is impossible to know whether the extent, in utero or in later childhood, is actually unprecedented or simply previously unreported. Modern diagnosis of the maltreatment of girls and boys includes, for example, witnessing domestic violence, a phenomenon that has always devastated many Canadians. In the past, however, it has not been interpreted as child abuse. Advanced medical technologies have similarly recognized injuries and conditions that previously escaped notice. In times past, in the context of much isolated or rural living, small bodies readily disappeared and inhabitants were little monitored by government agencies in health, welfare, and education. The same problem of assessing trends exists in charting sexual abuse, which became a major justification for apprehension during these years. For example, while "research in Canada and the US suggests a significant decline in substantiated child sexual abuse" early in the twenty-first century, experts remain uncertain about the findings. Did they constitute a "response to effective child sexual abuse prevention initiatives, more effective intervention to perpetrators, or changes in the system that may deter sexual abuse reporting"?[37] The problem of data interpretation worsens with each step back in time.

This enhanced awareness of the various dangers in the late twentieth century was a key development in Canadian child protection. Many girls and boys gained valuable knowledge of their rights and access to those who promised to believe them. Many were saved from terrible situations. Many Canadians learned to look beyond individuals for the origins of tragedy. Unhappily, awareness readily led as well to the familiar scapegoating of entire populations, notably young, working-class, and Aboriginal parents. Suspect individuals and deficient cultures readily emerged as leading explanations and villains. As had happened routinely in the past, poverty, racism, and male violence became readily sidelined in preoccupation with supposed social pathologies that might be "fixed" by experts and punished by the state. This tendency repeatedly undermined understanding and support for the adults in children's lives. The situation was made all the worse because of the massive increase in complaints regarding child abuse. In British Columbia alone, the surge from "3,500 to 32,000 between

1980 and 1990" drove "out the time and attention needed for family counsel-
ing, community, and a variety of preventive programs."[38]

Equally corrosive was the slippage of verdicts into general discourses of
despair, inevitability, and even bio-determinism. Child victims too easily joined
parents and kin groups as being beyond repair. Like "street kids," a term that
emerged after the Second World War in reference to the children of developing countries who entered Canada by the 1980s, entire categories of wounded
youngsters appeared simultaneously threatening and hopeless.[39] This conclusion,
which was so clearly evident in the withdrawal from much domestic adoption
by all but the most dedicated of Canadian adults, fuelled growing pessimism
regarding child welfare in general. Apprehended youngsters were increasingly
assessed as "commonly both disturbing to their foster families and emotionally
disturbed," displaying "a variety of mental, physical, emotional, and behavioural
problems." Remediation was always expensive and seemingly doubtful.[40] In face
of such conclusions, gloom haunted many millennial discussions of child protection. The message regarding violence and abuse that feminists, in particular, had offered for causes rooted in structural disadvantage and sexism was only
too readily ignored.

Aboriginal Tragedies and Resistance

A second major influence during these years was the centrality of First Nations
populations in all discussions of child protection.[41] Three points are particularly worth remembering. First, mainstream efforts failed early on; second, Native
communities quickly challenged state apprehensions; and, third, important initiatives came from First Nations communities and leaders themselves. Just as
feminists, who were sometimes also Aboriginal, offered ways to understand violence and abuse as something more than individual pathology, Aboriginal champions, who were also sometimes feminist, pointed to the impact of colonialism
and racism in undermining adult–child relations.

As they apprehended unprecedented numbers of Aboriginal youngsters,
provincial child protection workers initially assumed benefits. As Aboriginal
veterans of these years have attested, some good did indeed occur. Rescue from
communities devastated by colonialism was sometimes absolutely essential for
the survival of individual children, even if it involved placement in non-Aboriginal homes.[42] In the context of new constitutional recognition, which occurred
in 1982 with the *Canadian Charter of Rights and Freedoms*, court challenges, and
an energetic rights movement, child welfare became a highly charged symbol of
all that was wrong with Native–non-Native relations.[43] By the 1970s, some governments were trying to engage with Aboriginal communities in finding solutions. The BC ministry responsible for child welfare, which was buoyed by a

NDP government from 1972 to 1975, articulated the conclusions of many pro-gressive observers:

> Nowhere is the need for prevention more obvious than among our Indian peo-ple. Statistics show that Indian children, once removed from their family and cultural roots, remain in care for longer periods and are frequently lost to their tribe. The past year has been one in which there have been frequent meetings and discussions with the Indian people to plan with them toward the provision of a better child welfare and family service on the reserve ... Protective services to chil-dren must focus on the rehabilitation of the family and the eventual restoration of the child to his natural parents.[44]

The election of a generally unsympathetic Social Credit administration soon capsized these particular hopes, but similarly reactionary sentiments everywhere compromised new beginnings. At least as important was the depth of Aborigi-nal poverty on reserves and in cities that went well beyond anything that could be solved by individual rescue or apprehension.

Official reports, autobiographies, fiction, public protests, and the well-pub-licized failed adoptions by notables such as politician Jean Chrétien and broad-caster Barbara Frum increasingly publicized the downside of old policies. Aboriginal film director Alanis Obomsawin's prize-winning film *Richard Cardi-nal: Cry from the Diary of a Métis Child* in 1986 captured the recurring face of tragedy. This teen from Alberta's "Fort Chip" spent more than a decade bun-dled from one foster home to another. His eventual escape was suicide. The predicament of such Crown wards readily loomed as insurmountable. Even con-sultations with local bands and leaders were hard put to generate alliances or enough Aboriginal foster parents.[45] There was no ready answer to apparent contradictions such as when children required distant medical treatment to survive, when inadequate supports for subsequent reintegration threatened well-being, or when conflicts arose between Native mothers preferring offspring to be "raised outside his extended family" and communities that claimed rights "to make that decision."[46]

By the 1980s, two faculty members in social work from the University of Manitoba summed up the dawning professional recognition that Aboriginal child welfare was nothing more than Canadian "colonialism."[47] Within a short time, this was the dominant perspective in Native child welfare scholarship. This spurred initiatives in the same decade such as Manitoba's delegation of protection services to the Dakota Ojibway Tribal Council and Ontario's requirement that there be "due consideration of a child's cultural identity" when it came to determining best interest.[48] Prejudice and politics neverthe-less continued to stymie many attempts at redress and reconciliation. The federal Conservative government's rejection of the 2005 Kelowna Accord, which promised to close the health, education, housing, and economic gap between Aboriginal and non-Aboriginal Canadians, once again set back hopes.

Aboriginal communities maintained long-standing protests over the loss of youngsters.[49] Advocates of prevention and protection spoke out eloquently, cooperated with progressive policy makers, and forged their own instruments for addressing distress. In 1974, the Union of BC Chiefs presented the Native consensus in a brief on adoption and welfare services: "Leadership must be allowed to emerge from the Indian population."[50] Individual communities took concrete action. In the 1980s, Alberta's Yellowhead Tribal Council initiated searches for apprehended youngsters and British Columbia's Spallumcheen Band seized control over child welfare.[51] In 1984, in order to sidestep the city's Children's Aid Society, which was regarded as unhelpful, the Winnipeg Urban Indian Coalition joined with the Manitoba government to establish the Ma Mawi Wi Chi Itata Centre to support vulnerable families. Five years later, British Columbia's Nuu-Chah-Nulth child welfare program received delegated authority from the province.[52] The same decade also introduced the Vancouver Aboriginal Child and Family Social Services, which advocated for families involved with child protection and used cultural resources to help put them back on their feet. Over two decades, it built programs emphasizing family preservation and reunification and eventually became a delegated agency for the province.[53] By 1992, 207 of 592 First Nations communities had "service agreements enabling some form of control over child and family services."[54] By the time the new millennium started, First Nations child and family service agencies across Canada "represent[ed] the fourth largest child welfare service organization in Canada, exceeded only by the provinces of Quebec, Ontario, and British Columbia."[55]

Mainstream prejudice was not the only obstacle to progress. As Patrick Johnston, who coined "the sixties scoop" observed, child welfare often only received attention when women forced it on the indigenous agenda. Like their counterparts elsewhere, male leaders appeared frequently more interested in land and treaty rights.[56] Many proved reluctant to confront the "degree of difficulty of the tasks" that they asked child protection staff, once again women, for the most part, to assume.[57] In both government and Aboriginal agencies, child welfare workers were readily scapegoated. They remained, as elsewhere, "highly vulnerable," "held accountable for the many children at risk in their communities and for conditions not within their power to alter."[58] When resource-rich bands, such as those in southern Alberta, proved unwilling or unable to distribute resources equitably, children suffered. This failure too was not unique.

Familiar problems haunted indigenous programs as they tackled the heritage of colonialism and patriarchy. As one 2000 critic observed, "allegations that political considerations outweighed concern about child welfare ... surrounded reports in 1987 of child abuse resulting from improper placement of children by the Awasis Agency into homes on reserves in Northern Manitoba."[59] Cheryl Swidrovich has convincingly argued that a widespread misunderstanding of what had actually happened during the sixties scoop contributed to the birthing problems of Aboriginal agencies. As she emphasizes, evidence demonstrates that most youngsters came into care not because of any enthusiasm for apprehension by authorities who, as this volume emphasizes, were always concerned with funding shortfalls but, rather, because something had gone badly wrong in children's lives. In particular, colonialism had seriously undermined the caring capacity of many Native households, and their needs went well beyond communities simply acquiring control of child welfare.[60]

Native child protection workers struggled with familiar conditions. In the 2000s, children and youth in Manitoba's Cree Nation Kinship Care Program lived on average with twelve different foster parents, with 25 percent living with four or fewer, and 50 percent with fourteen or more.[61] Many Aboriginal communities and agencies remained ill equipped and ill supported in dealing with the extent of damage that had earlier similarly stymied mainstream efforts.[62] Nonetheless, they had to face increasing numbers coming into care. This was hardly surprising. As Manitoba commentators have pointed out, "the lack of child welfare services on reserves prior to the 1980s, widespread recognition of physical and sexual abuse within First Nations communities, poor economic and social conditions, the limited funding available for prevention, the lack of complementary social services, and the relatively recent adoption of a community-based service model are likely to contribute to higher case findings."[63] Alcohol and other drug addictions, as well as violence, sometimes proved overwhelming, just as they did in Canada generally.[64]

Although the inauguration of the federal Aboriginal Head Start program in 1995 helped, inequities proved hardy. A 2000 study pointed out that federal funding per child for First Nations child and family service agencies "was on average 22 percent lower than the provinces" and that it failed to take into account "special needs services and least disruptive measures services."[65] The situation was all the worse because Native families received far less support in recreation, education, healthcare, housing, and mentoring from the voluntary sector than did other citizens.[66] Disputes between federal and provincial governments over responsibility for costs further hindered solutions. One Native toddler, Jordan from Norway House, Manitoba, spent an unnecessary two years in hospital before his death because no jurisdiction would agree to fund homecare costs.[67]

Since almost 70 percent of Aboriginal youngsters lived off-reserve at the beginning of the new millennium, there was also the growing challenge of an increasingly diverse population—in other words, the same sort of situation that regularly
overwhelmed other social workers.[68] Race-based solutions to the crisis in care
were additionally challenging when charges reflected the diverse origins of
Canadians as a whole. Such was the case with one small boy, born of a status
mother from Manitoba, who was herself adopted by White Americans, and a
Black American biological father. In response to claims by both his maternal birth
grandfather and adoptive grandparents, the Supreme Court of British Columbia recognized African ancestry as "equally deserving of preservation and nurturing."[69] What such preservation meant in practice would have to be negotiated
in countless individual cases.

In the face of multiple challenges, new Aboriginal child protection authorities have developed significant strategies focused on cultural revival, group solidarity, and alliance building. The formation of the First Nations Child and
Family Caring Society (FNCFCS) has promised to provide important collaboration with partners such as the Child Welfare League of Canada.[70] In
Saskatchewan, where the twenty-first century promises to usher in an Aboriginal majority of citizens, initiatives have been ubiquitous. Between 2004 and
2006, elders, community members, agencies, and researchers from the province's
two social work faculties cooperated in a "Transmission of Values Project" to get
beyond the prevailing pessimism. It set out to raise consciousness "of all of the
work that is being done to support children, youth, and their families and to
strengthen the community."[71] In 2005, a meeting in Ontario's Six Nations Territory discussed the redesign of child welfare practices for Aboriginal youngsters in both Canada and the United States. Participants embraced the principles
of "self-determination," the significance of "culture and language," "holism,"
or decision making "within the context of their contextual and cultural reality,"
the strategic targeting of "structural risk factors," and "non-discrimination,"
including access to voluntary sector services.[72] In the same year, the FNCFCS
produced two major reports—Wen:de: We Are Coming to the Light of Day and
Wen:de: The Journey Continues—which emphasize chronic under-funding and
the need for new formulas to address historic prejudice and despair. Experiments with "restorative justice" and "family conferencing," programs that aim
"to restore balance to the individual, family and community" set out to realize
the promise of indigenous caregiving.[73]

Many new Aboriginal agencies proved willing to make hard decisions. In
2007, the executive director of Ottawa's First Nations Child Family Caring
Society reported Native-run child protection societies making "mass removals"
from households judged to be dangerous.[74] That same year, in response to var-

ious controversies, including the evacuation of twenty-one youngsters from a reserve-based group home, the Federation of Saskatchewan Indian Nations set up the First Nations Family and Community Institute to formulate guidelines, training materials, and on-reserve programs. A year later, British Columbia's representative for children and youth, Mary Ellen Turpel-Lafond, a member of the Cree Nation and a former Saskatchewan judge, acknowledged an unpleasant necessity for Native and non-Native communities alike with the demand for background checks for adults in the "children in the home of a relative" program.[75] Even Aboriginal kinship and investment in dreams of previous domestic Edens proved no guarantee of good treatment.

From the 1960s into the first decade of the twenty-first century, Aboriginal activists presented their own solutions to the problems of child welfare that officials had everywhere to take into account. Cooperative possibilities confronted a long history of mistrust, misunderstanding, and racism. Building capacity to protect youngsters in First Nations communities proved as difficult an endeavour as it had long been in the mainstream of Canadian society. Their challenge was central to the general Canadian conundrum of child welfare.

Deinstitutionalization and Community Living

Wrongs done to children with physical and mental disabilities joined other unsettling public discoveries in the last decades of the twentieth century. Horrific revelations of institutional violence across a range of service realms sensitized a generation. In 1990, Ontario's provincial auditor targeted unreported deaths in two nursing homes for children with mental handicaps.[76] In 1991, the Quebec Human Rights Commission awarded $1 million in damages to the former residents of Pavillion St. Theophile.[77] Exposures of mistreatment at Vancouver's Jericho Hill School for the Deaf, St. John's Mount Cashel Orphanage, and New Westminster's Woodlands School kept failings front page. When the Law Commission of Canada's report entitled *Restoring Dignity: Responding to Child Abuse in Canadian Institutions* linked residences housing Aboriginal, delinquent, mentally handicapped, and otherwise marginalized youngsters across the country with incidences of child abuse, the reputations of institutions and childcare authorities were in tatters.[78]

Just as feminists and Aboriginal activists highlighted the larger context of structural inequities in these years, advocates of inclusion of Canadians with impairments pointed to the social construction of disadvantage. While the drug therapies of the 1950s and 1960s offered one basis for deinstitutionalization, philosophical critiques that embraced human diversity and rights inspired outspoken champions such as Wolf Wolfensberger, an international crusader working in Canada.[79] By 1970, the Canadian Association for the Mentally Retarded had placed inclusion firmly on the national agenda.[80] UN declarations on the rights of the "mentally retarded" and the handicapped during this decade further highlighted the value of deinstitutionalization and social recognition. In 1972, the National Institute on Mental Retardation published Wolfensberger's influential *The Principle of Normalization in Human Services*. In Quebec, where the 1962 Bedard Commission on Psychiatric Services had earlier proposed the removal of citizens with mental handicaps from asylums and the provision of "life training,"[81] integration became "a recognizable movement" about the same time.[82] In 1981, a Special Parliamentary Committee on the Disabled and the Handicapped recommended independent living. Seven years later, the federal government endorsed deinstitutionalization. At the grassroots level, the "people first" movement emerged by the early 1990s to popularize inclusion for all ages, and community living groups flourished across Canada.[83] The founding of the Canadian Academy of Child Psychiatry in 1980 (later the Canadian Academy of Child and Adolescent Psychiatry/Academie canadienne de psychiatrie de l'enfant et de l'adolescent), like the Ontario Child Health Study that identified that one in five children had a serious mental health problem,[84] also brought unprecedented attention to long-standing injury. In response to mounting indictment, many institutions shrank, disappeared, or transformed, as Chapter 2 suggests.[85]

These decades' renewed awareness of institutional shortcomings contributed to the changing character of youngsters coming into fostering.[86] Mental hospitals responded to historic overcrowding by encouraging external placements. The so-called normalization of institutionalized populations became especially popular in British Columbia during the 1970s when community resource boards advocated "citizen participation, integration, and decentralization of services." This promising start, like those elsewhere, struggled to generate sufficient popular support. Even before the defeat of a sympathetic government, child welfare planners and practitioners discovered that local supports required more resources and met more opposition than they had hoped.[87] Even as institutional options deteriorated, children with handicaps and their parents found too little respite or treatment care. The result was recurring hardship. By the 1980s, a leading child psychiatrist summed up the result: "More older and seriously disturbed children are coming into care" that is ill equipped to meet their needs.[88]

Ultimately, provinces largely "accepted the inevitability of preserving at least a minimal number of residential care programs in perpetuity."[89] In the 1960s and 1970s, group homes emerged as a popular way of keeping especially vulnerable youngsters more or less in home communities and out of larger congregate operations. In particular, there was significant agreement that collective care helped particular populations, such as adolescents, who found accepting family life more difficult. The experts of the day concluded, and many parents agreed, that "for those who have deep-seated effects of trauma and who have difficulty controlling their acting-out pain behaviour, the more formal and professionalized attention of staff can make the difference between real person change and another failure experience."[90]

In his text *The Principle of Normalization*, Wolfensberger anticipates the benefits of group homes.[91] What he did not foresee was that they would become the mainstay "of residential needs for young people with special needs."[92] This solution appeared to be easier and frequently cheaper than retrofitting original homes, providing respite options, or preparing highly trained foster parents. In any case, group homes proved regularly hard to run and staff, and they also produced abuse much like the type they were supposed to remedy. Nonetheless, they became a feature of the child protection landscape for older youngsters, particularly when many provinces downloaded responsibilities to religious and for-profit agencies in the 1980s and beyond.

First parents of children with disabilities, commonly but not only mothers, often led campaigns for deinstitutionalization. They worked hard for locally available supports. Some also questioned the use of foster parents. Some doubted "the ability of a substitute family to perpetuate placement in the face of demands so onerous as to defeat their own efforts to provide care for their children."[93] Many wondered why governments refused them sufficient in-home and emergency care. One mother typically asked: "If I had the support I needed and asked for, my son would never have gone into care. Why were they able to give the foster family supports but could not give them to me?"[94] Answers remained in short supply. In many jurisdictions, "families (including Aboriginal families) are [still] forced to surrender custody of their children to the child protection system because the necessary care is not available in their own community."[95]

Although foster parents sometimes had easier access to services, options for them also remained hit and miss. In the new millennium, despite a decade of (relative) prosperity and recurring demands for investment in community development, matters remained regularly desperate. In 2008, Canadian "children with disabilities are more likely to be living in households where household income is below the national average," "slightly more than half of children with disabilities do not have access to needed aids and devices," and "children with disabilities are overrepresented in provincial/territorial child welfare systems."[96] Even as disability rights activists made Canadians more cognizant of problems, assistance was hobbled by preference for private solutions and general prejudice. The failures of many mainstream public services in education and health to sustain real inclusion made challenging old patterns more difficult. Like women and

Natives, governments too frequently appeared to regard young and old Canadians with disabilities as demanding, but essentially second-class, citizens.

Searching for Best Interest

The deaths of youngsters known to child protection agencies at the end of the twentieth century, such as Ontario's Kim Anne Popen (1975–76), British Columbia's Matthew John Vaudreuil (1986–92), and Manitoba's Sophia Lynn Schmidt (1995–96), confirmed the devastation and the dilemmas confronting Canadian policies and practices in child protection.[97] Growing recognition of abuse fuelled dramatic, although intermittent, increases in apprehension over these decades, even as social workers negotiated commitment to family preservation principles that were also embraced both as a matter of principle and for their potential cost savings. In 2007, the number of Canadian children in care approached 80,000, and close to half of these children had Aboriginal ancestry.[98] The report of Saskatchewan's child advocate in 2009 captured the tragic trajectory in one city: "Historically, between January 2004 and July 2008, the total number of foster children in the Saskatoon Service Centre grew from 670 to 1,067. This is a 159 per cent increase in just four years." Even those grim statistics were partial. They failed to include "children in the care of First Nations' child and family services agencies in Saskatoon and surrounding area."[99] Indeed, overlapping jurisdictions and poor reporting meant that numbers across the country were never certain.

These years brought intense concern with unstable foster placements. "Drift" among homes was not new, but it was now widely recognized as a major failing everywhere. Two major National Film Board exposés of foster care— *Richard Cardinal: Cry from a Diary of a Métis Child* (1986) and *Wards of the Crown* (2007)—profiled victims of dozens of placements. Their tragedies haunted all discussion of child protection as knowledgeable observers concluded that long-term foster care was generally too uncertain to promote attachment and well-being. Thoughtful responses turned more than ever to strengthening adults' capacity to parent even as overtaxed social workers knew too well the reality of domestic violence in original families.

Despite difficulties in procuring ongoing funding, the end of the 1980s and early 1990s saw important experiments in empowering disadvantaged families, including some 2,000 "primary and secondary prevention and promotion projects in the Montréal area" alone.[100] Manitoba's Neighbourhood Parenting Support Project and Ontario's Highfield Community Enrichment Project and Child Welfare Demonstration Project aimed at the same result. The first involved helping residents of some of Winnipeg's most disadvantaged communities gain skills to take control of their own lives.[101] The second, a part of a series of community projects under the *Better Beginnings, Better Futures* initiative, connected parents and neighbourhood partners in building capacity.[102] The third, the Child Welfare Demonstration Project, was a "social support intervention with the primary goal of preventing out-of-home placements of children at risk of neglect or abuse." Like the others, it promoted "social integration," "emotional support," "education," and "concrete support."[103] Success was demonstrated when multi-problem participants were "significantly" less likely to lose children.[104] British Columbia's *Empowering Women Project* was a comparable endeavour, setting out to build on "survival-related strengths" and "correctly naming conditions like poverty." Women were treated "as partners" and "active participants in any planning affecting their lives as well as contributors to social and policy change."[105] Such initiatives, which were often fuelled by feminist insights, made inequalities, not mothers, the problem to be tackled.

Emphasis on the "least intrusive measures" became the leitmotif of many public agencies as they tried to help parents discover longer-term strategies for helping themselves and their offspring. When apprehensions occurred, up-to-date planning persistently favoured cooperation with original parents. In order to facilitate contact and even reunification, social workers developed care plans with extended family members, the community, and the children themselves.[106] Such commitment affected the provision of services both positively and negatively. Positive effects included improved efforts to support original households and the development of family support programs. Negative results have been delays in intervention in families where children's well-being could not be assured.[107]

Despite a continuing reliance on gender-neutral terms, such as the "Child in the Home of a Relative Program," grandmothers and aunts also moved to the forefront of preferred solutions in these years. Kinship care offered the special promise of cost savings. Relatives were expected to be cheaper than other parental substitutes, and they routinely received the "lowest level of compensation."[108] Mainstream officialdom's recognition of the need to work with First Nations agencies and communities also encouraged the resort to kin care.[109] Such placements, wherever they occurred, were rarely as closely supervised as those provided by non-relatives. Until close to the end of the first decade of the twenty-first century, most of these substitutes escaped criminal checks and formal standards. In 2004, the Ontario Association of Children's Aid Societies summed up the downside by stating that policies, caregiver assessment practices, payment, and supervision, all lacked "clarity and consistency."[110] Once again, families were presumed to function effectively with scant resources and with women expected to subsidize the endeavour and to control potentially abusive men in their lives.

Mounting expectations of continued contact with birth families added significantly to the duties of foster parents and childcare workers. In the 1970s, the Vancouver Children's Aid Society described the implications:

> Previously our foster parents' main focus was to care for the child until the child went for adoption. Our foster parents had little or no experience with the mother who wanted to visit the child in the foster home—take the child out for a day, etc. The focus today is to assist the mother, inexperienced as she might be in some areas, to take her child back. Many foster parents have to almost train the mother in parenthood. This has required a different type of foster parent who plays a different role with different demands being made on her. Many of our traditional foster parents refuse to accept this new role.[111]

Up-to-date foster parents were more than ever asked to serve as quasi-therapists and councillors even as they acted as housekeepers, nurturers, appointment keepers, and disciplinarians.

Dr. Paul Steinhauer, a leading Canadian child psychiatrist of the day, was a key figure in the therapeutic turn that became increasingly visible in foster care. In particular, he emphasized youngsters' need to mourn the loss of first families. He joined many other observers in concluding that a child's past could not be as readily discarded as some agencies had hoped. In arguments reminiscent of sociologist David Kirk's insights regarding adoption in the previous period, Steinhauer argued that separation required opportunities to grieve and that "terminating contact encourages idealization of the parent and fantasies of reunion, and thus deprives the child of opportunity to address the reality of the loss and its causes ... and interferes with attachment to new caregivers."[112] Such conclusions informed the period's legal decisions that favoured Crown wardship with access.[113] In theory at least, connection with the past was acknowledged, sometimes embraced, as essential to a child's future well-being. However, properly recognizing and coping with this connection required attention that both child protection agencies and foster parents were hard put to supply.

As demands on host families mounted, child welfare and treatment programs scrambled for suitable substitutes and training. One solution, as we shall see in Chapter 6, which considers foster parents in detail, was to train fostering professionals who could embrace and sustain programs of therapy, conciliation, and recovery. This never proved easy. An enhanced clinical and therapeutic orientation always threatened other important attributes of good fostering. As a thoughtful critic noted, it largely failed to take account of "the feeling and caring aspects of the job, the real invisible work that often spells the difference between success and failure."[114] The for-profit suppliers of service that flourished as cost-cutting state administrations withdrew from duties of care would be especially hard put to recognize and supply these essential elements.

In order to support new roles and to address the continuing shortfall in recruitment of kin and non-kin caregivers, child welfare authorities promoted various recognition programs for individuals and associations of foster parents. At the beginning of the twentieth century, efforts along these lines included the Child Welfare League of Canada's PRIDE program and the Parenting Resources for Information Development and Education program, which were both imported from the United States.[115] In their empowerment of foster parents, such initiatives offered the potential for both partnerships and criticism. By the late twentieth century, foster parents, as we shall see later, demanded more than ever a voice in the shaping of policy and practice. Their insistence promised both to strengthen and to complicate the provision of child protection everywhere.

As they sought remedies, provincial and territorial child welfare programs reduced distinctions between adoption and fostering. Greater stress on permanency planning aimed to reduce the drift of youngsters among caregivers. In particular, social workers experimented with subsidizing adoptive homes and creating "fostering with a view to adopt" programs. The same inspiration informed the growing provision for "post-adoption services, such as therapeutic support, consultation and including mediated open-adoption."[116] Such strategies built on the commitment of families who wanted permanent relationships but who needed additional financial and other supports. Results were everywhere difficult to judge, but solutions did not meet the rising numbers of children in care.

The seeming incorrigibility of many problems gnawed at Canadian social workers. Like foster parents, they became increasingly difficult to recruit and to retain. They likewise suffered from overload, bureaucratic barriers, insufficient resources and information, and a lack of respite and recognition. The rewards of (women's) caring work, for them as for others, were increasingly questioned.[117] When women's opportunities were limited, maternalism and altruism could be sustained, if only barely. By the late decades of the twentieth century, some potential and actual social workers had backed away from efforts to salvage the victims of state policies. Only a few hardy or hardened souls could sustain the recurring attack on their credibility and commitment by the public and their political masters.

One scholarly appraiser of child protection summed up the only too common situation in many jurisdictions: "Impossible working conditions contributed to 'creativity' being 'replaced with conformity;' 'idealism' with cynicism; collective sharing with turf protection; and where critical questions, challenges, and new ideas are oftentimes feared and avoided." These results, in turn, "contribute[d] to ever increasing emphasis on control, efficiency, accountability, technical proficiency, and on endeavouring to find clinical solutions to structural problems." As he went on to add, "the irony is that these are the same experiences and feelings of the parents and children with whom they work."[118]

The growing strain on everyone involved in foster care sometimes prompted a reconsideration of the old options. In 1991, Paul Steinhauer summed up the new case for institutions:

> The value of foster care as a service for children requiring placement has recently been challenged by a number of prominent mental health professionals and government officials who question whether long-term foster care is so innately unstable that children unable to be raised in their own family would be better served by a return to institutional placements. A number of factors have contributed to their taking this position: difficulties in both recruiting and retaining foster parents; the frequency with which placements break down; the high numbers of foster children requiring institutional placements; the number of failures of the foster care system who leave care showing severe and persistent disorders of personality, socialization, behaviour, and emotion regulation; the frequency with which these patterns recur in the next generation, repeating the cycle of neglect, abuse, and multiple separations that the parents, as children, experienced. In some jurisdictions the result has been a serious call for a return to institutionalization as an alternative possible less detrimental than foster care.[119]

Like many other progressive experts, he resisted this conclusion. For many Canadians labouring in the minefields of child protection, greater community supports for both birth and foster parents offered far better prospects for good outcomes.

Conclusion

To end on an entirely negative note would do a disservice to Canada's many champions of children from the nineteenth to the twenty-first century. Several modern developments justify optimism over the long term. The first is the period's compelling documentation of the real needs of children and youth in care and, with this data, a widespread and largely unprecedented recognition of systemic failure. Contemporary feminism has been another significant force in rejecting long-standing assumptions about the naturalness of violence and abuse and has done much to inspire the broader research agenda. Above all, it has pointed to the need to take proper account of racism, poverty, ableisim, and dependence on women for caregiving.[120] The commitment of many First

Nations communities to placing child welfare at the top of their agenda offers another reason for hope. Their determination, in the face of the devastation of colonialism, should inspire mainstream Canadians to do better as well. Disability rights advocates have similarly provided unprecedented challenges to the system that currently injuries so many children and adults.

At the beginning of the twenty-first century, such wide-ranging criticism has inspired renewed interest in community development and organizing. This promises to empower ordinary citizens left behind when governments prioritized debt reduction and disengaged from equality agendas. This orientation to social problems and inequalities has strong roots in English Canada, notably in the early twentieth-century settlement houses, the Company of Young Canadians from the 1960s, and social democratic movements more generally.[121] Community development initiatives also have a significant history in Quebec in long-standing Catholic social action movements and the Quiet Revolution of the 1960s.[122] Brian Wharf, one of Canada's most thoughtful social work scholars, suggests that mainstream modern agencies such as Winnipeg's Child and Family Services may regard community organizing with far greater interest. In this case, enthusiasm for "a community kitchen and parent–child recreation programs" and advocacy for public housing invoked a holistic approach that locates children's well-being firmly within their communities.[123] The introduction of provincial and territorial child advocates and representatives of children and youth from the 1970s onward similarly provides important institutional instruments for ensuring a hearing for critical voices.[124] These resources were invaluable as Canadians confronted the future of child protection in the context of a world economic crisis (beginning 2008) that clearly demonstrated the failure of old ways of thinking. Canadians were asked as never before to examine their consciences and to tackle the fundamental inequities of gender, class, race, and ability that consigned so many to lives of pain.

5

FIRST FAMILIES AND
THE DILEMMA OF CARE

"First" PARENTS FIGURE IN MOST POPULAR AND PROFESSIONAL accounts as deeply problematic, to be assisted, remade, or rejected by authorities and others. Women frequently emerge, as Alice Parizeau lamented in the 1970s, as "monstres" or, as a more recent observer notes, objects of "contempt," apparent violators of deeply held conventions about what constitutes normalcy.[1] In such assessments, Aboriginal Canadians and their racialized counterparts have loomed as especially predisposed to incompetence, but they have never been unique. Perspectives commonly fluctuate between pity and horror, with little inclination to consider individuals in the context of systemic failure to support the nurture of children. A recurring tendency to summary judgment and individual indictment readily stereotypes, even demonizes, first families. In many cases, however, parents have been as desperately placed as their sons and daughters who enter fostering and other types of care.

This chapter begins by reviewing how poverty has always made some adults susceptible to difficulties as parents and to the loss of progeny. It then turns to women whose maternal roles have been especially suspect as well as central— especially the racialized, the unwed, the battered, those with perceived mental or physical disabilities, and the criminalized. It next considers biological fathers, the central but often offstage actors who haunt the narratives of many youngsters who are transferred to state care; rarely do these fathers receive close attention. Finally, it sets out Canadians' evolving response to the original parents of children who are in, or are candidates for, care.

The Particular Vulnerability of the Poor

Poverty and class, which is often its unacknowledged shadow, commonly propel children into the hands of non-biological adults. Women, negatively racialized groups, and Canadians with impairments have had more limited access to good waged employments and to resources in general than healthy Anglo-Celtic males. Although abuse has always attracted much more attention, neglect or a failure to provide the necessities of life—commonly the inability to do so—has always explained the loss of most daughters and sons from the nineteenth century to the present.[2] The gap between resources and demands fundamentally undermines adult ability to nurture or to protect the young. Disadvantage and its consequences have been regularly passed from one generation to another. Take, for example, a child emigrated by the Barnardo Homes, who was swept out of Britain to arrive as a ten-year-old with a younger brother in Canada in 1912. With little formal education and less adult support, she became a servant. Soon enough, unwed pregnancy forced her to surrender her only child to the local Children's Aid Society. This daughter then moved through a series of foster homes where her mother visited as often she could. At age fifteen, Helen rejoined her mother, but their relations remained unsettled and often difficult throughout their long lives. Despite hard work and loyalty, survival could never be taken for granted.[3] In another trajectory of pain, Lucy Cardinal, a veteran of a northern mission school, was forced to surrender her son Gil when Edmonton proved too hard for a young woman without marketable skills and with uncertain relations with her Native family.[4] An examination of admissions from 1957 to 1959 by Hamilton's Children's Aid Society and its Catholic counterpart confirmed commonplace patterns in revealing that 42.3 percent and 23.3 percent respectively had grandparents "known" to social agencies.[5]

A hand-to-mouth existence has been the best guarantee of attracting the attention of child protection agencies and the related criminal justice system. As Linda Gordon concludes in her classic study of family violence in the United States, clients of both services were disproportionately poor and racialized, not because they were the only offenders but, rather, "because they were more likely to be 'caught.'"[6] Much the same has always been true in Canada. The rise of the New Right in the 1980s and 1990s, with its agendas of "welfare-bashing and moral hyper-sensitivity," invoked long-standing prejudice to construct "mothers, who were mostly poor and single, and involved with the child protection system as 'dangerous parents,' who are likely to harm or even kill their own children." The result "directs attention to mothers' faults as individuals, when in fact most mothers get tangled in the child protection system as a result of structural inequality and exclusions."[7] Those with comfortable accommodation, access to education, respite, medical care, therapy, and ties to those in authority have always been much more sheltered from observation and intervention.

Poor wages, dangerous workplaces, pervasive ill health, and seasonal labour markets have long stalked Canadian families. The loss of male breadwinners by death or desertion and ubiquitous female economic disadvantage have readily catapulted youngsters onto the streets and into other households. The appearance of creches, orphanages, and settlement houses in nineteenth-century Canada testified to their founders connecting a pervasive economic vulnerability with parental failure. So too did the slow emergence, beginning in Newfoundland in 1872, of state programs in aid of deserted wives. Personal tragedies were not always, however, immediately visible. Historian Bettina Bradbury has observed that in pre–First World War Canada, the "reshuffling of the child population into other people's homes through fostering means that only some children of single parents can be seen in the censuses."[8] As the Great Depression of the 1930s merely reiterated, many families stood only a single harvest from land or sea or one adult wage away from disaster.[9] The introduction of family allowances at the end of the Second World War, which initially represented a significant addition to the coffers of the poor, had several aims, including allowing the impoverished to keep sons and daughters at home and in school. It also, as Dominique Marshall suggests, made such families, especially mothers, more responsible for their offspring's school attendance and general well-being and their failures all the more egregious.[10]

As the social welfare state uncertainly expanded, poverty largely disappeared as a public issue, but it never vanished in real life. Rare public housing projects such as Toronto's Regent Park and Vancouver's Little Mountain never met demand. As one Saskatchewan social worker remembered of the 1940s and 1950s, "municipalities didn't like dirty people; they didn't like citizens who might become a charge on the community—[they preferred to] apprehend the children and let the parents starve!"[11] Governments were not alone in disliking the poor. When urban housing markets were especially inhospitable, as they were after both world wars and again at the turn of the twenty-first century, landlords were highly selective of tenants—those with insecure employments or offspring stood at the bottom of their hierarchy of preference.[12] For example, between 1 January 1957 and 31 December 1959, Hamilton, the nation's steel city, saw 21.5 percent of admissions to the Children's Aid Society and 10.0 percent of those to its Catholic counterpart occurring because of eviction; "accommodation difficulties" accounted for a further 6.7 percent and 9.3 percent respectively.[13] In Canada's centennial year, a family of nine living in a two-bedroom house had to give up its five oldest children because "the parents are guilty of Toronto's terrible housing sin: Too many kids and too little money." They were on the list for municipal housing. They were not alone. The director of Toronto's Children's Aid Society reported that "more than 150 other children of low income families have been placed in foster homes—'temporarily'—because of the city's housing nightmare."[14] The overdue systematic compilation of data at the end of the twentieth century confirmed familiar links between accommodation and child protection. Metropolitan Toronto discovered that housing problems drove 18.4 percent of children into care and delayed the return home of 8.6 percent of cases.[15]

The reports of the Royal Commission on the Status of Women (1970) and the Special Senate Committee on Poverty (1971) gradually dispelled postwar faith that bad times were largely a relic of the past. In 1975, a National Council of Welfare study offered a further wake-up call. It reported that 21.2 percent of youngsters in two-parent families, 33.7 percent in single-father, and 69.1 percent in single-mother households lived in poverty. Three Manitoba mothers with five to seven youngsters apiece, for whom social assistance meant a cold Christmas, demonstrated the limits of the contemporary welfare state in the same decade. Only occasional prostitution made ends meet, a strategy that made mothering immediately suspect.[16] The 1966 Canada Assistance Plan offered hope with its promise of greater federal support for social security, but advocates of a guaranteed annual income had largely lost that debate by the late 1970s. This great defeat set the stage for rising levels of child apprehension. In the 1980s and beyond, "years of cutbacks by the federal government in cost-shared funding for social and welfare programs and increasing provincial budget deficits" hit hard at "families at the lower end of the socioeconomic scale." Such households could easily be "forced to move to even cheaper housing and would have lost any social support system that may have been in place. These are the very families that are most at risk of having their children taken into care due to neglect and abuse."[17] In the next decade, the "client profile" of British Columbia's Ministry of Social Services revealed the recurring pattern: 80 percent were single-parent women and 75 percent received social assistance.[18] This group was always vulnerable to slipping still further from respectability and having their children apprehended.

Even as the gap between rich and poor expanded, poor bashing, which had fallen into disfavour since Canada's instructive encounter with the Great Depression in the 1930s, emerged to defend the rights of the better-off and to slander the parenting of the poor.[19] Where the latter might have been regarded as potential rights-bearers in the upbeat 1960s and 1970s, they came increasingly to be regarded as creators of their own misfortune. Single mothers, or "welfare queens" as they became in the Reaganite United States,[20] became special targets of the "national sport" of victim blaming.[21] Modern media coverage readily concen-

trated on "unusual cases for scrutiny, while ignoring or diminishing routine situations" of limited opportunity and inadequate supports. As Jean Swanson, one
of Canada's long-time anti-poverty activists, explains, "poor-bashing means constantly being afraid that someone will take your children."[22] Since "the idea of
the lone mother as a benefit scrounger is the obverse of the married mother
who turns happily and confidently to her husband for support,"[23] conservatives
demanded a return to traditional values that obliged women and men to act out
gender roles that made caregiving the duty of the former. Moreover, female
obligations were increasingly combined with full-time engagement in the labour
market, at least for those who otherwise would have needed state support to survive. "Good" mothering now required income generation, and modern studies
have confirmed once more that "parents' income level is the best predictor of
a child's removal from the home."[24]

Even when they were expanding, social services were in no position to
tackle structural factors that propelled so many Canadians into poverty. Whatever the origins of youngsters, modern state strategies concentrated on shifting
the parental attitudes believed to produce inadequacy. Ottawa's post–First
World War "Little Blue Books" of instruction to the nation's mothers, and their
imitators over the years, identified the thinking and the practice of individuals
as the prime determinant of troubles for Natives and non-Natives alike. Not surprisingly, adults who lost offspring knew that they might well be compared
"unfavourably with foster mothers who may have had more resources and
time."[25] A report on one Labrador Innu community in the 1990s noted that
"the financial aid provided to approved foster parents is substantially greater than
the aid provided for informal child support (regular social assistance). Social
assistance is grossly inadequate and does not provide sufficient money for the
proper food, clothing, and shelter which these children deserve."[26] Mothers,
such as one Newfoundlander who put her youngsters into voluntary foster care
after she suffered a nervous breakdown, sometimes wondered "if her children
would be better off staying in foster care."[27]

Housing, health, education, and employment conditions on First Nations
reserves and among urban indigenous populations remained especially desperate over the entire period covered by this volume. The federal Department of
Indian Affairs provided at best niggardly support, long preferring residential
schools as arm's length solutions to distress. These institutions also frequently
took for granted the "natural" incompetence of original households. Provinces
were little more generous when they reluctantly included Aboriginal families in
their child protection mandates after the Second World War.

African Canadians were also especially suspect clients to whom little was
presumed due. Solutions, such as the destruction of Nova Scotia's Africville in

the 1960s, echoed remedies that targeted Native extended households as one source of inadequacy.[28] There were also important differences. While Ottawa expressed its obligations to indigenous citizens through subsidies for residential schools and occasional aid from Indian agents, the hardships facing Black parents were largely ignored. For many years relief, such as that provided by the Nova Scotia Home for Coloured Children, was for the most part private. After the Second World War, slowly changing sensibilities required greater inclusion of minorities. Ironically, as with Native populations, this entailed growing apprehension of African-Canadian progeny.[29] The racialization of welfare fraud control in British Columbia and Ontario at the end of the twentieth century and racial profiling more generally also suggest that the credentials of certain Canadians continue to be found wanting.[30]

Immigrant status has similarly provided a source of recurring economic vulnerability. As early reformer James Shaver Woodsworth revealed in his pioneering studies *Strangers within Our Gates* and *My Neighbor*, impoverished arrivals, especially non-northern Europeans, were readily deemed culpable for inadequacies of housing, cleanliness, industry, and discipline.[31] Franca Iacovetta has documented more recently this continuing disadvantage and prejudice in *Gatekeepers: Reshaping Immigrant Lives in Cold War Canada.*[32] At the end of the twentieth century, negatively racialized arrivals from many corners of the world were in a familiar pattern, "often isolated, lack family and community supports, are poor, are unemployed or underemployed, may not speak English or French, and are often unfamiliar with the resources available to them. Along with this they may be completely baffled by the intervention of the child welfare system."[33] From the vantage point of the longer settled, the domestic cultures of newcomers both explained their disadvantage and made them deserving of only limited taxpayer support.

Ill health and chronic disability preceded and accompanied much economic distress and regularly compromised parenting. Conditions such as tuberculosis, anaemia, blindness, deafness, polio, and arthritis combined with poor nutrition and inadequate accommodation to drain time and energy. Investigations by Hamilton's Children's Aid Society and its Catholic equivalent from 1957 to 1959 demonstrate a commonplace reality: 22.3 percent and 15.6 percent respectively of clients were directly credited to the "illness or hospitalization of the mother."[34] The introduction of Medicare in the last decades of the twentieth century helped immeasurably, but preventive options, in matters of public health and recreation as well as counselling and physiotherapy, remained difficult to access. Insufficiency set the stage for behaviours and outcomes, such as depression, lack of self-care, erratic attention, addiction, and episodic desertion, which encouraged observers to distrust and even despise first parents. As the decades passed, diagnoses of precipitating conditions became increasingly clinical. In 1992, one study typically summed up the plight of many adults whose children came before public agencies: "54% of the mothers and 29% of the fathers had been treated for psychiatric illnesses," while "54% of mothers and 84% of fathers abused alcohol and/or drugs."[35] Another Montreal study from early in the twenty-first century suggests that "48% of mothers and 30% of fathers" had "a personality disorder" that impeded effective relations with off-spring and professionals.[36] While better-off households could hope to down-load responsibilities or to camouflage the impact of illness and addiction, the poor and the racialized faced easier public observation of their troubles. Indeed, sometimes the only hope for respite for parents and treatment for offspring lay in apprehension.

Limited resources have sometimes driven disadvantaged parents to seek assistance from courts and child protection authorities and to surrender impaired and difficult youngsters. Tamara Myers has described how poor Montrealers attempted to use external legal authorities to discipline daughters from 1869 to 1945, while Franca Iacovetta has pointed to later Toronto immigrants' resort to judges to curb disobedience.[37] Calls for help persist. Early in the twenty-first century, one couple of hard-pressed immigrants to Quebec echoed other parents in asking for the apprehension of their "out-of-control" thirteen-year-old.[38] Many families' recurring lack of resources was visible as well in the stories of the four young graduates of Ontario's foster care system portrayed in the National Film Board documentary *Wards of the Crown* (2007). Their surrender was deter-mined by the ultimate inability of their mothers to cope with poverty. Their fathers seemed, in contrast, largely absent. Parents who are comfortably well off have rarely been as vulnerable to desperate remedies that commonly involve institutions and foster homes.

Measuring Up: The Predicament of Mothers

Women have always made up the majority of poor adults. This unenviable sta-tus is closely related to their recurring designation as primary caregivers. The powerful dogma of the naturalness of maternal self-sacrifice and its associated subsidy of male public life has informed opportunities and outcomes. Both reli-gious and secular experts have emphasized that women's highest calling lies in maternity. Female nature, aided and abetted by proper socialization, has made them, it was persistently held, both natural and unmatched custodians of the young. Ontario's first superintendent of child welfare, J.J. Kelso, summed up long-standing beliefs in his conclusion that "in 99 cases out of 100 it is either the want of a good woman's influence or the influence of a bad woman that has brought the child within the meshes of the law."[39] Women who rejected or failed at their calling were presumed to defy the natural order, not to mention gods and men.

Assumptions about what constituted authenticity for women extended well beyond public authorities. Subject to a steady diet of maternal propaganda, in matters from Mother's Day to poems such as Rudyard Kipling's "Mother o' Mine" (1891) with the classic lines: "If I were hanged on the highest hill … I know whose love would follow me still," Canadians in general have concurred. Many daughters and sons have endorsed this picture. As a study of single mums observed, "it was also obvious that children took it for granted that their mothers keep them and even tolerate unpleasant behaviour." As one six-year-old put it, "'it's your natural duty.'"[40] Mothers in contact with child welfare agencies have frequently concurred. Many have justified fertility and retention of their offspring by reference to the supposedly innate desires and rights of their sex.[41] Even as they struggled or failed to match ideals, women have taken pride and comfort in the promise embodied in pregnancy, childbirth, and child rearing.

Many mothers have also believed that their sex's special duties merited state support when individual men floundered. Commonplace requests for public and private assistance in everything from dealing with newborns and violent husbands to getting temporary respite in order to regain mental and physical bearings convey assumptions of entitlement, if sometimes also embarrassment or shame.[42] Such seems the case with the Victoria woman with disabilities, the mother of five who was living on social assistance, who responded when told that she could not choose to do without supervision: "I felt very hurt with that. Because I didn't think it was fair."[43] Like others before her, she assumed reproduction to be natural to her sex, a right of all human beings and deserving of external support, although not necessarily scrutiny. In face of a mainstream culture that prizes independence and autonomy, requiring external aid nevertheless readily causes considerable distress.

Even when they could not take responsibility for day-to-day care, most first mothers have remained concerned about their offspring. Child protection records show them lining up to visit orphanages and residential schools, sending letters and gifts, visiting substitute households, and contacting authorities about outcomes. Sometimes this has involved great distances as with mothers of British "home children" sent to Canada. They would have understood the repeated efforts of biological mothers who over the years typically used messages and gifts to maintain contact and to affirm affection with kids who had been apprehended. Many have made plans for better times, to escape welfare and eventually to reunite.

Feelings of continuing connection are not unique. Mothers who send sons and daughters to boarding schools feel much the same. The continuing concern of female migrants forced to leave sons and daughters behind has also been well documented and sometimes termed "transferred motherhood."[44] A similar link has been described as "phantom mothering" in the case of incarcerated women.[45] The connection to the predicament of first mothers of youngsters in care is all the clearer when researchers investigating migrants to Canada discovered that "feelings of shame about abandoning children" kept women from identifying themselves for study.[46] Subsequent problems also seem familiar: "After months or years of infrequent long distant contact, estrangement occurred and became evident when reunification eventually happened."[47]

In the process of investigating the needs of girls and boys, child welfare authorities have often paid limited attention to maternal "situations and strengths," and client mothers have existed largely to "be fixed or bypassed."[48] Their struggles too frequently win little acknowledgement. As a result, over the decades, "poverty, class and race relations, gender issues, and fathers all vanish. Mothers are produced and reproduced as the "causal variable."[49] As one Canadian scholar has recently argued, "the study of child neglect is in effect the study of mothers who 'fail.'"[50]

Over the decades, even as they gained rights in guardianship and custody of children upon marital breakdown, women faced steadily toughening standards of performance. A shifting response to infanticide conveyed a deepening culture of blame. At the beginning of the twentieth century, explanations emphasized "socio-economic disadvantage." Such acts were later "understood as a psychiatric illness linked to childbirth and lactation," and gradually "no justification is legitimate because it is presumed that the infant-victim has a 'right-to-life' that the courts must protect by punishing fully responsibilized mothers."[51] The rights of the unborn readily obscured the predicament of the living. Much the same assumption of original sin or at least inadequacy has inspired many adopters' resistance to conveying contact information to birth mothers. As one individual from the 1960s put it, "'it is none of her business ... she had many days after the baby was born to make up her mind.'"[52] Where living offspring once constituted success, modernity has increasingly demanded "supermoms," hardly an accessible role for the vast majority of women.[53]

Responsibility for children originally gave women (limited) rights to stay out of full-time waged employment, but the end of the twentieth century saw mothers directed more than ever to the labour market. Neo-conservative citizenship regimes envisioned women's obligations as encompassing both voluntary service in the private sphere and paid work beyond its borders. Women were expected to move into waged labour as relatively unskilled workers commanding limited salaries as soon as possible. Training programs for those deemed "'at risk' of neglecting or abusing their children" were regularly "time-limited." The emphasis was placed on gaining paid work of any sort that might reduce state liability, and very little emphasis was placed on employment that might generate a good standard of living and even fulfilment. When jobs brought signs of financial improvement, recipients of social assistance often lost auxiliary services, such as public transit passes and dental care. Such losses readily destabilized fragile budgets of women commonly earning little more than the minimum wage and made children more likely to be apprehended as neglected. Once this happened, situations readily deteriorated. As "self-esteem, the regard of family and friends, a reduced income assistance allowance, the child tax benefit, and eligibility for social housing" all slipped away, the retrieval of youngsters became more difficult.[54]

One modern study of fifteen Canadian mothers involved with child protection agencies in two small Canadian cities conveyed recurring realities. All had "lives of little privilege and reduced expectations" and reported chronic fatigue in negotiating maternal duties. Investigators found histories "of family alcoholism, sexual and other maltreatment when they were children, abusive relationships with male partners, social isolation, disruptions in living arrangements and involvements with social services." Another assessment of 380 parents described similarly high levels of deprivation, violence, heavy duties, and little relief.[55] Bad times were often long standing. British Columbia's Verna Vaudreuil was far from typical in murdering her son, but her personal history was familiar:

> Between 1974 and 6 April 1985, the day she was discharged from care at age nineteen, Verna was nearly always a child in care. During the first seven years, Verna lived in eight different foster homes. From age fifteen to eighteen, she lived in a ministry-supported Skills Development Community Residence in Fort St. John. Finally, she lived independently while being supported financially by the ministry's independent-living program. When she was returned home to her parents in 1978 for one year, she was sexually abused by her older brother. A 1981 assessment noted that Verna was developmentally delayed and emotionally insecure, and she displayed such behavioural problems as lying and stealing.[56]

As one of British Columbia's most thoughtful social work scholars concluded about such cases, "children suffer because their mothers are assigned their care yet do not have the power to provide for or protect them. Women's behaviour toward their children is better understood in terms of their powerlessness than their perversity."[57] Never able to protect herself, Verna proved no better at protecting Matthew. Disadvantaged mothers ultimately face a recurring "catch 22":

Children [are] increasingly upset and perhaps difficult to manage as they move
back and forth from home to foster care, each move accompanied by attendant
strains of loss of friends, schools, belongings, and so on ... ongoing scrutiny and
criticism ... conditional on her lifestyle and relationships. If she has relatives
with similar addictions, she may be asked to sever ties with them, which means
cutting herself off from the very family we are taught to revere ... Since the child
welfare mandate does not include protecting children from poverty and racism
or helping the mother enrich her own life, the case will likely be closed—until
the next crisis.[58]

The recurring neglect of women's economic and other needs cannot be separated from the neglect of children.

The Particular Jeopardy of Negatively Racialized Mothers
Authorities and the public in general regularly saw mothers in the context of
particular communities. Those distinguishable from the mainstream by skin
colour, language, or culture have always been especially suspect, but race is a fluid
category. In the nineteenth century, Catholic Irishness was frequently sufficient
condemnation. One historian has described characterization that other populations encountering racism would have found familiar:

Accounts of Irish-Catholic couples lying on their babies in a drunken stupor, of
inebriated Irish labourers beating their children or kicking their pregnant wives
in the belly, and of stabbings, fights, and late-night brawling parties further confirmed anti-Catholic prejudice. Even relatively mild reports, such as the story of
Bridget Judge, appearing "in puris naturalibus" and with disheveled hair, who
was found "fighting with herself" and pummeling "a fence most lustily," or that
of Ann McCabe, "found lying in the gutter ... with her children playing about
like little pigs," reinforced the image of Irish Catholics as a drunken and degen-
erate blight upon the landscape of the Queen City [Toronto].[59]

Early twentieth-century Italians were likewise credited with primitive and bes-
tial traits that made them violent, overly fertile, and frequently unsuitable parents. The much-publicized 1911 trial of twenty-eight-year-old Angelina
Napolitano, who murdered an abusive husband, provided an opportunity for prejudice, even as it also aroused champions of maternity. She went to prison, and
her daughters and sons went into care. After a shortened sentence, she and
some of her offspring were reunited.[60]

First Nations have always been particular objects of prejudice in Canada.
Civilized mothering was commonly believed to require the elimination of their
extended households, itinerant wage earning and resource harvesting, polygamy,
female independence, premarital sex, matrilineal inheritance, and permissive

child rearing.[61] Even when populations, such as those in Fort/Port Simpson, a BC mission settlement, took up many European practices, they were rarely able to escape assumptions of inferiority.[62] Women with any hint of Aboriginal heritage were everywhere dismissed as "squaws." As Marlee Kline has explained, such mothers were not credited as being in the "best interest" of any child.[63] In face of what has been termed the "inferiorization of Aboriginal motherhood," church-run schools, Indian agents, and White adoptive and foster parents were regarded as improvements.[64]

Calumny was always challenged. Individuals such as the Mohawk writer and performer E. Pauline Johnson (Tekahionwake) before the First World War, Carrier activist Mary John after the Second World War, and Cree-Salish activist and writer Lee Maracle in the last decades of the twentieth century as well as groups such as BC's Indian Homemakers and the Inuit Pauktuutit offered alternative visions.[65] Maracle's revealingly titled novel *Daughters Are Forever* describes how child protection agencies and mainstream prejudice undermined mothers. Her central character, Marilyn, ultimately draws on indigenous tradition to move from neglect to empowerment as a caring mother and effective social worker.[66]

Other non-White women have also been suspect. Until the second half of the twentieth century, the entry into Canada of Chinese, Japanese, and South Asian women was restricted. Stereotyped as docile and subservient, they were regarded as far from proper mothers of the nation.[67] African-Canadian women were equally stigmatized.[68] They, in turn, laboured in the historic Black churches and groups such as Ontario's Coloured Women's Councils to reject demeaning depictions.[69] By the late twentieth century, public rebuttal included documentaries such as *Black Mother, Black Daughter* (1989) by Nova Scotia filmmaker Sylvia D. Hamilton and *Older, Stronger Wiser* (1989) on five Black women from across Canada by Claire Prieto.

Mainstream suspicions have fuelled the failure to recognize domestic strength. While the flexibility of Native and immigrant households holds possibilities for mutual support, they remain regularly stigmatized and discounted.[70] Observers have focused on indulgence and deficient cultural practices as explanations for domestic disasters. Response has rarely addressed colonialism's impact on many lives, such as the fact that 90 percent of single parent clients in one urban Native child and family service agency were former foster children and very often granddaughters of residential school students.[71]

Unwed and Solo Mothers

In the nineteenth and early twentieth centuries, the unwed tended to be viewed either as largely innocent victims of male lust—that is, if they were deemed previously chaste—or as promiscuous, probably mentally deficient, and "foreign."[72] Ontario child welfare authorities regularly diagnosed "feeblemindedness with its consequent shiftlessness, inefficiency, and dirt" as the cause of sexual impropriety and vulnerability.[73] Many unwed mothers could nevertheless hope for some redemption by marrying, preferably the father of the child, or by sacrificing themselves on the altar of maternal duties. In neither case would they entirely escape the taint of immorality. Continued responsibility for illegitimate offspring constituted both punishment and instruction. As Lori Chambers has recently concluded in her study of early twentieth-century legislation aimed at enforcing paternal obligations, "the unwed mother—and her exclusion and poverty—provided an object lesson in sexual ethics."[74]

By the 1920s and into the years after the Second World War, experts, influenced by the psychological theories of the day, shifted their assessment. Unwed White mothers were not so much immoral as maladjusted.[75] Increasingly conceptualized with little explicit reference to class and as essentially or potentially respectable, they might recover by immediately transferring offspring to married couples. In a memory-sapping exercise of compartmentalization that recalled experiments with twilight sleep in childbirth in the same period they might forget.[76] In essence, such young women were regarded as being too immature to know their own best interest. Those who were truly adults, notably social workers but also religious and medical authorities and older relatives, were presumed to be in the best position to make decisions. Surrender was further encouraged by the tardy extension of provincial mothers' allowances. Ontario's inclusion of unmarried mothers in 1946 (not extended to Métis applicants until 1953) still battled "old prejudices and arguments" about "condoning illegitimacy" and encouraging girls to have babies "in order to receive financial help.[77]

By the late 1960s and 1970s, Canadians showed greater tolerance. Young mothers did not necessarily need to lose their infants or their reputations. Fewer surrendered their offspring. Official initiatives such as the 1966 *Canada Assistance Act* and the 1967 Ontario *Family Benefits Act* "no longer singled [them] out as undeserving of social assistance and provided a new discourse of welfare as a right, not a privilege."[78] Tolerance was, however, conditional. By the end of the twentieth century, women without financially supportive male partners appeared to be increasingly a burden for state finances, a symptom of a crisis of heterosexuality, a sign of promiscuity, especially on the part of racial and ethnic minorities, and a reflection of female, even feminist, independence.[79] In 2001, Canadian media dealt in all of these tropes in censoring two BC single mothers, one a blond twenty-something involved with a Black American basketball player and the other, a much-married thirty-something Palestinian immigrant.[80] Once "living together" gained wide acceptance in late twentieth-century

Canada, sexual morality was not so important as financial capacity.[81] The unwed attracted greatest censure when they sought external support.

Most single mothers have remained on the economic margin throughout Canadian history. In the modern period, they clustered "below the low income cutoffs" established by Statistics Canada.[82] A late twentieth-century study of 353 unwed adolescent mothers in Nova Scotia confirmed comprehensive disadvantage. Far more often than their age group, they came from

> families that were not intact, either because of divorce, separation, death or illegitimacy. By the time they were 16 years of age, one out of every three nonmarried mothers no longer lived with both natural parents. For the majority of their first years, approximately one-quarter were not raised by both natural parents. They had very limited schooling, with only 20% having completed a high school education or better, compared to 65% of the married mothers. Eighty percent (compared to 35% of the married mothers) were without any job training, and at the time of conception, 34% were working, 38% were in school and the remaining 28% were at home.[83]

Not surprisingly, female lone parents struggled with "finances, housing, friends, self-esteem, job or main activity, and life as a whole."[84] Paul Sachdev's pioneering investigations of Newfoundland birth mothers in the 1980s captured common hardship. Not until 1967, in an omission that implied shame across the country, did that province's protection files supply sufficient data for identification. Even in the more tolerant period in which the study was conducted, many mothers feared disclosure.[85] Poverty and lack of family support tarnished lives before and during pregnancy.

While comparisons are difficult, young mothers have nevertheless sometimes found it easier than others in contact with child welfare to contemplate reunions. They always elicited some sympathy, especially if they were White. Like print and radio journalist Anne Petrie, who was sent away to give birth in the 1960s, they could be understood as youthful victims of times, circumstances, or unworthy men.[86] They appeared far better candidates for redemption than mothers accused of neglect or abuse. Not surprisingly, unwed teenagers and those in their twenties have loomed largest in searching accounts by birth parents, adoptees, and fosterlings.

The more distant mothers stood from mainstream ideals, the less public sympathy they received. Lori Chambers' study of Ontario's unmarried mothers from 1921 to 1969 suggests that non-Anglo-Saxon, but White, immigrants evoked less concern, had fewer supports, and were significantly more likely to surrender babies.[87] Aboriginal Canadians once again remained the most vulnerable.[88] Visibly racialized babies were also, however, in far less demand by mainstream adopters. Aboriginal and Black mothers, who knew the racial score of their day, had good reason to attempt to keep offspring who otherwise might drift in and out of institutions and foster homes.[89]

Whatever their origins, unwed mothers confronted a terrible contradiction. Most of them desperately needed paid employment but "not being in the home ensured that they would be censured as 'bad' mothers."[90] Their predicament was all the more inevitable because day nurseries have been, as one angry social worker noted in 1950, "few and far between in Canada."[91] All things being equal, few women ever choose entirely to be a single parent. As one British study has argued, "even when well-loved, illegitimate children were a terrible burden, financially, emotionally, and socially: some ambivalence from their mothers was all but inevitable."[92] One Canadian teen, despite her own supportive parents, spoke for many before and after in concluding: "I have to give up my child, not because I really wanted to, but because I knew it would be better for him. I was only 15, with a grade 10 education, no husband and no means of support ... I wish I could have kept him."[93] Since single mothers have been regularly trashed, their choices have made perfect sense.

Battered and Bruised[94]

Canada's major study of so-called "bad" mothers confirms that violence perpetrated by fathers, husbands, and lovers has always pervaded files of neglect in all parts of the country.[95] Angelina Napolitano in Sault Ste. Marie just before the First World War was unusual because she ultimately murdered her tormentor, but the beatings she endured were familiar. In 1897, Ontario legislation recognized their pervasiveness by allowing women "to petition the lower criminal courts for a maintenance order on the grounds of marital cruelty" and extended the definition of a "'deserted wife' to include those who voluntarily separated from husbands because of 'repeated assaults and other acts of cruelty.'"[96] Demanded by some parliamentarians since at least the 1880s, "wife beating" entered the federal *Criminal Code* in 1909.[97]

State support for escaping violent partners came far more slowly. In 1935, one Ontario applicant found the Ontario Mothers' Allowances Board typically uninterested even as she explained: "My children have seen scenes since babyhood of absolute terror for them, and many times have been in real fear of being killed by him ... he has kicked me all the way as I crawled across the floor on my hands and knees while carrying his babies."[98] While acceptance of abuse gradually diminished, its reality haunted national life. Canada's authoritative 1993 *Violence against Women Survey* found that one-half (51%) of all surveyed women had experienced at least one incident of sexual or physical assault since age sixteen ... Of the women who had ever lived with a male partner, 29% had been physically or sexually assaulted by him at some time in the relationship. Among women with disabilities or a disabling health concern this increased to 39% ... Despite the frequency and seriousness of the violence and the fact that 34% of the women feared for their lives, 22% of the women did not mention the violent incidents to anyone.[99]

In the 1990s and 2000s, Canada's neo-conservative governments nevertheless cut legal aid, support for battered women's shelters, and social assistance rates, ensuring that women's independence of dangerous partners remained difficult.[100]

Fear of reprisals kept many women from leaving. Even violent breadwinners might mean food and accommodation. Women have also been reluctant to expose private agonies to outsiders and to deprive children of their fathers. In First Nations and other racialized communities, mothers have often understood the effects of prejudice and preferred "healing of all members of the family." They might feel that "the abuser in the family does not need to be sacrificed." If he returned to community roots, he could be salvaged as a father and a husband.[101] Whatever their origins,

> mothers who are being battered have no good choice to make. Should they choose to leave, they are endangering themselves and their children, often plunging their children into poverty and stigmatizing themselves as single mothers. Should they choose to stay, they live in fear that the abuse may spread to their children.[102]

Equally daunting is that "leaving also increases the likelihood that a mother will lose her children" to state agencies.[103]

Father–daughter incest and children's observation of domestic violence have offered further opportunities to accuse mothers of shirking their paramount obligation. As feminist scholars note of incest, such blame largely ignores the subjection of adult women and reflects "the availability of mothers and daughters as chief informants and as participants in treatment" as well as the fact that "treating the mother is easier and fits more with professional training than taking strong action against the father," who looms as far more threatening.[104] Most women are themselves victims of abuse and hardly in a position to keep assailants from their children. Many late twentieth-century laws requiring the reporting of child abuse implied collective oversight but nevertheless repeatedly directed attention at a practical level to mothers, as the likely on-site custodians of the state's protective mandate.[105]

A few daughters and sons have ultimately died at the hands of their fathers, confirming the dominant pattern of male perpetrators of homicide. Such deaths, notably of the very young, are, however, the one area of violence where mothers have occasionally equalled or surpassed male offenders. The fact that they regularly spend much more time with their offspring, that most of them are themselves abused, and that they have fewer options of escape than fathers helps explain female perpetrators.[106] Ontario social work scholar Cyril Greenland captured this special vulnerability when he observed that maternal abusers in Ontario, like many in the United Kingdom and the United States, have commonly been teenagers, pregnant, depressed, previous state wards, brutalized, abandoned by adult men, and/or economically marginal.[107] Most have long histories of family violence. At the end of the twentieth century, a study of two groups of Quebec mothers in contact with authorities because of the fear or presence of child neglect revealed just such patterns: 46.7 percent of one group and 64.3 percent of the other reported marital abuse, 60.0 percent of one and 71.4 percent of the other experienced violence, while 40.0 percent and 78.6 percent were victims of neglect in their original family.[108] Such suffering hardly served them well as parents.

As conditions deteriorate, many women engage in help-seeking behaviours before they reach "the end of their tether, fearful that they may lose control and harm their children."[109] They may run away, leave youngsters with others, or complain to neighbours, relatives, and social workers of exhaustion, despair, and illness. This was true of notorious mothers in the last decades of the twentieth century—Jennifer Poppen of Ontario, Verna Vaudreuil of British Columbia, and Nora Jean Sinclair of Manitoba—all of whom communicated distress well before they killed those in their care. Offspring are commonly only the latest of casualties.

(Dis)Abled

Although the hierarchy of worthiness is impossible to define precisely, Canadians with physical and mental impairments have stood far from parental ideals. In this brutal calculation, women are once again additionally liable because of their greater likelihood of poverty. Even as they struggle against "barriers in the economy and the built environment, mothers with disabilities face stigmatizing public perceptions of them as inadequate or inappropriate in the role of mothering."[110] Those with mental impairments have been a persisting focus of criticism and anxiety. In 1914, the *Report upon the Feeble-Minded in Ontario* typically included unwed mothers in its mandate, arguing that their predicament was largely a product of mental inferiority.[111] The inauguration between the two great wars of eugenics legislation targeted mentally challenged women in non-mainstream groups. As one Canadian commentator concluded, "the simultaneous operation of child protection law, mental health law, and the power of the psychiatric paradigm almost inevitably severs the relationship between mothers with mental health histories and their children."[112] Newspapers have referenced "myth and fairy tale genres" to treat "women with mental illnesses as dangerous and incapable mothers."[113] In fact, they suffer abuse five times more often than other Canadians.[114]

Although modern technologies have made the promise of normality more possible, the introduction of risk assessment in the 1990s as a major predictor for child neglect and abuse, easily reified old prejudices.[115] In British Columbia, legislation established that "a child may be found in need of protection on account of being 'deprived of necessary care through the death, absence or disability of the parent.'" As lawyer Judith Mosoff has concluded, "linking disability with death or absence of a parent is an astonishing codification of disability as a signal to the state of risk."[116] Such perceptions have ensured that such parents suffer greater than average prospects of "child apprehension or disrupted parenting."[117] Indeed, disadvantage precedes risk since "helping professionals and family members often discourage women with disabilities from becoming pregnant." They foresee incompetence and future genetic threat.[118] In such cases, fertility clearly emerges as a highly conditional right of citizenship.

Drug-using mothers arouse similar hostility. This pattern is also not new. Nineteenth- and twentieth-century reformers interpreted female alcoholics not only as more unusual but also as more dangerous than their male counterparts. Male violence and financial failure wreaked havoc, but female intemperance threatened the home's moral and emotional heart.[119] By the end of the twentieth century, simmering concern about addiction boiled into panic. Alarmed by prospects of fetal alcohol syndrome and coke babies, provincial social services drug-tested obstetrical patients and considered restraints on pregnant women.[120] The plight of adults facing long waiting lists for rehabilitation programs largely disappeared in the preoccupation with potential infant victims. As scholar Susan C. Boyd, the founder in 1991 of "one of the first woman-centred, harm-reduction programs for women from the Downtown Eastside of Vancouver," has pointed out, "pregnant women and mothers who used illegal drugs were often depicted by health, social service and criminal justice professionals as manipulative liars, immoral criminals, threats to both themselves and their infants, and more deviant than their male counterparts." As a result, "permanent child apprehension was the norm rather than exception for poor women suspected of illegal drug use in Vancouver." Most were "poor, on social assistance, and First Nations, even though First Nations women's narcotic use rates were no higher than those of non-Aboriginal women."[121] The 1997 ruling by the

Supreme Court of Canada that pregnant women could not be forced to take treatment contributed to less "intervention" than in the United States, but First Nations' women still faced special jeopardy.[122]

In 2008, Canadians with mental impairments made child protection head-lines. British Columbia's Barbara Gamble (twenty-seven years of age) and her partner Vince Kinney (thirty years of age), who were both diagnosed with below-normal mental capacities and with histories of violence and foster care, lost a sixth infant to the state. Deemed unsuitable by experts and others, they remained determined to parent.[123] Ultimately, however, neither was trusted to justify the high costs of the 24/7 support that was judged to be necessary. Their lack of kin resources stands out, especially in comparison with a Victoria, BC, mother of five, who tested with a similarly low IQ and who received public assistance in the same period. Her mother, who cared full time for her grandson at one point and who supplied the backbone of an extended care team, clearly made the difference. The absence of a male partner seemed unimportant, except to reduce the prospect of violence, which haunted the Vancouver couple.[124] Like others of their sex, both women insisted that mothering was central to their self-worth and identity. The absence of much public sympathy for such claims has con-tributed to additional external scrutiny and stress. The result may very well compromise the ability to nurture.[125]

While, in the past, mothers with less visible disabilities might have escaped notice, late twentieth-century regimes of diagnosis and monitoring spotlight shortcomings, even when youngsters may not be in jeopardy. As they now also increasingly access modern technological and other supports to which they may be entitled as citizens, some women with impairments are nevertheless newly able to embrace maternity. This possibility further unsettles child protection agendas, raising the question once more of rights to caregiving and caretaking and the interests of both women and children and the public good.

The Criminalized

First mothers have sometimes been involved in criminal activities. While far fewer in number than male prisoners, imprisoned women have been generally poorer, less educated, and more addicted than the men. Some lose children to foster care even before they are apprehended.[126] When charged and incarcer-ated, they have been likely to see daughters and sons go to family members or into state care. Motherhood is not new for prisoners. In the nineteenth cen-tury, inmates gave birth and weaned children who were subsequently dis-patched to kin or orphanages.[127] In the 1970s, Alice Parizeau reported on the predicament of mothers in Quebec jails.[128] In 1990, the *Report of the Task Force on Federally Sentenced Women* highlighted their presence.[129] At the beginning of the twenty-first century, two-thirds of incarcerated women had offspring and two-thirds of these were single parents. Over two-thirds also suffered "unaddressed physical or mental health problems." They also experienced a high rate of HIV infection. More than 80 percent had been physically or sexually abused and most had been transient and uncertainly housed.[130] Only 25 percent of mothers, but 90 percent of jailed fathers, had partners caring for their sons and daughters.[131] Not surprisingly, "probably the most significant difference between male and female inmates relates to mothering and caregiving and the feelings of despair that women particularly experience being separated from their children."[132]

Once again, certain populations have remained especially vulnerable to incarceration. A 1989 survey discovered that 77 percent of Aboriginal women serving federal sentences had four to five children each.[133] While Aboriginal Canadians represented less than 3 percent of the entire population at the beginning of the twenty-first century, they constituted some 30 percent of female prisoners. In 2009, the Correctional Service of Canada reckoned that "the Aboriginal woman offender is generally 27 years old with a grade nine education and single with two or three children. She has limited education and employment skills and she is usually unemployed at the time of her crime."[134] Most have also been sexually abused. Black women face similar circumstances. In 2000, they were reckoned 9 percent of the federally incarcerated women, far out of proportion to their share of the population.[135]

Despite their numbers and the fact that "mother-child separation has been an on-going concern for federally sentenced women for many years," Canadian jails and prisons have a poor record in making provision for mothers.[136] American efforts to maintain ties with fostered offspring appeared by the 1970s.[137] A rare initiative, the Mother-Baby program at the provincial Allouette Correctional Centre was cancelled in 2008 despite the opposition of the BC Association of Social Workers.[138] Studies have also noted that the female inmates have greater difficulty maintaining contact because Canada's small number of women's prisons means that there is a likelihood that the women will be greater distances from their offspring.[139] Shortfalls continue in part at least because it is easier "for the community to question the criminalized woman's capabilities of raising her children, hence shaping the citizens of tomorrow."[140]

On the Sideline but also at the Centre: First Fathers

The 2008–9 Canadian reality show *The Week the Women Went* featured small-town Alberta and Nova Scotia and suggested that mainstream culture readily regards fathers, whatever their disposition and circumstances, as incompetent.

Child protection authorities have often shared this perspective. While regularly critical of men for their economic failures and their responsibility for emotional, physical, and sexual injury, they have largely taken for granted an inferior capacity for nurture and never held men to the same standard as maternal caregivers. Indeed, since women are regularly faulted for not reforming violent partners, their caregiving clearly extends to male adults. Given such views, and the frequent paternal determination to avoid "the centre of attention" in child protection investigations, first fathers are little studied. A rare exception sums up the default opinion, finding them sources of stress and violence.[141]

In the decades after Confederation, Christian and secular social reformers worried about paternal retreat from responsibility, particularly the failure to model good citizenship for sons. Groups such as the YMCAs joined church leaders in demanding "lifestyle changes" with renewed commitment to family life. In 1918, Canada's leading Methodist monthly went so far as to editorialize: "Far be it from us to belittle the power and influence of the mother, but the task of bringing up the boys and girls in the home isn't all hers, and oughtn't to be more than half hers, and the father that leaves it with her is a coward and a shirk."[142] While both world wars provoked anxiety about absent patriarchs, concern about mainstream performance was intermittent. Non-Anglo-Celtic fathers, and especially those who were of Aboriginal, African, and Asian ancestry, were considered more likely delinquents at parenting's hard work. Even then, however, they never attracted the interest shown to mothers.

Only at the end of the twentieth century did social work scholars and practitioners, often inspired by feminism, begin "reframing child welfare practice, policy and discourse in ways that are more inclusive of fathers and less blaming of mothers."[143] This shift did not prove to be easy. Many social workers tended to avoid, even to fear, fathers who were encountered in the course of child protection.[144] Most proved to be less seemingly pliant than their womenfolk. Such was the case in the mid-twentieth century when female social workers fled, never to return, after a Native single father brandished a shotgun.[145] Here, as elsewhere, race, class, and gender offered potent opportunities for misunderstanding. Male recalcitrance and anger at the intrusion of outside experts in so-called private matters sometimes crippled efforts "to reweave the social ties within the grassroots community"—in other words, the very endeavour to get away from holding mothers in particular to account.[146] The question of how "dangerous" men, or even those that I have elsewhere termed "casual fornicators," "delinquent dads," and "young lovers," could be made to contribute to better outcomes for their offspring has not been readily answered.[147]

Continuing patriarchal privilege has also allowed men to gain respect simply by making financial contributions. They have been likely to receive kudos for any attention or concern that from women would be considered unremark-able. As Robert Adamoski discovered, the early twentieth-century Vancouver's Children's Aid Society was grateful to single fathers who paid even token amounts of attention. Unlike mothers, they needed to demonstrate no other enthusiasm nor be held accountable for household cleanliness or order. When hard-pressed, fathers "expected public agencies such as the society to fulfill a quasi-contractual obligation to house, feed and educate their children."[148] Nor have experts or popular opinion expected men to find complete fulfilment as fathers. Indeed, natural men are regarded as generally just not very interested in youngsters. This perspective is in keeping with ready suspicion of male homo-sexuals as pedophiles even when male heterosexuals are more likely offend-ers.[149] Not surprisingly, Canadians have readily assumed that it was abnormal for women to surrender children and equally peculiar for unwed dads to want to parent.

While defaulters cannot be readily summed up,[150] drinking, drugs, unemploy-ment, promiscuity, and violence have all been offered as explanations for "worth-less men."[151] Problematic dads, such as journalist Victor Malarek's wife-beating father in post–Second World War Montreal, regularly demonstrated overall inad-equacy by expecting wives to work outside the home, thus establishing the basis for charges of child neglect. Two of Malarek's sons paid the penalty and were apprehended by child welfare. They were brutally fostered in other families and institutions.[152] On Native reserves, apprehensions have been similarly linked to male violence and addiction.[153] Not all mistreatment was immediately visible: "Often overlooked is the array of emotional and psychological abuse tactics designed to maintain control over a spouse without leaving physical marks."[154] Sons and daughters supply sideline tragedies to this situation as well.

Family members have sometimes joined authorities both in letting fathers off the hook and condemning them. An abandoned birth mother from the 1960s made her feelings plain: "It takes two to tangle. When he gave up his responsibility to marry me and care for the child he gave up all his rights as father. As far as I'm concerned there is no such thing as a birth father."[155] Another commentator, who as a child had been surrendered to Newfoundland authorities, concluded similarly: "God only knows about the birth father. The birth mother is the only real attachment I have. The circumstances could have been that Daddy came and Daddy went."[156] Such "visitors" to the womb deserved neither respect nor consideration. Although a modern fathers' rights movement has claimed injustice, many children and mothers have reported terror about those who admitted paternity and stayed around to reveal their limitations. Mandatory charging policies were introduced beginning in the 1980s to deal with just such fears.[157]

In the second half of the twentieth century, experts nevertheless recognized that not all fathers were equally culpable. As psychological explanations for the fall from grace became increasingly popular, young parents of both sexes emerged as ripe for rehabilitation. Manitoban social workers typically credited both with similar "emotional problems."[158] As Simma Holt, a BC journalist and later Liberal member of parliament, similarly argued: "To the boy, this experience is one of ego identity; the child is part of himself. Despite the difference in the nature of their possessiveness towards this child, the strong natural bond of flesh and blood is with the boy as much as with the girl. But there are no social workers, counselors, nurses, or doctors to help him."[159] The dereliction from adult duties, such as three-fifths of Toronto birth fathers cited in one study who failed to spend any time at all over four weeks with teen mums, was increasingly credited to psychological maladjustment and less to moral failure.[160] By 1975, BC's Royal Commission on Children and Family Law acknowledged unmarried fathers' efforts "to have a voice in planning for their children" and that some at least were "also willing, and able, to raise their children as single parents."[161] Nineteen years later, the province's panel to review adoption legislation agreed that birth fathers deserved legal recognition.[162] In 1999, Newfoundland made its first legislative reference to "birth fathers."[163] The special predicament of some fathers also drew new attention. A study of 116 child protection cases involving adolescent mothers in one mid-sized Canadian city between 1997 and 2005 demonstrated just such awareness. Typically, a few years older and without high-school completion, most male partners were "indigenous" with "histories of incarceration, alcohol misuse, or drug misuse." Although almost 50 percent were judged "irrelevant" and 60 percent a risk, "a small, but significant, proportion of young fathers provided either financial or in-kind support to mothers and/or children."[164] They clearly intended some meaningful input. Unprecedented sympathy, especially for Aboriginal fathers who were acknowledged to have special demons, began to encourage cautious consideration. As one scholar, both Aboriginal and feminist, concluded, "it is true that not all men who grew up with family violence have become perpetrators, [but] every Aboriginal perpetrator that I have ever been involved with has a background of childhood family violence."[165] The remedy for this cycle of violence, similarly identified with other male offenders, continues to perplex child protection at the beginning of the twenty-first century.

By the beginning of the twenty-first century, first fathers nevertheless clearly remained on the sidelines of child protection. Such was the case with the parent of the murdered Matthew Vaudreuil, who spent much of his son's brief life in jail, never offered support, and escaped close attention from welfare and justice authorities.[166] Others remained equally invisible even as their recurring violence set the stage for children's apprehension.[167] Nor has any Canadian or American man apparently lost offspring because of "failure to protect" them from the other parent.[168] Women remain uniquely responsible for the well-being of sons and daughters.

Various and Shifting Judgments on First Parents

Child welfare authorities have never been alone in standing in judgment. Communities produce their own critics of members who do not meet standards. Even before laws required reporting child abuse, Canadians found ways to communicate what constituted "*limites raisonnables*" in family discipline. In the 1890s, the local doctor and neighbour who bore legal witness against a Quebec grandmother who inflicted "*des tortures atroces*" upon her grandchildren, like the four disguised men who tarred and feathered an Ontario woman "for allegedly abusing her stepdaughter," testified to wider surveillance.[169] Foster parents have similarly often scorned predecessors reckoned "immoral, inconsistent, or antisocial" with a history of "inadequate care and supervision."[170]

As Canadians grew familiar with child-rearing standards endorsed by modern experts and revelations of child mistreatment, they also became more willing to report apparent infractions. Their suspicions were also not always reckoned as warranted. In 1997–98, 75.6 percent of investigations into reports of abuse and neglect in British Columbia could not be substantiated. A year later, the proportion was 76.9 percent and in 1999–2000 it increased to 81.9 percent.[171] While difficult to interpret, such patterns demonstrate real limits to public tolerance of child abuse. Even the appearance of significant deviation from community standards could well provoke incomprehension, disgust, and fear and justify apprehension. The very possibility of such attention has reminded parents of the external sanctions that are best avoided.

Definitions of normal caregiving have nevertheless been somewhat fluid. To compare the nineteenth century with the twenty-first is to discover shifting attitudes to the relations of men and women, adults and children, different classes and races, and differently abled persons. At the beginning, interchanges more often reflected taken-for-granted, supposedly natural hierarchies. While neglect and cruelty were never approved, superiority in one domain or more was assumed to confer rights of discipline and preferential treatment. Inferiority involved subjection to physical control and limited options. Inattention to violence against women and children in the decades between the two feminist movements made life all the worse for victims. Its rediscovery in the last decades of the twentieth century has encouraged unprecedented levels of intervention in families and sometimes apprehension. This has sometimes saved lives.

While regularly uncertain, the decades leading to the twenty-first century saw unparalleled supports for different families—notably Native, poor, and those with parents who were single, lesbian, queer, or suffering disabilities. While those who were European in origin and comfortably off remained the common ideal, there was less certainty about the right to dictate the reproduction and child-rearing choices of others. Growing reconsideration of old prejudices prompted Alberta to repeal its *Sexual Sterilization Act* in 1972, efforts to improve options for incarcerated mothers in the 1990s and 2000s, and the legalization of same-sex marriage in 2005. In 2008, the desire of a developmentally delayed couple to parent was endorsed by the BC Association for Community Living, which argued that "being a loving and responsible parent has little to do with education, intellect or income," a position that would have been far more unusual earlier.[172] Support for Native-run child welfare agencies spoke to the same shift. Many Canadians slowly benefited from an enlarged appreciation of what constituted good parenting.

Feminist scholars have been prominent in questioning the normality of any single style of responsible adult–child interaction. More particularly, they point to the benefits men acquire when women are held singularly responsible for caring work. They provide ample reminders that there is no such thing as "a level playing field upon which all families carry out their child-rearing activities."[173] Even when public policy has been slow to respond, this insight has become a powerful presence in expert discourses. Canadian modern social work experts now commonly reconsider old practices:

> On one side is the power to name the problem, the solutions, and document the official reality of a mother's parenting and lifestyles; on the other side are the women doing the daily work of caring for their children, but without access to the resources required. Their world and work is *invisible* in the official systems ... Those at the receiving end of reports, investigations, support/treatment, and apprehension are overwhelming poor, single mothers with young children ... neglect rather than sexual or physical cause is the key reason for apprehending a child.[174]

Most also now insist that "positive parenting practices" can be "found in rich and poor families alike" and endorse "universal programs" of support rather than stigmatizing interventions as the best hope for children and adults alike.[175]

Deeply rooted racism, sexism, and ableism nevertheless continue to undermine Canadians' ability to move beyond commonplace contempt and horror at findings of neglect and abuse. In failing at supposedly natural duties, first mothers and fathers do not generally present as the kind of adults that merit sympathy or the expenditure of public funds. Nor is the task of assisting them straightforward. Destructive individual and collective histories make it tremendously difficult to shift parent–child behaviours or to offer realistic alternatives. Apprehension sometimes appears and is indeed the only option. When social workers consider the limited support for successful parenting, the temptation to remove children, especially in face of recurring public demands that they do so more quickly, is often immense.

Despite growing awareness of their frequent vulnerability, original parents remain largely subject to a public gaze that readily sums them up, mothers in particular, as unworthy of official trust or offspring. As a Canadian social work scholar observed at the beginning of the twenty-first century, "the public portrait is of lazy, incompetent, unmotivated, anti-social, even immoral, parents who are the architects of their own and their children's misfortunes. Racial fears mix in with these stereotypes as the media draws our attention to the First Nations and other "non-European" groupings."[176] The 2008 demand from many observers that a mentally disabled BC woman expecting a sixth child be sterilized invoked long-standing opinion.[177]

First parents in contact with child protection understand that their character and capacity are doubted. Many have resisted such an evaluation. One Saskatchewan social worker summed up "the normal reaction to the first visit as hostility. Parents felt guilty and their first line of defence was often denial."[178] They have been likely, as one sympathetic psychiatrist noted, to "defend against their guilt and their sense of failure by projecting the blame onto someone else, such as the child, the foster parents, the child-welfare agency, or the courts … often, their own self-esteem is so low and the need to deny and rationalize their overwhelming sense of failure so great that any realistic perception of the child's needs is impossible."[179]

While some birth parents have accepted verdicts that judged them incapable of raising offspring, few have left lengthy explanations. A very rare exception is a book-long account provided by Canadian Elizabeth Camden (1948–) whose nine-year-old son became a Crown ward. Assisted by a sympathetic social worker, she told her own history of neglect and abuse by a mother and stepfather. Like others before and after her, she sought unconditional love by having a baby, but violence soon followed. This got worse as he grew "more difficult to deal with." Eventually, she called the Children's Aid Society and the police. She accepted the "disgust and contempt" that she identified in the eyes of the foster mother: "I didn't blame her for it. I felt the same way about myself." When she gave him up permanently, she hoped that "someday he'd understand why things happened the way they did, and that he'd know how much I loved him and what strength it took for me to give him up. I knew I had done the right thing for me and my son."[180] Her confession and actions were highly unusual, but her shame and regret were not.

The end of the twentieth century also saw some birth parents make tentative efforts to organize against accusations of abuse. In the 1990s, at least one Canadian attempted to establish "local chapters of the U.S.-based Victims of Child Abuse Laws."[181] Others took their cases to the courts and the newspapers. In spring 2009, Canadians watched two BC parents, who had lost two sons and an infant daughter to child protection after they were deemed to have shaken the baby, challenge accusations.[182] In the previous year, an Ontario pathologist whose findings convicted parents of battering babies was discredited in part because of parental protests.[183] Some parents resorted to the courts when foster care proved to be its own nightmare. One "resilient, resourceful," and loving mother from British Columbia surrendered her sons so that they could escape abuse at the hands of their father. To her horror, many years later she discovered their subsequent mistreatment and demanded punishment for the offenders.[184] Such efforts remained nevertheless highly unusual. They run up against the disgrace of any contact whatsoever with child protection authorities. However, unprecedented official recognition that birth parents might well deserve legal representation began slowly to acknowledge vulnerability to false charges.[185] Such assistance was nevertheless far more the exception than the rule.

Ultimately, impoverished birth parents have had limited resources to call on in bad times. Only a small minority have ever been reckoned without guilt and thus worthy of significant sympathy. The histories that undermined their capacity to parent, and sometimes made them irresponsible and occasionally dangerous, were rarely adequately addressed. Individuals, especially mothers, have been blamed and shamed, but the conditions that commonly give rise to their difficulties and inadequacies remain too often insufficiently addressed. So frequently made risky parents by conditions that have been in part at least beyond their control, they continue to lose offspring and reap pity or revulsion in the early twenty-first century.

6

NEGOTIATING SURROGACY
The Construction of Foster Parents

F OSTER PARENTS STAND IN FOR THE COMMUNITY AT LARGE.
For many children and youth, they may be the closest thing to responsible and caring adults that they encounter. The transitive verb, to foster, invokes care, development, and growth, which are just those qualities that benefit all girls and boys. This type of care remains the ideal. Its achievement is, however, various and sometimes uncertain. The work of foster mothers and fathers has unfolded in the context of social relations that make some groups and individuals more likely, acceptable, or able candidates. It has been highly gendered and has ideally required expressions of model maternity and paternity. In the last half of the twentieth century, such surrogates also increasingly emerged as part of therapeutic teams working towards the physical and psychological salvation of disadvantaged children and young people.

Canada's fostering adults have always negotiated an essentially border status. In modelling superior mothering or fathering or in operating alongside experts, they have confronted a recurring dilemma of authenticity. On the one hand, most have received money and been subject to state supervision for duties judged to be preferably voluntary and private. On the other hand, most have lacked formal credentials in child study and protection agencies and governments have rarely paid professional wages. As surrogates and amateurs, they have always struggled to be treated as more than inferior mimics of "real" parents or "real" experts. Women stand at the centre and men to the side of both conundrums.

This chapter examines foster parenting in five stages. First, it turns to the ways that class, race, and notions of respectability position certain Canadian women and men as potential candidates. Second, it focuses on mothers, always the central symbolic and practical players in domestic dramas. They are judged and often judge themselves by reference to a nurturing essentialism. Next it considers fathers for whom cultural ideals of paternity have been much less demanding. Fourth, it sums up the growing sense of crisis that has engulfed foster parents and the response of authorities as the twentieth century faded into the twenty-first. Ultimately, surrogates have encountered the same contradiction that has shipwrecked so many first parents—namely the recurring failure to sufficiently value caring labour.

Class and Race Construct Respectability

Many foster parents have enjoyed children and youth in their lives. Some Canadian families have fostered over generations, and the care of unrelated youngsters has been integral to many personal histories. Such commitment has offered one way of demonstrating responsibility and maturity. Respectability, or at least the appearance of what was regarded as normality, has been central to the assumption of surrogate roles. Governments and agencies aimed to recruit those who could successfully integrate charges into acceptable mainstream behaviours that were believed suitable for their class, race, and gender and that were best productive of good citizenship. In their turn, foster mothers and fathers hoped through superior parenting and additional home-based income to secure their status as successful adults.

Class

Modern child welfare authorities have occasionally toyed with the possibility of middle-class rescuers, but they have learned that their charges had little general appeal for this group. Few such candidates applied for, or persisted in, such labours.[1] Deterrents were many. The work was hard; the pay was poor; the status at best uncertain; and opening up private space for external scrutiny was never attractive. In particular, women with good employment prospects or similarly fortunate spouses had options that appeared more rewarding. Receptivity to domestic strangers also diminished over the course of the twentieth century as an earlier "culture of household sharing" gave way to "a preference for independence and privacy in living arrangements."[2]

The handful of middle-class foster parents who enlisted in fostering's cause over the years have appeared especially motivated by various feelings of service. Some, like Sheila Jane Carlisle Jones, who held a 1949 graduate social work degree from the University of British Columbia, met disadvantaged children in the course of their work and extended commitment into their personal life.[3] Judith Mary Kennedy (1937–2009), of Prince George, British Columbia, and "a pioneer and leader in the fields of social work, education, and community development," was another example. Three girls and a boy lived with her for years. It was said that "her intelligence, strength of character, sharp wit, and zest for life made her an anchor for others." She also turned her energies "to encouraging and assisting the education system and local community agencies to transition from practices of segregation to models of inclusion for special needs children and youth."[4] Fostering was one way of many that she demonstrated her commitment to, and leadership of, her community.

For some middle-class citizens, religion proved a prime motivator. In 1957, a couple from Richmond, British Columbia, who were celebrated in an article entitled "Little Rock [Arkansas] Could Learn a Lot," were typically inspired by their Baptist faith to welcome four "coloured" sisters and their brother from the Children's Aid Society.[5] Similar motives moved an Albertan United Church minister and his wife who fostered babies in the 1960s.[6] In 2008, a minister of St. Andrew's United in Markham, Ontario, pursued a "crusade to find a loving home for every waiting child in Canada." Over thirteen years, he and his wife fostered nearly 1,100 state charges who were received as "children of God."[7] Inspiration to outreach could also be explicitly political. In the decades after the Second World War, one foster father, identified as a hippie and a rebel, adopted an infant and two older sisters, and then fostered three children, as part of his lifelong dedication to "helping troubled young people."[8] Whether religious or secular in motivation, such middle-class Canadians frequently emphasized their contribution to social betterment.

Some better-off candidates also simply confessed to enjoying children. Many women in particular clearly liked having them around and found deep fulfilment in the mothering role. Such seems the case with Kingston resident, Sharon Beck, Ontario's Foster Parent of the Year for 2005. A former schoolteacher married to another teacher, she fostered more than 200 children over eighteen years as well as adopting and rearing her own. As she explained, "when my own children were getting older, I still wanted to be around babies."[9] More unusual was the immediate economic motivation visible in the 1960s when a lawyer and his wife, with two young children, took in six teenage girls to foster as one strategy for acquiring a house in Toronto.[10] Such efforts, unless buttressed by other incentives to service, rarely, however, lasted once careers and economic stability were achieved. Nor were authorities always convinced of the value of middle-class recruits. Governments and agencies, especially before the Second World War, regularly feared lest youngsters be placed above their station, either too readily turned into servants or rendered discontented and unsettled at the contrast with original lives.

Certain working-class households promised a better fit. As Bryan Hogeveen has noted in his study of juvenile delinquency, Canadian elites in child protection sharply distinguished among the lower orders when they considered whom to trust:

> To put it simply, there were two broad groupings. First, respectable working-class males were industrious, took their role as breadwinners seriously, ensured their children attended school, and followed a sober, law-abiding course of life. Second, dangerous working-class males were the reverse of this proletarian propriety. Unlike the respectable working class, the dangerous classes lived in abject poverty as a result of their disconnection from the labour market. They dodged domestic obligations, were habitually criminal, fond of alcohol, and flouted what élites considered decent and honest conduct.[11]

The worthy stratum, with their taken-for-granted stay-at-home wives, supplied the intended bedrock of fostering programs as they emerged in the nineteenth and twentieth centuries. It was to discipline and absorb the unfortunate offspring of the disreputable and dangerous.

Such hopes coincided with the needs of many Canadians. As Bettina Bradbury and David Frank have demonstrated, working-class economies depended on a patchwork of contributions for survival.[12] In both Native and non-Native households, adults were used to doubling up and making do, with all of the sacrifices in privacy this might require. When they could, respectable working-class households long preferred to keep mothers at home where their activities could reap greatest return in terms of health, comfort, and productivity and exemplify breadwinner ideals. As opportunities for domestic production declined in urban settings, even ill-paid fostering held attractions. Its appeal for many country dwellers was much the same. The care of young kin and unrelated youngsters has always been regularly integrated into familial economies, but with modern governments and agencies came unprecedented security of payment.[13] This is a partial explanation of the appeal of even small sums, such as those in New Brunswick in the mid-1960s:

> The foster parent receives $7.28 per week to feed and shelter the ward. There is no possibility that this amount of money will cover the indirect costs of a child in the home and certainly no financial regard at all for the 24-hour, seven-day-a-week care and supervision of the child.[14]

The cash helped steady fragile budgets even as women were expected to donate time and labour.[15]

Suzanne Morton has aptly described the evolution of modern working-class respectability in Richmond Heights, a 1920s Halifax suburb. A dedication to privacy as a reflection of worthiness was expanding to inform working-class, as well as middle-class, aspirations in the twentieth century. At its heart lay a highly gendered familialism that "strengthened patriarchy within the household and the maintenance of the private household at the expense of community," while offering women status and pride in their security and homes. Its attraction also helped explain difficulties with supervision from child protection agencies.[16] Fostering's potential benefits had to be reconciled with the scrutiny involved.

Respectable working-class Canadians knew something of the consequences of social and economic failure. Many might be better armed than their more comfortably off contemporaries to deal with shipwrecked children and youth. At the very least, challenging behaviours might be familiar. Living proof as it were of the promise of making it, at least on a modest scale, these respectable householders could be both judgmental and helpful. Proud traditions of harbouring unrelated youngsters of families down on their luck help explain the financial and moral support of the Oshawa and District Labour Council for Ontario's best-known foster parent, "Mom" Whyte and her houseful of informally fostered charges in the 1950s. As the wife of a labourer, she appeared to embody, at least at first glance, the moral rectitude of working people.[17]

Although quantitative assessments of fostering households are rare, there is evidence of a recurring profile. In 1948, a social work study from the University of Toronto found a majority to be heterosexual couples, aged between twenty-five and fifty-five, most with less than high-school education, with at least one child of their own, though some had none, and with an annual household income of less than $2,500. Most husbands were skilled or unskilled workers and women were housewives. Most owned their own homes of five or six rooms. Most requested children between six and twelve, old enough to be relatively independent while not presenting the challenge of infancy or adolescence. The majority also believed that youngsters were essential to normal homes. While the additional income clearly made a real difference, these adults publicly emphasized the benefits of companionship, either for themselves or for their own offspring.[18]

Several later studies are similarly suggestive. British Columbia's Federation of Foster Parent Associations surveyed its membership between 1984 and 1987, claiming

the foster parents who participated in this study tend to have incomes below $25,000, are between 30 and 50 years old, and have completed their high school

education. About half of the respondents have some formal child care education. Most are somewhat religious. They were introduced to fostering by friends
and "others." Most are members of the BCFFPA, although half do not attend
meetings.[19]

Other late twentieth-century investigations discovered that

> most foster parents begin fostering in their mid to late thirties, and take in about
> fourteen children in six years. They are married and live in the city. Often nei-
> ther parent completed high school. Usually the father is a blue-collar worker,
> and the sole wage earner. The father's income is about $29,000—well below the
> Ontario average of $41,775.

BC. foster parents were summed up as "solid, firm" and sensible citizens who
took in children in order "to follow their church's teaching that they should
help the less fortunate."[20]

In the 1970s, a rather less positive portrait emerged in an investigation of
Canadian family daycare. This characterized most female caregivers as handicapped by having young children at home, poor English, a lack of waged alternatives, and chronic illness or injury. Many confessed that they did not really
like children. A very few were deemed "warm and trustworthy."[21] Commonplace difficulties were conveyed even in the case of a relatively well-off subject.
This woman had two school-aged children of her own, fostered another two
under ten years of age for the Children's Aid Society and provided homecare
to nine youngsters from five families. As the investigator concluded,

> it takes a large crowd of children in one home to produce meager stab at a living
> wage. And that kind of overcrowding simply adds to the caregiver's problems—
> and the children's ... How can you make a villain out of a woman with health
> problems and low self-esteem who is trying to add a few dollars to her modest fam-
> ily income by taking in other people's children?[22]

While evidence is fragmentary, fostering appears to have become less attractive for more securely established working-class households over the decades.
By the end of the twentieth century, most of Canada's married women with
school-aged children no longer worked solely at home. Widespread availability
of contraceptives enlarged their options. Economic respectability could be
increasingly ensured without sacrificing privacy. As a result, the pool of foster
parents appeared to be less sturdily respectable than in the past. Recruits were
also likely to come from populations with a particular investment in keeping
women at home and in the service of children and husbands or in saving particular communities of children, notably First Nations in the 1960s and later.

Farm and rural householders supplied one alternative to the homes of urban workers. Authorities and many Canadians long believed such settings promised moral and physical health. Such faith persisted despite continued out-migration, especially of young people.[23] The loss of farm offspring, ironically enough, kept strangers in demand for both companionship and labour. In comparison with city-dwellers, women on hard-pressed family operations also had fewer economic alternatives and generally less education with which to maximize income.[24] Even at the end of the twentieth century, jurisdictions such as Nova Scotia reported up to 81 percent rural placements.[25]

Much like the "home children" brought in from Great Britain for more than a century, somewhat older youngsters were commonly preferred candidates for farm homes and their chores. The tragic subject of Alanis Obomsawin's documentary *Richard Cardinal: Cry from a Diary of a Métis Child* appears to have spent most of his short life helping Alberta's rural foster parents.[26] He and his brother were variously incorporated into marginal domestic economics to ensure their survival. Geography also meant that these foster parents could expect less supervision from urban-based authorities. Since Canada's rural population dropped steadily over the twentieth century to 23 percent by 1991, candidates were in dwindling supply.[27] Up-to-date authorities were also decreasingly confident that rural living remedied problems presented by disadvantaged urban youth.

Difficulties in finding suitable adults worsened when hard-pressed agencies sometimes allowed foster care to become an unsupervised dumping ground for unwanted children. The 1927 survey of child welfare in Vancouver found that bad practices damaged the reputation of all fostering households.[28] By the mid-twentieth century, recurring reports of brutal and lazy surrogates similarly hurt the name of all. Speaking in the 1960s, one blunt social worker assessed foster parents as being in general "disrepute" since so many were "marginal members of the community who are too often economically unstable, socially disorganized and emotionally disadvantaged."[29] They were far from the stalwart working-class and rural citizens who were to display their worthiness in assisting unrelated girls and boys.

Race

In city and in country, foster parents from racial and cultural minorities were always less common than such children in care. Many such families may have been preoccupied with informal assistance to their own compatriots and not responsive, but certain adult populations were not readily regarded as supplying guidance that would restore children to usefulness and well-being. In the beginning, authorities took for granted "a common-sense racial logic which associated whiteness with the "clean and the good, the pure and the pleasing."[30] Pioneers such as J.J. Kelso and others assumed the superiority of northern Europeans in fostering as in most else. Despite occasional early efforts to seek racial and, even more so, religious matching of children and substitute parents, non-mainstream numbers continued small.[31] Public agencies had few ties to minorities and recruitment was always impeded by mutual suspicion. This mismatch was not, however, generally regarded as a problem so long as Aboriginal, Black, Asian, and otherwise racialized youngsters remained relatively unusual among state charges. Their numbers, however, rose sharply in the second half of the twentieth century. By its end, authorities increasingly sought "culturally appropriate child welfare services" that included the search for greater diversity among child protection professionals as well as foster parents.[32]

Montreal faced issues that were typical of major urban centres. In the 1950s and 1960s, the city's Children's Service Centre, assisting the Anglophone and Allophone population, found its foster mothers predominantly among those born in Britain and to some degree from continental Europe. Such immigrants were both acceptable and likely to need additional funds. At times, "the agency did not have a single foster family that was wholly North American-born" even as "the natural family background of most of its foster children was wholly American (inclusive of the Caribbean area)." Not surprisingly, the Montreal Centre found that fostering households had "culturally-based expectations which were foreign to the children's society."[33] Approved applicants in post–Second World War Toronto presented a similar picture with "98% of the men and 99% of the women" being "British-born [this designation included the Canadian-born], one of whom was a "Negro" and one a French-Canadian; 2% of the men and .5% of the women were European born.[34] It is unlikely that this group included many eastern or southern Europeans as this would have been considered worthy of mention.

Explanations for such patterns extend beyond agency prejudice. Many non-mainstream households struggled to survive and were already crowded with additional kin in need of help. Even as authorities frequently remained equally uncertain of their qualifications, many minorities have also been highly suspicious of child protection activities as involving little more than child theft. A few representatives nevertheless took up fostering as part of their community duties. This scenario seemed to be the case with a Toronto-born activist from the Brotherhood of Sleeping Car Porters, a political candidate for the Cooperative Commonwealth Federation, and, much later, a Citizenship Court judge, and his wife, Stanley and Kate Grizzle, who fostered a child alongside their own after the Second World War.[35] While late twentieth-century California reported success with Hispanic recruits and the creation of "a kind of ethnic community care" that included sympathy for young mothers and "surrogate extended family networks not only for the children but often also for the mothers," such a phenomenon has not been readily visible in Canada.[36]

This nation's long-standing shortfall of Aboriginal foster parents in state employment reflected the larger absence of diverse representation.[37] Differences have also been crucial. In many Native communities, mainstream agencies were especially suspect as part of broader efforts at cultural genocide. Even when child protection authorities aimed to help and campaigned actively for Native surrogates, recruitment was rarely easy. One BC study from the 1980s discovered that "many Native people" had different expectations of fostering. Many, like others in settler society before them, would only consider the care of related children. When they were asked to accept unrelated youngsters, they required compatibility with the natal band and family. Many were also fully engaged in helping their own kin and had no space and energy left for strangers. Somewhat to the surprise of investigators, potential First Nations candidates were also much like other prospective applicants in their reluctance to subsidize the state. They too demanded fair rates and benefits.[38] They knew full well that they had fewer resources than most Canadians to subsidize child protection. In 1980, grandmothers at a BC Indian Homemakers conference made the recurring case for adequate compensation: "Give us the resources and we will do the best job of taking care of our own children."[39] Another BC study at much the same time discovered reluctance because Natives believed they faced almost automatic rejection.[40] They rightly feared that their traditions and practices would not be regarded as the equal of mainstream households. In their suspicion of governments, Native citizens resembled working-class counterparts who sometimes regarded child protection agencies, like the police and the courts, as representatives of an essentially alien and unfriendly power.[41] As Cheryl Swidrovich has argued, however, perhaps the most important disincentive was the poverty and disarray of many Native households injured by colonialism.[42] Alternatively, families discovering economic success by assimilation or some other route may have discarded or even feared demands for additional caregiving lest they derail their own prospects. The Native counterparts of the mainstream middle class were also likely to have women employed full time and perhaps also to have invested more in privacy and individualism. Such trajectories, like those in other communities since the advent of modernization, could create distance from the offspring of others.

When Native foster parents enrolled in increasing numbers with tribal and provincial agencies at the end of the twentieth century, their motives also seemed familiar. Many appreciated additions to their limited income, especially when employment prospects were otherwise slight as they were on most

Canadian reserves. Many were also inspired by desires to contribute to a better future for their communities. Fostering was one way to show social and political leadership and to model behaviours that demonstrated the worthiness of indigenous traditions.

Respectability and Conservatism

Recruitment efforts and interest in application over the years reflected prevailing assumptions about what constituted propriety or respectability. Since many in care were understood to come from disordered or dangerous households with limited attachment to the labour market and problematic habits and morals, their antithesis was the ideal. Not surprisingly, foster parents frequently appear to have been conservative or more traditionally minded members of their communities. Evidence often suggests deep commitment to gendered domestic values and a sensitivity about obligations to children whose parents had failed. In the 1950s, "Mom" Whyte of Bowmanville, Ontario, was a self-righteous proponent of such opinion. This middle-aged factory worker's wife who at one time or another took in some eighty children, including five of her own, bluntly blamed wage-earning mothers for neglect. She also vigorously opposed birth control and held that "men today are sissies because women have made them sissies."[43] Such traditional values often had disciplinary implications. Like "Mom," another religious couple who fostered provincially and adopted internationally in Alberta in the 1970s was firm about the need for obedience. The father frankly admitted to "spanking" his sixteen-year-old foster ward "on the bottom" after she "falsely" accused him of abuse. He challenged the government to charge him and was subsequently cleared.[44] Corporal punishment might have been increasingly out of fashion in liberal circles, but such Canadians considered it to be a necessary part of achieving order. Perhaps not surprisingly, an assessment of ninety-eight foster mothers and fifty-three fathers from 1980s British Columbia concluded that the majority "held to traditional views of their roles as substitute parents."[45]

Regular church going has been a commonplace marker of respectability. In the 1980s, one study found that most surrogates were at least "somewhat religious."[46] A later Nova Scotia survey reported that 89 percent of its sample engaged in church activities.[47] Evangelical sentiments surfaced regularly, often proving essential in shoring up willingness to receive challenging youngsters. Here, the sole entry in Paul Magocsi's monumental *Encylopedia of Canada's Peoples* to mention fostering specifically is notable. Both Catholic and Protestant Dutch Canadians were described as committed to "the family as the most important institution in society and child rearing as an honourable and rewarding task." The author believed that agencies found that the Dutch-Canadian family generally provided a stable home with fair and impartial discipline. These homes also came to be a refuge for abused and neglected children in need of protection. Such care often led to the adoption of children who were regarded as difficult to place ... Even today, many second-generation Dutch families carry on the tradition of foster care and adoption that was begun by their parents.[48]

In the 1960s, one such foster mother, commenting on a Métis "premie" and two earlier additions to her household, concluded: "These children have given us more than we have given them. We have learned much, and felt our Christian lives grow and mature."[49]

Religious inspiration similarly encouraged an Alberta couple to take in "23 children, more or less" in the 1970s. They had "promised God never to turn away a child in need." Provinces and territories appreciated such dedicated recruits because they "would take the hard cases, the children that no one else would have." Faith could also make them effective adversaries. These same Albertans pursued a reluctant government in court and won permanent wardship of four siblings whose birth father they distrusted. Like the Tasmanian foster parents assessed by Janet McCalman, such highly motivated Canadians showed little "social and political deference."[50] Much like "Mom" Whyte, they also proved capable of generating support. When the Albertans campaigned to become international adopters, they found Mennonite neighbours eager to help "with the gardening, freezing and baking as well as outside chores such as logging and guiding. Stores gave clothing and shoes (or discounts); a construction firm in Calgary gave the gift of a carpenter for the summer months, an 80-year-old woman in Calgary bakes cookies by the bushel."[51]

Protestantism has been highly visible, but it was not unique in mobilizing recruits. A Catholic Ukrainian Canadian, Katherine Hrynewich Labiuk (born in 1915) was similarly prompted to seek foster children in Alberta after the Second World War.[52] In 1958, when the provincial Catholic Women's League campaigned for applicants, a small-town volunteer, and wife of an engineer for Northern Electric, in eastern Ontario visited Kingston's orphanage and walked out with two sisters to foster. Her faith gave her the confidence and support to assume additional duties.[53] In 1961, the national Catholic Women's League devoted its convention to foster care. Religious-minded women were everywhere encouraged by such an affirmation of maternal labour.

Attendance at church, however, did not guarantee good treatment for youngsters. There was the early example cited in Chapter 1 of an Anglican minister and his wife beating their young charges. In her investigation of girls in trouble with the law, historian Joan Sangster has discovered another supposedly Christian couple beating a ward whom the husband had also impregnated. Ontario authorities did not prosecute these individuals then, nor did they in the case of a twelve-year-old whose foster father, a "respected "church elder," kept her close to starvation.[54] Professions of faith could sometimes camouflage sin.

Closely related to foster parents' pervasive conservatism was the assumption that children should contribute to their keep, much like working-class and farm offspring in general and pauper apprentices in the past.[55] This necessity sometimes led to youngsters' exploitation as cheap rural or domestic labourers.[56] Surrogates might be better off than original families, but many dwelt only a mouth, a paycheque, or a healthy body away from disaster. Additional charges required economic inputs, either in direct transfers of labour, a solution made increasingly more difficult by requirements for schooling, or by cash for care. This calculation sometimes resulted in abuse.

As they set about the work of fostering, Canadians, like their counterparts in Hope Children's Services in Los Angeles County, the largest foster care system in the United States, often seemed eager

> to construct a "Family myth" defining men as the exclusive breadwinners and women as the full time nurturers ... These traditional families masked women's economic contribution, as foster mothers' work remained invisible in the private sphere and resembled the work they did daily as mothers."[57]

Self-consciously worthy citizens prided themselves on upholding the roles and practices of authority and obedience that distinguished them from first parents. State payment was accepted as a proper, if inadequate, reward for a critical social service.

Not surprisingly given such views, and all the more so because of the commitment many often developed to youngsters in their care, foster couples, notably mothers, regularly found it difficult to cooperate with natal kin. Despite recurring evidence that youngsters did better with "ongoing contact with their natural families," many surrogates resisted access. The early twentieth-century efforts of the Toronto's Infants' Home to have foster and unwed mothers collaborate ran into just such reluctance.[58] Much like adopters who feared original families, fostering adults regularly argued that contact upset charges and households.[59] At the end of the twentieth century, a leading Canadian psychiatrist concluded that the commonplace hostility of "traditional foster families" made them unsuitable but admitted that the shortfall in applications left agencies "little option."[60]

The emergence of formally recognized kin foster care in the last decades of the twentieth century confirmed the value of contact. It also offered an opportunity for original communities to assert respectability. Parents may have failed, but other kin would not. Such potentially worthy caregivers nevertheless presented a special problem. Relatives could share in the odium so often attached to original parents. This was especially likely for racial minorities. Grandmothers and aunts, the most common substitutes for mothers and fathers, might have much to offer, but they were tainted by their association with parental dereliction from duty and sometimes by their own histories. Many shared the economic deprivation that undermined parental care. Previous run-ins with child protection agencies made some kin susceptible to negative assessment even as they struggled to save the next generation. In 2002, this was the dilemma facing the BC Native grandmother who sought the return of youngsters who had been in her care since birth. She had to counter the assessment of agency workers and her own lawyer that she herself had been an abusive mother, a charge she vigorously denied.[61] Situations were all the more difficult because relatives often struggled with conflicting loyalties to both children and their parents.[62] When Native agencies took over child welfare duties beginning in the 1980s, they could be more understanding, but they also encountered related challenges, sometimes made more difficult in the context of political interference from elites in small communities.

Recent Canadian studies show grandmothers giving up jobs and compromising retirement. Hard-won late twentieth-century initiatives, such as the "Child in the Home of a Relative" and "Guardian Financial Assistance" programs, recognized kin commitment.[63] Such benefits, which often involved both somewhat lower funding and less supervision, reflected simultaneous assumptions that relatives should properly subsidize care. Governments were not the only advocates of this position. Native communities sometimes held that "family should take care of their own as part of their traditional responsibility without any remuneration." Nor was that the only dilemma. The shortage of reserve employments meant that additional income was jealously prized and a potential cause of conflict.[64]

Whatever the opposition to financial support for kin care, this perspective ignored recurring findings that

> children in kin care are more likely to live in disadvantaged neighborhoods, public housing, and in poorer households than children placed with non-kin ... the effort kin caregivers must expend in order to protect their children from the hazards associated with poverty may be considerable, yet there are few formal social services supports available to assist them in their regard.[65]

Equally serious, the whole turn to official kin care, including the possible cost-savings and cultural affirmation it potentially invoked, sidestepped the harsh fact that blood relations have stood centre front in the history of abuse. At the start of the twenty-first century, repeated instances of child deaths at the hands of kin caused BC's Advocate for Children and Youth to demand higher levels of scrutiny.

For all of their different inspirations and shortcomings, many Canadian communities have shared feelings that the care of youngsters is a proper expression of respectable adulthood. Many surrogates remain inspired by notions of service to children. They have enlisted to rescue children and valued results such as the success of a young woman who first lost her "grandmother in Guyana" and was then "rejected and abused by her relations in Canada." She attributed "her hard-won sense of strength and self-confidence today largely to her years with these first foster parents who, above all, treated her with respect."[66] Some Native veterans of fostering with White families, such as film director Gil Cardinal, remember similar kindness and support, observations that have contradicted conventional understanding of their apprehension.[67] Such results rarely have made the headlines, but they have meant all the difference to the people involved.

Real Mothers

Parenting of every sort benefits from both affection and material resources. Both contribute to feelings of self-worth and respectability. For modern mothers, however, love and money have often been judged incompatible. A pervasive "cult of true womanhood" that dated from the eighteenth century found first expression in regulating and empowering middle-class women. Over time, it became broadly pervasive as an ideal for others as well. Good women, so this gender ideology went, subsumed themselves in service to children and husbands. Affection was a rightful, even sufficient, reward. Indeed, pecuniary considerations could tarnish character and relations. This paradox dogged foster mothers, just as it has female teachers, nurses, and social workers. How could they express womanhood's supposedly natural impulses while demanding a fair wage?

Most foster mothers have viewed care as being deeply congruent with their sense of who they were as respectable gendered beings. While compensation has generally been essential for the maintenance of the household, this necessity did not mean lack of commitment. Prospects for service and affection have always encouraged application.[68] Most women have taken pride in sheltering children in need—those who have been failed by the less competent or fortunate. They trusted that their particular capacity for nurture could benefit young lives. Child protection workers early on recognized determination to mother. Indeed J.J. Kelso, Ontario's first superintendent of neglected and dependent children, and others like him have counted on it to save their charges. Later observers have made the comparison with a dedication to other employments. In her depiction of a Toronto foster mother in 1945, one journalist argued:

> There are some women who make careers out of writing or painting; some who choose secretarial work or become nurses or doctors; but in the case of Mrs. Rogers and others like her, child care is the most important and satisfying job in life. Homemaking and motherhood is not something that merely "happens"; they deliberately seek it as a career.[69]

Commitment to maternal duties could be powerful as the choice of a Scarborough, Ontario, resident in 1965 suggested. This wife of a "stationary engineer" cared for "three adopted children, three in the process of adoption, six on the foster plan and one by birth" and refused to surrender any when their ten-room bungalow went up in smoke. Maternalism seemed the great motivator.[70] Some forty years later, a special education teacher married to a bus driver explained her dedication this way: "I've had a deep love for kids all my life," and "we've had to teach ourselves self-control and to create the calmest environment for them that we possibly can."[71] Another foster mother at the end of the twentieth century summed up her feelings: "I have a lot of love to give and I love kids. I have been babysitting since I was twelve and I loved kids. It is hard on the nerves at times, but I love kids."[72] In a testament to such feelings, a Native veteran of child protection since age seven remembered being treated like a granddaughter in "a warming atmosphere and a loving atmosphere."[73] Such sentiments explain recurring examples of foster parents adopting those they have fostered, even as they worried about the reduced income.[74]

A 2006 study of a large sample of Ontario foster parents has emphasized the significance of altruism. Its investigators also demonstrated a marked inattention to the class of respondents, although indications of total income, with over 50 percent earning below $49,000 year and some 22 percent earning $20,000–29,000, are suggestive.[75] They also did not deal with gender, although 80 percent of respondents were mothers. They did, however, discover that "the two most frequently endorsed reasons fostering were wanting to provide loving parents to children and wanting to save children from harm."[76] Another twenty-first-century study of motivations for fostering youngsters with disabilities similarly stressed personal, rather than financial, rewards. Once again, however, authors made nothing of the fact that 86 percent of participating parents were female.[77] Mothers seemed after all the prime authors of altruism.

Many surrogates or their close relations appear to have been themselves fostered or otherwise raised separately from their birth parents. Such adults were determined to help others as they had been helped or, indeed, to do better. One

Ontario woman, recalling her own "miserable" childhood as a ward of Children Aid Societies in the 1930s, set out on a rescue mission. After toiling as a domestic servant, she married a compositor and raised two sons but saw a daughter die. She fostered girls for the province.[78] Another woman (1934–2000), inspired by her own unhappy adoption and subsequent exploitation, grew up to marry, produce two sons, and work as a foster mother and daycare provider for some 112 children. Just before her death, she received a thank-you card upon the college graduation of twin brothers who had lived with her for years. Her husband explained, "she always wanted to make sure the kids were okay. She was a good woman."[79]

Some spoke explicitly of playing good deeds forward. One late twentieth-century Nova Scotian determined to repay kindness shown to her father and husband by parenting "someone in need." Another accounted for her efforts as part of a family project: "Originally we started because my husband had spent time in a N.B. [New Brunswick] orphanage and he wanted to repay the debt."[80] A former Barnardo child drew on her own hard experience when she

> boarded children from the Children's Aid—as many as seventeen and eighteen children. I was so wanting to give some poor children the love and care they needed ... Some of the children I raised from the time they were little. They got a high school education and good jobs and they think of us as Mom and Dad and come to see us just the same as our own children and grandchildren.[81]

Similar inspiration moved the fifty-five-year-old director of Calgary's Foster Parent Association, who had been abandoned as an infant and fostered by a Ukrainian family who kept her in contact with her Native roots. In 2007, she testified: "They were a strong and loving family. I want to give the kids I care for the same kind of chance that I was given." She began to foster at the age of twenty-one and eventually partnered with an Aboriginal man, who was himself fostered by family members. Of him, she said: "The best part of fostering is knowing he's serving as a positive male role model."[82] Such figures have formed part of a persistent contingent over the decades.

In some families, successive female generations have developed a strong domestic culture associated with taking in children in need. Such seemed to be true of one Albertan, who was honoured by the Order of Canada. Her English settler mother had sheltered homeless girls and boys in the 1920s and 1930s. When she was eighteen, Zoe Gardner moved next door to make room for additional youngsters and eventually to embark on her own career as a foster parent.[83] Similar commitment caused the first Canadian winner of the Foster Parent of the Year award from the Child Welfare League of America to assume that her daughter would take over her charges when she died. In the meantime, she could not contemplate retirement, saying: "How do you retire from life, and this is a way of life."[84] As another champion explained, "we are only part of a lend-lease arrangement … Foster parenthood for us became a worthwhile family project."[85] Much the same commitment emerged in some First Nations families. A 2005 Manitoba study suggests that kinship care sometimes "crossed and extended" through generations.[86] Such adults formed the bedrock of the fostering system from its origins until the present.

Although couples were everywhere preferred, and unpartnered status was treated as a liability by most agencies, spinsters and widows were always present in fostering's ranks. Insufficient numbers of more acceptable recruits and faith in women's particular qualifications kept them on the rolls.[87] They were considered most suitable for very young children, but they received others for whom no couples could be found. One divorcée remembered that as late as the 1960s, "the only foster children single mothers were allowed to care for were mentally handicapped ones [since] the belief was a single parent could not give a proper upbringing to a normal child."[88] This fact may explain the long-term fostering career of spinster Marguerite Hein of Port Alberni, British Columbia, who began taking in otherwise hard-to-place children from the local Native residential school and from the provincial ministry in the 1960s. Like many other recruits, she discovered a vocation. Despite the hard work, she insisted: "I never considered looking after these children as work, in fact I always felt bad in that I didn't have a job."[89]

Single and widowed candidates were regarded more favourably when charges maintained contact with fathers. Their marginal welcome, as well as the popularity of psychological interpretations, informed the conclusion of a Toronto social worker in 1948:

> Even though a child has no father these homes could be used as long as the woman realized the child's need of some contact with a father person which might be met by some outside club or organization. The important thing here, as at any time, is that the foster mother is a mature person and does not expect the child to be the answer to all her needs. She must be able to let him grow up as an individual. Single women might be used even more frequently for babies who are being placed temporarily.[90]

Since their marital situation resembled that of many first parents who had faltered, suspicions regarding unmarried women were hardly surprising.

Even as maternal enthusiasm supplied a critical inspiration, it posed special challenges in dealing with first parents or in subsequently surrendering youngsters. One Halifax single mother of four, with a long history of personal hardship, including the consignment of her own children to an orphanage while she worked to retrieve them, typified the possibility of inclusive sympathies. While welcoming young strangers for over twenty years "to supplement her income," she showed "a special empathy for single women with young children." They too came under her wing and into her heart.[91] Her response was the ideal. For many women, however, deep investments in their own mothering skills meant that they could only regard those who surrendered and possibly abused offspring as transgressing nature and perhaps god.[92]

Devoted foster mothers had to confront loss when agencies moved children to new homes. Many have wished to stay in touch.[93] Hopes were regularly stymied by provincial policies that commonly forbade contact. Prohibitions only lapsed when wards reached the age when they could leave care. When separation happened with insufficient preparation and consultation, as appears common, foster mothers were often upset. Some resisted and took "their stories to the press" where they hoped for greater recognition of their natural maternal love.[94] Such was the case with the Anglican foster mother, Mrs. Timbrell, who engaged in a highly public struggle to adopt two Roman Catholic foster daughters in the 1960s. Ontario's Waterloo County Children's Aid Society intended them to be separately adopted by Catholic parents. Before working for the province, Timbrell had cared for the child of a serviceman whose wife could not find housing during the Second World War and subsequently became "a sort of den mother for the area, taking children through newspaper ads or on the recommendations of friends and neighbors." As she explained, "I like children. Before I got the first one, I was sitting at home doing nothing and I thought I would like to do something to occupy my time." Her desire to keep her fosterlings ran afoul of the criminal records of her construction worker husband, a veteran on a pension, and two sons and a young daughter's unwed pregnancy. One social worker termed this mother of nine a "psychopath." Supposed shortcomings had not, however, previously been sufficient to bar her from employment with the Children's Aid Society.[95] Nor did they deter neighbours who joined family members in opposing officials.[96]

Such confrontations have persisted as a feature of fostering's complicated relations. In 2002, British Columbia saw an evangelical foster mother, supported by the Foster Care Support Network, struggling to retain a four-member sibling group and another fosterling. The youngsters who had resided with her and her husband for some seven years were to be removed after he was charged with assault on another foster child. In this case, the kids, aged eight to thirteen, were old enough to join the protest. They refused to attend school until child protection authorities relented.[97] Such incidents formed part of the recurring contests of authority between foster parents and welfare agencies.[98]

When it came to child rearing, most foster mothers valued experience over professional qualifications. They were readily suspicious of young, unmarried social workers and uncomfortable with external supervision in general. A substantial social divide further complicated many interactions. In the early twentieth century, investigations of intelligence, cleanliness, and finances by Toronto's Infants' Home typically upset applicants. Its experts doubted "foster mothers' knowledge of modern child welfare practices." They worried about their attendance at weekly baby clinics where conversation sometimes included criticism of the Infants' Home. Eventually, the Infants' Home sent nurses on home visits rather than having foster mothers share their experiences.[99] The 1948 judgment of one social work student aptly conveyed how social inferiors might be assessed more as potential clients than as co-workers:

> The foster mother may say she wishes a child as a companion for one of her own, when really she means she cannot control her own youngster and would like to try with another one to prove she is not a failure as a mother. She may say she is fond of children and wants to give a child a home, when really she is in need of the extra financial support and yet does not want to go out to work. She may say she needs the financial help, while really she is lonely and wants to mould a child into her life to make up for some of the affection she is not getting from her husband.[100]

While some clearly appreciated assistance with difficult youngsters, most foster parents valued childcare for the autonomy it offered. This contrasted sharply with the factory, clerical, service, or sales jobs otherwise most often available to less educated women. Yet, even as they cherished managing on their own, they have been likely to be undermined. As Teresa Tooguchi Swartz has pointed out in her study of California's foster mothers, "the bureaucratic, regulatory, and supervisory nature of the foster care system" positioned professional women as "matriarchs" licensed to intervene in the domestic management of others ultimately judged to be less competent.[101] Since Canadians, like their counterparts identified in Tasmania, were also frequently "independent, resourceful women," they found "inspections, with the inference that their homes were suspect, difficult to bear."[102] Ultimately, however, maternal desires combined with the need for more income to induce some women to accept surveillance.

Material recompense supplied, however, its own dilemma. Right from the beginning, foster mothers wrestled with the perception that payment somehow made them less authentic. Recurring public sentiments that "good" mothers did not require money to perform natural functions undermined their claims. Once cash changed hands, their contribution to human relations, not unlike that of prostitutes, was often effectively regarded as contaminated. In 1919, a journalist summed up just such sentiments: "The woman who boards babies for money may or may not be a good person to have them, but the woman who takes a baby out of sympathy and love is a pretty safe risk."[103]

State payments were nonetheless essential in permitting most recipients to remain housewives and mothers. Few prospective households did not need to add to the income of male wage earners. This requirement could sometimes be desperate. In the 1930s, British Columbia discovered families on relief request-ing charges as one means of survival.[104] Governments early on learned to accept that budgets did not readily "stretch to the care and feeding of extra children." At a bare minimum, reimbursement of costs was a necessity to secure "the right kind of boarding homes." Payment rarely extended, however, to include the value of maternal labour. Fears persisted of putting "foster parenthood on a mercenary basis."[105]

Authorities firmly connected women's efforts to good citizenship not profit making. Ontario's post–Second World War public welfare bureaucrats cele-brated mothers as "the very core of effective child placing services" and "socially minded citizens who provide such good care at a minimum of expense to the Society and to the taxpayer." These stalwarts "need[ed] the encouragement and co-operation of every citizen in the community."[106] The fear of cash as a con-taminant nevertheless persisted. As Baukje Biedema, the author of a major Canadian study on late twentieth-century foster mothers, has concluded, "the notion that foster mothers entered into fostering because of the money was a sore point for many, if not all."[107] Fears of not adhering to codes of maternal altru-ism in which most were deeply invested handicapped claims for remuneration.

Yet for all their recurring hesitation, many foster mothers ultimately demanded more than admiration. Such was the case, for example, in 1926 when a foster mother refused to release a child to his mother until she was compen-sated. The latter had apparently assumed that the care was free in return for the satisfaction of rearing a child.[108] The long-standing shortage of recruits for fos-ter care pointed to the most common form of resistance. In 1942, Canadian social agencies typically reported a "shortage of such homes caused by various wartime circumstances," most notably improved job prospects for women and more stable family income.[109] Some forty years later, the president of Metro Toronto's Foster Parent Association in 1983 summed up the stark reality: "We have enough love in our hearts, but our husbands don't have enough money in the bank ... we aren't supposed to make money by being foster parents. But what it's come down to is that we're subsidizing foster children."[110] Canada was not the only nation where women increasingly declined to subsidize child pro-tection. One observer of the late twentieth-century United States concluded, "changes in employment patterns, family composition, and other demographic shifts contributed to a decline of almost a third in the number of active foster families between 1987 and 1991."[111] The supply of maternal self-sacrifice was clearly exhaustible.

Co-Starring Fathers

Child protection agencies and scholars have devoted little attention to fathers in fostering.[112] They are difficult to find in government records, public accounts, or individual memory. They attract most notice when they surface as abusive monsters.[113] Illustrative of persisting disregard was the observation of one 1970 commentator that suggested that most foster families were "matriarchal" and that fathers were "forgotten" men in a world where "foster mothers are basically women that like having children around."[114] In such scenarios, men seemed little more than ciphers in a maternal project. Over the years, authorities have never wavered in regarding women's pledge to mother as being pivotal. Good men's dedication to waged employment and to respectability allowed maternal vocation. They served best in performing essential tasks quietly and aiding and abetting the more central efforts of their wives.

When passing acknowledgement has been positive, paternal surrogates have been likely to win applause for involvement in recreation and for offering vocational support and guidance, especially to boys. Like the "fathers of the community" in post–World War II suburbs identified by Robert Rutherdale, foster dads were paying their obligations to the next generation. Participation in fostering could affirm male respectability and leadership. Payment nevertheless once again raised questions of legitimacy. Conservative gender codes presumed that true men supported families without dependence on female earnings or state assistance. Fostering was in both regards transgressive. State oversight could readily be judged as interference in properly private matters and a source of possible embarrassment.

Some fathers, however, resisted sidelining. In 1960, a Toronto couple shared honours from the Catholic Children's Aid Society as Foster Father and Foster Mother of the Year. Over the years, they had taken in twenty-five children, "most of them handicapped, as well as raising their own son." The wife took the opportunity to emphasize her service station operator husband's "extra efforts to be a 'father.'"[115] In the same decade, Saskatchewan child protection services had to organize joint teas to thank parents when fathers protested their exclusion.[116] As gender roles slowly relaxed, more grew restive. In 2004, a foster dad from Niagara Falls, Ontario, publicly rejected suggestions that his charges grew up "without the love and security they'd get from committed parents." He proudly claimed joint responsibility for the twenty-four children, aged four to ten, who had entered their home over five years: "These children like our own. We are loving, committed, and a lot of children who have passed through our home and family have wished to return. Ask the kids, they'll tell you."[117] Another man, who self-consciously took "to heart that he may be the only loving father figure these kids ever know," communicated the same message a few years later.[118] Such assertions were part of a growing appreciation for the value of children and men alike of nurture. They remained hard put, however, to make a substantial dent in the pre-eminent reliance on women for nurture and the heightened fears of male pedophiles that characterized late twentieth-century Canada.

Crisis and Recognition

From their origins, state foster programs relied on respectable communities and traditionally gendered roles to provide home care at the least possible cost. A continuing shortage in applications, high turn over, and the uneven quality of recruits increasingly revealed the flaws of this calculation. By the 1960s, in the face of rising numbers of married women employed outside the home and growing caseloads, the situation had become desperate in many jurisdictions. As the characteristics of children in care shifted, it became more so. In the beginning, fostering programs chiefly concerned themselves with seemingly healthy and largely mainstream, or at least White, wards, but after the 1960s more disadvantaged populations previously segregated into asylums, hospitals, reformatories, and residential schools, or those who had been ignored altogether, began to arrive in unprecedented numbers. Social workers discovered that "many foster parents, with the best intentions in the world, can't cope with unhappy children, and are likely to reach the breaking point."[119]

By the end of the twentieth century, drug and alcoholic addictions swept further distraught youngsters into care. Canada, much like the United States, Britain, and Australia, had to deal more than ever with

> special needs' children, most of whom come into care with well-established physical, mental, emotional and behavioural problems. As a result, they can considerably disrupt the life of the foster family, forcing foster parents, whether or not they recognize it, to function as parent therapists, providing specialized management, if not a prescribed treatment program, in addition to supplying basic care. They may or may not be paid for the specialized time and services offered over and above the boarding and maintenance allowance they receive ... Today, however, there is probably little difference in the children cared for in foster homes that have and have not been designated specialized, so that routine foster care, to be adequate, must usually be specialized care.[120]

As the gap between rich and poor Canadians deepened at the end of the twentieth century, the situation deteriorated still more.

Particularly needy youngsters intensified the labour and complicated relations for both foster parents and social workers. The period's recurring restructuring of child protection in a desperate search for solutions as well as the growing pains of First Nations–managed programs joined with systemic underfunding to generate crisis.[121] In 2009, Saskatchewan's child advocate condemned the result. He described foster parents who were ill equipped to cope with the intensity of distress. One foster mother told the inquiry that "when I first started nine years ago there were a few [children] with behavior problems, now they are more severe. Eight-year-olds pulling their own hair, scratch themselves ... five and six-year-olds who hurt themselves ... chew toe nails until they bleed."[122] The report generated great upset for a few weeks, but its bad news had been available for some time.

As charges struggled with difficult histories, more and more surrogates found themselves living in a pressure cooker, far from any semblance of normal family life. Like child welfare in general, fostering burned out multitudes who found it impossible to cope with vulnerable youngsters, inadequate assistance, and limited resources. Many foster parents discovered that they or other family members lacked the temperament or stamina to handle needy strangers. Reports were commonplace of "natural children" complaining "of feeling ignored and unloved" as their parents sought to meet the needs of others.[123]

As the population of youngsters in care shifted, foster parents also became increasingly vulnerable to charges of abuse. In the context of late twentieth-century panics and generally inadequate reporting, it is impossible to know if the situation was worse than in the past or even than that in so-called intact families. Failures also sometimes went unreported—part of the taken-for-granted nature of domestic violence—but some surfaced publicly as charges grew up and were better able to defend and speak for themselves. Certainly, not all foster parents have been up to the demands of the job. Some succumbed to circumstances similar to those that had already toppled previous caregivers. Some were driven by dangerous motives when it came to youngsters. In the process, the reputation of foster caregivers dipped once more.

Upgrading Foster Parents

In the last half of the twentieth century, authorities responded to the crisis with efforts to upgrade the employment. This took three forms: first, the singling out of outstanding foster parents; second, the encouragement of foster parent associations; and, third, experimentation with therapeutic teams. "Foster Parent of the Year," "Foster Parent Weeks," and "Foster Parent Months" began across

Canada in the 1950s and 1960s and were subsequently joined by diverse awards for community service. Winners and runners-up, who were overwhelmingly women but occasionally men as well—most generally as part of couples but sometimes on their own—were publicly applauded for good citizenship. Such recognition deliberately set out to reward contributors, enhance the reputation of the employment, and recruit newcomers. The *sub voce* agenda was symbolic compensation for inadequate payment. In many ways, awards captured the preferred qualities and the personal character of community mothers and fathers.

In 1959, Mrs. Ernest Whalen became Foster Mother of the Year for Toronto's Catholic Children's Aid Society. Much of the publicity omitted her first name. Standing in the shadow of her breadwinner spouse, she epitomized respectable womanhood. For eighteen years, twelve of them as a widow, she had cared for close to sixty crown wards. In her fifties, she lived with nine wards, plus "the chum of one of them." She also counted two married daughters, seven grandchildren, and over 100 foster grandchildren. She confessed to embarrassment over the honour: "I love children and they have been a great comfort to me. I feel guilty about accepting an honor for doing something I like." Self-effacement helped make her emblematic of what was hoped for in associated campaigns for foster mothers.[124] A year later, the Bannons of Weston, one of Toronto's working class suburbs, were awarded Foster Parents of the Year. They had adopted four children and housed a further twenty-five charges, most with physical and mental disabilities. Public recognition confirmed such worthy heterosexuals as representative of community values.[125]

By the new millennium, award winners frequently reported long periods of involvement. Alberta's Zoe Gardner started taking in homeless youngsters, who eventually numbered in the hundreds, in the 1930s. She received the Order of Canada and the YWCA Tribute to Women Award and was termed Canada's Mother Teresa before her death in 1998.[126] Ontario's 2001 Foster Parent, Emma Vinson, celebrated a half-century of achievement and over 125 children under her care. Her career included the adoption of three brothers and a sister who took her family name. They thanked her by saying "they couldn't have had a better home." She also kept in touch with many others who had passed through her home more briefly.[127]

Descriptions of later award winners signalled shifts in what was valued in caregivers. While maternal qualities remained front and centre, other traits also became significant. Canada's Child Welfare League chose a Digby, Nova Scotia, couple, Darlene and Rodney Peck, as recipients of the 2000 Canadian Achievement Award, which recognized the "outstanding contribution of Canadian foster parents." Since 1984, they had rescued nearly ninety children and taken two youngsters as "permanent members of the family." Such achievements were not new among Canadians judged publicly worthy, but emphasis on success with first parents and contributions to teams composed of "the social workers and agency, as well as staff of the schools the child attends" was far less common. The Pecks were also applauded for service to the local, provincial, and national foster parent associations that were a growing feature of the child protection landscape.[128]

Late twentieth-century awards also identified new groups whom child protection authorities wished both to honour and to recruit. In 1998, David Stewart, a former Edmonton police officer and the chief of police for the Blood Tribe Indian Reserve in Standoff, Alberta, received the Governor General's Caring Canadian Award as a foster and adoptive parent of children with special needs.[129] Diversity was similarly invoked in the 2004 recognition of Montrealer Bertolette Démosthène, who had fostered since 1991, five years after her arrival from Haiti. She brought a newly appreciated cultural background to her service to some sixty-two girls and boys. A participant in the development of "publications to assist foster parents" and a "member of a support group for other foster families," she advocated "within the Haitian community on behalf of vulnerable children."[130] Peck, Stewart, and Démosthène represented the team-playing and diverse Canadians that authorities hoped represented the future of foster care.

Even public recognition did not eliminate the fact that foster parents were junior, and, ultimately, especially vulnerable, partners in child protection. In the 1990s, Lyn Platz of Nanaimo, British Columbia, received the Lieutenant Governor's Award for her efforts since 1972 with well over 200 children. In 1997, even as young charges lived with her, she found herself fired by the province. Platz resolved not to go quietly but to capitalize on previous recognition. In October 1998, she defended her record before the BC Human Rights Commission, arguing

> that moving the children from her home was an act of recrimination for her long record of going to bat for her kids, her habit of getting into squabbles with ministry staff. She will tell them that the closure cost her $300,000, including the loss of her home. She will tell them that the price paid by her foster kids was much, much higher.[131]

Despite her spirited defence, her credentials were hard put to withstand public suspicion that always lurked about the motives and behaviours of mothers in the service of the state.

Foster parent associations offered a further option for both agencies and surrogates when it came to mobilizing resources in the last decades of the twentieth century. Just as with the awards, initiatives often came from child protection authorities. From at least the 1960s onwards, experts hoped to improve morale, training, and recruitment and to create allies in lobbying for additional resources. In 1967, such sentiments inspired the creation of the BC Federation of Foster Parent Associations with fifteen local offices. Other such initiatives appeared in Ontario beginning in 1973, Alberta in 1974, Newfoundland and Labrador in 1981, and the Yukon in 1989. Most, if not all, initiatives had close ties with public agencies. The Foster Parents Society of Ontario (FPSO) started under the auspices of the Toronto Children's Aid. Until 1987, the Ontario Association of Children's Aid Societies had final veto over amendments to FPSO bylaws.[132] The BC Federation of Aboriginal Foster Parents similarly depended on government funding after its founding in 1997.

In general, associations seemed to have drawn relatively few active members. Many foster parents clearly felt it sufficient to devote time and energy to the tasks they faced at home. Many preferred their own practical knowledge to any training offered through such groups. Some were simply unwilling to make long-term commitments to the employment. Another deterrent was the long-standing suspicion of external supervision. Some foster parents saw too close an affiliation with officialdom. More bureaucracy was never popular.

On the other hand, a few foster mothers and fathers appeared enthusiastic. Some hoped to use the associations on behalf of themselves and their charges. In the process of coming together, members occasionally went head to head with authorities. In 1967, ten foster parents at an unprecedented Victoria conference, which assembled them alongside youngsters in state care, issued a typical complaint: "Due to the heavy case load they [social workers] seem unable to get close to the situation."[133] Both parents and youngsters insisted on their wish "to be accepted as they are, to be listened to, to be trusted."[134] Cooperation offered opportunities for collective militancy. In this spirit, foster parents in several Ontario Children's Aid Societies threatened to strike in 1988 for better working conditions.[135] In the 1990s, the head of BC's Federation of Aboriginal Foster Parents blamed Victoria for the difficulties encountered by a family ranch: faults lie not with its foster parents but with people who "are, and have for some time been, removed from the reality of child care" and social workers "who don't have a clue about kids."[136] In 2001, the same group publicized a survey setting out the top five issues for caregivers:

- recrimination/intimidation by ministry personnel (55 percent of respondents);
- wrongful allegation/closure (52 percent);
- poor case planning (52 percent);
- poor relationship with ministry (44 percent); and
- lack of support (43 percent).[137]

Such outspokenness was far from the friendly, but subordinate, alliance desired by many authorities. It testified to the recurring conflicts between the two groups, both of which valued their own expertise.

For all of their merits, awards and associations never produced sufficient numbers of recruits to the occupation. Across Canada, modern agencies, just like their predecessors, constantly held publicity campaigns that came up short.[138] While youngsters with few problems aroused interest, some groups, notably teenage boys, charges with disabilities, and Aboriginal youngsters, remained difficult to place. At the end of the twentieth century, team-based approaches, often involving non-profit organizations and sometimes the reprivatization of child protection services,[139] represented a further effort to generate households for difficult-to-place wards. Old time foster service that emphasized maternalism and preparation for respectability was deemed no longer sufficient for more-demanding duties. Foster parents needed specialized preparation to cope with, and re-socialize, difficult clients.

Initiatives to organize foster parents within therapeutic teams appeared and disappeared depending on the ebb and flow of budgets and personnel. In 1976, British Columbia's provincial Ministry of Human Resources experimented with the employment of three experienced foster mothers as part-time foster family workers. They helped less experienced counterparts develop strategies for high needs youngsters and were intended to improve the retention of parents and outcomes. Despite the "energy, warmth, intelligence and enthusiasm" of participants, the program, like many others, fell victim to multiple agendas and scarce budgets.[140]

Experiments often embraced treatment foster care, variously termed "therapeutic foster care, professional parenting, specialized foster care, and treatment family care." All shared

- a focus on youth with special needs;
- a focused recruitment of treatment foster parents;
- extended pre-service training and in-service supervision/support for treatment parents;
- placement of children in treatment parents' own homes;
- parent stipends that are substantially higher than those of traditional foster care;
- planned treatment that combines technologies from more restrictive settings with an emphasis on daily interactions with treatment parents and others as opportunities for treatment and development; and
- within these general parameters, intervention is individualized to meet the needs of a particular child.[141]

Several experimental projects variously embraced such principles: the parent-therapist program developed at the McMaster Medical Centre in the 1970s, the Alberta Parent Counsellors Program operating between 1974 and 1977, and the Toronto Foster Care Research Project in the 1980s.[142] The parent-therapist model combined institutional and foster care for emotionally disturbed children and won a gold medal from the American Psychiatric Association Achievement Award in 1977. It trained thirteen "parent-therapists to serve both as foster parents and as surrogate therapists." They acted as "the primary treatment resource." It also constructed "an extended-family system, whereas, without them, the only alternative when a placement broke down would have been a referral for institutional placement." It also prioritized contact with first parents and reported considerable social and academic success for the original thirty-four youngsters.[143] The Parent Counsellors Project, which originated with Alberta Social Services, defined foster parents as central and social workers as auxiliaries in working with children and birth families. It aimed to get "all participants to work as a team, using group methods."[144] Fostering adults were to be involved at every level, to be treated as colleagues, and to receive "appropriate support, recognition, and financial remuneration." First parents were again ideally part of the team.[145]

The Foster Care Research Project developed by Metro Toronto's Children's Aid Society and the University of Toronto's Division of Child Psychiatry involved both control and experimental groups of foster parents. The first "received all routine services and educational opportunities," while the latter assigned members

> to one of four foster-parent support groups, each of which was jointly led by an experienced foster parent couple (the FPCLs) and a social worker (the SWCLs). The FPCLs provided relief for group members in times of crisis and shared leader of the support group ... Once each month, the leaders of the four support groups spent two hours with a senior child psychiatrist (the author) who directed the project.[146]

As the key psychiatrist in the project explained, the transition to more therapeutic expectations proved frequently difficult:

> Many foster parents today are unclear as to whether they are *parent surrogates* (which they traditionally were, and which many would still like to consider themselves) or *surrogate therapists* (which, with the older age and higher levels of disturbance of children coming into care, they are increasingly forced to be) ... While exceptions exist, by and large foster parents need to begin to see themselves—and to be treated by social workers and agencies—as surrogate therapists and colleagues instead of as parent surrogates and clients, since increasingly

they are expected to provide not just accommodation but a therapeutic milieu within their home and family.[147]

Such goals required a significant change in orientation for the vast majority of Canadians, who more often considered fostering either a passion, a vocation, or a simple employment.

Studies have suggested that "those serving adolescent and special needs children" were especially willing to view "themselves as quasi- or para-professionals and want to be seen by the agency as essential and significant members of the child's treatment team.[148] Such adults found employment as house mothers, house fathers, and residents in the group homes that increasingly occupied the middle ground between traditional foster care and the old institutions. Ultimately, however, meagre budgets and the unwillingness of the public and most foster parents to rethink their relations with youngsters regularly curbed the development of professionalized options. An employment that had always relied on maternalism and women's restricted options could not be readily transformed into a therapeutic practice requiring high levels of professionalism, abstraction, and competitive payment.

In the third millennium, foster parents encountered dilemmas that had no ready remedy. In 2009, Saskatchewan's child advocate found them complaining of having to deal with lies and intimidation rather than respect and cooperation from government officials.[149] Their experiences bore little resemblance to the therapeutic ideals invoked by professionals or to normal family life. As the report noted,

> one foster parent who operates an overcrowded foster home with hired home-help reported that they felt that they were not in a home but an institution, with their role as a foster parent being replaced for that by a Director of a program, responsible for not only the children in their care, but also the management of staff and a program. The Ministry of Social Services needs to stop turning foster homes into de facto "institutions" by endorsing overcrowding and compensating foster parents to hire home-help. If the Ministry wants to create facilities for children, then set them up as such, but regulate them and provide the proper resources and supervision that is required of other child care facilities.[150]

Such findings describe foster parents in crisis, as they try to deal with tragedies that neither altruism nor professionalism can readily handle. Like other mothers and fathers, most could cope with a small number of essentially healthy kids. The world of child protection in Canada has for some time, however, matched that of many disadvantaged households. Too few adults with too few resources have been asked to do too much.

Conclusion

Foster parents act in effect as substitutes not only for original families but also for Canadians' overall capacity to nurture the young. Not surprisingly, they present a contradictory picture. On the one hand, commitment to the daunting task of nurturing injured girls and boys has frequently been apparent. On the other, there is abundant evidence of insufficient emotional and material capacity. Fostering adults face conundrums that are common to many Native and non-Native Canadian households that live precariously. Many routinely expect women to bear the brunt of kin keeping and domestic maintenance. Such highly compromised realities undermine application and persistence in fostering. Not surprisingly, when kids are strangers or far from cultural ideals, relations are especially fragile. Long-term commitments have proven hard to make.

Fundamental to these problems is many Canadians' overall failure to value caring labour. Foster mothers and fathers have been expected to bear burdens that governments and many other citizens have been reluctant to share or adequately reward. Children are not commodities. They require attention from the heart. Their needs cannot be met until citizens acknowledge that caregiving is an exhaustible resource that needs to be nourished and regularly renewed to flourish.

7

"DEAR MOM AND DAD"
Canada's Children

IN 2000, CANADA'S NATIONAL YOUTH IN CARE NETWORK SENT an open letter to Ottawa directed to "Dear Mom and Dad."[1] They took the nation to task. Like other offspring, they challenged the gap between parental claims and everyday reality. This chapter focuses on that story. The picture is again complex. Individual temperaments and actions always matter. It is hard, however, to escape the sense of a recurring nightmare endured by many Canadian youngsters. Good stuff happens in care but far less than it should. As the National Longitudinal Survey of Children and Youth has told all who would listen, these particular daughters and sons of the nation live lives that are far harder than good mothers and fathers would wish.[2]

This chapter explores this story in six stages. It begins with uncertainty, namely the actual numbers and characteristics of the children involved. It next explores the legacy of disadvantage with which they have entered government care, and how this has often been further compounded by abuse and unmet needs while under supposed state protection. The third part turns to what happens after care or when they "age out" of the system. The fourth considers continuing relations with original families and communities. The next section acknowledges the reality of rescue but points out the recurring problem of stigma. The final part of this chapter considers the resistance and courage demonstrated by foster kids.

A Medium-Sized Town

In 1980, Philip Hepworth published his invaluable *Foster Care and Adoption*, and Patrick Johnston followed three years later with his equally important *Native Children and the Child Welfare System*.[3] These volumes supply the authoritative benchmark with regard to descriptions of the population in care until the 1980s. Both conclude, as has every scholar in the field, that the numbers and traits of youngsters have always been uncertain. Even at the beginning of the twenty-first century, precision remains impossible. Jurisdictions have different reporting bodies, shifting criteria for assessment, agencies uninterested in, or overwhelmed by, statistics, changing diagnostic standards, and limited or nonexistent provision for information storage. Sometimes the little that was collected has not survived. And these are only the problems with the official documentation. At the grassroots, families and children in crisis and the social workers and others who deal with them may well be missing critical information, be too preoccupied to collect or to share it, and lack the words or the confidence to describe experiences. The commonplace stigma of involvement with child protection further obscures reporting. Only as Canadian First Nations tackled the apprehension of youngsters has a personal history of fostering occasioned much more than embarrassment or shame. Native champions have very properly made it an inspiration for redress and reform. Full disclosure of the situation facing Canada's children is the necessary first step in securing justice.

Contemporary examples demonstrate the persisting shortfall in information, without which good planning is undermined. Race, sexuality, and (dis)ability remain contested categories. Claims of status according to the *Indian Act* and actual ancestry have many different meanings. Lesbian, gay, and bisexual Canadians are not new but naming them is. Mental and physical conditions may be ignored, unknown, or variously diagnosed, depending on the presence, capacity, and interest of observers. Meaning is also highly dependent on related social trends. Two examples point to the difficulty of judging what we seem to see: more state wards in general or their origins in particular backgrounds may reflect a greater tendency to apprehension, worsening domestic situations, or larger birth cohorts. Fewer babies in care may reflect rising rates of abortion, adoption, retention, or mortality. In other words, generalizations based on statistics must be made with care.

Keeping such complications in mind, the population of young Canadians in care from the nineteenth to the twenty-first century can nevertheless be broadly described. In any period, its numbers have corresponded more or less to those of a medium-sized Canadian town of the day, and its residents have likewise often been highly transient. Many more girls and boys spent periods in

care than official records ever captured. During the 1930s, some 40,000 youngsters were reported as receiving institutional and foster care, but many more
would have come and gone over the decade. Overall, the reported levels have
stayed about the same, with fewer in institutions, until about 1959 when totals
reached nearly 50,000. The post–Second World War baby boom occasioned a
sharp increase to 83,279 in 1967, and by the end of that decade 98,379 youngsters lived in various forms of state-supported care. By 1977, numbers fell to
78,392 with relatively good times, social security programs, and falling fertility
rates all having a role to play.[4] From the 1960s to the 1980s, foster homes were
credited with accommodating some 68 to 80 percent of the in-care population.[5] As child protection authorities struggled to sustain first families and the
baby boom group aged out, overall numbers, with the conspicuous exception of
youngsters with First Nations heritage, dropped to less than 50,000 in the mid-
1990s. By the start of the new millennium, however, they were once again
mounting to some 60,000.[6] Two years later, the Child Welfare League estimated
that some 75,000 children and youth, or about 1 percent of Canadians aged
nineteen and under were state wards.[7] In 2007, the number was close to 80,000.[8]
Just as in the past, this figure, more or less the size of towns such as Drummondville, Kawartha Lakes, or Grande Prairie and significantly larger than
Charlottetown, Brandon, or Penticton in 2006, deserves the close attention of
all Canadians.

Ethnicity and race have been key in determining which children do not
reside with birth families. Certain broad trends are again obvious. Native, Black,
and Asian children rarely appeared in public care before 1960. Throughout the
decades covered by this volume, most kids have been European in origin. Part
of the racial mainstream, they were considered most worthy of rescue. Only in
the last decades of the twentieth century have the caseloads changed significantly.
In 2005–6, Toronto, in which "55% of families and 60% of the 3,326
children/youth served in foster or residential" care self-identified "as members
of a minority culture or race," supplied the new Canadian reality.[9] Boys and
girls with Aboriginal ancestry were the most regularly overrepresented. While
they constituted, for example, a mere twenty-nine of the 3,433 youngsters in care
in British Columbia in 1955, the "sixties scoop" quickly changed the story. In
1961–62, the province had 3,000 "registered Indian children in care"; in
1966–67, it had 3,637; in 1971–72, it had 5,531; and in 1976–77, it had 5,336.[10]
Across the country, the Aboriginal proportion of overall numbers has varied
widely. The 1996 report of the Royal Commission on Aboriginal Peoples cited
1981–82 figures, ranging from "a low of 2.6 per cent in Quebec to a high of 63
per cent in Saskatchewan." In general, official rates were lower in the Maritimes and higher in the western provinces and northern territories. They also

differed within individual jurisdictions—parts of northern Ontario credited some 85 percent of those in care with Native origins, while the province as a whole recorded only 7.7 percent.[11] In 1998, 25 percent of all girls and boys admitted to the Canadian child welfare system were Aboriginal.[12] In 2006, the Assembly of First Nations claimed more than 27,000 youngsters in care in Canada, more than were enrolled in the residential schools at their height.[13] Using various definitions of "in care" and "Aboriginal," early twenty-first-century estimates range between 30 and 40 percent of all children in care.[14] While very far from a majority of Aboriginal offspring, most of whom, like other Canadians, reside with birth parents, they alone constitute the equivalent of a small Canadian municipality.

The size of the population with disabilities or "special needs" is similarly uncertain but significant. Since early in the nineteenth century, commentators have identified dependent youngsters with impairments in body and mind. Poverty, with its results in untreated illness and disability, has supplied the obvious common denominator. Michael Reid sums up the fundamental problem in his assessment of the wards of Ontario's Brantford Children's Aid Society between 1894 and 1906: "Their parents were too poor to take care of them."[15] Over the course of the twentieth century, observations of disabilities became steadily more detailed. Modern calculations regularly indicate rising levels from "30–40% in the 1970s–1980s to 48–80% in the mid-1990s."[16]

Once again, calculations need to be placed in context. Definitions and diagnoses are chronically uncertain and subject to reconsideration. Recurring evidence also suggests that those with disabilities face significantly "greater risk for maltreatment" and "involvement with child protection systems."[17] A review of "shaken baby syndrome" cases in Canada at the end of the twentieth century, for example, revealed 42 percent had been taken into foster care after their discharge from hospital. They joined many others whom modern sciences now identified as suffering "serious neurological and developmental consequences including profound mental retardation, spastic quadriparesis or severe motor function impairment."[18] In the past, many such youngsters would have died without attracting attention much beyond the immediate family. In 2004, one-third of Manitoba's children in care were reckoned to suffer a disability; 60 percent were boys and just over two-thirds were First Nations. Fetal alcohol syndrome was diagnosed in just over one-third of the group, and it was suspected in slightly more than half.[19] The persisting connection of impairments to economic distress is again readily apparent. Canada's National Longitudinal Survey of Children and Youth found that "the odds of a child having a behaviour problem decrease by about 1 percent for every $10,000 increase in income."[20]

Other conditions also created prejudice and vulnerability. Canada has always had a significant prison population, and this number has been closely associated with child welfare. Many inmates have been its alumnae. Many too have had offspring in care but

> no Province or Territory in Canada keeps any statistics on the number of children under guardianship care that have a parent in prison. No Province or Territory officially recognizes the problems for children related to parental incarceration nor do any recognize that the child of an incarcerated parent is at increased risk of criminal justice involvement or provide any training for social workers regarding the risk profile for these children.[21]

There is, however, plenty of scattered evidence about this group. In 1911, the notorious Angelina Napolitano saw her four youngsters placed by an Ontario Children's Aid Society after she murdered her battering husband.[22] Her predicament was far from unique. Male prisoners could anticipate female partners looking after their offspring; mothers far more frequently resorted to relatives, neighbours, and, ultimately, child protection. In 1979, Alice Parizeau's study of Quebec prisoners told such a story. In her sample, "les enfants des prisonniers vivent généralement avec leur mère ou les concubines," unless illness put them out of commission. In stark contrast, female prisoners saw 36.37 percent of their offspring in group, foster, or adoptive homes and a further 20 percent with neighbours or kin. A significant group was also old enough to be independent. Only 25.45 percent lived with fathers.[23] Few authorities have ever made much effort to serve such vulnerable girls and boys. No wonder Parizeau noted that many prisoners had spent part of their own youth in care.

When it comes to describing crown wards, little is known about the precise role of gender and age. In-care numbers reflect the fact that young charges have been variously in demand for their labour, regarded as variously difficult or easy to manage and adoptable. Boys have appeared somewhat less likely to be retained in original or foster families and more often directed to institutions. The absence of effective fathers has seemed especially important. Single mothers have been regularly reported as needing special help with sons, while relations with daughters have seemed somewhat more manageable.[24] Girls have generally been more readily useful in straitened domestic economies and sometimes more compliant. Kin and non-kin seem to have found many girls easier to keep. On the other hand, their sexual abuse and, sometimes, promiscuity made them additionally vulnerable and attracted scrutiny less often directed to similarly situated boys. Inappropriate sexual knowledge, including incest, brought many more girls into care. Such was the case with teenage Priscilla who suffered "recurring rages and depressions" in Ontario in the 1940s.[25] In their encounters with child protection systems, both sexes have been likely to be set on paths to becoming the next generation of mothers and fathers who could not keep their sons and daughters.

Age has mattered a good deal in shaping experience. Children and youth have entered and departed state custody from birth to legal maturity. Always at least potentially fragile, infants and toddlers have represented special challenges to parents and particularly so to those with few material and human resources. In the nineteenth and early twentieth centuries, agencies were often loath to accept the very youngest. As commercial baby formulas, better control of disease, and an optimistic environmentalism changed brutal calculations, infants and babies increasingly appeared briefly in state care. Most readily headed towards adoptive parents and only returned to public notice if those relations collapsed. Older children often entered care once problems of neglect or abuse became visible in schools and other public settings that increasingly characterized modern life. One unanticipated result of social work efforts to shore up original households in the later twentieth century was the greater appearance of older, sometimes more severely damaged, youngsters who were also more bound to original parents. Over time, teenagers supplied larger proportions of provincial and territorial caseloads. They proved especially suspicious of adults and less inclined to accept the discipline of strange families.

Since the capacity to parent easily diminishes with every extra mouth to feed, state wards have also often been part of sibling groups. This information also has never been systematically recorded. Many brothers and sisters, including twins, have been split up, sometimes by great distances. The reasons for separation have been diverse—not all siblings may enter care; ages, sex, or perceived problems may be regarded as requiring different settings; and few foster homes have been equipped to take larger groups. As the British immigrant children from the nineteenth and twentieth centuries have remembered, the separation of siblings has frequently proved a special hardship. The new millennium has continued both the breakups and the importance of such relations. A study of BC youth who had aged out of care found "a solid majority (74–82 percent)" who felt connected with siblings whatever the separations they had experienced.[26]

In short, foster children have never been homogeneous. They have demonstrated diverse characteristics and abilities. In this respect, they are very normal. They are also products of a situation that has been "normal" since the nineteenth century—girls and boys have entered care suffering far more physical, mental, and social disabilities than their age group as a whole. Many are malnourished, inappropriately dressed, and badly housed, and their educational and health needs have rarely been met. They are only too likely to be born underweight, premature, with worrying indications of future problems to young mothers and to parents with few resources and often facing significant social barriers to success. Over-stressed and angry adults, domestic violence, and frequent community despair have set them up for future hardship. As one observer noted, "one reason why foster children are so difficult to manage is that they don't become wards of the government until a succession of awful things has happened to them."[27] "Family chaos, conflict, and inconsistency" produce youngsters who, as a sympathetic psychiatrist concluded, often regard themselves "as unlovable and deserving of rejection.[28] This outcome is frequently consistent with what had occurred to their parents, many of whom shared comparable histories of pain.

Disadvantage Compounded

Youngsters commonly arrive in care scarred, scared, sad, and angry. Many have good reason not to trust adults, perhaps especially those they have loved. Many are nevertheless deeply attached to kin and sometimes understand their predicament or even blame themselves for their troubles. Many are not easy to transplant nor readily appealing to unrelated adults. Fostering and apprehension by child welfare agencies nevertheless promises to improve situations. Conditions and ailments can be diagnosed, sometimes for the first time, and addressed. Basic security and safety can be improved. As one male and Native alumnus of prairie child protection efforts in the 1960s remembered, "it was safety—number one … It made me feel safe, right, because there was no drinking involved. There was no violence … cause it was a lot better than the life I was living in the community."[29] Real benefits did not, however, easily dissolve pain. Gil Cardinal, a Métis veteran of a generally positive experience of fostering in 1950s and 1960s Alberta regretted his transformation into "a little brown white man" who was suspicious of Indians.[30]

Prejudice regularly worsened outcomes. Those people racialized as inferior encountered daily slights before and after their entry into the child welfare system. The persistent lack of racial matches between youngsters and host families added to the potential for misunderstanding and mistreatment. In 1931, the Ontario superintendent for child welfare concluded unhappily that it was hard enough to get "good foster homes for children of Anglo-Saxon race but when it comes to mixed nationality, especially where there is half Chinese or half negro blood, the difficulties become infinitely greater."[31] Racialized youngsters have been especially vulnerable to the insecurities of foster care. Georges Thurston (1951–2007), the son of a White Québécoise and Black American and best known as the Quebec singer "Boule noire," initially found a happy refuge, but this home fell apart with the serious illness of his foster mother. He then drifted, like many of his counterparts, among various settings. Labelled a "problem," he ended up in reform school. Music rescued him, but poor starts in life kept salvation unlikely for many more.[32]

At the beginning of the 1960s, one Vancouver journalist identified just the sort of injuries that could linger: "Billy is an example of an unwanted child. He is part Indian, son of an unmarried mother and in his 13 short months of life has been shunted around in four foster homes. He is irritable, cranky, won't eat, is afraid of strangers, whines all the time, and nothing is right in his world."[33] In the 1980s, a twenty-nine-year-old Native woman described her own history of traumatization. Her parents' early death precipitated entry into a residential school that denied her religion and culture. Vacations spent with her grandmother offered little help. As she recalled,

> I never felt too protected there. One of my aunts used to beat me brutally and her husband was always trying to molest me. Because I was adopted, I felt a bit like Cinderella. I didn't have nobody to look after me. I didn't belong to anybody. I think I was abused a lot just for amusement and also so that the older ones wouldn't have to do any work. I got to be very tough.[34]

At twelve, she gave up on home and school and discovered drugs. Her grandmother had her charged with "unmanageability," and she entered child protection. When she summed up her life, she confessed:

> The problem is I felt like I didn't belong all the time when I was a kid and I still feel that way today. Like I'm an alien, an outsider ... I'm not white, but I don't feel Indian, and I don't feel accepted by the Indian people here either. I know I'm Indian by race and blood, but I don't know much about my culture ... I'd like to learn about it.[35]

Prejudice similarly undermined the reception of non-Aboriginal youngsters who looked or behaved other than what was considered normal. As Michael Reid has pointed out, Ontario's early Children's Aid Societies regularly devalued those "with disabilities. The reality that such children were hard to market to foster parents often combined cruelly with child savers' own attitudes that such children were secondary to the CAS project of regenerating the nation."[36] As he concluded, "if the child savers believed that a child had an incurable flaw, then they could not imagine the child in their future Canada, which they implicitly assumed would be populated by unmarked, able citizens.[37] The rise of eugenic thinking in the first half of the twentieth century made life immeasurably more difficult. Kids with perceived disabilities were very likely to be hidden away in institutions and in natal homes.

Canada's centennial year offered one observer the opportunity to sum up the recurring lack of welcome:

Because they are disturbed or retarded or physically disabled, or of a minority race or religion, or just too "old," they are not the kind of children a normal family welcomes easily. Some of the children themselves rejected for years would now recoil from a close family. They are, to our disgrace, the children nobody wants.[38]

Rejections have been deeply felt. A boy from southwestern Ontario captured possible outcomes. Turned away by a series of surrogate parents, he began to inhabit a fantasy world in which he was a dog who "pretended to be very loving, and was 'adopted' by loving owners." His behaviour, however, soon disappointed, and he was returned to the kennel. This cycle was endlessly repeated.[39] Such feelings haunted the nation's unwanted as the sad tales told in the documentary films *Richard Cardinal: Cry from a Diary of a Métis Child* and *Wards of the Crown* attest.

Ironically, early child savers intended foster families to do much better than institutions in supplying a sense of stability and inclusion. For some youngsters, this clearly worked as with Gil Cardinal who grew up with one family, the Wilsons. When he sought his birth kin, he could still conclude: "I belong to two realities. I have two mothers, two families, two cultures."[40] The uncertain needs and abilities of both private households and youngsters, however, have always made fits uncertain. While children born outside of Canada, such as young Jewish and Hungarian refugees after the Second World War, found resettlement especially difficult, youngsters everywhere wrestled with impermanency and instability and associated alienation. Foster parents might well aggravate pre-care problems and "thereby increase the risk of placement failure."[41] Modern social workers identified "drift" through multiple placements as a running sore. As Ontario's Sparrow Lake Alliance Children in Limbo Task Force concluded, children repeatedly learned the lesson of adult abandonment.[42] In 2009, Saskatchewan's child advocate heard about a three-year-old "who had been to so many homes that she did not want to go in the car to the zoo because she was afraid that if she left the house that she might be moving."[43] Not surprisingly, many boys and girls sought to protect themselves by avoiding attachment. In their turn, they then became less likely to be successful parents.

Lessons in surrogate households sometimes included instruction in further neglect and abuse. As is the case with first families, the precise extent of such failings is unknown. Youngsters were always, however, vulnerable. Even religious respectability and modern kin care programs have not prevented mistreatment and indifference. Limited state support for room and board, not to mention therapies and supports, has often strained surrogates in much the same ways as their predecessors. A British Columbia case that was heard before the

Supreme Court of Canada illustrates the dangers. In the 1960s, a mother desperate to save her four sons from a violent father committed them to child protection and, ultimately, to two sets of new parents. Decades later, the Court agreed that "the children suffered abuse in both foster homes. Instead of being treated as family members and shown love and trust, they were subjected to harsh and arbitrary disciplinary measures. They were blamed for things they did not do, humiliated in front of each other, and made to feel worthless." Despite warnings, overwhelmed social workers provided little supervision since few foster parents were willing to accept such sibling groups.[44]

Although it is often difficult to distinguish previous injuries from what occurs after apprehension, the title of a research study by a former ward, "'We Get a Life Sentence,'" has often appeared only too true.[45] The conclusions of the provincial children's advocate regarding foster homes in Saskatoon in 2009 were terribly familiar. They were blamed for rampant "head banging," "hoarding," "non-stop" eating, "speech delay," "motor delay," "increased aggression," "decreased impulse control," and "attention deficit disorder." While damage preceded the move to state care, worsened conditions were deemed "more likely due to the child's ongoing needs for attachment being denied in their overcrowded foster home."[46] Youngsters who, in contrast, sat quietly had simply given up.

Many child welfare workers have long tried to prevent such outcomes. By the 1940s and 1950s, they had turned to child guidance clinics and techniques of psychology and psychiatry to obtain better results. In the following decades, some youngsters were directed to individual and group psychiatric and psychotropic therapies. Modern agencies such as the Vancouver Children's Aid Society have deployed psychiatrists, disability specialists, psychologists, social workers, and foster parents in programs of psychiatric consultations. Individual treatments, generally however, have proven more expensive and time-consuming than governments were prepared to support. One 1974 assessment was typically bleak:

> Recommendations were often not carried out because of lack of facilities (35 percent), specifically, lack of closed therapeutic, adolescent psychiatric, and appropriate detoxification units. The next commonest reason was lack of motivation on the part of the child (31 percent) or the foster parents (11 percent) in pursuing treatment or accepting the treatment recommended. Six percent of the children ran away, and occasionally the board interfered with the carrying out of recommendations.[47]

The shortfall continued despite the diagnosis of 75 percent of youngsters with "moderate or severe character disorders which were complicated by delinquent behavioural patterns." Many potential patients ultimately became runaways and drug abusers, in patterns that were familiar across the nation.[48]

The last decades of the twentieth century saw growing pessimism about the possibilities of many counselling-based therapies.[49] In the context of insufficient, often worsening resources and caseloads involving "more severe precare experiences than those entering care a generation ago," drugs moved to the forefront.[50] By the 1980s, "the extensive use of child psychopharmacologic treatments without adequate documentation in the medical literature became commonplace."[51] In 2007, an estimated 47 percent of Ontario's crown wards took medication for "depression, attention deficit disorder, anxiety and other mental-health problems." Much consumption was improperly supervised, left the responsibility of "often low-paid, inexperienced staff working in privately owned, loosely regulated group homes and to overburdened caseworkers legally bound to visit their charges only once every three months." Not surprisingly, many foster children turned to self-medication on and off the street.[52]

Since the vast majority of Canada's experts have been White and trained in mainstream methods, their efficacy could well be limited. Psychiatrists and psychologists found it especially difficult to help Native youngsters. Dr. Clare C. Brant, a Mohawk and Canada's first psychiatrist of Native origin, explained that his professional colleagues found such clients "passive, difficult to assess, and not forthcoming. This behaviour, which affects the individual Native child's attitude and performance in an assessment situation, is understandable in view of the child's cultural background." Ignorance readily resulted in the "overuse of antidepressants and the all too frequent diagnosis of "personality disorders."[53] Such labelling and the search for acquiescence resemble in both perspective and intent the persisting response to the offspring of racial majority but nevertheless "dangerous" classes.

Working-class kids had long revealed troubles communicating with middle-class experts. Take, for example, bedwetting or enuresis, which is a frequent expression of fear and anxiety. In the past, it was readily interpreted as a sign of moral turpitude and genetic inferiority in European-origin populations. In dealing with expressions of disagreement and unhappiness that they could not understand, mainstream institutions readily resorted to pathologizing and sedating the deviant and the non-compliant.[54] As Joan Sangster has observed in her investigations of judgments of delinquent girls, the vast majority of whom were working class and/or Native, few adults were prepared to take incest, sexual abuse, or desires for freedom seriously.[55] Results were predictable. As one teen explained of her resort to violence and theft, "I just was angry at everything. Nothing was going right. I felt I'd never achieve anything—so what the hell. What am I doing here?"[56]

Schools sometimes offered escape. Lucky youngsters found that study, teachers, and other pupils provided a critical counterweight of stability and safety. One
individual remembered: "School was the most consistent thing in my life. I moved
around a lot and I went to nine different elementary schools. But I always knew
that my teacher was going to be there when I got there every morning and I don't
have that at home."[57] Understandable temptations to act out or to retreat had
academic consequences. Ultimately, positive educational outcomes remained
rare. Very typically, only one of the four youngsters profiled in the 2007 documentary *Wards of the Crown* found solace and a future in schooling.

Older youngsters entering care commonly suffered prior histories of disrupted education.[58] It was particularly hard for them to settle in environments
that were dependent on skills of sitting, listening, and study for which they were
ill prepared. For many years, households taking children also routinely kept
them home to work. As old traditions of pauper apprenticeship demonstrated,
labour was generally regarded as a proper part of growing up for everyone but
especially for non-kin residents. Many juvenile immigrants to Canada before and
after the First World War found expectations for time away from chores unmet.
As child protection officials knew during the Great Depression and other times
as well "if a girl was not going to help scrub the floors, many households did not
want her."[59] In rural and remote homes, children were especially likely to see little of classrooms. As one remembered, "I was supposed to go to school every winter. No. Never sent to school, or to church or Sunday school."[60] In many
instances, their labour freed the natural offspring for education and its promise of upward mobility.[61] Preceding disadvantage became a rationalization for further absence from the classroom—kids in care had lost or were incapable of
the "habits" of literacy and numeracy, and they could never catch up. Few fostering adults had the skills or the inclination to organize the homework assistance that benefited so many middle-class offspring. Remedial help in addressing
the common problems of "emotional and behavioural development" that needed
to be sorted out if academic potential was to be realized was likely to be less than
what was needed and often entirely absent.[62]

By the end of the twentieth century, scholarly studies confirmed decades
of anecdotal evidence: "Children in foster care consistently perform below the
national average for their age group, even when they are in long-term placements,
and they are at greater risk of dropping out."[63] A 2002 report located 36 percent of children in care in special education programs as compared to only 5 percent in the general student population. By Grade 10, almost 25 percent of those
in care, but only 4 percent of others, appeared in alternative classes. By Grades
10 and 12, almost 50 percent in comparison with 22 percent and 35 percent
respectively of their peers, were behind a grade for their age.[64] In 2007, only 21

percent of British Columbia's wards graduated from Grade 12 in the standard time unlike 79 percent of the overall student population.[65]

Over the twentieth and twenty-first centuries, undereducated youngsters fell further behind. While initiatives such as BC's Youth Education and Assistance Fund (or Public Guardian and Trustee Education and Assistance Fund) promised post-secondary bursaries to high school graduates, small sums hardly addressed the breadth and depth of deprivation or the real costs of prolonged schooling.[66] Unlike other offspring, those in care could not "boomerang" home. They would not be subsidized to save, enjoy life, or return to school like the 32 percent of adults aged twenty to twenty-nine in 1986 and the "60.3 percent of Canadian young adults aged 20–24 and 26 percent of those aged 25–29 [who] were living in a parental home" at the dawn of the new millennium.[67] Modern "preparation for independence" programs begun by provincial and territorial agencies did little to confront long-standing inequality.[68] Right from the beginning, "for youth leaving care, entry into adulthood is more akin to an 'expulsion' than a transition."[69] Nor surprisingly, veterans of fostering stress the importance of ongoing and sufficient support for post-secondary education.

Outcomes

A 1980s graduate of Canada's child protection system summed up the recurring predicament of kids leaving care in one well-chosen phrase: "To Be on Our Own with No Direction from Home."[70] In the last years of the twentieth century, foster and group homes generated homeless youth in familiar patterns. In 1993, some 40–60 percent of youngsters on Calgary streets had been, or were, provincial wards. Among them was "half Cree" Rich, one of eight siblings "spread around in foster homes." His mum died when he was three, and he fell victim to sexual and physical abuse. Then there was Phil, born to an unwed seventeen-year-old who struggled to keep him. She ultimately surrendered him for adoption, but he ended up in foster and group homes.[71] A few years later, Toronto's Covenant House found that 51 percent of street kids were veterans of state care.[72] In 2007, in the aftermath of the murder of dozens of women in the Vancouver Downtown Eastside, an investigation commissioned by the BC Federation of Foster Parents Associations estimated that "65 percent of people who live on the street are former kids in care."[73]

As the BC killings demonstrated, street life constitutes a special threat for girls. Beatrice Culleton's bestselling In Search of April Raintree (1983) drew on her family history of fostering and the deaths of her sisters to depict the dangers. Cheryl, the younger of the Métis siblings at the centre of the story, succumbed to Winnipeg's mean streets in the 1960s, while April only narrowly escaped.

Another successful autobiography, *Runaway: Diary of a Street Kid* (1989), describes the same search for acceptance and vulnerability to predators. The escape of this teenager, Evelyn Lau, was eventually aided by social assistance. Very importantly as well, Lau, unlike the Manitoba young women, did not have to deal with a family history of residential schools. Disaster was always more common on the streets than was fame and fortune. In 2009, the non-governmental organization Justice for Girls described the representative "Zara" living in Downtown Eastside. She had suffered childhood sexual abuse and school bullying. Full of rage, she readily resorted to knives and her mother found her unmanageable. She was moved to a group home and then to various foster homes. Claiming to feel like nothing more than a "paycheque," she sought refuge in public spaces and couch surfing. A twenty-five-year-old man got her hooked on heroin at age fifteen. Her future looked typically all too grim.[74]

The descent of youngsters through more and more desperate situations has often accompanied the move from foster to group care. One young woman made the connection explicit in a complaint to the Ontario children's advocate:

> I feel I have been living in limbo since my arrival [at this group home]. My experience so far has been one of uncertainty and confinement which has fostered violent behaviour from me and some of my co-residents. I feel that the spirit of the youth offender still lingers in these halls. As a resident I have been threatened by calls to be locked in my room and have witnessed other residents being shipped off during the night. I feel that these experiences have fed our perception of being held in prison. We feel as if we are constantly being watched, bedrooms feel like holding cells ... I would like small things like having my hygiene products in the bathroom as I would at home, a cozy bedroom decorated to my liking with my personal belongings but most of all an environment we can call home temporarily.[75]

In *Wards of the Crown*, the conclusion of eighteen-year-old Emily, a veteran of multiple placements, that "love is inappropriate in a group home" summed up the emotional costs. Modern youngsters nevertheless regularly get transferred to congregate residences, just as they previously ended up in reformatories and industrial schools, because surrogate parents could not cope. By this time, the overall prognosis has generally deteriorated as well.[76]

For many, the next step has led to the courts. In 1974, Aboriginal scholar Don McCaskill reported that over 50 percent of Native youth offenders in Ontario reformatories had experienced placements in White foster homes. This especially estranged group demonstrated "limited knowledge and participation in Indian affairs, a low degree of Indian culture and a great sense of alienation from the mainstream society."[77] As the "sixties scoop" aged, growing numbers of adult offenders revealed the same pattern. While vastly overrepresented,

Natives were never alone in this background. In 1979, Alice Parizeau surveyed male and female prisoners in Quebec jails and fostering, either as children or as parents, trailed through lives gone wrong.[78] A later west-coast study, entitled "Promoting Positive Outcomes for Youth from Care," made familiar connections: "Within 2.5 years after leaving [care]: 85 percent had been charged with a crime; 38 percent had been diagnosed with depression; and 41 percent reported using marijuana at least a few times per week."[79] A veteran of the system summed up a common sequence of events:

> If you were interested in creating a criminal you would have a pretty good chance if you took a young person from a seriously troubled home, put them into a series of foster and group homes, changed their primary worker on a regular basis, let them run away from "home" at an early age, allowed them to drop out of school and enabled them to develop a drug and/or alcohol addiction. Your chances would improve if, somewhere in their lonely and painful existence, they had been sexually, physically or emotionally abused. If in those few instances that they sought help you would ensure that there were no accessible services, that the workers they encountered were rushed and overwhelmed by heavy caseloads, and that they would be seen first and foremost as trouble rather than troubled, is it surprising that these young people would become perpetrators or victims of crime?[80]

Like pupils from residential schools, graduates of child welfare were also likely, whatever their racial background, to become the parents of another vulnerable generation.

Recurring hardship heightened mortality. Deaths in care or subsequently, whether by suicide, neglect, accident, or murder, are rare. They are, however, far more frequent than in the general population and are often avoidable. Such was clearly true of a Barnardo boy murdered after much abuse by a male householder in 1895.[81] A pattern of preventable mistreatment similarly preceded the 2001 death in care of First Nations toddler Savannah Hall in Prince George. Six years later, a BC inquest judged it as homicide.[82] By the end of the twentieth century, growing observation of self-mutilation signalled the recurring desperation of older youngsters in particular.[83] A few wards have also died by their own hands. Richard Cardinal, a seventeen-year-old, killed himself in 1984 after moving through more than two dozen Alberta child welfare placements. In 2005, fourteen-year-old Tracia Owen of Winnipeg, the survivor of sixty-four moves, drug use, and prostitution, hung herself. Like Richard, she saw no end to despair.[84]

In 2003, John Dunn, a child-in-care veteran of Ontario, instituted 6 October as "Victims of Child Welfare Memorial Day" to commemorate such recurring suffering. In 1972, he and three siblings were made wards of the Crown. From aged eighteen months to eighteen years, he moved through over a dozen placements. He has demanded that Canadians "remember the innocent foster children who have been killed by the improper use of physical restraints in group homes, to remember those innocent foster children who have committed suicide while under government protection, and to remember those innocent foster children who have died by other means while under government protection." He has also emphasized wider devastation, notably "the natural family members who have committed suicide as a result of the severe trauma of having their children apprehended into government protection." His mother, Mickey McLeod, took her own life at age fifty-six. "Guilt and despair" proved overwhelming when she discovered the abuse that her son had to bear in foster care.[85]

Continuing Relations

Distress in care has encouraged desires to connect with first families, but even the recognition of benefits does not eliminate desires for reconnection. Right from the start of state child protection, original relations, even when they have involved neglect and abuse, have proven extraordinarily resilient. Kin of all types have regularly contacted agencies and ministries about each other's fate. Much to the chagrin of would-be rescuers, some 16 percent of the Barnardo youngsters who had emigrated to Canadian families returned permanently to Britain in hopes of connecting with their pasts.[86] They were not alone. One boy dispatched by a Scottish philanthropy to New Brunswick described a commonplace sentiment: "My mother is anxious for me to go back home to Glasgow and she wrote and asked me to apply to your department to repatriate me."[87] A major survey of juvenile immigrants brought to Canada in 1910 and 1920 described "pathetic" appeals for "their own people."[88] In 1932, the executive secretary of Montréal's Ladies' Benevolent Society acknowledged the throng of former clients returning to learn of "relatives, lost to them forty, fifty years ago, even brothers and sisters who were with them in the institution but who were allowed to slip away into the outside world without a trace." Even if searchers had made good lives, they sorrowed at losses. One transplant to the United States returned to Montreal for answers and protested when these were not forthcoming:

> I wrote and got an answer that you had no information, but I just refused to believe it, and I have been saving for years to make this trip. I had a mother, and four brothers and sisters, and you let me be adopted out [in fact probably fostered].

I have a lad now ... just reaching manhood, and he needs some background to tie up to.[89]

In 1939, the director of Toronto's Children's Aid Society and a consultant to the League of Nations on child welfare acknowledged such feelings when he reminded audiences that "parents who have given up their children frequently want them back again." Mothers and fathers, he warned, "are not interchangeable."[90] A year later, in a speech before supporters of the Hamilton, Ontario, Boys' Home, he again emphasized the significance of friends and relatives even when they were a

> "blessed nuisance" to those who are chiefly interested in running the institution. The job for them would be very much easier if parents would be wiped out of the picture entirely. However, to those primarily interested in the children themselves, parents and relatives are of the greatest importance. If modern psychology has taught us anything worthwhile, it certainly has taught the importance of a sense of security; and the feeling of really "belonging" in a family group is, without doubt, the greatest possible contributor to that fundamental "security."[91]

Almost two decades later, the Children's Aid Society of New Brunswick's Westmoreland County made the same argument—children remained upset and resentful over the loss of even abusive and negligent parents. At legal majority, most former wards tried to renew relations.[92]

Even youngsters who have expressed gratitude for rescue, admitted sadness about "the breaking up of family ties."[93] Métis filmmaker Gil Cardinal credited an Albertan foster family as making him one of their own when he arrived as a toddler in 1952, but more than three decades later he set off to search for his mother Lucy whom he could not remember.[94] Another individual from British Columbia vividly described sadder memories. Her original home had included "physical, emotional and sexual abuse, an alcoholic mother, an unstable father, and unbelievable poverty." These occasioned moves to foster homes, a reformatory, and an institution for the mentally impaired. Years later, she still had trouble "understanding how I could have felt so angry and hurt and still want to be with her [mother]."[95] As she recalled, the shadow of her first family hobbled fresh starts:

> The foster home wasn't something I could have imagined, because I'd never experienced anything like a real home before. None of us had. It may have been a perfect foster home, but it didn't work for me ... At home we always slept whenever we could, which was usually when the party was over, when my mother passed out and the noise died down. In the foster home we had to put on pyjamas and lie down alone, one to a bed. At home we always slept in our clothes, all together

in one bed. In the foster home we were supposed to brush our teeth but I'd never had a toothbrush. At nine-thirty the lights went out and it was so quiet it was scary. There was no way I could "settle down and get to sleep." At meal time we sat together around a table to eat, something we never did at home, and had prayers before dinner. I'd never done that either. While everyone had their heads bowed, I grabbed bread and whatever food I could reach quickly and put it in my lap. I had no "manners," I didn't know how to have a conversation. Everything they took for granted was new to me.[96]

In *Wards of the Crown*, sixteen-year-old Leah repeatedly sought to live with her mother who had placed her in care at age twelve and who shared her addiction to drugs. Despite the bad news of the relationship for both of them, she could not disengage even as they cycled downward together. Links to the past could be even more destructive. At the beginning of the third millennium, a First Nations child welfare agency found it impossible to wean Manitoba's Tracia Owen from her desire to reconcile with violent and alcoholic parents and a sexually abusive brother.[97]

In the face of such determination, Canadian child welfare authorities increasingly concluded that it was generally preferable to attempt to reform natal families. Their mounting insistence on the collection and retention of detailed case histories reflected, at least in part, a recognition that connections were not readily surrendered. In her study of foster care in mid-twentieth-century Philadelphia, however, Laura Curran has correctly cautioned about over-emphasizing and even romanticizing original kin and the links to them.[98] Some boys and girls have desperately desired to escape chaotic and violent early histories. This is very much the story of the now generally well educated and happily settled Native foster care veterans interviewed by Cheryl Swidrovich.[99] Some had been terrified by any prospect of reunion. Some remained furious about the failures of their first parents. The young unwed mothers who refused to let their babies be returned to Native communities were not alone in rejecting contact. As a community panel in British Columbia in the 1990s more generally observed as well, some boys and girls

grew up angry, blaming their parents for not providing for them. Going to school without proper clothing or school supplies they were targets of bigotry and discrimination that increased with every year of their young lives. And, worse of all, they said—worse than the deprivation and discrimination and the thousand and one other injuries and insults that go with being poor—poverty left them with unshakable feelings of being neglected, unloved and worthless.[100]

When sexual abuse and other assaults occurred, there was plenty of reason to wish to obliterate all associations with the perpetrators.

The Promise and the Predicament of Life in Foster Families

For all of the bad news that makes headlines, diverse outcomes have followed kids after care. Even a disturbing study of Calgary's street kids concluded that most "foster children do in fact succeed while in care."[101] Indeed, their very success makes them difficult to track. Few have wished to draw attention to a stint as one of the state's offspring. In many cases, apprehension constituted rescue from dire straits that they wish to put firmly behind them. It remains of course impossible to know for certain whether life would have been better or worse without intervention. Would their initial circumstances have changed or could preventive measures and programs have been put into place before permanent damage was done? On the other hand, some graduates of so-called intact families recall horrifying and demeaning treatment that dogs them throughout their maturity. Adult survivors of incest, for example, could sometimes only dream of rescue.[102] Child protection sometimes has offered far happier prospects. Even as he began to meet members of his birth family, Gil Cardinal had to conclude that fostering had "probably" been "the best thing for me."[103]

Explanations for success in care are complex. Is it due to something intrinsic in individual children, in their experience with their birth families or communities, or to contacts with social workers, teachers, neighbours, foster families, or even judges or police officers? The search for answers has helped drive the new field of resiliency studies and the "Looking after Children" approach that has preoccupied some child protection workers since the 1990s.[104] Early conclusions affirm multiple influences. Findings from a 2002–3 multi-province study that examined positive experiences in care are worth quoting at length:

Approximately 24% of the young people nominated positive events focusing on activities/events, including playing a sport, participating in clubs, and going to camp or on trips. Similarly, 23% of the young people reported a relationship as being a key positive occurrence, nominating mainly biological family members (11.2%) and to a lesser extent foster family members (5%). Closely related to the relationship category, living in a foster home was flagged as a positive event by a fair number of young people (18%). A smaller proportion specified living in the current placement as a positive life event (8%). Approximately 13% of young people identified education, particularly academic achievements (8%) such as graduating from school, receiving an award for good grades, or attending school (4%), as being a positive occurrence in their lives. An additional 8% of them nominated events reflecting instances of personal growth, such as being in good health (3%), belonging to a religion or possessing a sense of spirituality (1%), or experiencing a life changing event such as, for example, going to prison (3%) [!]. One theme that was identified by young people (6%) as favouring their well-being comprised instances reflecting their coming of age (i.e., a transition to adulthood). Events grouped under this theme included being employed (3%) and acquiring personal possessions such as a bike or a stereo (2%). Finally, about 4% of the positive events cited involved activities with the biological family (2%) or the foster family (1%).[105]

Several implications of these findings seem clear. Obviously striking is their evident normality. Like most kids, those in care treasure activities, relationships, school achievement, and possessions. What also stands out is the significance of biological relations. While this study did not appear to take race into account, the prominence of kin confirms long-standing observations. Finally, the stress on recreational and material pleasures suggests the depth of previous deprivation. Youngsters lived better than they had in economically disadvantaged households, and they understandably prized this improvement.

Some girls and boys obviously found hope and sustenance in new settings. Younger wards in particular have been likely to seek and receive security and affection. Even as they grew to recognize differences between themselves and members of the fostering family, many discovered something better than what they had known. Right from the beginning, some foster parents and their charges developed meaningful, even lifetime, bonds.[106] There were always stories such as the one from a pre–First World War migrant from Birmingham, United Kingdom, who was handed over to a Quebec couple. They turned out to be "real parents." As she remembered decades later,

> they thought as much of me as they did of their own. I went to school until I was 16. Then I stayed at home to help my mom as she wasn't always too well. She passed away in May 1919, and I stayed with dad until I was married in 1923 ... My dad stayed with me until he died in 1933 at the age of 80. I thought as much of them as if they had been my own flesh and blood ... I do not know anything about my parents. I have never been back to England, and I have never had any desire to go.[107]

Such sentiments were not restricted to any single group. Earl Einarson, one of three brothers and a member of the Ktunaxa First Nation, was another veteran of the system who valued a loving fostering mother. His picture book *The Moccasins* fondly depicts her encouragement of a First Nations youngster to take pride in his heritage.[108] In real life, upon the birth of his first child, she gave him the small shoes she had saved to help connect him to his first family. He planned to pass them on to his son.[109] The stories of safety, care, education, and love told to Cheryl Swidrovich by Native women and men who had been adopted and fostered in the 1960s and 1970s repeatedly pointed out how much better life became in care.[110] The encounters of April Raintree with nurturing institutions and foster homes helped insulate, although never entirely shield, her from the trauma and prejudice that eventually overwhelmed her younger sister.

In new families, youngsters sometimes discovered unprecedented kindness and patience. There could be second, third, and even more chances to recuperate and find their way in the world. Early in the new millennium, one young ward from British Columbia, who was accustomed to shoplifting and "kicking holes in walls," found support to move ahead, "thanks to foster parents who finally managed to get through all that anger and resentment. He settled down with one couple in his mid-teens and says they showed him how a 'real' family was supposed to be, how you could feel secure and loved and still have fun."[111] Another success story credited a household that had "welcomed her into their hearts and hearth" from age eleven to twenty-one. She went on to complete two university degrees, get married, and have two babies of her own.[112] Such good news demonstrates that hope need not be abandoned when early starts fail. Caring adults in the service of the state have strengthened many charges.

Even in good situations, foster kids nonetheless wrestle with prejudice. To lack birth parents has readily signalled that something is wrong, whether with you, your kin, or your community. Private business that was not supposed to need explanation was bared to the world in ways that made youngsters feel self-conscious, uncertain, and often ashamed. Like many other child protection authorities, Ontario's child and youth advocate has heard the same sad lament over and over again: "'When someone learns that I am in care, they always ask me, 'What did you do to come into care?' Of course I tell them I did not do anything. Something happened to me.' The stigma of being in care, many say, is terrible."[113]

Such feelings are not new. Early child savers have often encouraged children and fostering adults to be silent about their relations. Young charges have regularly endeavoured to appear as natural products of new households—the use of kin terms, such as auntie or uncle, or even mum and dad, has been commonplace and even encouraged especially for younger girls and boys.[114] One escapee from incest, incompatible foster care, and British Columbia's Woodlands School for the developmentally delayed found rescue with a widow and a teacher whom she fondly called "Aunt Gwen."[115] Such assertions of kinship helped normalize and disguise relations.

Various strategies have evolved to hide history from gossips and critics. In choices that would be familiar to many others, British girls and boys at the completion of their Canadian indentures have often chosen "to change their location, often their names, and even, in some cases, their accent in an effort to lose their identity as "immigrant" or 'Home' children."[116] April Raintree elected another similarly popular remedy to deflect the gaze of strangers: "[As] an excuse for being with the Children's Aid. I told my friends that my parents died in a plane crash."[117] She knew that to be a ward of Canada was to be repeatedly singled out as personally inadequate or the product of inadequate ancestry. While modern youngsters no longer wear the badge of institutional dress that sometimes distinguished inmates of orphanages and other institutions, they are still hard put not to be targeted for opprobrium. The letter to "mom and dad" with which this chapter began pointed out "the embarrassment that I went through with clothing and food vouchers, which broadcast that I was in care. Not being able to have sleep-overs because I lived in a group home."[118]

Resistance and Advocacy

Youthful agency has not been restricted to efforts to normalize what has happened. Child welfare reports have offered repeated glimpses of boys and girls finding allies in improving conditions or in escaping bad situations in original homes and later on as well. Foster kids have also tried to provide their own version of events. Surviving evidence has frequently tended to stress bad times. Those with happy memories often felt little need to tell their stories; they might well settle into lives that looked little different from those of their contemporaries. Native girls and boys in particular may be reluctant to offer observations that in any way call into question the larger horror of colonialism and oppression. Good experiences have also been less likely to appear newsworthy or even to attract scholarly attention.

In any case, the younger the foster children the more difficult it is to recover their stories. The evidence of those of "tender years," commonly under twelve or fourteen years of age, has always been suspect without adult corroboration.[119] Still more prohibitive has been the recurring failure to ask for their opinion. Foster boys and girls have often felt like pawns in the games of others. One survivor typically recollects shifting casually from household to household as a domestic in early twentieth-century Ontario: "No one seemed to have anything to do with where or with whom I lived. I cannot remember anyone ever asking me how I was treated or coming to see me in such a way."[120] Modern child protection promised to address inadequate or absent supervision for both immigrant and native-born youngsters but neglect persisted right into the twenty-first century.

Fostered charges sometimes waited years to let the world know what had happened. In the last decades of the twentieth century, researchers, such as Phyllis Harrison and Joy Parr, offered them unprecedented opportunities to make their case. Their interviews portray youngsters as active agents as well as sometime victims. Many seized occasions to take decisions, whether to go or to stay, sometimes against the advice of authorities. As in Australia, "protests encompassed a range of 'disobedient' behaviours, some more conscious than others. Bad language, unpunctuality, truancy, stealing, telling lies, and absconding are common examples."[121] Suicide and violence directed against themselves and others supplied other solutions.

Some efforts to seize control of lives involved rejection of origins. Take the case, of "Sarah," a Sto:lo foster child, living with a White foster family in British Columbia's Fraser Valley at the start of the twenty-first century. She and her sister had been in care for over a decade when her nation demanded their repatriation. Both took their opposition to the provincial Supreme Court. Their refusal occurred in the context of a public outcry after the September 2002 death of a baby returned by the band child welfare agency to a father with a history of abusive behaviour. Sarah, who had been diagnosed with fetal alcohol syndrome, claimed no interest in her Native heritage or in reunion. After losing in court, she was sent to a Saskatchewan treatment centre as the Sto:lo wished. Eventually, she returned to her White foster parents and to school in British Columbia.[122] The full meaning of such actions are not readily clear. In this instance, choices may well reflect the self-hatred and other damage of colonialism. Sarah's resistance nevertheless also demonstrates that even injured youngsters have their own agendas and that these do not necessarily fit adult priorities.

Over the years, fostered youngsters also combated demeaning treatment by pursuing education and careers and committing to happy marriages and responsible parenting and, as Chapter 6 has indicated, foster parenting. Take, for example, the response of Vancouver's "sports mother of the year" in 2009. By age eleven, she was orphaned, moved first to an aunt's and then to a series of provincial foster homes. She quickly took on part-time jobs and eventually forged a successful life as the hospitality manager for a major hotel and a "soccer" and more single mum to four teenagers.[123] Her achievements appear to be a repudiation of the time she was unwanted.

The decades leading up to the new millennium supplied significant new and long overdue opportunities to hear from kids in care. Social workers grew increasingly conscious that

> for a youth to speak up and make a complaint takes hope and courage. Children and young people come into care for reasons of neglect or abuse, certainly not by their own choice. They speak about the feelings of being removed from their home while in many cases the person whose actions caused them to come into care stays put. They meet worker after worker and move from home to home, despite the sys-

tem's best efforts to maintain continuity and stability. It is not surprising that many of them feel their lives are spinning out of their control. These are conditions rife for hopelessness. Even at the best of times, life in care is not easy.[124]

As such observers have understood, wards needed and deserved a full hearing.

In the 1960s, influenced by the liberation politics of the day, such sympathizers helped set up unprecedented platforms for young voices. In 1967, in a fitting commemoration of the nation's centennial, British Columbia's child welfare ministry assembled teens in care, foster parents, and experts in the provincial capital to learn from one another in planning the future. The youth delegates made a good impression. Their answers to conference questionnaires demonstrated how much they had to offer.

Question: "What have you personally found to be the least helpful part of the child welfare system?"

Answer:

- "lack of communication between myself and affairs concerning myself. My social worker and foster parents would talk things over and reach a conclusion without consulting me ... act of excommunication affected me emotionally";
- "placing you in a home where it is entirely different and meeting new people. You have to adjust to their way of living which most of the time is extremely difficult";
- "the absence of regular meetings with your worker, the changing of social workers without your knowledge and the inability to get in touch with your worker when you want";
- "when you need a doctor or dentist appointment all the red tape you have to go through—and then you end up having to go far away to get there"; and
- "the tendency to forget a child when he is considered to be doing well."

Question: "What have you personally found to be the most difficult to understand part of the overall child welfare programme?"

Answer:

- "no medical plan and the money problems";
- "the system by which the foster parent is able to be compensated from my family allowance account ... I still don't understand why I wasn't consulted even though I was only 13 years old";
- "the welfare program's lack of concern for the opinion and feelings of a child";

- "the constant change of social workers"; and
- "I will first set the scene. A child is living with his mother, is happy, but the income is such that it is impossible to stay. Why instead of giving the welfare amount for child and parent, give the parent the single amount for herself ($75), the amount given the foster parent ($70) and the child's clothing allowance. With a few more dollars earned ($25) this family could live happily without being broken up. This is not allowed. It would be sensational for me. Why can't it be done?"

Question: "What are your suggestions to improve the child welfare programme?"

Answer:
- "It was suggested that a Foster Children's Association be formed. This I think may be too extreme, but it would be a start. I think that the child should be told and shown that he or she may consult his or her social worker in the strictest confidence. Everything said should not be repeated back to the foster parent. The child should have freedom of speech without fear of persecution. Is that not one of the principles of the *democratic* way of life?"

Question: "What have you personally found to be the most helpful part of the child welfare programme?"

Answer:
- "It has kept me out of the slums and provided for my clothing and education";
- "sending me through school, buying my clothes and keeping a roof over my head";
- "giving me a feeling that I'm a person who's important to them—not just a number on a filing card";
- "the right to be able to continue my education"; and
- "I am in a home which I can and have called my own and you can make a mistake without thinking, 'Will I get kicked out?'"

Question: "What else would you like to add?"

Answer:
- "One other thing I feel very strongly about is that after a child has been living since he was small in a foster home, the foster parent should be given full guardianship. Because after a kid is taken out of that foster home when he's older there is never any hope of getting adopted because people never adopt older kids, but they re willing to when the kid is younger,

and then the kid will just end up getting tossed from one home to another—and then his real problems will begin."[125]

In their breadth and their balance, responses movingly summarize the good and bad in fostering up to the 1960s. After that date, observations would not be complete without attention to the impact of colonialism and prejudice on surging numbers of First Nations and Black kids.

In the subsequent decades, Canadians began to learn this additional story. Aboriginal veterans of child welfare did much to help raise the "buckskin curtain" that Cree leader Harold Cardinal coined to characterize mainstream blindness to justice for the First Nations.[126] Poet and activist Duke Redbird, who was born to a Saugeen woman and Métis man on an Ontario reserve in 1937, signalled the personal connection to child apprehension that motivated many activists. After the death of his mother in a house fire, his father could not manage his five children. Like many other parents, he turned to the local Children's Aid Society for help. His offspring were dispersed. While Redbird experienced good and bad foster families, he never recovered from losing his own. In the context of Red Power in the 1960s, self-hatred turned to activism.[127] Like singer Buffy Saint Marie, who was born on a Saskatchewan reserve but grew up adopted in the United States, Redbird's enlistment in Native rights campaigns needs to be understood in the context of Canada's politics of child protection. The same can be said of Chief Wayne Christian, a former foster child, who led the successful crusade of British Columbia's Spallumcheen nation to gain control of child welfare in 1980.[128]

Although much attention has been appropriately focused on Aboriginal activism, the late twentieth century has also brought a burgeoning of organized protest from a range of former foster kids. Two groups—the National Youth in Care Network (NYCN) and the Foster Care Council of Canada (FCCC)—assembled founders and allies, most of whom appear to be of European origin, who were passionate advocates of listening to kids in care. Brian Raychaba and others founded the NYCN in 1985 for those aged fourteen to twenty-four presently or formerly in care. It developed active networks that often worked closely with local child welfare authorities and a strong research program focusing on youth voice and experience. Through bringing youngsters in care into public forums such as the Canadian Child Welfare Research and Policy Symposium, which was first held in Alberta in 1994, it helped ensure that conversations about child protection "include the voices of youth."[129] The similarly non-profit and activist FCCC was created in 2002 by another former ward, John Dunn. Less research oriented than the NYCN and seemingly with much less official support, it appears to concentrate on identifying and mobilizing public and official opinion against violence and abuse within state care.[130]

Nor is modern activism solely the preserve of the normally abled. An obituary in May 2009 recognized a lifetime of commitment to social justice for developmentally delayed Canadians. Bill Van Buren (1953–2009) was an early and outspoken champion of L'Arche, which was founded by Jean Vanier. He was born into an impoverished Toronto family of eight to a mother with mental impairments. At the age of ten, he entered a group home, and his future seemed permanently curtailed. At sixteen, however, he seized the opportunity to help initiate the first North American L'Arche home, Daybreak House in Richmond Hill, Ontario. At his death over four decades later, he was recognized as "a wisecracking artistic, sociable, globe-trotting ambassador for L'Arche."[131] Like other Aboriginal and non-Aboriginal veterans of child welfare, he refused stigma and silencing.

This chapter began with the difficulties of knowing who exactly has been in care in Canada. It ends with the voices and engagement of the sons and daughters of the state. Bravery and determination punctuate a picture of continuing prejudice and disadvantage. Canada's offspring too often enter, experience, and leave public care with little attention to their needs. In particular, the wellspring of tragedy has never been systematically addressed. As the example of imprisoned populations demonstrates only too well, disadvantage in one generation generally begets disadvantage in the next. Just as the rich in Canada are very often the consequence of a circle of inherited options, so too are the kids in care. This history makes their frequent courage all the more remarkable.

CONCLUSION

Canada's fostered girls and boys have always been the offspring of disadvantage. From the nineteenth century to the present, poverty, and unequal relations more generally, has undermined health, fomented discord, and left victims with few of the alternatives that have allowed the better-off and the more powerful to face child rearing's inevitable strains. Although assistance has generally improved over time, state programs have frequently offered little more than a band aid over a chronic wound created in the first instance by lack of good adult jobs, comfortable accommodation, and physical well-being. For the most part, the loss of youngsters has been treated as if it involved little more than personal failure. This hemorrhage has been the special legacy of unequal adult access to resources in Canada as elsewhere. Too often, as Dominique Marshall has concluded in her careful study of the evolution of the Canadian welfare state, "the promotion of the rights of children aided governments by providing an ideological detour around the harsh debates about the welfare of adults."[1]

Families have been generally determined to do well by their offspring, but efforts have been hobbled by crippled abilities to parent and the significant needs of injured girls and boys. The history of kin care, children's institutions, birth parents, foster households, and kids in care generally demonstrates the essential and the highly contingent nature of adult nurture. Without this basic resource, children have failed to thrive, lives have been foreshortened, and entire communities have been endangered. Caregiving, which is so commonly sentimentalized, should never be taken for granted as a natural legacy of bio-logical relations. Mothers and fathers often struggle with personal demons and prevailing circumstances. Would-be substitutes sometimes fare little better. The poor have had few attractive remedies when child rearing goes wrong. The inau-guration of public child welfare programs in the nineteenth century recognized this fundamental reality. Over the ensuing decades, Canadian authorities have endorsed various remedies from fostering to adoption, institutions, and enhanced social security to deal with the young victims. As *Fostering Nation?* has sug-gested, policies and practices, for all their frequent good will, have rarely been equipped to address the root of much distress.

A century and more of Canadian efforts in child protection has revealed ultimately a substantial deficit in care. When it has come to promoting the best interests of the young, the nation has clearly too often failed to deliver. When they have considered the gap between modern ideals of childhood and the actual experience of many young citizens, governments and many Canadians have regularly blamed individuals whom custom and law, ironically enough, have simultaneously encouraged to produce offspring, women for maternal inad-equacy, and entire communities of the poor for incompetence and delinquency. One of Canada's most thoughtful social work scholars, Marilyn Callahan, has provided an effective summation of the damage:

> Child welfare as it is presently constituted does not just ignore the poverty and powerlessness of women and exacerbate these, it also perpetuates the division between public and private realms at the heart of women's inequality and their inability to enjoy full citizenship ... Although pursued through the auspices of a public agency, the work is actually carried out very privately, family by family, woman to woman, confidential case by confidential case, and the work is divided as family work is often divided—women doing the caring; men managing the operations. Instead of seizing the opportunity to make some aspects of private fam-ily needs a public business, a public agency often buries them as deeply as private families do.[2]

This temptation to sidestep the dilemmas faced by women as mothers and social workers reflects an abiding tendency to undervalue caring work and ignore structural inequalities in Canadian life.

Responsibility for children, as for the elderly and others in need of assistance, has routinely been underrated in terms of skill and significance. Female labours in the home and with persons, what Olena Hankivsky has termed women's "perilous project,"[3] have been assumed to properly subsidize public relations, including those in the marketplace, which are presided over by men. Since love was to be its own reward, material reimbursement for such tasks has regularly been meagre. Recurring sentimentalization of caring labour has hobbled child protection in at least three direct ways. First, birth mothers, and fathers too, have received inadequate support; second, foster parents and surrogate households in general have faced the same dilemma; and, third, the social work profession, with its lower ranks overwhelmingly dominated by women, has been undermined and overtaxed in its efforts to assist families.

The individualistic orientation of most explanations for failures in child rearing has left origins too often unaddressed. As one anti-poverty champion, H. Philip Hepworth, concludes in his comprehensive assessment of adoption and fostering in Canada, "governments have had difficulty moving philosophically from a traditional rescue orientation to a more preventive approach."[4] The attraction of rescue was its implication that unpredictable forces and possibly disreputable individuals were at work. Both could be dispatched in an ad hoc fashion without questioning the fundamentals of the nation itself. Social work's own recurring preoccupation with casework solutions, for all their utility in specific instances, has helped direct attention away from structural causes of misfortune.[5] At the dawn of the new millennium, as Paul Kershaw notes, a pervasive neo-liberal policy orientation once again "risks theoretically removing children's well-being from the circumstances of their parents or other guardians."[6]

Observation of recurring tragedies has, in the context of explanations rooted in prejudice, readily worked to encourage preoccupation with morality and biological determinism. This was notably so at the beginning of Canada's experiment with child protection when fostering and related initiatives emerged. Early initiatives emphasized the restoration of responsible masculine oversight as the solution to problematic families. More progressive critics identified women's and workers' unequal access to resources as a problem. The lessons of the Great Depression, the Holocaust, and the post–Second World War civil rights campaigns slowly generated widespread recognition of socially created inequalities and fuelled the uneven expansion of social security programs and support for a guaranteed annual income. For all of their recurring shortfall and the greater surveillance they entailed, benefits such as free public education, medicare, and family allowances have greatly improved life for many families.[7] By the 1970s and 1980s, however, even cautious confrontation with continuing structural inequalities ran into increasing opposition. In the context of budget crises and revived conservatism, pessimism returned with a vengeance. Explanations for child injury, street kids, addiction, and violence readily blamed problematic mothers and communities, notably but never only First Nations, not to mention incompetent social workers and their fellow travellers. The resulting culture of frustration and despair signalled bad news for Canada's most disadvantaged citizens.

Preventive policies and practices admit the reality that prevailing gender, class, and racial arrangements can unreasonably let down citizens. They even raise the possibility that resources and power would have to be at least minimally reconstituted and reallocated if parenting were to be undertaken with dignity and hope. Not surprisingly, prevention has been more readily endorsed in theory than in practice. Children's best interests have suffered as a result. Ninety deaths in care in Ontario in 2007 offered ample reminder of the costs that have been exacted.[8]

By the dawn of the third millennium, Canadian child protection efforts appeared close to the rocks around the country. The expanding gap between rich and poor, mounting caseloads, continuing scandals and tragedies, and savage and sometimes covert attacks on social security everywhere threatened morale and well-being. As Judge Ted Hughes, the author of the BC Child and Youth Review: An Independent Review of BC's Child Protection Services, concluded in 2006: "The strongest impression I have gleaned from this inquiry is one of a child welfare system that has been buffeted by an unmanageable degree of change ... much of this has gone on against a backdrop of significant funding cuts.[9] His words found tragic echo in the damning report on foster care by the Saskatchewan's child advocate in February 2009:

> We reveal merely the tip of the iceberg and that if we were to delve deeper into the provincial foster care system and broader child welfare system, we would find the same symptoms of too few resources, non-compliance with policy, demoralized government staff and community members, and indifferences to the rights and best interests of those children in receipt of child welfare services.[10]

None of this information was new. As the advocate pointed out, the "crisis" had been "raised, criticized and condemned by the Provincial Ombudsman, Children's Advocate and Provincial Auditor for over twenty years."[11] Much the same could be said of every jurisdiction in the country.

Yet, even when disaster appeared ever-present, Canada's children found important champions. Investors in the status quo faced significant opposition over the entire period covered by Fostering Nation? Possibilities for reconsidering policy and practice emerged from many quarters. First, there was many Canadians' mounting embrace of childhood as a distinct life stage in need of special protection and of the succour of girls and boys as a public as well as a private good. Failure to secure the optimal development of young citizens was increasingly understood to threaten the nation's economic and social foundations. Over time, this doctrine slowly extended its embrace to diverse groups of youngsters and increasingly recognized that improving life for parents was the best means of helping children. This perspective treated the welfare of youngsters as a bellwether of the welfare of Canada in general, and it has persisted as a powerful influence.

Right from the beginning, some Canadians have also been inspired by various religious and secular ideologies to challenge disadvantage located in the power of men and dominant classes and races. Even as they emphasized the need for personal reforms in parenting, many reformers agreed that children's ultimate well-being required reorganization of society and governments to meet the needs of a broader spectrum of citizens. Such conclusions drove early initiatives such as workmen's compensation, mothers' allowances, public education, public health, and the introduction of personal taxation. After the Second World War, growing sensitivity to human rights encouraged Canadians to tackle the origins of much disadvantage. Enhanced liberalism helped reveal the extent of disparities originating in gender, class, race, and ability. Social security, adoption, and fostering programs evolved to confer greater entitlement to the benefits of modern childhood on First Nation, non-European, and other marginalized populations. Although Canadians' endorsement of more inclusionary ideals and practices never escaped prejudice, it represented a major advance over many previous views. Pressed by the evolving consensus that governments properly protected citizens in the exercise of parenthood, Ottawa, the provinces, and the territories have improved life for many Canadians.

The extension of mainstream child protection efforts to First Nations youngsters also provided the occasion for significant rethinking of the very sinews of traditional practices. The sheer numbers of Aboriginal girls and boys in care became increasingly impossible to ignore, and the symbolic centrality of Native people to the Canadian story, not to mention their growing visibility in cities, further spotlighted tragedy. More than anything else, the abject failure of Aboriginal inclusion in traditional delivery of services from the 1960s on demonstrated the need for much closer attention to relations of power, beginning with but not limited to those originating in colonialism. The emergence of Native-administered initiatives in child welfare, ranging from band agencies to Aboriginal Head Start programs, suggested the benefit of root and branch reforms. While the federal Conservative government's repudiation of the 2005 Kelowna Accord between Ottawa and the provinces, which had promised to return child welfare fully to Aboriginal communities, was an undeniable setback, colonial practices were increasingly on the defensive. By the end of the first decade of twenty-first century, racism and its injustices were difficult to ignore as central to the vulnerability of so many girls and boys.

Aboriginal challenges to the status quo have not stood alone. In the last decades of the twentieth century, they have occurred alongside, and were often effectively partnered with, feminist, disability rights, and community development critics of social policy. Together with their international counterparts, many Canadian scholars and child protection practitioners have produced broad-ranging condemnations of traditional policies and practices. They have increasingly emphasized the consequences of the refusal to value caring labour properly, the vulnerability of women and children to male violence, the necessity of involving communities in the identification and solution of problems, and the benefits of programs of inclusion and empowerment. They have helped to shift attention from individual failure to collective jeopardy and the need, as Olena Hankivsky has persuasively argued, for an "adequate concept of citizenship" that has the equality of domestic and public contribution at its core.[12] Setbacks, such as failures to gain a guaranteed annual income and national childcare policy, have hurt, but new consciousness and an associated vocabulary that provides more convincing explanations for the child protection tragedy have found audiences across the land.

The appearance of an organized rights' movement among Canadians who have experienced foster care is equally important. Canada's offspring now have platforms to present their own case for a fair deal. Their voices have made it especially difficult to ignore the consequences of poverty and violence in everyday lives. At the beginning of the third millennium, their input is essential for finding ways of moving ahead that offer hope for the future.

Although the collapse of the global economy that began in 2008 seemed far from auspicious, it confirmed the bankruptcy of old ways of proceeding built on entitlement and inequality. While conservative commentators have continued to encourage reactionary agendas that once again scapegoat the vulnerable for child-rearing failures, a generation and more of Canadians have had their consciousness raised and their consciences informed by Natives, feminists, foster care veterans, and other challengers. As never before, a chorus of agreement from children and adults, from amateurs and experts, from Aboriginal and non-Aboriginal citizens has pointed to the paths forward that lie with honouring caregiving and guaranteeing both parents and children the resources with which to maintain dignity and to realize potential. *Fostering Nation?* ultimately takes comfort from the ever-widening recognition that justice for children requires justice for adults as well.

NOTES

Notes to Introduction

1 UN General Assembly, *Convention on the Rights of the Child*, 20 November 1989, United Nations, Treaty Series, vol. 1577, p. 3, available at http://www.unhcr.org/refworld/docid/ 3ae6b38f0.html.

2 UNICEF Canada, *What's Rights for Some 18@18: A Portrait of Canada's First Generation Growing Up under the UN Convention on the Rights of the Child* (Toronto: UNICEF Canada, 2007), 5.

3 See *Aboriginal Children's Health: Leaving No Child Behind: Canadian Supplement to the State of the World's Children 2009* (Toronto: Canadian UNICEF Committee, 2009).

4 Senate of Canada, *Children: The Silenced Citizens: Final Report of the Standing Senate Committee on Human Rights* (Ottawa: Senate of Canada, 2007).

5 Canada, *The Report of the Royal Commission on the Relations of Capital and Labour* (Ottawa: Queen's Printer, 1889); Peter Bryce, *Report on the Indian Schools of Manitoba and the North-West Territories* (Ottawa: Queen's Printer, 1907); Patricia T. Rooke and R.L. Schnell, "Child Welfare in English Canada, 1920–1948," *Social Science Review* 55, no. 3 (September 1981): 484–506; Canada, *The Report of the Special Senate Committee on Poverty: Poverty in Canada* [Croll Report] (Ottawa: Senate of Canada, 1971); Law Commission of Canada, *Institutional Child Abuse—Restoring Dignity: Responding to Child Abuse in Canadian Institutions* (Ottawa: Minister of Public Works and Government Services, 2000).

6 Veronica Strong-Boag, *Finding Families, Finding Ourselves: English Canada Confronts Adoption from the Nineteenth Century to the 1990s* (Toronto: Oxford University Press, 2006).

7 Olena Hankivsky, *Social Policy and the Ethic of Care* (Vancouver: UBC Press, 2004), 1. See also her discussion in Ch. 6 "Caregiving: Reconceptualizing the Public/Private Divide."

8 Paul Kershaw, *Carefair: Rethinking the Responsibilities and Rights of Citizenship* (Vancouver: UBC Press, 2007), 187.
9 Paul Kershaw, Jane Pulkingham and Sylvia Fuller, "Expanding the Subject: Violence, Care, and (In)Active Male Citizenship," *Social Politics: International Studies in Gender, State and Society* 15, no. 2 (Summer 2008): 182–206.
10 See Alvin Finkel, *Social Policy and Practice in Canada: A History* (Waterloo, ON: Wilfrid Laurier University Press, 2006), Chapter 12 for the conservative assault on social security.

Notes to Chapter 1

1 Gordon Darroch, "Families, Fostering, and Flying the Coop: Lessons in Liberal Cultural Formation," in *Household Counts: Canadian Households and Families in 1901*, ed. Eric W. Sager and Peter Baskerville (Toronto: University of Toronto Press, 2007), 198.
2 Deena Shorkey and Barbara Mitchell, "Grandparents Raising Their Grandchildren," in *Child Welfare: Connecting Research, Policy, and Practice*, ed. Kathleen Kufeldt and Brad McKenzie (Waterloo: Wilfrid Laurier University Press, 2003), 1.
3 See Stompin' Tom Connor, *Stompin' Tom: Before the Fame* (Toronto: Penguin, 1995). Like many others, Isabel had eventually to surrender her son to the foster care system.
4 Gordon Darroch, "Home and Away: Patterns of Residence, Schooling, and Work among Children and Never Married Young Adults, Canada, 1871 and 1901," *Journal of Family History* 22, no. 2 (April 2001): 246.
5 Nancy Christie, "A 'Painful Dependence': Female Begging Letters and the Familial Economy of Obligation," in *Mapping the Margins: The Family and Social Discipline in Canada, 1700–1975*, ed. Nancy Christie and Michael Gauvreau (Montreal and Kingston: McGill-Queen's University Press, 2004), 80. See also Françoise Noel, *Family Life and Sociability in Upper and Lower Canada, 1780–1870: A View from Diaries and Family Correspondence* (Montreal and Kingston: McGill-Queen's University Press, 2003).
6 John R. Gillis, *A World of Their Own Making: Myth, Ritual, and the Quest for Family Values* (New York: Basic Books, 1996), 11.
7 Lucy Maud Montgomery, *Anne of Green Gables* (1908).
8 Shurlee Swain, "Sweet Childhood Lost: Idealized Images of Childhood in the British Child Rescue Literature," *Journal of the History of Childhood and Youth* 2, no. 2 (Spring 2009): 208.
9 See, for example, the resort to matriarchies in Sharon D. McIvor, "Self-Government and Aboriginal Women," in *Feminisms and Womanisms: A Women's Studies Reader*, ed. Althea Prince and Susan Silva-Wayne (Toronto: Women's Press, 2004), 25–42.
10 See the thoughtful and passionate assessments in D. Memee Lavell-Harvard and Jeannette Corbiere Lavell, ed., *"Until Our Hearts Are on the Ground": Aboriginal Mothering, Oppression, Resistance and Rebirth* (Toronto: Demeter Press, 2006).
11 Joanne Barker, "Gender, Sovereignty, Rights: Native Women's Activism against Social Inequality and Violence in Canada,"? *American Quarterly* 60, no. 2 (June 2008): 262. See also her "Gender, Sovereignty, and the Discourse of Rights in Native Women's Activism," *Meridians: Feminism, Race, Transnationalism* 7, no. 1 (2006): 127–61. See also the *Report of the Royal Commission on Aboriginal Peoples*, volume 3 of *Gathering Strength* (Ottawa: Ministry of Supply and Services 1996), 66; Rosemary Kuptana, *No More Secrets: Acknowl-*

edging the Problem of Child Sexual Abuse in Inuit Communities: The First Step towards Healing (Ottawa: Pauktuutit, 1991); and Nancy MacDonald, Joan Glode, and Fred Wien, "Respecting Aboriginal Families: Pathways to Resilience in Custom Adoption and Family Group Conferencing," in Handbook for Working with Children and Youth: Pathways to Resilience across Cultures and Contexts, ed. Michael Ungar (Thousand Oaks, London, and New Delhi: Sage Publications, 2005), 360.

12 Richard Wagamese, Keeper'n Me (Toronto: Doubleday Canada, 1994), 9.

13 Sandra Lovelace Sappier in Enough Is Enough: Aboriginal Women Speak Out, as told to Janet Silman (Toronto: Women's Press, 1987), 244.

14 Cindy Baskin, "Systemic Oppression, Violence and Healing in Aboriginal Families and Communities," in Cruel but Not Unusual: Violence in Canadian Families, ed. Ramona Maggia and Cathy Vine (Waterloo: Wilfrid Laurier University Press, 2006), 21.

15 Barker, "Gender, Sovereignty, and the Discourse of Rights," 148.

16 Encyclopedia of Canada's Peoples, ed. Paul Robert Magocsi (Toronto: Multicultural History Society of Ontario and University of Toronto Press, 1999).

17 Anita Beltran Chen, "Filipinos," in Magocsi, Encyclopedia of Canada's Peoples, 506.

18 Peter D. Chimbos, "Greeks," in Magocsi, Encyclopedia of Canada's Peoples, 620.

19 Rasesh Thakkar, "Gujaratis," in Magocsi, Encyclopedia of Canada's Peoples, 635.

20 Franca Iacovetta, Gatekeepers: Reshaping Immigrant Lives in Cold War Canada (Toronto: Between the Lines, 2006).

21 For a start to understanding mothers-in-law, see Olivia Slaughter and Jean Kubelun, Life as a Mother-in-Law: Roles, Challenges, Solutions (Indianapolis, IN: Dog Ear Publishing, 2008); and Luisa Dillner, The Complete Book of Mothers-in-Law: A Celebration (London: Faber, 2008).

22 Gillis, World of Their Own Making, 75.

23 Indeed, immigrant communities face the problem of inventing their past even as their original homelands change. See, for example, the case of the Gujaratis, who worry about the pressure on traditional domestic arrangements, even as "in rapidly urbanizing India, the joint family, defined by a common residence, common property, and a common purse, is fast disappearing." Thakkar, "Gujaratis," 634.

24 Cheryl Marlene Swidrovich, "Positive Experiences of First Nations Children in Non-Aboriginal Foster or Adoptive Care: De-Constructing the 'Sixties Scoop'" (MA dissertation, University of Saskatchewan, 2004).

25 Karen V. Hansen, Not-So-Nuclear Families: Class, Gender, and Networks of Care (New Brunswick, NJ: Rutgers University Press, 2005), 131.

26 Carolyn J. Rosenthal and James Gladstone, Grandparenthood in Canada (Ottawa: Vanier Institute of the Family, 2000), http://www.vifamily.ca.

27 See the reminder in Bettina Bradbury, "Canadian Children Who Lived with One Parent in 1901," in Sager and Baskerville, Household Counts, 247–301.

28 Statistics Canada, http://www.statcan.gc.ca/pub/89–625-x/2007001/t/4054991-eng.htm and http://www.statcan.gc.ca/daily-quotidien/020711/dq020711a-eng.htm. On the psychological implications, see the report of social work scholars from Lakehead University, Nancy Shalay and Keith Brownlee, "Narrative Family Therapy with Blended Families," Journal of Family Psychotherapy 18, no. 2 (2007): 17–30.

29 See Vern L. Bengtson, "Beyond the Nuclear Family: The Increasing Importance of Multigenerational Bonds," Journal of Marriage and the Family 63, no. 11 (Feb. 2001): 1–16.

30 Lisa Dillon, *The Shady Side of Fifty: Age and Old Age in Late Victorian Canada and the United States* (Montreal and Kingston: McGill-Queen's University Press, 2008), 218. I would like to thank Dr. Dillon for sending me a prepublication version of the chapter on grandparenting.

31 For a start at this story, see Veronica Strong-Boag, "Sisters Are Doing It for Themselves, or Not: Aunts and Caregiving in Canada," *Journal of Comparative Family Studies* 40, no. 5 (Autumn 2009): 791–807.

32 Midge Michiko Ayukawa and Patricia E. Roy, "Japanese," in Magocsi, *Encyclopedia of Canada's Peoples*, 850.

33 See Madeline A. Kalbach, "Ethnic Intermarriage in Canada," *Canadian Ethnic Studies* 34, no. 2 (2002): 25–69; and "Canada's Ethnocultural Mosaic, 2006 Census: National Picture," Statistics Canada, http://www12.statcan.ca/english/census06/analysis/ethnicorigin/increased.cfm; and Alexander von Gernet, "Aboriginals: Iroquoians," in Magocsi, *Encyclopedia of Canada's Peoples*, 61.

34 See the acknowledgement of diversity in Bengtson, "Beyond the Nuclear Family," especially 9–11.

35 Mary C. Marino, "Aboriginals: Siouans," in Magocsi, *Encyclopedia of Canada's Peoples*, 96.

36 Laura Peers and Jennifer Brown, "'There is no end to relationships among the Indians:' Ojibwa Families and Kinship in Historical Perspective," *History of the Family* 4, no. 4 (1999): 533.

37 See J.H. van den Brink, *The Haida Indians: Cultural Change Mainly between 1876–1970* (Leiden: E.J. Brill, 1974).

38 Brian P. Clarke, *Piety and Nationalism: Lay Voluntary Associations and the Creation of an Irish-Catholic Community in Toronto, 1850–1895* (Montreal and Kingston: McGill-Queen's University Press, 1993), 24. For extended comparison of Natives and Highlanders that makes this point, see Colin G. Calloway, *White People, Indians, and Highlanders: Tribal Peoples and Colonial Encounters in Scotland and America* (Oxford: Oxford University Press, 2008). See also the earlier introduction to this comparison in Veronica Strong-Boag, "'A People Akin to Mine': Indians and Highlanders within the British Empire," *Native Studies Review* 14, no. 1 (2001): 27–53.

39 Nancy Christie, "Introduction," in Christie and Gauvreau, *Mapping the Margins*, 12.

40 David Moody, *Scottish Family History* (Baltimore: Genealogical Publishing Company, 1994), 90–94.

41 On this point, see Sharon A. Roger Hepburn, *Crossing the Border: A Free Black Community in Canada* (Urbana and Chicago: University of Illinois Press, 2007), especially 102.

42 See Native Women's Association of Canada, *Claiming Our Way of Being: Matrimonial Real Property Solutions* (Ohsweken, ON: Native Women's Association of Canada, 2007).

43 Theodore R. Marmor, Jerry L. Mashaw, and Philip L. Harvey, *America's Misunderstood Welfare State: Persistent Myths, Enduring Realities* (New York: Basic Books, 1992), 26.

44 Leslie Anderson et al., *Best Practice Approaches: Child Protection and Violence against Women* (Victoria: Ministry of Children and Family Development, May 2004), 7.

45 See Jan Beise, "The *Helping* and the *Helpful* Grandmother: The Role of Maternal and Paternal Grandmothers in Child Mortality in the Seventeenth and Eighteenth Century Population of French Settlers in Quebec, Canada," Working Paper no. 2004–004, *Max-Planck-Institute for Demographic Research* (January 2004; revised September 2004).

46 See Dillon, *Shady Side of Fifty*, Chapter 6, especially 246–47.

47 Statistics Canada, *Aboriginal Children's Survey: First Nations Children Living off Reserve* (Ottawa: Statistics Canada, 2008), 2.

48 See Joy Parr, *The Gender of Breadwinners: Women, Men, and Change in Two Industrial Towns, 1880–1950* (Toronto: University of Toronto Press, 1990).

49 Mary E. Rand, "Implications when Grandmothers Assume Responsibility for the Care of Children Whose Mothers Are Working for Pay" (MSW dissertation, Maritime School of Social Work, May 1956), 17.

50 Harry MacKay and Catherine Austin, *Single Adolescent Mothers in Ontario: A Report of Eighty-Seven Single Adolescent Mothers' Experiences, Their Situation, Needs, and Use of Community Services* (Ottawa: Canadian Council on Social Development, 1983).

51 Carolyn J. Rosenthal and James Gladstone, *Grandparenthood in Canada* (Ottawa: Vanier Institute of the Family, 2000), 8–10, http://www.vifamily.ca.

52 Suzanne Morton, "Nova Scotia and Its Unmarried Mothers, 1945–1975," in Christie and Gauvreau, *Mapping the Margins*, 341.

53 Barb Whittington, Tina Pearson, Pat Mackenzie, David Burns, Leslie Brown, and Marion Gracey, *Supporting Grandparents Raising Grandchildren: Resource Booklet*, 2nd edition (Victoria: University of Victoria, January 2007), 15; and Esme Fuller-Thomson, "Grandparents Raising Grandchildren in Canada: A Profile of Skipped Generation Families," SEDAP Research Paper no. 132, McMaster University, October 2005, 2, http://socserv.mcmaster.ca/sedap/.

54 Fuller-Thomson, "Grandparents Raising Grandchildren in Canada," 18.

55 Ibid., 1.

56 Marilyn Callahan, Leslie Brown, Patricia Mackenzie, and Barbara Whittington, "The Underground Child Welfare System: Grandmothers Raising Grandchildren," *Perspectives* 27, no. 5 (November 2005): 12–13.

57 Lynn M. Meadows, Wilfreda E. Thurston, and Laura E. Lagendyk, "Aboriginal Women at Midlife: Grandmothers as Agents of Change," *Canadian Woman Studies* 24, no. 1 (2004): 161.

58 Dillon, *The Shady Side of Fifty*, 219.

59 Meadows, Thurston, and Lagendyk, "Aboriginal Women at Midlife," 163. See also L.E. Krosenbrink-Gelissen, "Caring Is Indian Women's Business, But Who Takes Care of Them? Canadian Indian Women, the Renewed Indian Act and Its Implications for Women's Family Responsibilities, Roles and Rights," *Law and Anthropology* 7 (1992): 107–30; and Jo-Anne Fiske, "Child of the State, Mother of the Nation: Aboriginal Women and the Ideology of Motherhood," *Culture* 13, no. 1 (1993): 17–35.

60 Verna Patronella Johnston, quoted in *I Am Nickomis Too* in Heather Howard-Bobiwash, "Women's Class Strategies as Activism in Native Community Building in Toronto, 1950–1975," *American Indian Quarterly* 27, no. 3 (2003): 566.

61 Stephen Workman, "Lives Lived: Irene Revels Lydiard," *Globe and Mail*, 3 March 2000, A20.

62 Laura C. Johnson and Janice Dineen, *The Kin Trade: The Day Care Crisis in Canada* (Toronto: McGraw-Hill Ryerson, 1981), 65 and 72.

63 Betsy M. Wearing and Christine G. Wearing, "Women Breaking Out: Changing Discourses on Grandmotherhood?" *Journal of Family Studies* 2, no. 2 (October 1996): 165, 167, 174.

64 Bonita F. Bowers and Barbara J. Myers, "Grandmothers Providing Care for Grandchildren: Consequences of Various Levels of Caregiving," *Family Relations* 48, no. 3 (July 1999): 303.

65 Katrina Bell McDonald and Elizabeth M. Armstrong, "De-Romanticizing Black Inter-generational Support: The Questionable Expectations of Welfare Reform," *Journal of Marriage and the Family* 63, no. 1 (February 2001): 213–23.

66 Fuller-Thomson, "Grandparents Raising Grandchildren in Canada," 9.

67 Shorkey and Mitchell, "Grandparents Raising Their Grandchildren," 153.

68 See B. Barer, "The 'Grands and Greats' of Very Old Black Grandmothers," *Journal of Aging Studies* 15, no. 1 (March 2001): 1–11; and K. Fingerman, "The Good, the Bad and the Worrisome: Emotional Complexities in Grandparents' Experiences with Individual Grandchildren," *Family Relations* 47, no. 4 (1998): 403–14.

69 Quoted in Mario Toneguzzi, "When Grandparents Have to Raise the Kids: Caregivers Can Claim a Range of Benefits," *The [Montreal] Gazette*, Canwest News Service, http://www.canada.com.

70 See, for example, J. Strawbridge, Margaret I. Wallhagen, Sarah J. Shema, and George A. Kaplan, "New Burdens: More of the Same? Comparing Grandparent, Spouse, and Adult-Child Caregivers," *The Gerontologist* 37, no. 4 (1997): 505–10.

71 Peers and Brown, "'There is no end to relationships among the Indians.'"

72 See Ian Gillespie, "Grandparent-Caregivers Deserve Our Full Support," *London Free Press*, 24 November 2008), http://freedominion.com.pa/phpBB2/viewtopic.php?t=107898&view=next&sid=c30416447b9a46e2918a93ec89b9d064.

73 Garry Cooper, "Lives Lived: James Fenimore (1910–2004)," *Globe and Mail*, 14 October 2004, A14.

74 "Re Whitfield," *Dominion Law Review* 70 (1922): 658–59.

75 Debates about these marriages began in Britain in the 1840s, but the removal of this pro-hibition was not enacted until 1907, twenty-five years after similar legislation was passed in Canada, For a discussion of these protracted debates, see Nancy F. Anderson, "'Marriage with a Deceased Wife's Sister Bill' Controversy: Incest Anxiety and the Defense of the Family Purity in Victorian England," *Journal of British Studies* 21, no. 2 (Spring 1982): 67–86; and Mary Jane Corbett, "Husband, Wife, and Sister: Making and Remaking the Early Victorian Family," *Victorian Literature and Culture* 31, no. 1 (2007): 1–19.

76 Anne Langton, *The Story of Our Family* (Manchester: Thos Sowler and Company, 1881), 147–48.

77 Dillon, *The Shady Side of Fifty*, 248.

78 Darroch, "Families, Fostering, and Flying the Coop," 211.

79 Denyse Baillargeon, *Making Do: Women, Family and Home in Montreal during the Great Depression* (Waterloo: Wilfrid Laurier University Press, 1999), 88.

80 Sharon Anne Cook, "Lives Lived: Harriet Ethel (Fry) Killins," *Globe and Mail*, 9 July 2003, A18.

81 Rita Joe, "The Honour Song of the Micmac: An Autobiography of Rita Joe," in *Kelusul-tiek: Women's Voices of Atlantic Canada*, coordinator, Renate Usmiani (Halifax: Institute for the Study of Women, Mt. St. Vincent University, 1993), 46. See also Susie Doxta-tor in Elizabeth Graham, *The Mush Hole: Life at Two Indian Residential Schools* (Water-loo, ON: Heffle Publishing, 1997), 438–39.

82 Library and Archives Canada, http://www.collectionscanada.gc.ca/women/002026-615-e.html.

83 "Parents on Kids: How Do Fathers Bring Up Children Single-Handed?" *Star Weekly*, 24 May 1969, 6.

84 Alexandra Wright, Diane Hiebert-Murphy, Janet Mirwaldt, and George Muswaggon, *Summary Report Factors That Contribute to Positive Outcomes in the Awasis Pimicikamak*

Cree Nation Kinship Care Program (Winnipeg: Centre of Excellence for Child Welfare and Health Canada, 2005), 3, 15.

85 Hansen, *Not-So-Nuclear Families*, 184.

86 Farley Mowat, *Lost in the Barrens* (1956).

87 See Yousuf Karsh, *In Search of Greatness: Reflections of Yousuf Karsh* (Toronto: University of Toronto Press, 1962).

88 Charles Dickens, *A Christmas Carol* (1843).

89 Ingrid Arnet Connidis, "Sibling Ties across Time: The Middle and Later Years," in *Cambridge Handbook of Age and Ageing*, ed., Malcolm L. Johnson (Cambridge: Cambridge University Press, 2005), 431.

90 Dorothy Scott and Shurlee Swain, *Confronting Cruelty: Historical Perspectives of Child Abuse* (Melbourne: Melbourne University Press, 2002), 8.

91 Ben Wicks, *Yesterday They Took My Baby: True Stories of Adoption* (Toronto: Stoddart, 1993), 31.

92 Jeannine Carriere-Laboucane, "Kinship Care: A Community Alternative to Foster Care," *Native Social Work Journal* 1, no. 1 (1997): 43–53.

93 Quoted in Lori Chambers, *Misconceptions: Unmarried Motherhood and the Ontario Children of Unmarried Parents Act, 1921 to 1969* (Toronto: University of Toronto Press, 2007), 116.

94 See Ginger Suzanne Frost, "'The Black Lamb of the Black Sheep': Illegitimacy in the English Working Class, 1850–1939," *Journal of Social History* 37, no. 2 (Winter 2003): 293–322; and Peter Ward, "Unwed Motherhood in Nineteenth-Century English Canada," in *Historical Papers*, ed., Canadian Historical Association (Halifax: Canadian Historical Association, 1981), 34–56; Constance A. Maguire, "Kate Simpson Hayes, Agnes Agatha Hammell, and 'the Slur of Illegitimacy,'" *Saskatchewan History* 50, no. 2 (Fall 1998): 7–23; Leslie Savage, "Perspectives on Illegitimacy: The Changing Role of the Sisters of Misericordia in Edmonton, 1900–1906," in *Studies in Childhood History: A Canadian Perspective*, ed. Patricia T. Rooke and R.L. Schnell (Calgary: Detselig Enterprises Limited, 1982), 105–33; Andrée Lévesque, *Making and Breaking the Rules: Women in Quebec, 1919–1939*, trans. Yvonne M. Klein (Toronto: McClelland and Stewart, 1994); and McDonald and Armstrong, "De-Romanticizing Black Intergenerational Support," 221.

95 See Susan McDaniel and Robert Lewis, "Did They or Didn't They? Intergenerational Supports in Families Past: A Case Study of Brigus, Newfoundland, 1920–1945," in *Family Matters: Papers in Post-Confederation Canadian Family History*, ed. Lori Chambers and Edgar-André Montigny (Toronto: Canadian Scholars' Press, 1998), 475–98.

96 See Karen Bridget Murray, "Governing 'Unwed Mothers' in Toronto at the Turn of the Twentieth Century," *Canadian Historical Review* 85, no. 2 (2004): 253–76; and Lévesque, *Making and Breaking the Rules*.

97 Doris Anderson, *Rebel Daughter: An Autobiography* (Toronto: Key Porter Books, 1996).

98 Geertje Boschma, "A Family Point of View: Negotiating Asylum Care in Alberta, 1905–1930," *Canadian Bulletin of Medical History* 25, no. 2 (2008): 381–82. See also Geoffrey Reaume, "Mental Hospital Patients and Family Relations in Southern Ontario, 1880–1931," in Chambers and Montigny, *Family Matters*, 271–88.

99 Kirsten Johnson Kramar, *Unwilling Mothers, Unwanted Babies: Infanticide in Canada* (Vancouver: UBC Press, 2005), 60–62.

100 BC Social Welfare Branch, Department of Health and Welfare, *Annual Report for the Year Ending March 31st, 1948*, Review of the Social Services of the Government of British Columbia, 82.

101 Quoted in Ellen Adelberg and Claudie Currie, "In Their Own Words," *Too Few to Count. Canadian Women in Conflict with the Law*, ed. Ellen Adelberg and Claudia Currie (Vancouver: Pressgang Publishers, 1987), 85.

102 *Re Hart*, Ontario High Court, Middleton, J., in Chambers, *Dominion Law Reports* 4 (18 May 1912): 294.

103 "Mary Walsh," Library and Archives Canada, http://www.collectionscanada.gc.ca/women/002026–615-e.html.

104 Susan Houston, "The 'Waifs and Strays' of a Late Victorian City: Juvenile Delinquents in Toronto," in *Childhood and Family in Canadian History*, ed. Joy Parr (Toronto: McClelland and Stewart, 1982): 129–42.

105 Gillis, *World of Their Own*, 15.

106 Helen Creighton, *A Life in Folklore* (Toronto: McGraw-Hill Ryerson, 1975).

107 Donald Wright, *The Professionalization of History in English Canada* (Toronto: University of Toronto Press, 2005), 105.

108 See the recognition of this by W.E. Mann, "The Social System of a Slum: The Lower Ward, Toronto," in *The Community in Canada. Rural and Urban*, ed. Satadal Dasgupta (Lanham, MD: University Press of America, 1996), 294–310.

109 Mary Anne Poutanen, "Bonds of Friendship, Kinship, and Community: Gender, Homelessness, and Mutual Aid in Early-Nineteenth-Century Montreal," in *Negotiating Identities in Nineteenth- and Twentieth-Century Montreal*, ed. Bettina Bradbury and Tamara Myers (Vancouver: UBC Press, 2005), 29.

110 Rachel Crowder, "Lives Lived: James Albert (Al) Crowder," *Globe and Mail*, 20 November 2002, A24.

111 Franc Sturino, "Italians," in Magocsi, *Encyclopedia of Canada's Peoples*, 806.

112 Isabel Kaprielian-Church, "Armenians," in Magocsi, *Encyclopedia of Canada's Peoples*, 221.

113 Milda Danys, "Lithuanians," in Magocsi, *Encyclopedia of Canada's Peoples*, 925.

114 See Tanya L. Gogan, "Surviving as a Widow in Late Nineteenth-Century Halifax" (MA dissertation, Dalhousie University, 1994), 138–39.

115 Claude Morin, "Beyond Kinship and Households: Godparents and Orphans: An Introduction," *The History of the Family* 5, no. 3 (November 2000): 255–57. For a popular celebration that invokes their continuing significance, see Michelle DeLiso, *Godparents: A Celebration of Those Special People in Our Lives* (New York: McGraw-Hill, 2002).

116 Jan Noel, *Family Life and Sociability in Upper and Lower Canada, 1780–1870* (Montreal and Kingston: McGill-Queen's University Press, 2003), 142. See also Bruce S. Elliott who notes of Irish migrants that "godparents were usually chosen from among relatives where possible." *Irish Migrants in the Canada: A New Approach* (Montreal and Kingston: McGill-Queen's University Press, 2004), 315, n 106.

117 Franc Sturino, "Italians," in Magocsi, *Encyclopedia of Canada's Peoples*, 805.

118 Anita Beltran Chen, "Filipinos," in Magocsi, *Encyclopedia of Canada's Peoples*, 506.

119 On recent recognition of the importance of informal care by scholars and policy makers, see Michael Bittman, Janet E. Fast, Kimberly Fisher, and Cathy Thomson, "Making the Invisible Visible: The Life and Time(s) of Informal Caregivers," in *Family Time: The Social Organization of Care*, ed. Nancy Folbre and Michael Bittman (London: Routledge, 2004), 69–90.

120 Peter C. Pineo, "The Extended Family in a Working-Class Area of Hamilton," in *The Community in Canada: Rural and Urban*, ed. Satadal Dasgupta (Lanham, MD: University Press of America, 1996), 328–38.

121 Deborah Crawford, "Lives Lived: Isabel Strickland," *Globe and Mail*, 21 April 2003, A14.

122 Rose Barton, "The Child Who Adopted Me," *Chatelaine*, September 1958, 34–35, 101–5.

123 "Parents on Kids," 6–7.

124 Ibid., 2.

125 On these conflicts, see Veronica Strong-Boag, *Finding Families, Finding Ourselves: English Canada Confronts Adoption from the Nineteenth Century to the 1990* (Toronto: Oxford University Press, 2006), passim.

126 Margaret Philp, "A White Man Struggles to Reclaim His Children," *Globe and Mail*, 11 May 2007, A15.

127 Angela Hall, "Advocate Tells Goverment to Put Children First," *[Regina] Leader Post*, 16 May 2007, A5.

128 Quoted in "Priorities Askew," *[Saskatoon] Advocate-Star Phoenix*, 16 May 2007, B7.

129 See McDonald and Armstrong, "De-Romancing Black Intergenerational Support," 213–23.

130 "Pram in River," *Toronto Star*, 18 January 1950, 1.

131 This case was heavily covered in the 2008 press. See, for example, "Ontario Introduces New Laws to Protect Women, Children in Custody," CBC News, 24 November 2008, http://www.cbc.ca/canada/toronto/story/2008/11/24/bentley-katelynn.html.

132 James Shaver Woodsworth, *My Neighbour* (1911; reprinted Toronto: University of Toronto Press, 1972), 144.

133 Paul Steinhauer, *The Least Detrimental Alternative: A Systematic Guide to Case Planning and Decision Making for Children in Care* (Toronto: University of Toronto Press, 1991), 82-83.

Notes to Chapter 2

1 Terry Glavin and Former Students of St. Mary's, *Amongst God's Own: The Enduring Legacy of St. Mary's Mission* (Mission, BC: Longhouse Publishing, 2002), 11.

2 See Alvin Finkel, *Social Policy and Practice in Canada: A History* (Waterloo: Wilfrid Laurier University Press, 2006), 68–75 and passim.

3 See Michael Harris, *Unholy Orders: Tragedy at Mount Cashel* (Markham, ON: Viking, 1990); and Jean Barman, "Separate and Unequal: Indian and White Girls at All Hallows School, 1884–1920," in *Indian Education in Canada: the Legacy*, ed. Jean Barman, Yvonne Hebert, and Don McCaskill, volume 1 (Vancouver: UBC Press, 1986), 110–31.

4 Carol T. Baines, "The Children of Earlscourt, 1915–1948: All in the Same Boat: 'Except we were in a better boat,'" *Canadian Social Work Review* 11, no. 2 (Summer 1994): 196.

5 See Jean Barman, *Growing Up British in British Columbia: Boys in Private School* (Vancouver: UBC Press, 1984); and Sharon Wall, *The Nurture of Nature: Childhood, Anti-Modernism, and Ontario Summer Camps, 1920–55* (Vancouver: UBC Press, 2009), especially Chapter 2, "Socialism for the Rich: Class Formation at the Private Camp."

6 Charlotte Neff, "The Role of Protestant Children's Homes in Nineteenth Century Ontario: Child Rescue or Family Support," *Journal of Family History* 34, no. 1 (2009): 48–88.

7 See Megan Sproule-Jones, "Crusading for the Forgotten: Dr. Peter Bryce, Public Health, and Prairie Native Residential Schools," *Canadian Bulletin of Medical History*, 13, no. 2 (1996): 199–224; and Baines, "The Children of Earlscourt, 1915–1948," 186.

8   Sara Posen, "Examining Policy from the 'Bottom up': The Relationship between Parents, Children and Managers at the Toronto Boys' Home, 1859–1920," in *Family Matters: Papers in Post-Confederation Canadian Family History,* ed. Lori Chambers and Edgar-André Montigny (Toronto: Canadian Scholars' Press, 1998), 9.

9   See *Welfare Services in Nova Scotia,* typescript at Dalhousie University Library (Halifax: Nova Scotia Ministry of Public Welfare, August 1964); and Paul M. Gouett, "The Halifax Orphan House 1752–87," *Nova Scotia Historical Quarterly* 6, no. 3 (1976): 281–91.

10 As quoted in Finkel, *Social Policy and Practice in Canada,* 67.

11 *Welfare Services in Nova Scotia,* 19. On workhouses, see Finkel, *Social Policy and Practice in Canada,* 67–70.

12 Charlotte Neff, "Government Approaches to Child Neglect and Mistreatment in Nineteenth-Century Ontario," *Histoire sociale/Social History* 41, no. 81 (May 2008): 188.

13 Nova Scotia, House of Assembly, *Journals and Proceedings of the House of Assembly,* Session 1901, Appendix no. 3 (B) "Report on Public Charities for the Year ending 30th September 1900," 32–33.

14 Nova Scotia, *Journal and Proceedings of the House of Assembly,* Session 1917, Part 1, 5–6.

15 Janet Guildford, "The End of the Poor Law: Public Welfare Reform in Nova Scotia before the Canada Assistance Plan," in *Mothers of the Municipality: Women, Work, and Social Policy in Post-1945 Halifax,* ed. Judith Fingard and Janet Guildford (Toronto: University of Toronto Press, 2005), 57.

16 Ibid., 55.

17 See Sophie Boucher et al., "Consequences of an Institutionalized Childhood: The Case of the 'Duplessis Orphans,'" *Santé mentale au Québec* 33, no. 2 (Autumn 2008): 271–91; and Rose Dufour and Brigitte Garneau, *Naître rien: des orphelins de Duplessis, de la crèche à l'asile* (Ste-Foy, QC: Éditions multimondes, 2002).

18 This is most fully explored for Canada by Patricia T. Rooke and Rodolph L. Schnell, *Discarding the Asylum: From Child Rescue to the Welfare State in English Canada* (Landham, MD: University Press of America, 1983).

19 Arthur Saint-Pierre, *Témoignages sur nos Orphelinats: Recueillis et commentés* (Montreal: Fides, 1946), 51 and 52. See also Chs.-E. Bourgeois, *The Protection of Children in the Province of Quebec,* trans. Paul E. Marquis (Trois-Rivières, QC: Bishop of Trois-Rivières, 1948), which makes the same point (34–36).

20 Charlotte Neff, "The Use of Apprenticeship and Adoption at the Toronto protestant Orphans' Home, 1853–1869," *Histoire sociale/Social History* 30, no. 60 (November 1997), 338. See also Neff, "The Role of Protestant Children's Homes in Nineteenth-Century Ontario," 58.

21 Neff, "Government Approaches to Child Neglect and Mistreatment,"195.

22 Janice Harvey, "The Protestant Orphan Asylum and the Montreal Ladies Benevolent Society: A Case Study in Protestant Child Charity in Montreal, 1822–1900" (PhD dissertation, McGill University, 2001), 289 and 282.

23 See the important reminder in Charlotte Neff, "The Education of Destitute Homeless Children in Nineteenth-Century Ontario," *Journal of Family History* 29, no. 1 (January 2004): 3–46.

24 Posen, "Examining Policy from the 'Bottom up," 16.

25 Heidi Macdonald, "Doing More with Less: The Sisters of St. Martha (PEI) Diminish the Impact of the Great Depression," *Acadiensis* 33, no. 1 (Autumn 2003): 21–46.

26 Saint-Pierre, *Témoignages sur nos Orphelinats,* 53.

27   Baines, "The Children of Earlscourt, 1915–1948," 190.

28   Ibid., 188. See also Carol T. Baines, "From Women's Benevolence to Professional Social Work: The Care of the Wimodausis Club and the Earlscourt Children's Home, 1902–1971" (PhD dissertation, University of Toronto, 1990); and Carol T. Baines, Patricia M. Evans, and Sheila M. Neysmith "Women's Caring: Challenges for Practice and Policy," *Affilia* 7, no. 1 (Spring 1992): 21–44.

29   Bettina Bradbury, "The Fragmented Family: Family Strategies in the Face of Death, Illness, and Poverty, Montreal, 1860–1885," in *Childhood and Family in Canadian History,* ed. J. Parr (Toronto: McClelland and Stewart, 1982), 117.

30   Diane Purvey, "Alexandra Orphanage and Families in Crisis in Vancouver, 1892–1938," in *Dimensions of Childhood: Essays on the History of Children and Youth in Canada,* ed. Russell Smandych, Gordon Dodds, and Alvin Esau (Winnipeg: Legal Research Institute of the University of Manitoba, 1991), 115.

31   Baines, "The Children of Earlscourt, 1915–1948," 193.

32   Saint-Pierre, *Témoignages sur nos Orphelinats,* 62 and 65.

33   Bourgeois, *The Protection of Children,* 12.

34   Ethel M. Chapman, "An Orphanage That Is a Home," *Maclean's,* 15 July 1920, 69–71.

35   See David T. Beito, *From Mutual Aid to the Welfare State: Fraternal Societies and Social Services, 1890–1967* (Chapel Hill and London: University of North Carolina Press, 2000), Chapter 4, "The Child City."

36   Reuben Slonim, *Great to Be an Orphan* (Toronto: Clarke, Irwin and Company, 1983), 12.

37   David Maunders, "Awakening from the Dream: The Experience of Childhood in Protestant Orphan Homes in Australia, Canada and the United States," *Child and Youth Care Forum* 23, no. 6 (December 1994): 393–412.

38   See, in the instance of the English experiments, Lydia D. Murdoch, "From Barrack Schools to Family Cottages: Creating Domestic Space for Late Victorian Poor Children," in *Child Welfare and Social Action,* ed. Jon Lawrence and Pat Starkey (Liverpool: Liverpool University Press, 2001), 148.

39   Mary Alban Bouchard, "Pioneers Forever: The Sisters of St. Joseph of Toronto and Their Ventures in Social Welfare and Health Care," in *Catholics at the "Gathering Place": Historical Essays on the Archdiocese of Toronto 1841–1991,* ed. Mark G. McGowan and Brian P. Clarke (Toronto: Canadian Catholic Historical Association, 1993), 115. See also James A. Knight, "Where Children Get a Second Chance," *Star Weekly,* 3 June 1961, 6–9, on a cottage experiment in London, Ontario.

40   Murdoch, "From Barrack Schools to Family Cottages," 161.

41   Maurice N. Cote, "The Children's Aid Society of the Catholic Diocese of Vancouver: Its Origins and Development, 1905 to 1953" (MSW dissertation, University of British Columbia, 1953), 32–33.

42   Stompin' Tom Connors, *Stompin' Tom: Before the Fame* (Toronto: Penguin, 1991), 113, 115, and 120.

43   See Karen Bridget Murray, "Governing 'Unwed Mothers' in Toronto at the Turn of the Twentieth Century," *Canadian Historical Review* 85, no. 2 (2004): 253–76.

44   Mary Ellen Wright, "Unnatural Mothers: Infanticide in Halifax, 1850–1975," *Nova Scotia Historical Review* 7, no. 2 (1987): 16.

45   See *Winnipeg Free Press,* 12 May 1938, 6.

46   Suzanne Morton, "From Infant Homes to Daycare: Child Care in Halifax," in *Mothers of the Municipality: Women, Work and Social Policy in Post-1945 Halifax,* ed. Judith Fingard

218 NOTES TO CHAPTER TWO

and Janet Guildford (Toronto: University of Toronto Press, 2004), 169. See also Wright, "Unnatural Mothers," 12–29.

47 Neff, "Government Approaches to Child Neglect and Mistreatment," 202 and 204; and Wright, "Unnatural Mothers," 29.

48 See Andrée Lévesque, *Making and Breaking the Rules: Women in Quebec, 1919–1939,* trans. Yvonne M. Klein (Toronto: McClelland and Stewart, 1994).

49 See Betty Flint, *The Child and the Institution: A Study of Deprivation and Recovery* (Toronto: University of Toronto Press, 1967); and the documentary, *Difference between Institutionally Reared and Home Reared Children* (National Film Board of Canada, 1967). On a similar transition in the United States, see Nurth Zmora, *Orphanages Reconsidered: Child Care Institutions in Progressive Era Baltimore* (Philadelphia: Temple University Press, 1994), 10.

50 On industrial schools as institutions for the protection of non-criminal children in England, see Marianne Moore, "Social Control or Protection of the Child? The Debates on the Industrial Schools Acts 1857–1894," *Journal of Family History* 33, no. 4 (October 2008): 359–87. See also Andrew Jones and Leonard Rutman, *In the Children's Aid: J.J. Kelso and Child Welfare in Ontario* (Toronto: University of Toronto Press, 1981), 29.

51 Christelle Burban, "Les origines institutionnelles de la protection de l'enfance au Québec : l'école d'industrie de Notre-Dame de Monfort (1883–1913)" (Mémoire en histoire, Université de Rennes II, 1997).

52 *Criminal Code, Act Respecting Procedure in Criminal Cases,* found in "The Evolution of Juvenile Justice in Canada," Canada. Department of Justice, http://www.justice.gc.ca/eng/pi/icg-gci/jj2-jm2/sec01a.html.

53 See Prue Rains and E. Teram, *Normal Bad Boys: Public Policies, Institutions, and the Politics of Client Recruitment* (Montreal and Kingston: McGill-Queen's University Press, 1992); and Prue Rains, "La justice des mineurs et The Boy's Farm: 1909–1968," *Criminologie* 18, no. 1 (1985): 103–27.

54 Neil Sutherland, *Children in English-Canadian Society* (Waterloo: Wilfrid Laurier University Press, 2000): 104.

55 See Manitoba Archives, Knowles Home for Boys/Knowles School for Boys (from 1924) 1907–ca. 1950, http://www.mbarchives.mb.ca/orphanage/ccinstitution.asp?id=21.

56 *Juvenile Delinquents Act,* found in Canada, Department of Justice, http://www.justice.gc.ca/eng/pi/icg-gci/jj2-jm2/sec01a.html.

57 *Young Offenders Act,* found in Canada, Department of Justice, http://www.justice.gc.ca/eng/pi/icg-gci/jj2-jm2/sec01a.html.

58 W.G. Clark, "Life in Residential Schools," *Maclean's,* August 1909, 24 and 26.

59 For the comparisons between the view of elite and middle-class mothers and those among the poor, see Baines, Evans, and Neysmith, "Women's Caring, 33.

60 An assessment of parents' role in the Maritime Home for Girls is discussed in George F. Davidson, IV, *Report on Public Welfare Services,* Royal Commission on Provincial Development and Rehabilitation (Halifax: King's Printer, 1944), 144.

61 Joan Sangster, *Girl Trouble: Female Delinquency in English Canada* (Toronto: Between the Lines, 2002).

62 Robin W. Winks, *The Blacks in Canada,* 2nd edition (Montreal and Kingston: McGill-Queen's University Press, 1997), 495.

63 Manitoba, Department of Health and Social Services, *Annual Report* (1969), 187 [emphasis in original].

64 Bryan R. Hogeveen, "Toward 'Safer' and 'Better' Communities? Canada's Youth Criminal Justice Act, Aboriginal Youth and the Processes of Exclusion," *Critical Criminology* 13, no. 3 (January 2005): 287–305.

65 See James C. Hackler, *The Prevention of Youthful Crime: The Great Stumble Forward* (Toronto: Methuen, 1973), especially 96–99.

66 MP Nicholas Davin, *Report on Industrial Schools for Indians and Halfbreeds* (Ottawa: Queen's Printer, 1879).

67 See James R. Miller, *Shingwauk's Vision: A History of Native Residential Schools* (Toronto: University of Toronto Press, 1995); and John Milloy, *"A National Crime": The Canadian Government and the Residential School System, 1879 to 1986* (Winnipeg: University of Manitoba Press, 1999).

68 Mary-Ellen Kelm, "'A Scandalous Procession': Residential Schooling and the Re/Formation of Aboriginal Bodies, 1900–1950," *Native Studies Review* 11, no. 2 (1996): 51–88.

69 Bryce published his findings much later as *The Story of a National Crime: Being a Record of the Health Conditions of the Indians of Canada from 1904 to 1921* (Ottawa: J. Hope, 1922).

70 Jo-Anne Fiske, "Gender and the Paradox of Residential Education in Carrier Society," in *Women of the First Nations: Power, Wisdom, and Strength*, ed. Christine Miller and Patricia Chuchryk (Winnipeg: University of Manitoba Press, 1996), 167–82; and Baines, "The Children of Earlscourt, 1915–1948," 195.

71 Elizabeth Graham, *The Mush Hole: Life at Two Indian Residential Schools* (Waterloo: Heffle Publishing, 1997), 10.

72 Elizabeth Graham, "The Uses and Abuses of Power in Two Ontario Residential Schools: The Mohawk Institute and Mount Elgin," in *Earth, Water, Air and Fire: Studies in Canadian Ethnohistory*, ed. David McNab (Waterloo: Wilfrid Laurier University Press, 1998), 237.

73 Graham, *The Mush Hole*, 42.

74 Bill Williams, "Foreword," in Glavin and Former Students of St. Mary's, *Amongst God's Own*, 10.

75 Shirley Mitchell, "These Pictures Are Dear to My Heart," *Kelusultiek: Women's Voices of Atlantic Canada*, coordinated by Renate Usmiani (Halifax: Institute for the Study of Women, Mt. St. Vincent University, 1993), 208–9.

76 Review Committee on Indian and Metis Adoptions and Placements, *Transcripts and Briefs, Public Hearings, Special Hearings*, chaired by Judge Edwin C. Kimelman (Winnipeg: Manitoba Community Services, 1985), 420.

77 Miller, *Shingwauk's Vision*, 290.

78 See the discussion in Veronica Strong-Boag, "Children of Adversity": Disabilities and Child Welfare in Canada from the Nineteenth Century to the Twenty-First," *Journal of Family History* 32, no. 4 (2007): 413–32.

79 Jessa Chupik, "'I know that I can handle him now': The Relationship between Families, Confined Children, and the Orillia Asylum, 1900–1935," paper presented before the Canadian Historical Association, Toronto, May 2003, 4.

80 Quoted in Nic Clarke, "'Sacred Daemons': Exploring British Columbian Society's Perceptions of "Mentally Deficient" Children, 1870–1930," *BC Studies* no. 144 (Winter 2004–5): 75. See also on the difficulties of families, Thierry Nootens, "'For Years We Have Never Had a Happy Home': Madness and Families in Century Montreal," in *Mental Health and Canadian Society: Historical Perspectives*, ed. James E. Moran and David Wright (Montreal and Kingston: McGill-Queen's University Press, 2006), 49–68; and

Geoffrey Reaume, "Mental Hospital Patients and Family Relations in Southern Ontario," in Chambers and Montigny, *Family Matters,* 271–88.

81 On this extensive literature, see, for example, Clare Connors and Kirsten Stalker, *The Experiences and Views of Disabled Children and Their Siblings: A Positive Outlook* (Philadelphia: Jessica Kingsley Publishers, 2003); Michel E. Dunn et al., "Moderators of Stress in Parents of Children with Autism," *Community Mental Health Journal* 31, no. 1 (February 2001): 39–52; and J.L. Tanner and American Academy of Pediatrics, Committee on Psychosocial Aspects of Child and Family Health Pediatrics, "Parental Separation and Divorce: Can We Provide an Ounce of Prevention? Commentary," *Pediatrics* 110, no. 5 (November 2002): 1007–9.

82 On the significance of maternal care, see Melanie R. Panitch, "Accidental Activists: Mothers, Organization and Disability" (PhD dissertation, City University of New York, 2006), 3; and Geertje Boschma, "A Family Point of View: Negotiating Asylum Care in Alberta, 1905–1930," *Canadian Bulletin of Medical History* 25, no. 2 (2008): 381–82.

83 Boschma, "A Family Point of View," 372.

84 For an introduction to the issues, see Steven Hick, *Social Work in Canada: An Introduction* (Toronto: Thompson Educational Press, 2004) and his *Social Welfare in Canada: Understanding Income Security* Toronto: Thompson Educational Press, 2004). On the reality for a Toronto family with an autistic son, see Thelma Wheatley, *My Sad Is All Gone: A Family's Triumph over Violent Autism* (Lancaster, OH: Lucky Press, 2004).

85 Boschma, "A Family Point of View," 377.

86 Mrs. J.B. McGregor, "The Care of the Child Who Is Different," in *Proceedings of the Sixth Canadian Conference on Child Welfare* (Ottawa: Canadian Council on Child Welfare, 1928), 119.

87 See Margaret A. Winzer, *The History of Special Education* (Washington, DC: Gallaudet University Press, 1993).

88 See Christopher Rutty, "'Do something! ... Do anything!' Poliomyelitis in Canada 1927–1962" (PhD dissertation, University of Toronto, 1995); and K. McCuaig, *The Weariness, the Fever, and the Fret: The Campaign against Tuberculosis in Canada, 1900–1950* (Montreal and Kingston: McGill-Queen's University Press, 1999).

89 L.E. Lowman, "Mail-Order Babies," *Chatelaine*, April 1932, 34.

90 Wolf Wolfensberger, "A Contribution to the History of Normalization, with Primary Emphasis on the Establishment of Normalization in North America between 1967–1975," in *A Quarter-Century of Normalization and Social Role Valorization: Evolution and Impact*, ed. Robert J. Flynn and Raymond A. Lemay (Ottawa: University of Ottawa Press, 1999), 59.

91 Manitoba, Department of Human and Social Development, *Annual Report* (1970), 27.

92 For a rare discussion of the phenomenon, see Ruth Ellen Homrighaus, "Wolves in Women's Clothing: Baby-Farming and the *British Medical Journal*, 1860–1872," *Journal of Family History* 26, no. 3 (July 2001), 350–72.

93 Sidney Katz, "What Can We Learn from Mom Whyte?" *Canadian Welfare* 33, no. 7 (15 March 1958), 331; and his "Missing Persons: Whatever Became of Mom Whyte?" *Star Weekly*, 24 April 1971, 10.

94 On the shift in psychiatry from psychoanalytical explanations, often "blaming mummy" to "organic explanations and treatments for mental illness," see Andrea Tone, "Listening to the Past: History, Psychiatry, and Anxiety," *Canadian Journal of Psychiatry* 50 (2005): 373–80.

95 Alan Phillips, "The Home That Rebuilds Children's Lives," *Maclean's*, 28 March 1958, 13.

96 Wolfensberger, "A Contribution to the History of Normalization," 52–55.

97 André Blanchet, "The Impact of Normalization and Social Role Valorization in Canada," in Flynn and Lemay, *A Quarter-Century of Normalization*, 437.

98 For developments in one province, see Ontario, Ministry of Community and Social Services, Policy Development, *Three Decades of Change: The Evolution of Residential Care and Community Alternatives in Children's Services* (Ottawa: Queen's Printer, November 1983).

99 Rains and Teram, *Normal Bad Boys*, 54.

100 Pat Kariel, *New Directions: Stepping Out of Street Life* (Calgary: Greenways Press, 1993), 26.

101 See Debra J. Pepler and Kenneth H. Rubin, eds., *The Development and Treatment of Childhood Aggression* (Hillsdale, NJ: Lawrence Erlbaurn Associates, 1991).

102 Raymond Lemay and Hayat Chazal, *Looking after Children: A Practitioner's Guide* (Ottawa: University of Ottawa Press, 2007), 10.

103 Dulcie McAllum, *Abuse of Deaf Students at Jericho Hill School* (Victoria: Ombudsman of British Columbia, 1993); and her *The Need to Know. Woodlands School Report: An Administrative Review* (Victoria: Ministry of Children and Family Development, 2001).

104 Law Commission of Canada, *Restoring Dignity: Responding to Child Abuse in Canadian Institutions* (Ottawa: Law Commission of Canada, 2000).

105 Gerry Fewster and Thom Garfat, "Residential Child and Youth Care," in *Professional Child and Youth Care*, ed. Roy V. Ferguson and Alan R. Pence, 2nd edition (Vancouver: UBC Press, 1993), 33.

106 Clifton F. Carbin, *Deaf Heritage in Canada; A Distinctive, Diverse, and Enduring Culture* (Toronto: McGraw-Hill Ryerson, 1996), 407.

107 Kathy Jones, "Listening to Hidden Voices: Power, Domination, Resistance and Pleasure within Huronia Regional Centre," *Disability, Handicap and Society* 7, no. 4 (1992): 340.

108 Saint-Pierre, *Témoignages sur nos Orphelinats*, 18.

109 John Bowlby, *Maternal Care and Mental Health* (Geneva: World Health Organization, 1951).

110 Fewster and Garfat, "Residential Child and Youth Care," 21.

111 See Premier Gordon Campbell of British Columbia to the Union of BC Municipalities in Victoria on 27 October 2006. For one criticism, see Gary Mason, "For the Most Helpless of the Homeless," *Globe and Mail*, 31 October 2006, A15.

112 Xiaobei Chen, *Tending the Gardens of Citizenship: Child Saving in Toronto 1880s-1920s* (Toronto: University of Toronto Press, 2005), 123.

113 See Renée Joyal, *L'évolution de la protection de l'enfance au Québec: des origines à nos jours* (Quebec City: Presses de l'Université du Québec, 2000); and Gilbert Dale, *Dynamiques de l'institutionnalisatin de l'enfance délinquante et en besoin de protection: le cas des écoles de réforme et d'industrie de l'hospice Saint-Charles de Québec, 1870–1950* (MA dissertation, Laval University, 2006).

114 Anna G. Singleton, "Child Welfare Administration under Protection Acts in British Columbia: Its History and Development, 1901–1949" (MSW dissertation, University of British Columbia, 1950), 59.

115 Peter Sypnowich, "Society's Child," *Saturday Night*, August 1983, 30 and 31.

116 Fewster and Garfat, "Residential Child and Youth Care," 18.

117 See the four-part study of the Niagara region of Ontario by Joel Emberson, "The For-
     gotten Children," originally published in the *St. Catharine's Standard* in 2008, http://
     www.stcatharinesstandard.ca/ArticleDisplayGenContent.aspx?e=4525.
118 Fewster and Garfat, "Residential Child and Youth Care," 28.
119 Peter Silverman, *Who Speaks for the Children? Giving Voice to a Forgotten Generation*
     (Toronto: Stoddart, 1989), 107.
120 Rains and Teram, *Normal Bad Boys*, 9.
121 Fewster and Garfat, "Residential Child and Youth Care," 29.
122 Bob Couchman, "From Precious Resource to Societal Accessory: Canada's Children Six
     to Twelve Years of Age," paper presented by the National Children's Alliance, National
     Symposium, 22–24 March 2002, typescript, 10.
123 Heather J. Whiteford, "Special Needs Adoption: Perspectives on Policy and Practice"
     (MSW dissertation, University of British Columbia, 1988), 22.
124 On the danger of homelessness for children whose families can no longer cope with
     their conditions and can find no substitute caregiving arrangements, see Jayne Barker,
     "Out-of-Home Care for Children and Youth with Serious Emotional Disturbances" (MA
     dissertation, Royal Roads University, 2000), especially 5.
125 See Jones, "Listening to Hidden Voices," 339–48.
126 See Ron Csillag, "Canada's First L'Arche Member Spread the Word," *Globe and Mail*,
     9 May 2009, S16. See also Pat Felt with Pam Walker, "My Life in L'Arche," in *Women
     with Intellectual Disabilities: Finding a Place in the World*, ed. Rannveig Traustadottir and
     Kelly Johnson (London and Philadelphia: Jessica Kingsley Publisher, 2000), 217–28.
127 See SOS Children's Village, BC, http://www.sos-bc.org/village.htm.

Notes to Chapter 3

 1 For a balanced explanation of the enthusiasm of social workers, see Marilyn Callahan
    and Christopher Walmsley, "Rethinking Child Welfare Reform in British Columbia,
    1900–60," in *People, Politics, and Child Welfare in British Columbia*, ed. L.T. Foster and
    B. Wharf (Vancouver: UBC Press, 2007), especially 29–30.
 2 I am indebted to Michael Reid's "Understanding Children's Aid: Means and Practice in
    Ontario Children's Aid Societies, 1893–1912" (MA dissertation, Trent University, 2009),
    for further insights about masculinity and child protection in Ontario. My thanks to
    him for sending me a copy of his thesis.
 3 Shurlee Swain, "Sweet Childhood Lost: Idealized Images of Childhood in the British
    Child Rescue Literature," *Journal of the History of Childhood and Youth* 2, no. 2 (Spring
    2009): 208.
 4 See Nellie L. McClung, *In Times Like These* (Toronto: McLeod and Allen, 1915).
 5 Diane Purvey, "Alexandra Orphanage and Families in Crisis in Vancouver, 1892–1938,"
    in *Dimensions of Childhood: Essays on the History of Children and Youth in Canada*, ed.
    Russell Smandych, Gordon Dodds, and Alvin Esau (Winnipeg: Legal Research Institute
    of the University of Manitoba, 1991), 114.
 6 Carol T. Baines, "The Children of Earlscourt, 1915–1948: All in the Same Boat: "Except
    we were in a better boat,"" *Canadian Social Work Review* 11, no. 2 (Summer 1994): 196;
    Janice Harvey, "The Protestant Orphan Asylum and the Montreal Ladies' Benevolent
    Society: A Case Study in Protestant Child Charity in Montreal, 1822–1900" (Ph.D. dis-

sertation, McGill University, 2001). On sympathies, see also Charlotte Neff, "The Role of Protestant Children's Homes in Nineteenth-Century Ontario: Child Rescue or Family Support," *Journal of Family History,* 34, no. 1 (2009): 48–88.

7 See James Struthers, "A Profession in Crisis: Charlotte Whitton and Canadian Social Work in the 1930s," *Canadian Historical Review* 62, no. 2 (March 1981): 169–85.

8 See Constance Backhouse, "Married Women's Property Law in Nineteenth-Century Canada," *Law and History Review* 6, no. 2 (1988): 211–57; Lori Chambers, *Married Women and Property Law in Victorian Ontario* (Toronto: University of Toronto Press, 1997); and Constance Backhouse, "Shifting Patterns in Nineteenth-Century Canadian Custody Law," in *Essays in Canadian Law,* ed. David Flaherty, volume 1 (Toronto: University of Toronto Press, 1981), 212–88.

9 Reid, "Understanding Children's Aid," 63.

10 Ibid., 119. See also Joan Sangster, "Masking and UnMasking the Sexual Abuse of Children: Perceptions of Violence against Children in 'The Badlands' of Ontario, 1916–1930," *Journal of Family History* 25, no. 4 (October 2000): 504–26; and Mariana Valverde, *The Age of Light, Soap, and Water: Moral Reform in English Canada, 1885–1925* (Toronto: McClelland and Stewart, 1991), 38.

11 Xiaobei Chen, *Tending the Gardens of Citizenship: Child Saving in Toronto 1880s–1920s* (Toronto: University of Toronto Press, 2005), 93.

12 Karen Swift, "Contradictions in Child Welfare: Neglect and Responsibility," in *Women's Caring: Feminist Perspectives on Social Welfare,* ed. Carol T. Baines, Patricia M. Evans, and Sheila M. Neysmith (Toronto: Oxford University Press, 1998), 162.

13 Marilyn Callahan and Christopher Walmsley, "Rethinking Child Welfare Reform in British Columbia, 1900–60," in Foster and Wharf, *People, Politics, and Child Welfare,* 11.

14 See the Chen, *Tending the Gardens of Citizenship,* passim.

15 Ontario, *Annual Report of the Superintendent of Neglected and Dependent Children,* Sessional Papers (1902), 12.

16 Swain, "Sweet Childhood Lost," 202.

17 Helen J. Macdonald, "Boarding-Out and the Scottish Poor law, 1845–1914," *Scottish Historical Review* 75, no. 2 (1996): 192.

18 Anne Margaret Angus, *Children's Aid Society of Vancouver, B.C. 1901–1951* (Vancouver: Vancouver Children's Aid, 1951), 20 [emphasis in original].

19 Ethel M. Chapman, "Could You Adopt a Baby?" *Maclean's,* December 1919, 116.

20 Chen, *Tending the Gardens of Citizenship,* 127.

21 Angus, *Children's Aid Society of Vancouver,* 21.

22 J.-M.-Rodrigues Cardinal Villeneuve, O.M.I., "Preface," in Arthur Saint-Pierre, *Témoignases sur nos Orphelinats: Recueillis et Commentés* (Montreal: Fides, 1946), 10.

23 Joseph E. Laycock, *Survey of Ottawa's Child and Family Services: Final Draft Report for Planning and Policy Committee* (Ottawa: Welfare Council of Ottawa, 5 June 1953), 4.

24 James Struthers, *The Limits of Affluence: Welfare in Ontario, 1920–1970* (Toronto: University of Toronto Press, 1994), chapter 3.

25 On this influence and its implications for fostering in the United States, see Laura Curran, "Longing to 'Belong': Foster Children in Mid-Century Philadelphia (1946–1963)," *Journal of Social History* 42, no. 2 (Winter 2008): 425–45.

26 Gale Wills, *A Marriage of Convenience: Business and Social Work in Toronto, 1918–1957* (Toronto: University of Toronto Press, 1995), 138.

27 Ibid., 5.

28 Mona Gleason, *Normalizing the Ideal: Psychology, Schooling, and the Family in Postwar Canada* (Toronto: University of Toronto Press, 1999).

29 The best overall discussion of this is Nancy Christie, *Engendering the State: Women, Work and Welfare in Canada* (Toronto: University of Toronto Press, 2000).

30 See H. Philip Hepworth, *Foster Care and Adoption in Canada* (Ottawa: Canadian Council on Social Development, 1980), chapter 4; and James Struthers, "'In the Interests of the Children': Mothers' Allowances and the Origins of Social Security in Ontario, 1917–1930," in *Social Fabric or Patchwork Quilt: The Development of Social Policy in Canada*, ed. Raymond B. Blake and Jeffrey A. Keshen (Toronto: University of Toronto Press, 2006), 59–87.

31 See Margaret Little, *"No Car, No Radio, No Liquor Permit": The Moral Regulation of Single Mothers in Ontario, 1920–1997* (Toronto: University of Toronto Press, 1998); and Struthers, "'In the Interests of the Children.'"

32 Lori Chambers, *Misconceptions: Unmarried Motherhood and the Ontario Children of Unmarried Parents Act, 1921–1960* (Toronto: University of Toronto Press, 2007).

33 See Sean Purdy, "'It was tough on everybody': Low-Income Families and Housing Hardship in Post-World War II Toronto," *Journal of Social History* 37, no. 2 (Winter 2003): 457–82.

34 Adele Saunders, "Short Term Mothers," *Chatelaine*, September 1945, 51.

35 See the recommendation for visiting homemakers in Laycock, *Survey of Ottawa's Child and Family Services*, 65.

36 See Christie, *Engendering the State*, chapter 7. On the conservative implication of similar British legislation, see also Colleen M. Forrest, "Familial Poverty, Family Allowances, and the Normative Family Structure in Britain, 1917–1945," *Journal of Family History* 26, no. 4 (October 2001): 508–28.

37 Nova Scotia, Bureau of Child Welfare, *38th Annual Report* (30 November 1951), 10.

38 Mildred E. Battel, *Children Shall Be First: Child Welfare Saskatchewan 1944–64* (Regina: Local History Program; Saskatchewan Department of Culture and Youth, 1980), 22 and 28.

39 *The Welfare of Canadian Children: It's Our Business* (Ottawa: Child Welfare League of Canada, 2007), 3.

40 Cynthia Comacchio, *Nations Are Built of Babies: Saving Ontario's Mothers and Children 1900–1940* (Montreal and Kingston: McGill-Queen's University Press, 1993), 40.

41 H. David Kirk, *Shared Fate: A Theory of Adoption and Mental Health*, 2nd edition (Port Angeles, WA, and Brentwood Bay, BC: Ben-Simon Publications 1984).

42 On David Kirk, see Veronica Strong-Boag, *Finding Families, Finding Ourselves: English Canada Confronts Adoption from the Nineteenth Century to the 1990* (Toronto: Oxford University Press, 2006), passim.

43 Hepworth, *Foster Care and Adoption in Canada*, 21. On the willingness to support unwed mothers, see Winona Armitage, "The Unmarried Mother and Adoption," *Proceedings of the Ninth Canadian Conference on Social Work* (Winnipeg: June, 1944), 79.

44 See Karen Dubinsky, "'We Adopted a Negro': Interracial Adoption and the Hybrid Baby in 1960s Canada," in *Creating Postwar Canada: Community, Diversity, and Dissent 1945–75*, ed. Magda Fahrni and Robert Rutherdale (Vancouver: UBC Press, 2008), 268–88; and Karen Dubinsky, *Babies without Borders: Adoption and Migration across the Americas* (Toronto: University of Toronto Press, 2010), especially chapter 3.

45 See Sarah Davies, "Adoption Crisis: 10,000 Kids with No Place to Go," *Chatelaine*, December 1967, 89.

46 On this industry, see Karen Balcolm, "'Phony Mothers' and Border-Crossing Adoptions: The Montreal-to-New York Black Market in Babies in the 1950s," *Journal of Women's History* 19, no. 1 (Spring 2007): 107–16.

47 Ethel M. Chapman, "Could You Adopt a Baby?" *Maclean's*, December 1919, 116.

48 Maurice N. Cote, "The Children's Aid Society of the Catholic Archdiocese of Vancouver: Its Origins and Development, 1905–1953" (MSW dissertation, University of British Columbia, 1953), 8.

49 Nova Scotia, Director of Child Welfare, *Annual Report* (31 March 1952), 7.

50 George F. Davidson, IV, *Report on Public Welfare Services*, Royal Commission on Provincial Development and Rehabilitation (Halifax: King's Printer, 1944), 143.

51 George Caldwell, *Child Welfare Services in New Brunswick: A Report to the Honourable W.R. Duffie, Minister of Welfare, Province of New Brunswick* (Ottawa: Canadian Welfare Council, October 1965), 18.

52 On the same philosophy in New Zealand until the 1970s and 1980s, see Bronwyn Dalley, *Family Matters: Child-Welfare in Twentieth-Century New Zealand* (Auckland: Auckland University Press and Historical Branch, Department of Internal Affairs, 1998), 322–23.

53 Sarah Davies, "Adoption Crisis: 10,000 Kids with No Place to Go," *Chatelaine*, December 1967, 87.

54 Ontario, Department of Public Welfare, *Annual Report*, 1949–50 (Toronto, 1950), 19.

55 Prue Rains and Eli Teram, *Normal Bad Boys: Public Policies, Institutions and the Politics of Client Recruitment* (Montreal and Kingston: McGill-Queen's University Press, 1992), 59–60.

56 W.D. McFarland, *Placement Resources Services: Children's Aid Society of Vancouver* (Vancouver: Children's Aid Society, November 1972), 17.

57 See Battel, *Children Shall Be First*, 59.

58 Patrick Johnston, *Native Children and the Child Welfare System* (Ottawa: Canadian Council on Social Development, 1983), 83.

59 McFarland, "Placement Resources Services," 55.

60 Marvin Bernstein, *A Breach of Trust: An Investigation into Foster Home Overcrowding in the Saskatchewan Service Centre* (Saskatoon: Children's Advocate, February 2009), http://www.cecw-cepb.ca/publications/987, 2–3.

61 Gérard Pelletier, *L'Histoire des enfants tristes* (Montreal: Action Sociale, 1950), http://orphelin.users2.50megs.com/triste01.html.

62 On these developments, see Renée Joyal, *Les Enfants, la société et l'état au Québec 1608–1989* (Montreal: Editions Hurtubise, 1999).

63 See Clio Collective, *Quebec Women: A History*, trans. Roger Gannon and Roslind Gill (Toronto: Women's Press, 1987).

64 Michael Gauvreau, *The Catholic Origins of Quebec's Quiet Revolution, 1931–1970* (Montreal and Kingston: McGill-Queen's University Press, 2007), 111.

65 Rains and Teram, *Normal Bad Boys*, 59–60.

66 Ibid.

67 Bridge Moran, *A Little Rebellion* (Vancouver: Arsenal Pulp Press, 1992), 41.

68 Battel, *Children Shall Be First*, 60.

69 Simma Holt, *Sex and the Teen-age Revolution* (Toronto: McClelland and Stewart, 1967), 142.

70 Quoted in Callahan and Walmsley, "Rethinking Child Welfare Reform in British Columbia, 1900–60," 25.

Notes to Chapter 4

1 See Paul Kershaw, *Carefair: Rethinking the Responsibilities and Rights of Citizenship* (Vancouver: UBC Press, 2005), chapter 4. See also Maureen Baker, *Restructuring Family Policies: Convergences and Divergences* (Toronto: University of Toronto Press, 2006).

2 Cheryl Farris-Manning and Marietta Zandstra, "Children in Care in Canada: A Summary of Current Issues and Trends with Recommendations for Future Research," in *The Welfare of Canadian Children: It's Our Business* (Ottawa: Child Welfare Council of Canada, 2007), 56.

3 Andy Wachtel, "Child Welfare in Canada: Framework for Action," in *The Welfare of Canadian Children*, 46.

4 The dilemmas for caregiving posed by this trend are effectively set out by Olena Hankivsky, *Social Policy and the Ethic of Care* (Vancouver: UBC Press, 2004), especially chapter 6.

5 Marlee Kline, "Complicating the Ideology of Motherhood: Child Welfare Law and First Nations Women," *Queen's Law Journal* 18, no. 2 (1993): 306–42.

6 Colin Hughes, *Greater Trouble in Greater Toronto: Child Poverty in the GTA* (Toronto: Children's Aid Society of Toronto, 2009), http://www.campaign2000.ca/GreaterTrouble GreaterTorontodec2008.pdf; and *2008 Report Card on Child and Family Poverty in Canada* (Toronto: Campaign 2000, 2009), http://www.campaign2000.ca/C2000ReportCard FINALNov10th08.pdf.

7 Alvin Finkel, *Social Policy and Practice in Canada: A History* (Waterloo: Wilfrid Laurier University Press, 2006), 300.

8 Ibid., 261.

9 For a critique of modern managerialism and the approach of "risk assessment," see Marilyn Callahan and Karen Swift, "Great Expectations and Unintended Consequences: Risk Assessment in Child Welfare in British Columbia," in *People, Politics, and Child Welfare in British Columbia*, ed. Leslie T. Foster and Brian Wharf (Vancouver: UBC Press, 2007), 158–83. On the growing gap, see Sandra Scarth and Richard Sullivan, "Child Welfare in the 1980s: A Time of Turbulence and Change," in Foster and Wharf, *People, Politics, and Child Welfare in British Columbia*, 83–96.

10 Patricia Evans, "Eroding Canadian Social Welfare: The Mulroney Legacy, 1984–1993," in *Social Fabric or Patchwork Quilt: The Development of Social Policy in Canada*, ed. Raymond B. Blake and Jeffrey A. Keshen (Toronto: Broadview, 2006), 263–74; R. Brian Howe and Katherine Covell, "Children's Rights in Hard Times," in *The Welfare State in Canada: Past, Present and Future*, ed. Raymond B. Blake, Penny E. Bryden, and J. Frank Strain (Concord, ON: Irwin Publishing, 1997), 230–45.

11 Kelly A. MacDonald, *The Road to Aboriginal Authority over Child and Family Services: Considerations for an Effective Transition* (Vancouver: Centre for Native Policy and Research and Canadian Centre for Policy Alternatives, 2008), 13

12 For these developments, see the various chapters in the excellent collection, Alexandra Dobrowolsky, ed., *Women and Public Policy in Canada: Neo-liberalism and After?* (Toronto: Oxford University Press, 2009).

13 Andrew Armitage, "Lost Vision: Children and the Ministry for Children and Families," *BC Studies* 118 (Summer 1998): 105–6.

14 Brian Wharf, "Addressing Public Issues in Child Welfare," in *Child Welfare: Connecting Research, Policy, and Practice*, ed. Kathleen Kufeldt and Brad McKenzie (Waterloo: Wilfrid Laurier University Press, 2003), 423.

15 Raymond B. Blake, "In the Children's Interest? Change and Continuity in a Century of Canadian Social Welfare Initiatives for Children," in Blake and Keshen, *Social Fabric or Patchwork Quilt*, 216.

16 Kathleen Kufeldt, "Inclusive Care, Separation, and Role Clarity in Foster Care: The Development of Theoretical Constructs," in *Child Welfare in Canada: Research and Policy Implications*, ed. Joe Hudson and Burt Galaway (Toronto: Thompson Educational Publishing, 1995), 388. See also Heather Whiteford, "Special Needs Adoption: Perspectives on Policy and Practice" (MSW dissertation, University of British Columbia 1988), 21.

17 Farris-Manning and Zandstra, "Children in Care in Canada," 60.

18 On the latter, see Wendy Chan and Kiran Mirchandani, *Criminalizing Race, Criminalizing Poverty: Welfare Fraud Enforcement in Canada* (Halifax: Fernwood Books, 2007).

19 See, for example, Nico Trocmé et al., "The Canadian Incidence Study of Reported Child Abuse and Neglect: Methodology and Major Findings," in Kufeldt and McKenzie, *Child Welfare*, 13–26.

20 Brian Wharf, "The Constituency/Community Context," in *Rethinking Child Welfare in Canada*, ed. Brian Wharf (Toronto: McClelland and Stewart, 1993), 109.

21 See *Changing the Landscape: Ending Violence—Achieving Equality* (Ottawa: Ministry of Supply and Services, 1993); Linda MacLeod, *Battered but Not Beaten: Preventing Wife Battering in Canada* (Ottawa: Advisory Council on the Status of Women, 1987); Peter Jaffe, David Wolfe, and Susan K. Wilson, *Children of Battered Women* (Newbury Park, CA: Sage Publications, 1990); Susan Prentice, ed., *Changing Child Care: Five Decades of Child Care Advocacy and Policy in Canada* (Halifax, NS: Fernwood Publishing, 2001); and Martha Friendly and Susan Prentice, *About Canada Childcare* (Halifax, NS: Fernwood Publishing, 2009).

22 Marilyn Callahan, "Feminist Approaches: Women Recreate Child Welfare," in Wharf, *Rethinking Child Welfare in Canada*, 173. See also Joan Gilroy, "Social Work and the Women's Movement," in *Social Work and Social Change in Canada*, ed. Brian Wharf (Toronto: McClelland and Stewart, 1990), 52–78.

23 James King, Morag MacKay, Angela Sirnick, with the Canadian Shaken Baby Study Group, "Shaken Baby Syndrome in Canada: Clinical Characteristics and Outcomes of Hospital Cases," *Canadian Medical Association Journal* 168, no. 2 (21 January 2003): 156 and 158.

24 Public Health Agency of Canada, Working Group, "Joint Statement on Shaken Baby Syndrome," http://www.phac-aspc.gc.ca/dca-dea/publications/jointstatement_web-eng.php.

25 Cyril Greenland, *Child Abuse in Ontario* (Toronto: Ministry of Community and Social Services, 1973); and Murray Fraser, J.P. Anderson, and K. Burns, *Child Abuse in Nova Scotia* (Halifax: no publisher identified, 1973).

26 Benjamin Schlesinger, *Child Abuse in Canada* (Toronto: Faculty of Education,University of Toronto, 1977).

27 Mary Van Stolk, *The Battered Child in Canada* (Toronto: McClelland and Stewart, 1972). See Sally Mennill and Veronica Strong-Boag, "Identifying Victims: Child Abuse and Death in Families," *Canadian Bulletin of Medical History* 25, no. 2 (2008): 11–33, for greater discussion of these reports.

28 Canada, Committee on Sexual Offences against Children and Youth, *Sexual Offences against Children: Report of the Committee on Sexual Offences against Children and Youth* (the Badgley Report), volumes 1 and 2 (Ottawa: Department of Supply and Services,

1984); and Christopher Bagley, *Child Sexual Abuse in Canada: Further Analysis of the 1983 National Survey* (Ottawa: Health and Welfare Canada, 1988). On earlier, much less publicized, discoveries, see Joan Sangster, "Incest, the Sexual Abuse of Children, and the Power of Familialism," *Regulating Girls and Women: Sexuality, Family and the Law in Ontario, 1920–1960* (Toronto: Oxford University Press, 2001).

29 See Charlotte Van Allen, *Daddy's Girl* (Toronto: McClelland and Stewart, 1980); Elly Danica, *Don't: A Woman's Word* (Charlottetown, PEI: Gynergy Books, 1988); and Sylvia Fraser, *In My Father's House: A Memoir of Incest and Healing* (Toronto: Doubleday, 1988).

30 Judy Steed, *Our Little Secret: Confronting Child Sexual Abuse in Canada* (Toronto: Random House, 1994).

31 Emma Laroque, "Culturally Appropriate Models in Criminal Justice Applications," in *Aboriginal and Treaty Rights in Canada,* ed. Michael Asch (Vancouver: UBC Press, 1998), 81.

32 Sheila McIntyre, "Feminist Movement in Law: Beyond Privileged and Privileging Theory," in *Women's Legal Strategies in Canada,* ed. Radha Jhappan (Toronto: University of Toronto Press, 2002), 70.

33 For a valuable study of the condition and its politics in the United States, see Janet Golden, *Message in a Bottle: The Making of Fetal Alcohol Syndrome* (Cambridge, MA: Harvard University Press, 2005). See also David T. Courtwright, "Drug Wars: Policy Hots and Historical Cools," *Bulletin of the History of Medicine* 78, no. 2 (Summer 2004): 440–50. For a related problem "discovered" in these years, see Wayne Hammond and David Romney, "Treatment Revisited for Aboriginal Adolescent Solvent Abusers," in Kufeldt and McKenzie, *Child Welfare,* 309–18.

34 See Caroline L. Tait, "Disruptions in Nature, Disruptions in Society: Aboriginal Peoples of Canada and the 'Making' of Fetal Alcohol Syndrome," in *Healing Traditions: The Mental Health of Aboriginal Peoples in Canada,* ed. Laurence J. Kirmayer and Fail Guthrie Valaskakis (Vancouver: UBC Press, 2009), 196–220.

35 See Public Health Agency of Canada, *Backgrounder on Government of Canada and FASD,* http://www.phac-aspc.gc.ca/fasd-etcaf/goc-bg-eng.php.

36 Chris Leischner et al., *Creating Solutions: Women Preventing FAS; Understanding Women's Substance Misuse* (Prince George, BC: Northern Family Health Society, 2001), 6.

37 Bruce MacLaurin and Megan McCormack, "Child Protection in Canada," in *The Welfare of Canadian Children,* 78.

38 Brian Wharf, "Organizing and Delivering Child Welfare Services: The Contributions of Research," in Hudson and Galaway, *Child Welfare in Canada,* 6.

39 Michel Parazelli, *La Rue attractive: parcours et partiques identitaires des jeunes de la rue* (Ste-Foy, QC: Presses de l'Université du Québec, 2002). See also Martin Goyette, Céline Bellot, and Jean Panet-Raymond, *Le Project Solidarité Jeunesse: dynamiques partenariales et insertion des jeunes en difficulté* (Ste-Foy, QC: Presses de l'Universié du Québec, 2006).

40 Paul Steinhauer, *The Least Detrimental Alternative: A Systemic Guide to Case Planning and Decision Making for Children in Care* (Toronto: University of Toronto Press, 1991), 6.

41 An excellent survey of the 1970s and 1980s in this regard is provided by Andrew Armitage, "Family and Child Welfare in First Nation Communities," in *Rethinking Child Welfare in Canada,* ed. Brian Wharf (Toronto: McClelland and Stewart, 1993) 131–71. See also Patrick Johnston, *Native Children and the Child Welfare System* (Ottawa: Canadian Council for Social Development, 1983); Cindy Blackstock, Ivan Brown, and Marilyn Bennett, "Reconciliation: Rebuilding the Canadian Child Welfare System to Better

Serve Aboriginal Children and Youth," in *Putting a Human Face on Child Welfare: Voices from the Prairies*, ed. Ivan Brown et al. (Regina: Prairie Child Welfare Consortium, 2007), 59–87; and Veronica Strong-Boag, *Finding Families, Finding Ourselves: English Canada Confronts Adoption from the Nineteenth Century to the 1990s* (Toronto: Oxford University Press, 2006), especially chapter 6.

42 For the most effective assessment of how mainstream child protection sometimes served child victims whose own nations were in little position to help, see Cheryl Marlene Swidrovich, "Positive Experiences of First Nations Children in Non-Aboriginal Foster or Adoptive Care: De-Constructing the 'Sixties Scoop'" (MA dissertation, University of Saskatchewan, 2004).

43 *Canadian Charter of Rights and Freedoms*, Part 1 of the *Constitution Act, 1982*, being Schedule B to the *Canada Act 1982* (U.K.), 1982, c. 11.

44 BC Department of Rehabilitation and Social Improvement, *Annual Report* (for the year ended 31 March 1972), 33–4.

45 See, for example, the reference to twenty years of efforts at recruitment on reserves in Review Committee on Indian and Metis Adoptions and Placements, *Briefs*, chaired by Judge Edwin C. Kimelman, Transcripts and Briefs: Public Hearings and Special Hearings (Winnipeg: Manitoba Community Services, 1985), 101.

46 Ibid., 103.

47 Peter Hudson and Brad McKenzie, "Child Welfare and Native People: The Extension of Colonialism," *Le Travailleur social/The Social Worker* 49, no. 2 (Summer 1981): 63–88. On the relationship of social work and the Native rights movement, see Yvonne House and Harvey Stalwick, "Social Work and the First Nation Movement: 'Our Children, Our Culture,'" in Wharf, *Social Work and Social Change in Canada*, 79–113.

48 Swidrovich, "Positive Experiences of First Nations Children," 22.

49 See Royal Commission on Aboriginal Peoples, *Public Policy and Aboriginal Peoples 1965–1992*, Summaries of Reports by Provincial and Territorial Bodies and Other Organizations, volume 3 (Ottawa: Royal Commission on Aboriginal Peoples, 1994).

50 Gene Elmore, Sharon Clark, and Sharon Dick, "A Survey of Adoption and Child Welfare Services to Indians of British Columbia (n.p.: Union of British Columbia Indian Chiefs, 18 February 1974), 8 and 22.

51 See Ann McGillivray, "Transracial Adoption and the Status Indian Child," *Canadian Journal of Family Law* 4 (1985): 466; and John A. MacDonald, "The Spallumcheen Indian Band By-Law and Its Potential Impact on Native Indian Child Welfare Policy in British Columbia," *Canadian Journal Family Law* 4 (July 1983): 75–95.

52 BC Ministry of Social Services and Housing, Services for People, *Annual Report* (1988–89), 44.

53 Vancouver Aboriginal Child and Family Services Society, http://www.vacfss.com/index .php?option=com_content&task=view&id=39&Itemid=286.

54 Peter Hudson and Sharon Taylor-Heley, "First Nations Child and Family Services, 1982–1992," in Blake and Keshen, *Social Fabric or Patchwork Quilt*, 251.

55 Cindy Blackstock, "First Nations Child and Family Services: Restoring Peace and Harmony in First Nations Communities," in Kufeldt and McKenzie, *Child Welfare*, 338.

56 Johnston, *Native Children and the Child Welfare System*, 126.

57 Hudson and Taylor-Heley, "First Nations Child and Family Services, 1982–1992," 251.

58 Ibid., 252 and 258.

59   Vic Satzewich and Terry Wotherspoon, *First Nations: Race, Class, and Gender Relations* (Regina: Canadian Plains Research Center, 2000), 93.

60   Swidrovich, "Positive Experiences of First Nations Children."

61   Alexandra Wright et al., *Summary Report Factors That Contribute to Positive Outcomes in the Awasis Pimicikamak Cree Nation Kinship Care Program* (Canadian Centre for Excellence for Child Welfare and Health Canada, 2005), 15.

62   See the argument in Joyce Timpson, "Four Decades of Child Welfare Services to Native Indians in Ontario" (PhD dissertation, Wilfrid Laurier University, 1993), 14.

63   Brad McKenzie, Esther Seidl, and Norman Bone, "Child Welfare Standards in First Nations: A Community-Based Study," in Hudson and Galaway, *Child Welfare in Canada*, 55.

64   G.C. Robinson, R.F. Conroy, and J.L. Conroy, *The Canim Lake Survey of Special Needs Children* (Vancouver: University of British Columbia, March 1985). This study, at the request of the Canim Lake Band, identified over 25 percent of children as handicapped and six of forty-five resident mothers as accounting for over 60 percent of youngsters affected by fetal alcohol (14 and 19).

65   Cindy Blackstock, "Aboriginal Children, Families and Communities," in *The Welfare of Canadian Children*, 86–87.

66   See S. Nadjiwan and C. Blackstock, *Caring across the Boundaries: Promoting Access to Voluntary Sector Resources for First Nations Children and Families* (Ottawa: First Nations Child and Family Caring Society of Canada, 2003).

67   Blackstock, "Aboriginal Children, Families and Communities," 87.

68   Ibid., 88.

69   *D.H. v. H.M*, [1999] 1 S.C.R. 328, No. F950814 (B.C.S.C.) (affirmed, J. Bauman) (Vancouver, 26 September 1997), cited on the website of the Continuing Legal Education Society of British Columbia, http://www.cle.bc.ca/Cle/Practice+Desk/Practice+Articles/Collection/02-app-custodysupport.

70   Cindy Blackstock, "First Nations Child and Family Services: Restoring Peace and Harmony in First Nations Communities," in Kufeldt and McKenzie, *Child Welfare*, 341–42.

71   Sharon McKay and Shelley Thomas Prokop, "Identity, Community, Resilience: The Transmission of Values Project," in *Putting a Human Face on Child Welfare: Voices from the Prairies*, ed. Ivan Brown et al. (Prairie Child Welfare Consortium and Centre of Excellence for Child Welfare, 2007), 48, http://www.uregina.ca/spr/prairechild/index.html/, Centre www.cecw-ceph.ca.

72   Blackstock, "Aboriginal Children, Families and Communities," 88–89.

73   See Nancy MacDonald, Joan Glode, and Fred Wien, "Respecting Aboriginal Families: Pathways to Resilience in Custom Adoption and Family Group Conferencing," in *Handbook for Working with Children and Youth: Pathways to Resilience across Cultures and Contexts*, ed. Michael Ungar (Thousand Oaks, CA: Sage Publications, 2005), 362–64.

74   Quoted in "Suffering Even in Care," *Globe and Mail*, 23 February 2007, A20.

75   Wendy Stueck, "Guardians Living on Reserves Subject to Screening," *Globe and Mail*, 24 November 2008, S1; and Gerry Bellett, "Foster Care Safety Probed," *Vancouver Sun*, 18 September 2008, A1 and A10.

76   See Diane Richler, "The Case for Community Living—The Case against Segregation," abilities.ca, http://www.abilities.ca/social_policy/1991/06/01/emerging_realities/.

77   B. Maltais-Valois, "The Right to a Quality Life," *Entourage* 6, no. 2 (1991): 12–13.

78   Law Commission of Canada, *Restoring Dignity: Responding to Child Abuse in Canadian Institutions* (Ottawa: Department of Justice, 2001).

79 Wolf Wolfensberger, "A Contribution to the History of Normalization, with Primary Emphasis on the Establishment of Normalization in North America between 1967–1975," in *A Quarter-Century of Normalization and Social Role Valorization: Evolution and Impact*, ed. Robert J. Flynn and Raymond A. Lemay (Ottawa: University of Ottawa Press, 1999), 93.

80 Ibid., 55.

81 André Dionne, "The Impact of Social Role Valorization on Government Policy in Quebec," in Flynn and Lemay, *Quarter-Century of Normalization*, 564.

82 Robert J. Flynn and Tim D. Aubry, "Integration of Persons with Developmental or Psychiatric Disabilities: Conceptualization and Measurement," in Flynn and Lemay, *Quarter-Century of Normalization*, 271.

83 André Blanchet, "The Impact of Normalization and Social Role Valorization in Canada," in Flynn and Lemay, *Quarter-Century of Normalization*, 439.

84 See the tribute to child psychiatrist and creator of the study, David (Dan) Offord (1933–2004) on the website of the Offord Centre for Child Studies, http://www.offord centre.com/about/dan.html.

85 Raymond Lemay and Hayat Ghazal, *Looking after Children: A Practitioner's Guide* (Ottawa: University of Ottawa, 2007), 10.

86 On developments in one province, see Brad McKenzie, "The Development of a Foster Family Care," in *Current Perspectives on Foster Family Care for Children and Youth*, ed. Brad McKenzie (Toronto and Dayton: Wall and Emerson, 1994), 59–73; and Don Fuchs et al., "Children with Disabilities Involved with the Child Welfare System in Manitoba: Current and Future Challenges," in *Putting a Human Face on Child Welfare: Voices from the Prairies*, ed. Ivan Brown et al. (Regina: Prairie Child Welfare Consortium, 2007), 127–45.

87 Wharf, "Introduction," in Foster and Wharf, *People, Politics and Child Welfare in British Columbia*, 5–7.

88 Paul D. Steinhauer, "The Management of Children Admitted to Child Welfare Services in Ontario: A Review and Discussion of Current Problems and Practices," *Canadian Journal of Psychiatry* 29, no. 6 (October 1984): 473.

89 James Anglin, "Staffed Group Homes for Youth: Toward a Framework for Understanding," in Kufeldt and McKenzie, *Child Welfare*, 191.

90 Ibid., 199.

91 Wolfensberger, *The Principle of Normalization* (Toronto: National Institute on Mental Retardation, 1972).

92 Carol Appathurai, Grant Lowery, and Terry Sullivan, "Achieving the Vision of Deinstitutionalization: A Role for Foster Care?" *Child and Adolescent Social Work* 3, no. 1 (Spring 1986): 50.

93 Ibid., 52.

94 Canadian Association for Community Living, *National Report Card 2008: Inclusion of Canadians with Intellectual Disabilities*, http://www.cacl.ca/english/documents/Report Cards/2008ReportCard_Nov26.pdf, 9 and 11.

95 Fraser Valentine, *Enabling Citizenship: Full Inclusion of Children with Disabilities and Their Parents* (Ottawa: Canadian Policy Research Networks, 2001), 7.

96 Canadian Association for Community Living, *National Report Card 2008: Inclusion of Canadians with Intellectual Disabilities*, 9 and 11.

97 On the significance of deaths in care, see the acknowledgement of the situation in Manitoba and Ontario in Brad McKenzie, Sally Palmer, and Wanda Thomas Barnard, "Views

from Other Provinces," in Foster and Wharf, *People, Politics and Child Welfare in British Columbia*, 217–25.

98 Farris-Manning and Zandstra, "Children in Care in Canada," 54–55.

99 Marvin Bernstein, *A Breach of Trust: An Investigation into Foster Home Overcrowding in the Saskatchewan Service Centre* (Saskatoon: Children's Advocate, February 2009), 21.

100 Nichole Dallaire et al., "Social Prevention: A Study of Projects in an Urban Environment," in Kufeldt and McKenzie, *Child Welfare*, 126.

101 Don Fuchs, "Preserving and Strengthening Families and Protecting Children: Social Network Intervention, A Balanced Approach to the Prevention of Child Maltreatment," in Hudson and Galaway, *Child Welfare in Canada*, 113–22.

102 Mark Pancer et al., "Promoting Wellness in Families and Children through Community-Based Interventions: The Highfield Community Enrichment Project," in Kufeldt and McKenzie, *Child Welfare*, 111–22.

103 Gary Cameron, "The Nature and Effectiveness of Parent Mutual Aid Organizations in Child Welfare," in Hudson and Galaway, *Child Welfare in Canada*, 66 and 69.

104 Ibid., 66 and 78.

105 Ibid., 93.

106 Child and Youth Officer for British Columbia [Jane Morley], *Heshook-ish Tsawalk: Towards a State of Healthy Interdependence in the Child Welfare System* (Victoria: Child and Youth Officer for British Columbia, June 2006), ii.

107 K. Kufeldt, J. Armstrong, and M. Dorosh, "How Children in Care View Their Own and Their Foster Families: A Research Study," *Child Welfare* 74, no. 3 (May-June 1995): 695–718.

108 Jane Morley, *Heshook-ish Tsawalk*, 5.

109 Leslie T. Foster, "Trends in Child Welfare: What Do the Data Show?" in Foster and Wharf, *People, Politics and Child Welfare in British Columbia*, 53; and M. Callahan et al., "Catch as Catch Can: Grandmothers Raising Their Grandchildren and Kinship Care Policies," *Canadian Review of Social Policy* 54 (Fall 2004): 58–78.

110 Jane Morley, *Heshook-ish Tsawalk*, 7.

111 W.D. McFarland, *Placement Resources Services: Children's Aid Society of Vancouver* (Vancouver: Children's Aid Society of Vancouver, November 1972), 5.

112 Paul Steinhauer, cited in Rita S. Eagle, 'The Separation Experience of Children in Long-Term Care: Theory, Research, and Implications for Practice," *American Journal of Orthopsychiatry* 64, no. 3 (July 1994): 424.

113 Ibid., 425.

114 Marilyn Callahan, "The Administrative and Practice Context: Perspectives from the Front Line," in Wharf, *Rethinking Child Welfare in Canada*, 87–90.

115 Farris-Manning and Zandstra, "Children in Care in Canada," 64.

116 Ibid., 65.

117 On this dilemma in the United States, see Teresa Toguchi Swartz, "Mothering for the State: Foster Parenting and the Challenges of Government-Contracted Carework," *Gender and Society* 18, no. 5 (October 2004): 568. On these difficulties in Canada, see the discussion of the "powerlessness" of social workers in Marilyn Callahan and Carolyn Attridge, *Women in Women's Work: Social Workers Talk about Their Work in Child Welfare*, Research Monograph no. 3 (University of Victoria, November 1990), 24–30.

118 Ken Barter, "Working Conditions for Social Workers and Linkages to Client Outcomes in Child Welfare: A Literature Review," in *The Welfare of Canadian Children*, 154.

119 Steinhauer, *The Least Detrimental Alternative*, 283. See also his "The Preventive Utilization of Foster Care," *Canadian Journal of Psychiatry* 33, no. 6 (August 1988): 461.

120 On feminism and Canadian social work, see the thoughtful assessment by Callahan,
"Feminist Approaches: Women Recreate Child Welfare," in Wharf, *Rethinking Child
Welfare in Canada*, 172–209.

121 See the various contributions to *Community Organizing: Canadian Experiences*, ed. Brian
Wharf and Michael Clague (Toronto: Oxford University Press, 1997). See also Mary
Joplin Clarke, "Report of the Standing Committee on Neighbourhood Work" (1917) in
Saving the Canadian City: The First Phase 1880–1920, ed. Paul Rutherford (Toronto:
University of Toronto Press, 1974), 171–93; Cathy James, "Reforming Reform: Toronto's
Settlement House Movement, 1900–20," *Canadian Historical Review* 82, no. 1 (March
2001): 55–90; Gale Wills, *A Marriage of Convenience: Business and Social Work in Toronto,
1918–1957* (Toronto: University of Toronto Press, 1995); Ian Hamilton, *The Children's
Crusade: The Story of the Company of Young Canadians* (Toronto: P. Martin, 1970); and
Margaret Daly, *The Revolution Game: The Short Unhappy Life of the Company of Young
Canadians* (Toronto: New Press, 1970). See also the possibilities glimpsed in Bryan D.
Palmer, *Canada's 1960s: The Ironies of Identity in a Rebellious Era* (Toronto: University of
Toronto Press, 2009).

122 See Jean Panet-Raymond and Robert Mayer, "The History of Community Development
in Quebec," in Wharf and Clague, *Community Organizing*, 29–61; Deena White, "Contradictory Participation: Reflections on Community Action in Quebec," in Wharf and
Clague, *Community Organizing*, 62–90; Linda Davies, Karen Fox, Julia Krane, and Eric
Shragge, "Community Child Welfare: Examples from Quebec," in Brian Wharf, *Community Work Approaches to Child Welfare* (Toronto: Broadview Press, 2002), 63–81; Jean-
Pierre Collin, "Crise du logement et action catholique à Montréal, 1940–1960," *Revue
d'histoire de l'Amérique française* 41, no. 2 (1987): 179–203; Gail Cuthbert Brandt and
Naomi Black, "'Il en faut un peu': Farm Women and Feminism in Québec and France
since 1945," *Journal of the Canadian Historical Association/Revue de la Société historique du
Canada* 1, no. 1 (1990): 73–96.

123 Wharf, "Addressing Public Issues in Child Welfare," 427.

124 Ontario's Advocacy Office, established in 1978, is the oldest office in this country.

Notes to Chapter 5

1 Alice Parizeau, *Protection de l'enfant: échec?* (Montreal: Les Presses de l'Université de
Montreal, 1978), 12; and Krista Robson, "'Canada's Most Notorious Bad Mother' The
Newspaper Coverage of the Jordan Heikamp Inquest," *Canadian Review of Sociology and
Anthropology* 42, no. 2 (2003): 217–32.

2 On the attention to "abuse" but the significance of "neglect," see Xiaobei Chen, "Con-
stituting 'Dangerous Parents' through the Specter of Child Death: A Critique of Child
Protection Restructuring in Ontario," in *Making Normal: Social Regulation in Canada*, ed.
Deborah Brock (Toronto: Nelson Thomson Learning, 2003), 209–34.

3 Ron Csillag, "She Was the First Anglican Woman Elected a Parish Warden in Toronto,"
Globe and Mail, 2 July 2007, S12. See also "Activist, Teacher and Counselor was Mainstay of the Community," *Toronto Star*, 23 July 2007, A13.

4 Gil Cardinal, Director, Foster Child (Ottawa: National Film Board of Canada, 1987).

5 Kathleen Arnott, *Analysis of a Selected Group of Families Whose Children Were Admitted to the Care of the Children's Aid Society in Hamilton between January 1st, 1957, and December 31st 1959* (Hamilton: Children's Aid Society, 1961), 16.

6 Linda Gordon, *Heroes of Their Own Lives: The Politics and History of Family Violence, Boston 1880–1960* (New York: Viking, 1988), 8.

7 Chen, "Constituting 'Dangerous Parents,'" 232.

8 Bettina Bradbury, "Canadian Children Who Lived with One Parent in 1901," in *Household Counts: Canadian Households and Families in 1901*, ed. Eric W. Sager and Peter Baskerville (Toronto: University of Toronto Press, 2007), 252.

9 See the letters of mothers in particular to the prime minister in L.M. Grayson and J.M. Bliss, eds., *The Wretched of Canada: Letters to R.B. Bennett, 1930–35* (Toronto: University of Toronto Press, 1971).

10 Dominique Marshall, "The Language of Children's Rights, the Formation of the Welfare State, and the Democratic Experience of Poor Families in Quebec, 1940–1955," *Canadian Historical Review* 78, no. 3 (September 1997): 418.

11 Mildred E. Battel, *Children Shall Be First: Child Welfare Saskatchewan 1944–64* (Saskatoon: Saskatchewan Department of Children and Youth, Local History Program 1980), 57.

12 See Jill Wade, *Houses for All: The Struggle for Social Housing in Vancouver, 1919–1950* (Vancouver: UBC Press, 1994); and Sean Purdy, "'It was tough on everybody': Low-Income Families and Housing Hardship in Post–World War II Toronto," *Journal of Social History* 37, no. 2 (Winter 2003): 81–98.

13 Arnott, *Analysis of a Selected Group of Families*, 3, Table 1.

14 "Five Children Given Up over House Shortage," *Toronto Star*, 30 October 1967, 1 and 9.

15 Miriam Cohen-Schlanger et al., "Housing as a Factor in Admissions of Children to Temporary Care: A Survey," *Child Welfare* 74, no. 3 (May-June 1995): 547.

16 Alvin Finkel, *Social Policy and Practice in Canada: A History* (Toronto: Wilfrid Laurier University Press, 2007), 258 and 249.

17 Leslie T. Foster and Michael Wright, "Patterns and Trends in Children in the Care of the Province of British Columbia," in *Too Small to See, Too Big to Ignore: Child Health and Wellbeing in British Columbia*, ed. Michael V. Hayes and Leslie T. Foster, Canadian Western Geographical Series no. 35, volume 35 (Victoria: Department of Geography, University of Victoria, 2002), 132.

18 Brian Wharf, "Organizing and Delivering Child Welfare Services: The Contributions of Research," in *Child Welfare in Canada: Research and Policy Implications*, ed. Joe Hudson and Burt Galaway (Toronto: Thompson Educational Publishing, 1995), 3. See also Jim Campbell, "Children and Youth: Ministry of Social Services Child Protection and the Legislative Review," *Perspectives* (1992), quoted in Andrew Armitage, "The Policy and Legislative Context," in Brian Wharf, ed., *Rethinking Child Welfare in Canada* (Toronto: McClelland and Stewart, 1993), 39; and Bruce MacLaurin, Nico Trocmé, and Barbara Fallon, "Characteristics of Investigated Children and Families Referred for Out-of-Home Placement," in *Child Welfare: Connecting Research, Policy, and Practice*, ed. Kathleen Kufeldt and Brad McKenzie (Waterloo: Wilfrid Laurier University Press, 2003), 39.

19 See Iglika Ivanova, *BC's Growing Gap: Family Income Inequality, 1976–2006* (Vancouver: Canadian Centre for Policy Alternatives, March 2008).

20 On the gendered and racialized calumny of the term, see Eileen Boris, "On Cowboys and Welfare Queens: Independence, Dependence and Interdependence at Home and

Abroad," *Journal of American Studies* 41 (2007): 599–621. On the situation in the United Kingdom, see Mary McIntosh, "Social Anxieties about Lone Motherhood and Ideologies of the Family: Two Sides of the Same Coin," in *Good Enough Mothering? Feminist Perspectives on Lone, Motherhood*, ed. Elizabeth B. Silva (London and New York: Routledge, 1996), 148–56.

21 Susan C. Boyd, *From Witches to Crack Moms: Women, Drug Law and Policy* (Durham, NC: Carolina Academic Press, 2004), 143.

22 Jean Swanson, *Poor-Bashing: The Politics of Exclusion* (Toronto: Between the Lines, 2001), 24.

23 McIntosh, "Social Anxieties," 150.

24 Duncan Lindsey, "Factors Affecting the Foster Care Placement Decision: An Analysis of National Survey Data," *American Journal of Orthopsychiatry* 61, no. 2 (April 1991): 272.

25 Marilyn Callahan, "Feminist Approaches: Women Recreate Child Welfare," in Wharf, *Rethinking Child Welfare*, 185.

26 Douglas Durst, Josephine McDonald, and Cecilia Rich, "Aboriginal Government of Child Welfare Services: Hobson's Choice?" in Hudson and Galaway, *Child Welfare in Canada*, 48–49.

27 Social Policy Advisory Committee, *Report of the Strategic Social Planning Public Dialogue: Newfoundland Labrador. Vol. I. What the People Said* (1997), http://www.gov.nl.ca/publicat/spac/volume1.htm#common.

28 See Jennifer J. Nelson, *Razing Africville: A Geography of Racism* (Toronto: University of Toronto Press, 2008), on the significance of extended households and officials' concern with poorly raised children.

29 Candace Bernard and Wanda Thomas Bernard, "Learning from the Past/Visions for the Future: The Black Community and Child Welfare in Nova Scotia," in Brian Wharf, *Community Work Approaches to Child Welfare* (Toronto: Broadview Press, 2002), 118.

30 Kiran Mirchandani and Wendy Chan, *The Racialized Impact of Welfare Fraud Control in British Columbia and Ontario* (Ottawa: Canadian Race Relations Foundation, October 2005), *The Racialized Impact of Welfare Fraud Control in British Columbia and Ontario* http://www.crr.ca/divers-files/en/publications/reports/pubRacialized_Impact_Welfare.pdf See also Frances Henry and Carol Tator, *Racial Profiling in Toronto: Discourses of Discrimination, Mediation, and Opposition* (Ottawa: Canadian Race Relations Foundation, September 2005), http://media.thestar.topscms.com/acrobat/bb/f3/b58171b8409a867335e64 edaf96a.pdf.

31 James Shaver Woodsworth, *Strangers within Our Gates* (1909; reprinted Toronto: University of Toronto Press, 1973); and James Shaver Woodsworth, *My Neighbour* (1911; Toronto: University of Toronto Press (reprinted 1972).

32 Franca Iacovetta, *Gatekeepers: Reshaping Immigrant Lives in Cold War Canada* (Toronto: Between the Lines, 2006).

33 Ramona Alaggia and Sarah Maiter, "Domestic Violence and Child Abuse: Issues for Immigrant and Refugee Women," in *Cruel but Not Unusual: Violence in Canadian Families*, ed. Ramona Maggia and Cathy Vine (Waterloo: Wilfrid Laurier University Press, 2006), 117.

34 Arnott, *Analysis of a Selected Group of Families*, Table 1, 3.

35 M.B. Thorpe and G.T. Swart, "Risk and Protective Factors Affecting Children in Foster Care: A Pilot Study of the Role of Siblings," *Canadian Journal of Psychiatry* 37, no. 9 (November 1992): 620.

36 Lise Laporte, "Un défi de taille pour les centres jeunesse. Intervenir auprès des parents ayant un trouble de personnalité limite," *Santé mentale au Québec* 32, no. 2 (2007): 97–114.

37 Tamara Myers, *Caught: Montreal's Modern Girls and the Law 1969–1945* (Toronto: University of Toronto Press, 2006); Franca Iacovetta, "Gossip, Contest, and Power in the Making of Suburban Bad Girls: Toronto 1945–1960," *Canadian Historical Review* 80, no. 4 (December 1999): 585–623. On the situation in English Canada in general, see Joan Sangster, *Girl Trouble: Female Delinquency in English Canada* (Toronto: Between the Lines, 2006).

38 Linda Davies et al., "Community Child Welfare: Examples from Quebec," in Wharf, *Community Work Approaches to Child Welfare*, 72.

39 Quoted in Xiaobei Chen, *Tending the Gardens of Citizenship: Child Saving in Toronto 1880s–1920s* (Toronto: University of Toronto Press, 2005), 43.

40 Anne-Marie Ambert, "Custodial Parents: Review and a Longitudinal Study," in *The One-Parent Family in the 1980s*, ed. Benjamin Schlesinger (Toronto: University of Toronto Press, 1985), 24.

41 See the case of developmentally delayed mother in Ian Mulgrew, "They Took My Babies," *Vancouver Sun*, 20 September 2008, A1 and A6–7.

42 See, for example, the initiatives described by Gordon, *Heroes of Their Own Lives*.

43 Quoted in "Developmentally Disabled Mother Raising Five Children," *Vancouver Sun*, 26 September 2008, Canada.com http://www.canada.com/vancouversun/story.html?id =69a9e684-5971-411a-841d-afe30ed9db9b.

44 On this phenomenon, see Geraldine Pratt, "'Is This Canada?': Domestic Workers' Experience in Vancouver, BC," in *Gender, Migration and Domestic Service*, ed. J.H. Momsen (London and New York: Routledge, 1999), 23–42; Judith K. Bernhard, Patricia Landolt, and Luin Goldring, "Transnationalizing Families: Canadian Immigration Policy and the Spatial Fragmentation of Care-giving among Latin American Newcomers," *International Migration* 47, no. 2 (2008): 3–31; and Yolanda Hernandez-Albujar, "Transferred Motherhood: Life Experiences of Latin American Mothers in Italy" (MA dissertation, University of Florida, 2004).

45 See Maria Christina Jose, "Women Doing Life Sentences: A Phenomenological Study" (PhD dissertation, University of Michigan, 1985).

46 Bernhard, Landolt, and Goldring, "Transnationalizing Families," 7.

47 Ibid., 18.

48 Fay Weller and Brian Wharf, "Contradictions in Child Welfare," in Hayes and Foster, *Too Small to See, Too Big to Ignore*, 147. In the case of the United States, see also Annette R. Appell, "On Fixing 'Bad' Mothers and Saving their Children," in *"Bad" Mothers: The Politics of Blame in Twentieth-Century America*, ed. Molly Ladd-Taylor and Lauri Umansky (New York and London: New York University Press, 1998), 356–80.

49 Karen Swift, *Manufacturing "Bad Mothers": A Critical Perspective on Child Neglect* (Toronto: University of Toronto Press, 1995), 125.

50 Ibid., 101.

51 Kirsten Johnson Kramar, *Unwilling Mothers, Unwanted Babies: Infanticide in Canada* (Vancouver: UBC Press, 2005), 16.

52 Paul Sachdev, *Unlocking the Adoption Files* (Lexington, MA: Lexington Books, 1989), 123.

53 See Canadian Kathy Buckworth, *The Secret Life of Supermom* (Napierville, KY: Source Books, 2005).

54 Callahan, "Feminist Approaches," 185.
55 Described in Gary Cameron, "Promoting Positive Child and Family Welfare," in Kufeldt and McKenzie, *Child Welfare*, 81–82.
56 Andrew Armitage and Elaine Murray, "Thomas Gove: A Commission of Inquiry Puts Children First and Proposes Community Governance and Integration of Services," in *People, Politics, and Child Welfare in British Columbia*, edited by Leslie T. Foster and Brian Wharf (Vancouver: UBC Press, 2007), 139–40.
57 Callahan, "Feminist Approaches," 177.
58 Karen Swift, "Contradictions in Child Welfare: Neglect and Responsibility," in *Women's Caring*, ed. Carol Baines, Patricia Evans, and Sheila Neysmith (Toronto: Oxford University Press, 1998), 175.
59 Brian P. Clarke, *Piety and Nationalism: Lay Voluntary Associations and the Creation of an Irish-Catholic Community in Toronto, 1850–1895* (Montreal-Kingston: McGill-Queen's University Press, 1993), 28.
60 Karen Dubinsky and Franca Iacovetta, "Murder, Womanly Virtue, and Motherhood: The Case of Angelina Napolitano, 1911–1922," *Canadian Historical Association* 57, no. 4 (1991): 305–31.
61 See Jean Barman, "Taming Aboriginal Sexuality: Gender, Power, and Race in British Columbia, 1850–1900," *BC Studies* 115/116 (Autumn/Winter 1997–98): 237–66; and Sarah Carter, *The Importance of Being Monogamous: Marriage and Nation Building in Western Canada to 1915* (Edmonton: University of Alberta Press, 2008).
62 See Jan Hare and Jean Barman, *Good Intentions Gone Awry: Emma Crosby and the Methodist Mission on the Northwest Coast* (Vancouver: UBC Press, 2006).
63 Marlee Kline, "Child Welfare Law: 'Best Interests of the Child' Ideology and First Nation," *Osgoode Hall Law Journal* 30, no. 2 (1992): 375–425.
64 J.-A. Fiske, "Child of the State, Mother of the Nation: Aboriginal Women and the Ideology of Motherhood," *Culture* 13, no. 1 (1993): 20.
65 See Carole Gerson and Veronica Strong-Boag, "Championing the Native: E. Pauline Johnson Rejects the Squaw," in *Contact Zones: Aboriginal and Settler Women in Canada's Colonial Past*, ed. Katie Pickles and Myra Rutherdale (Vancouver: UBC Press, 2005), 47–66; Bridget Moran and Mary John, *Stoney Creek Woman: The Story of Mary John* (Vancouver: Arsenal Pulp Press, 1989); and Lee Maracle, *Daughters Are Forever* (Vancouver: Raincoast Books, 2002).
66 Lee Maracle, *Daughters Are Forever* (Vancouver: Raincoast Books, 2002).
67 Vanaja Dhruvarajan, "Women of Colour in Canada," in *Gender, Race, and Nation: A Global Perspective*, ed. Vanaja Dhruvarajan and Jill Vickers (Toronto: University of Toronto Press, 2002), 99–122; and Tomoko Mkabe, *Picture Brides: Japanese Women in Canada* (Toronto: Multicultural History Society of Ontario, 1995).
68 See Tamari Kitossa, "Criticism, Reconstruction and African-Centred Feminist Historiography," in *Back to the Drawing Board: African Canadian Feminisms*, ed. Njoki Nathani Wane, Katerina Deliovsky, and Erica Lawson (Toronto: Sumach Press, 2002), 85–116; and Linda Carty, "African Canadian Women and the State: 'Labour Only, Please,'" in *"We're rooted here and they can't pull us up": Essays in African Canadian Women's History*, ed. Peggy Bristow et al. (Toronto: University of Toronto Press, 1999), 193–229.
69 See the various references in Dionne Brand, *No Burden to Carry: Narratives of Black Working Women in Ontario 1920s to 1950s* (Toronto: Women's Press, 1991).

70 See Gillian Creese, Isabel Dyck, and Arlene Tigar McLaren, "The 'Flexible' Immigrant: Household Strategies and the Labour Market," Working Paper no. 06–19, Research on Immigration and Integration in the Metropolis, Vancouver Centre of Excellence (December 2006).

71 Esme Fuller-Thomson, "Grandparents Raising Grandchildren in Canada: A Profile of Skipped Generation Families," SEDAP Research Paper no. 132, McMaster University (October 2005), 24.

72 On such distinctions, see Karen Dubinsky, Improper Advances: Rape and Heterosexual Conflict in Ontario, 1880–1929 (Chicago: University of Chicago Press, 1993).

73 James Struthers, "'In the Interests of the Children': Mothers' Allowances and the Origins of Income Security in Ontario, 1917–1930," in Social Fabric or Patchwork Quilt: The Development of Social Policy in Canada, ed. Raymond B. Blake and Jeffrey A. Keshen (Toronto: Broadview, 2006), 71.

74 Lori Chambers, Misconceptions: Unmarried Motherhood and the Ontario Children of Unmarried Parents Act, 1921 to 1969 (Toronto: University of Toronto Press, 2007).

75 For a typical version of this perspective, see Leontine Young, Out of Wedlock (New York: McGraw-Hill, 1959). On this phenomenon in the United States, see Ricki Solanger, Wake Up Little Susie: Single Pregnancy and Race before Roe v. Wade (New York: Routledge, 2000).

76 This was produced by a combination of morphine and scopolamine. See Cheryl K. Warsh, Prescribed Norms: Women and Health in Canada and the United States since 1800 (Toronto: University of Toronto Press, 2010), 121–23.

77 Battel, Children Shall Be First, 79.

78 Chambers, Misconceptions, 8.

79 On such tropes in the United Kingdom in the same years, see Ann Phoenix, "Social Constructions of Lone Motherhood: A Case of Competing Discourses," in Good Enough Mothering? Feminist Perspectives on Lone Motherhood, ed. Elizabeth B. Silva (London and New York: Routledge, 1996), 175–90.

80 Charmaine C. Williams, "Race (and Gender and Class) and Child Custody: Theorizing Intersections in Two Canadian Custody Cases," National Women's Studies Association Journal 16, no. 2 (Summer 2004): 46–69.

81 On this phenomenon in the United States, see Rosanna Hertz, Single by Chance, Mothers by Choice: How Women Are Choosing Parenthood without Marriage and Creating the New American Family (Oxford and New York: Oxford University Press, 2006).

82 Craig McKie, "An Overview of Lone Parenthood in Canada," in Single Parent Families: Perspectives on Research and Policy, ed. Joe Hudson and Burt Galaway (Toronto: Butterworth Publishing, 1993), 65.

83 Benjamin Schlesinger, The One-Parent Family in the 1980s: Perspectives and Annotated Bibliography 1978–1984 (Toronto: University of Toronto Press, 1985), 45.

84 Craig McKie, "An Overview of Lone Parenthood in Canada," in Hudson and Galaway, Single Parent Families, 70.

85 Paul Sachdev, Unlocking the Adoption Files (Lexington, MA: Lexington Books, 1989), 26 and 36–37.

86 See Anne Petrie, Gone to an Aunt's (Toronto: McClelland and Stewart, 1998).

87 Chambers, Misconceptions, 90.

88 Ibid., 137.

89 On a similar situation in the United Kingdom, see McIntosh, "Social Anxieties," in Silva, ed., Good Enough Mothering? 183.

90 Chambers, *Misconceptions,* 114.

91 Quoted in ibid., 112.

92 Ginger Suzanne Frost, "'The Black Lamb of the Black Sheep': Illegitimacy in the English Working Class, 1850–1939," *Journal of Social History* 37, no. 2 (Winter 2003), 311.

93 Mary Smith, pseudonym, "A Young Pregnant Girl Tells Her Story," *Canadian Nurse* (October 1975): 35.

94 Much of the argument here depends on Sally Mennill and Veronica Strong-Boag, "Identifying Victims: Child Abuse and Death in Canadian Families," *Canadian Bulletin of Medical History* 25, no. 2 (2008): 11–33.

95 Swift, *Manufacturing "Bad Mothers,"* 120. See also J. Humphrey, "Dependent-care by Battered Women: Protecting Their Children," *Health Care for Women International,"* 16 (1995): 9–20; I. Irwin, S. Thorne, and C. Varcoe, "Strength in Adversity: Motherhood for Women Who Have Been Battered," *Canadian Journal of Nursing Research* 34, no. 4 (2002): 47–57; C. Varcoe and L. Irwin, "'If I killed you, I'd get the kids': Women's Survival and Protection Work with Child Custody and Access in the Context of Woman Abuse," *Qualitative Sociology* 27, no. 1 (2004): 77–99; and Kathryn Harvey, "Amazons and Victims: Resisting Wife-Abuse in Working-Class Montréal, 1869–1879," *Journal of the Canadian Historical Association* (1991): 131–48.

96 Annalee Lepp, *Dis/membering the Family: Marital Breakdown, Domestic Conflict, and Family Violence in Ontario, 1830–1920* (PhD dissertation, Queen's University, 2001), 455.

97 Ibid., 456.

98 Margaret Little, *"No Car, No Radio, No Liquor Permit": The Moral Regulation of Single Mothers in Ontario, 1920–1997* (Toronto: Oxford University Press, 1998), 72.

99 Sarah Todd and Colleen Lundy, "Framing Woman Abuse: A Structural Perspective," in Maggia and Vine, *Cruel but Not Unusual,* 329.

100 On British Columbia, see Gillian Creese and Veronica Strong-Boag, *Still Waiting for Justice: Update 2009. Provincial Policies and Gender Inequality in BC* (Vancouver: BC Federation of Labour and the UBC Centre for Women's and Gender Studies, 8 March 2009).

101 Cindy Baskin, "Systemic Oppression Violence, and Healing in Aboriginal Families and Communities," in Maggia and Vine, *Cruel but Not Unusual,* 17. Data on the situation of other racialized groups are less complete, but some of the same fears exist. See Ramona Alaggia and Sarah Maiter, "Domestic Violence and Child Abuse: Issues for Immigrant and Refugee Families," in Maggia and Vine, *Cruel but Not Unusual,* 99–126.

102 Susan Strega, "Failure to Protect: Child Welfare Interventions When Men Beat Mothers," in Maggia and Vine, *Cruel but Not Unusual,* 240.

103 Ibid., 241.

104 Callahan, "Feminist Approaches, 185.

105 Swift, *Manufacturing "Bad Mothers"* 121. On the same problem in early twentieth-century Ontario, see Joan Sangster, "Masking and Unmasking the Sexual Abuse of Children: Perceptions of Violence against Children in 'the Badlands' of Ontario, 1916–1930," *Journal of Family History* 25, no. 4 (2000): 504–26.

106 Some recent studies also document a majority of male offenders. See Robert Silverman and Leslie Kennedy, *Deadly Deeds: Murder in Canada* (Toronto: Nelson Canada, 1993), which identifies fathers as the perpetrators in 323 of the 620 cases of a parent killing a child between 1961 and 1990 in Canada (77). The same study also concludes that the younger the child the more likely the murderer is female and very young themselves. (188–89). For a study that identified mothers, and step-mothers, as more common perpetrators, see Marlene L. Dalley, "The Killing of Canadian Children by a Parent(s) or

Guardian(s): Characteristics and Trends 1990–1993" (Ottawa: Missing Children's Registry and National Police Services, Royal Canadian Mounted Police, 2000). Disagreement may reflect the diverse and uncertain methods of identification and reporting and shifts from one reporting period to another. See also Michelle Oberman, "Mothers Who Kill: Cross-Cultural Patterns in and Perspectives on Contemporary Maternal Filicide," *International Journal of Law and Psychiatry* 26 (2003): 493–514.

107   See Cyril Greenland, *Preventing CAN Deaths: An International Study of Deaths Due to Child Abuse and Neglect* (London: Routledge Kegan and Paul, 1989), chapters 1 and 3.

108   Louise S. Ethier et al., "Impact of a Multidimensional Intervention Programme Applied to Families at Risk of Child Neglect," *Child Abuse Review* 9 (2000): 24.

109   Greenland, *Preventing CAN Deaths*, 165.

110   Claudia Malacrida, "Negotiating the Dependency/Nurturing Tightrope: Dilemmas of Motherhood and Disability," *Canadian Review of Sociology and Anthropology* (1 November 2007), http://www.accessmylibrary.com/coms2/summary_0286-33832059_ITM. See also Karen A. Blackford, "Erasing Mothers with Disabilities through Canadian Family-Related Policy," *Disability, Handicap and Society* 8, no. 3 (1993): 281–94.

111   Little, "*No Car, No Radio, No Liquor*," 6.

112   Judith Mossop and Kim James, "Motherhood, Madness, and the Law," *University of Toronto Law Journal* 45, no. 2 (Spring 1995): 108.

113   Colleen Varcoe and Gweneth Hartrick Doane, "Mothering and Women's Health," in *Women's Health in Canada: Critical Perspectives on Theory and Policy*, ed. Marina Morrow, Olena Hankivsky, and Colleen Varcoe (Toronto: University of Toronto Press, 2007), 309.

114   National Clearinghouse on Family Violence, *The Abuse of Children with Disabilities* (Ottawa: Family Violence Prevention Unit, Health Issues Division, Population and Public Health Branch, Health Canada, August 2000), 1.

115   See the very useful discussion in Karen J. Swift and Marilyn Callagan, *At Risk: Social Justice in Child Welfare and Other Social Services* (Toronto: University of Toronto Press, 2009).

116   Mossop and James "Motherhood, Madness, and the Law," 117.

117   Malacrida, "Negotiating the Dependency/Nurturing Tightrope: Dilemmas of Motherhood and Disability."

118   Claudia Malacrida, "Performing Motherhood in a Disablist World: Dilemmas of Motherhood, Femininity and Disability," *Journal of Qualitative Studies in Education* 22, no. 1 (2009): 112.

119   See the useful assessment of different responses to drinking on and by women and men by Lori Rotskoff, *Love on the Rocks: Men, Women, and Alcohol in Post–World War II America* (Chapel Hill, NC: University of North Carolina Press, 2002).

120   See Susan C. Boyd, "Women, Drug Regulation, and Maternal/State Conflicts," in Morrow, Hankivsky, and Varcoe, eds., *Women's Health in Canada*, 327–54; and her very useful *From Witches to Crack Moms: Women, Drug Law, and Policy* (Durham, NC: Carolina Academic Press, 2004). See also Laura E. Gomez, *Misconceiving Mothers: Legislators, Prosecutors, and the Politics of Prenatal Drug Exposure* (Philadelphia: Temple University Press, 1997).

121   Susan C. Boyd, "The Journey to Compassionate Care: One Woman's Experience with Early Harm-Reduction Programs in BC," *Women's Health Network Magazine*, 10, no. 1 (Fall/Winter 2007), http://www.cwhn.ca/network-reseau/10-1/10-1pg12.html.

122 Boyd, *From Witches to Crack Moms*, 18.

123 This couple is also considered in Mossop and James, "Motherhood, Madness, and the Law," 127.

124 "Developmentally Disabled Mother Raising Five Children." For another example, see the 1990 case of a mentally challenged mother losing custody in Manitoba in Mary Jane Mossman, *Families and the Law in Canada* (Toronto: Emond Montgomery Publications, 2004), 245–46.

125 See M.A. Feldman, M. Leger, and N. Walton-Allen, "Stress in Mothers with Intellectual Disabilities," *Journal of Child and Family Studies* 6, no. 4 (December 1997): 471–85.

126 American studies have recently made this point. See Marilyn C. Moses, "Does Parental Incarceration Increase a Child's Risk for Foster Care Placement?" *National Institute of Justice Journal*, No. 255 (November 2006), http://www.ojp.usdoj.gov/nij/journals/255/parental_incarceration.html.

127 "The Closing of the Prison for Women in Kingston," 6 July 2000, http://www.csc-scc.gc.ca/text/pblct/brochurep4w/2-eng.shtml.

128 Parizeau, *Protection de l'enfant*.

129 *Creating Choices: The Report of the Task Force on Federally Sentenced Women* (Ottawa: Ministry of Supply and Services, 1990).

130 Shawn Bayes, "A Snowball's Chance: Children of Offenders and Canadian Social Policy," Elizabeth Fry Society of Greater Vancouver, http://www.elizabethfry.com/A_SNOWBALLS_CHANCE.pdf, 11.

131 Ibid., 13.

132 Boyd, *From Witches to Crack Moms*, 248.

133 *Healing Lodge Final Operation Plan* (Ottawa: Correctional Service Canada, February 1993), http://www.csc-scc.gc.ca/text/prgrm/fsw/healing/toce-eng.shtml#21.

134 Norma Green, "Facts and Figures: Aboriginal Community Development in Corrections. Profile of an Aboriginal Woman Serving Time in a Federal Institution," Correctional Service of Canada, http://www.csc-scc.gc.ca/text/prgrm/abinit/know/5-eng.shtml.

135 "The Closing of the Prison for Women in Kingston," 6 July 2000, http://www.csc-scc.gc.ca/text/pblct/brochurep4w/2-eng.shtml.

136 Jamieson, Beals, Lalonde and Associates, *Guidelines for Parenting Skills Programs for Federally Sentenced Women* (6 January 1995), http://www.csc-scc.gc.ca/text/prgrm/fsw/parenting/guidelines_e.pdf, 7. See also K. Cannings, *Bridging the Gap: Programs and Services to Facilitate Contact between Inmate Parents and Their Children* (Ottawa: Minister of the Solicitor General of Canada, 1991); and Brigitte Blanchard, "Incarcerated Mothers and Their Children: A Complex Issue," *Forum on Corrections Research*, 16, no. 1 (2004): 45–46.

137 Phyllis Jo Baunach, *Mothers in Prison* (New Brunswick: Transaction Publishers, 1985), chapter 8.

138 Linda Korbin, "Taking Babies from Mothers in Prison Punishes the Children," Straight.com (13 March 2009), http://www.straight.com/article-206120/linda-korbin-taking-babies-mothers-prison-punishes-children.

139 Katherine Gabel and Denise Johnston, *Children of Incarcerated Parents* (Lanham, MD: Lexington Books, 1997), 24–25; and Lisa Watson, "In the Best Interest of the Child: The Mother-Child Program," *Forum on Corrections Research* 7, no. 2 (May 1995) http://www.csc-scc.gc.ca/text/pblct/forum/e072/e072h-eng.shtml.

140 Julie J. Fournier, "The Impact of Incarceration on the Mothering Role," *Forum on Corrections Research* 14, no. 1 (January 2002), http://www.csc-scc.gc.ca/text/pblct/forum/e141/e141ind-eng.shtml.

141 Carl Lacharité, Louise Ethier, and Germain Courture, "The Influence of Partners on Parental Stress of Neglectful Mothers," *Child Abuse Review* 5 (1996): 18–33.

142 Quoted in Patricia Dirks, "Reinventing Christian Masculinity and Fatherhood: The Canadian Protestant Experience, 1900–20," in *Households of Faith: Family, Gender and Community in Canada, 1760–1969*, ed. Nancy Christie (Montreal and Kingston: McGill-Queen's University Press, 2002), 307.

143 See Susan Strega et al., "Connecting Father Absence and Mother Blame in Child Welfare Policies and Practice," *Children and Youth Services Review* 30, no. 7 (July 2008): 705–16.

144 Strega, "Failure to Protect," 254.

145 Cited in Marilyn Callahan and Christopher Walmsley, "Rethinking Child Welfare Reform in British Columbia, 1900–60," in Foster and Wharf, *People, Politics, and Child Welfare in British Columbia*, 28.

146 Michèle Kérisit and Néré St.-Amand, "Taking Risks with Families at Risk: Some Alternative Approaches with Poor Families in Canada," in Hudson and Galaway, *Child Welfare in Canada*, 166.

147 Veronica Strong-Boag, "Casual Fornicators, Young Lovers, Deadbeat Dads, and Family Champions: Men in Canadian Adoption Circles in the 20th Century," in *Science, Polity, and Society in Canada: Essays in Honour of Michael Bliss*, ed. Elsbeth Heaman and Alison Li (Toronto: University of Toronto Press, 2008), 211–37.

148 Robert Adamoski, "Persistence and Privilege: Boarding and Single Fathers in the Practice of Child Rescue: 1901–1930," in *Child and Family Welfare in British Columbia: A History*, ed. Diane Purvey and Christopher Walmsley (Calgary: Detselig Ent, 2005), 47.

149 See the thoughtful assessment by Steven Angelides, "The Emergence of the Pedophile in the Late Twentieth Century," *Australia Historical Studies* 37 (October 2005): 272–95.

150 See Peter G. Jaffee, Nancy K.D. Lemon, and Samantha E. Poisson, *Child Custody and Domestic Violence: A Call for Safety and Accountability* (Thousand Oaks, CA: Sage Publications, 2002), 46.

151 L.E. Lowman, "Mail-Order Babies," *Chatelaine*, April 1932, 26.

152 See Victor Malarek, *Hey Malarek!* (Halifax: Formac Publishing, 1984).

153 See the controversial but well-documented novel featuring alcoholism on one Canadian reserve in Alan Fry, *How a People Die* (Toronto: Doubleday, 1970). See also Marie Wadden, *Where the Pavement Ends: Canada's Aboriginal Recovery Movement and the Urgent Need for Reconciliation* (Vancouver: Douglas and McIntyre, 2008).

154 Jaffee, Lemon, and Poisson, *Child Custody and Domestic Violence*, 48.

155 Quoted in Sachdev, *Unlocking the Adoption Files*, 148.

156 Quoted in ibid., 150.

157 See Myrna Dawson, "Rethinking the Boundaries of Intimacy at the End of the Century: The Role of Victim–Defendant Relationship in Criminal Justice Decision-Making over Time," *Law and Society Review* 38, no. 1 (2004): 105–38.

158 "Study of Services to Unmarried Parents in Manitoba" (Winnipeg: Welfare Council of Greater Winnipeg, 1 September 1960), 8. See also the indication that fathers were a recent concern in Alberta. *In the Matter of the Child Welfare Act, 1965*, Hearings held before His Honour Judge H.S. Patterson, Chairman Frank J. Fleming, Esq., and Mrs. W.F Bowke, volume 3 at the Court House, Calgary, 9–10 March 1965, 590.

159 Simma Holt, *Sex and the Teen-age Revolution* (Toronto: McClelland and Stewart, 1967), 93.

160 Harry MacKay and Catherine Austin, *Single Adolescent Mothers in Ontario: A Report of Eighty-Seven Single Adolescent Mothers' Experiences, Their Situation, Needs, and Use of Community Services* (Ottawa: Canadian Council for Social Development, 1983), ix.

161 BC Royal Commission on Family and Children's Law, *Fifth Report* (March 1975), 90 and 6.

162 Margaret Lord, *Final Report to the Minister of Social Services of the Panel to Review Adoption Legislation* (Victoria, BC, July 1994), 57–58.

163 *An Act Respecting Adoptions*, Newfoundland Statutes, 1999, chapter A-2.1, 215.

164 Susan Strega et al., "Connecting Father Absence and Mother Blame in Child Welfare Policies and Practice, *Children and Youth Services Review* 30, no. 7 (July 2007): 705–16.

165 Cindy Baskin, "Systemic Oppression, Violence and Healing in Aboriginal Families and Communities," in Maggia and Vine, *Cruel but Not Unusual*, 18. See also the similar conclusions regarding an American non-Aboriginal sample of abusive fathers, K.J. Francis and D.A. Wolfe, "Cognitive and Emotional Differences between Abusive and Non-Abusive Fathers," *Child Abuse and Neglect: The International Journal*, 32, no. 12 (2008): 1127–37.

166 Marilyn Callahan and Karen Callahan, "Victims and Villains: Scandals, the Press and Policy Making in Child Welfare," in *Child and Family Policies: Struggles, Strategies and Options*, ed. Jane Pulkingham and Gordon Ternowetsky (Halifax: Fernwood Publishing, 1997), 53.

167 Strega, "Failure to Protect," 247.

168 Ibid., 249.

169 Marie-Aimée Cliché, *Maltraiter ou punir? La violence envers les enfants dans les familles québécoises 1850–1969* (Montreal: Boréal, 2007), 48; and Lepp, *Dis/membering the Family*, 454, n. 9,.

170 Paul D. Steinhauer, *The Least Detrimental Alternative: A Systemic Guide to Case Planning and Decision Making for Children in Care* (Toronto: University of Toronto Press, 1991), 159.

171 Weller and Wharf, "Contradictions in Child Welfare," 144.

172 Rory Summers, "Government Should Not Discriminate," *Vancouver Sun*, 30 September 2008), http://www2.canada.com/vancouversun/news/editorial/story.html?id=2538dea 3–650e-4e61–8681-ef0505a9d6cd&k=9528.

173 Swift, *Manufacturing "Bad Mothers*, 10.

174 Weller and Wharf, "Contradictions in Child Welfare," 147.

175 Ruth K. Chao and J. Douglas Willms, "The Effects of Parenting Practices on Children's Outcomes," in *Vulnerable Children: Findings from Canada's National Longitudinal Survey of Children and Youth*, ed. J. Douglas Willms (Edmonton: University of Alberta Press, 2002), 165.

176 Gary Cameron, "Promoting Positive Child and Family Welfare," in Kufeldt and McKenzie, *Child Welfare*, 81.

177 Ian Mulgrew, "Support, Not Sterilization, Is the Missing Ingredient," *Vancouver Sun*, 23 September 2008, http://www2.canada.com/vancouversun/editorspicks/story.html?id =839fd622–5fbb-4edc-ba5b-c700372a19b0.

178 Battel, *Children Shall Be First*, 52. See the discussion of Ontario parents' accommodation and resistance to child protection workers in Gary C. Dumbrill, "Parental Experience of

Child Protection Intervention: A Qualitative Study," *Child Abuse and Neglect* 30, no. 1 (January 2006): 27–37.

179 Steinhauer, *The Least Detrimental Alternative*, 161.

180 Elizabeth Camden, *If He Comes Back He's Mine: A Mother's Story of Child Abuse* (Toronto: Women's Press, 1984), 96, 128, and 17.

181 Wharf, "The Constituency/Community Context," in Wharf, *Rethinking Child Welfare in Canada*, 111–12.

182 "Birth Parents Plead for Medical Treatment for Baby Girl in Foster Care, CBC News, 2 April 2009, http://www.cbc.ca/canada/british-columbia/story/2009/04/02/bc-surrey -parents-children.html.

183 See Ontario, *Report of the Inquiry into Pediatric Forensic Pathology in Ontario*, Hon. Stephen T. Goudge, Commissioner (30 September 2008), http://www.attorneygeneral.jus.gov.on.ca/ inquiries/goudge/report/index.html.

184 See the case reported in *K.L.B. v. British Columbia*, 2003 SCC 51, [2003] 2 S.C.R. 403 (2 October 2003), http://csc.lexum.umontreal.ca/en/2003/2003scc51/2003scc51.html,.

185 See Mary Jane Mossman, *Families and the Law in Canada* (Toronto: Emond Montgomery Publications, 2004), chapter 4.

Notes to Chapter 6

1   See, for example, the conclusion of Joscelyn Dingman, "An Unhappy Report on Foster Homes," *Chatelaine*, December 1970, 54–56.

2   Stacie D.A. Burke, "Transitions in Household and Family Structure: Canada in 1901 and 1991," in *Household Counts: Canadian Households and Families in 1901*, ed. Eric W. Sager and Peter Baskerville (Toronto: University of Toronto Press, 2007), 53.

3   "Jones [Carlisle]—Sheila Jane: 1923–2007," *Vancouver Sun*, 19 May 2007, F14.

4   "Kennedy—Judith Mary," *Vancouver Sun*, 16 May 2009, D15.

5   Anonymous, "Little Rock Could Learn a Lot," *Star Weekly*, 7 December 1957, 28 and 30–31.

6   Vera Cline, "Our Three Years as Foster Parents," *United Church Observer*, May 1965, 26. See also a letter to the editor from a foster mother in Fort St. John, British Columbia, who also planned to adopt. *United Church Observer*, July 1965, 2.

7   Sarah Boesveld, "Think Adoption and Babies Come to Mind ..." *United Church Observer,?* March 2008,? http://www.ucobserver.org/justice/2008/03/all_they_want_is_a_home/. See also the publications by this minister, John Niles, *The Art of Sacred Parenting* (2006), *How I Became Father to 1000 Children* (2004), and *The Power of Positive Believing* (2007) [copies on file with the author].

8   Miriam Swadron, "Herbert Sheldon Swadron," Lives Lived, *Globe and Mail*, 29 January 2001, A18.

9   Ian Elliot, "Foster Parent of the Year Has Been at Beck and Call of Hundreds," *Kingston Whig-Standard*, 2 May 2005, 1.

10 "243 New Lawyers Called to Bar," *Toronto Star*, 11 April 1962, 1 and 2.

11 Bryan Hogeveen, "'The Evils with Which We Are Called to Grapple': Elite Reformers, Eugenicists, Environmental Psychologists, and the Construction of Toronto's Working Boy Problem, 1860–1930," *Labour/Le Travail*, Spring 2005 http://www.historycooperative.org/ journals/llt/55/hogeveen.html. See also the portrait of Toronto's "unrespectable," but nevertheless "old Canadian," population in W.E. Mann, "The Social System of a Slum:

The Lower Ward, Toronto," in *The Community in Canada. Rural and Urban*, ed. Satadal Dasgupta (Lanham, MD: University Press of America, 1996), 294–310.

12 Bettina Bradbury, "Pigs, Cows and Boarders: Non-Wage Forms of Survival among Montreal Families, 1861–1891," *Labour/Le Travail* 14 (1984): 9–46; and David Frank, "The Miner's Financier: Women in the Cape Breton Coal Towns, 1917," *Atlantis* 8, no. 2 (Spring 1983): 137–43.

13 On the appeal of greater security, see Caroline Evans, "Excellent Women and Troublesome Children: State Foster Care in Tasmania, 1896–1918," *Labour History* 83 (November 2002): 133.

14 George Caldwell, *Child Welfare Services in New Brunswick: A Report to the Honourable W.R. Duffie, Minister and Welfare, Province of New Brunswick* (Ottawa: Canadian Welfare Council, October 1965), 18.

15 On the same philosophy in New Zealand until the 1970s/80s, see Bronwyn Dalley, *Family Matters: Child-Welfare in Twentieth-Century New Zealand* (Auckland: University Press and Historical Branch, Department of Internal Affairs, 1998), 322–23.

16 Suzanne Morton, *Ideal Surroundings: Domestic life in a Working-Class Suburb* (Toronto: University of Toronto Press, 1995), 35.

17 "'Mom' Whyte, Thirty Children on N.Y. Trip, TV," *Toronto Star*, 17 October 1956, 3. See also "'Mom' Whyte, "Carloads of Carpenters Building Home for Family," *Toronto Star*, 8 September 1956, 2; and "'Mom' Whyte, "Steel Union $500 Helps Whyte Fund," *Toronto Star*, 11 September 1957, 2.

18 Constance M. Harrison, "Foster Homefinding: A Study of Effective Ways of Increasing the Number of Foster Homes Available for Children" (MSW dissertation, University of Toronto, 1948), 83.

19 Lee Titterington, "Foster Care Training: A Comprehensive Approach," *Welfare* 69, no. 2 (March/April 1990): 157–65.

20 Peter Silverman, *Who Speaks for the Children? Giving Voice to a Forgotten Generation* (Toronto: Stoddart, 1989), 95.

21 Laura C. Johnson and Janice Dineen, *The Kin Trade: The Day Care Crisis in Canada* (Toronto: McGraw-Hill Ryerson, 1981), 61–65 and 67.

22 Ibid., 73.

23 On some problems of rural living for youth, see the British study, Hugh Matthews et al., "Growing-up in the Countryside: Children and the Rural Idyll," *Journal of Rural Studies* 16, no. 2 (April 2000): 141–267. See also Gill Valentine, "A Safe Place to Grow Up? Parenting, Perceptions of Children's Safety and the Rural Idyll," *Journal of Rural Studies* 13, no. 2 (April 1997): 137–48.

24 See *Rural Women. Employment Facts from ACTEW and Rural Woman Making Change Research Alliance* (2008), Rural Women Making Change, University of Guelph, http://www.rwmc.uoguelph.ca/page.php?p=1.

25 Baukje Biedema, *Mothering for the State: The Paradox of Fostering* (Halifax: Fernwood Publishing, 1999), 36.

26 Alanis Obomsawin, Director, *Richard Cardinal: Cry from a Diary of a Métis Child* Ottawa: National Film Board of Canada, 1986).

27 Ron Cunningham and Ray D. Bollman, "Structure and Trends of Rural Employment: Canada in the Context of OECD Countries," Statistics Canada, Agricultural and Rural Working Paper Series no. 28049 (1996), 3, http://ideas.repec.org/p/ags/scarwp/28049.html#provider.

28 Anne Margaret Angus, *Children's Aid Society of Vancouver, B.C. 1901–1951* (Vancouver: Vancouver Children's Aid, 1951), 28.

29 Annette Wigod, "Let's Ask the Middle Class," *Canadian Welfare,* November–December 1968, 14.

30 Hogeveen, "The Evils with Which We Are Called to Grapple."

31 See the mention of racial matching, even though religion seemed more important, in Harrison, "Foster Homefinding," 12.

32 No author, *Anti-Oppression, Anti-Racism Policy* (Children's Aid Society of Toronto, 9 November 2006), 2.

33 H.B.M. Murphy, "Foster Home Variables and Adult Outcomes," *Mental Hygiene* 48, no. 4 (October 1964): 595.

34 Harrison, "Foster Homefinding," 60.

35 See "CCF Twice Broke Tory Hold: 4 Names on York East Ballot," *Toronto Star,* 6 June 1959, 9; "Negroes Barred From Homes," *Toronto Star,* 21 February 1959, 9; "The Medium Online: The Voice of the University of Toronto at Mississauga," http://www.medium online.ca/news; and Stanley Grizzle and John Cooper, *My Name's Not George: The Story of the Sleeping Car Porters* (Toronto: Umbrella Press, 1997).

36 Teresa Toguchi Swartz, "Mothering for the State: Foster Parenting and the Challenges of Government-Contracted Carework," *Gender and Society* 18, no. 5 (October 2004): 576.

37 On the same problem in Australia, see Robert Van Krieken, *Children and the State. Social Control and the Formation of Australian Child Welfare* (North Sydney, Australia: Allen and Unwin, 1991), 108.

38 Bruce Cox, "Alternatives to Apprehending Native Children in Urban Settings: A Case Study" (University of Victoria, School of Social Work, Social Work 304 Practicum, 29 April 1988), 29.

39 Quoted in Kathleen Acosta, "McCarthy Shifts Responsibility of Finding Foster Care Homes to Indian People," *Indian Voice,* June 1980, 2.

40 *Child Care Task Force: A Report on B.C. Indian Child Care* (Ottawa: Program Evaluation Branch, Indian Affairs and Northern Development, May 1982), 1.

41 See Sheri Broder, *Tramps, Unfit Mothers, and Neglected Children: Negotiating the Family in Late Nineteenth-Century Philadelphia* (Philadelphia: University of Pennsylvania Press, 2002), 76.

42 Cheryl Marlene Swidrovich, "Positive Experiences of First Nations Children in Non-Aboriginal Foster or Adoptive Care: De-Constructing the "Sixties Scoop"" (MA dissertation, University of Saskatchewan, 2004).

43 Sidney Katz, "Should They Let "Mom" Whyte Keep Her Children?" *Maclean's,* 2 February 1957, 42.

44 Nancy Millar, "The Family That Grows and Grows and Grows," *United Church Observer,* October 1976, 30.

45 Mary-Anne Tinney, "Special Report: Role Perceptions in Foster Parent Associations in British Columbia," *Child Welfare* 64, no. 1 (1986): 76.

46 Titterington, "Foster Care Training," 161.

47 Biedema, *Mothering for the State,* 36.

48 PoHerman Ganzevoort, "Dutch," in *Encyclopedia of Canada's Peoples,* ed. Paul Robert Magocsi (Toronto: Multicultural History Society of Ontario and University of Toronto Press, 1999), 445.

49 (Mrs.) Phyllis Ljuden, "Foster Children," *United Church Observer,* July 1965, 2.

50 Caroline Evens, "Excellent Women and Troublesome Children: State Fostering in Tasmania, 1896–1918," *Labour History* (November 2002), http://www.historycooperative.org/journals/lab/83/evans.html.

51 Millar, "The Family That Grows," 29–30.

52 Ukrainian Canadian Congress, "Nation Builders" (2002), http://www.ucc.sk.ca/programs/nbuilders/2002/.

53 Betty Anne Brown, "Lives Lived: Lorraine Jeanne Valois Brown," *Globe and Mail*, 6 May 1998, A20.

54 Joan Sangster, *Girl Trouble: Female Delinquency in English Canada* (Toronto: Between the Lines, 2002), 137.

55 See this assumption in Scotland, a source of many Canadian attitudes to children, in Helen J. Macdonald, "Boarding-Out and the Scottish Poor Law, 1845–1914," *Scottish Historical Review* 75, no. 2 (1996): 192.

56 Michael Reid, "Understanding Children's Aid: Means and Practice in Ontario Children's Aid Societies, 1893–1912" (MA dissertation, Trent University, 2009), 124.

57 Swartz, "Mothering for the State," 572.

58 Karen Bridget Murray, "Governing 'Unwed Mothers' in Toronto at the Turn of the Twentieth Century," *Canadian Historical Review* 85, no. 2 (2004): 272.

59 Paul D. Steinhauer, *The Least Detrimental Alternative: A Systematic Guide to Case Planning and Decision Making for Children in Care* (Toronto: University of Toronto Press, 1991), 159.

60 Ibid., 185.

61 This is presented in the case of *D.B. v. British Columbia (Director of Child, Family and Community Services)* in Mary Jane Hatton, Nicholas Bala, and Carole Curtis, "Representing Parents," in *Canadian Child Welfare Law: Children, Families and the State*, ed. Nicholas Bala et al., 2nd edition (Toronto: Thompson Educational Publishing, 2004), 266–67.

62 Child and Youth Officer for British Columbia [Jane Morley], *Heshook-ish Tsawalk: towards a State of Healthy Interdependence in the Child Welfare System* (Victoria: Child and Youth Officer for British Columbia, June 2006), 9

63 See Marilyn Callahan et al., "Catch as Catch Can: Grandmothers Raising Their Grandchildren and Kinship Care Policies," *Canadian Review of Social Policy* 54 (2004): 58–77; and Jane Morley, *Heshook-ish Tsawalk*, 8

64 Alexandra Wright et al., *Summary Report: Factors That Contribute to Positive Outcomes in the Awasis Pimicikamak Cree Nation Kinship Care Program* (Winnipeg: Centre for Excellence for Child Welfare and Health Canada, 2005), 18.

65 Rob Geen and Jill Duerr Berrick, "Kinship Care: An Evolving Service Delivery Option," *Children and Youth Services Review* 24, no. 1/2 (2002): 10. See also Maria Scannagpieco and Rebecca L. Hegar, "Kinship Foster Care in Context," in *Kinship Foster Care: Policy, Practice, and Research*, ed. Rebecca L. Hegar and Maria Scannagpieco (New York: Oxford University Press, 1999), 7.

66 Susan Silva-Wayne, "Contributions to Resilience in Children and Youth: What Successful Child Welfare Graduates Say," in *Child Welfare in Canada: Research and Policy Implications*, ed. Joe Hudson and Burt Galaway (Toronto: Thompson Educational Publishing, 1995), 317.

67 Gil Cardinal, Director, "Foster Child" (Ottawa: National Film Board, 1987). See also the thirteen subjects interviewed by Swidrovich, "Positive Experiences of First Nations Children."

68 See, for example, the inspiration found among even poorer women in David Kertzer, Heather Koball, and Michael J. White, "Growing Up as an Abandoned Child in Nineteenth-Century Italy," *History of the Family* 2, no. 3 (1997): 211–28.

69 Adele Saunders, "Short Term Mothers," *Chatelaine*, September 1945, 16.

70 "She Won't Give Up Any of Her Thirteen Children," *Toronto Telegram*, 13 October 1965, 21.

71 Anne Bokma, "Families and Foster Care," *Canadian Living*, May 2007, 206.

72 Biedema, *Mothering for the State*, 39.

73 Carole quoted in Swidrovich, "Positive Experiences of First Nations Children," 56.

74 See Biedema, *Mothering for the State*, 59 and 116.

75 Susan Rodger, Anne Cummings, and Alan W. Leschied, "Who Is Caring for Our Most Vulnerable Children? The Motivation to Foster in Child Welfare," *Child Abuse and Neglect* 30, no. 10 (October 2006): 1135.

76 Ibid., 1134.

77 Jason Brown, "Rewards of Fostering Children with Disabilities," *Journal of Family Social Work* 11, no. 1 (May 2008): 36–39.

78 "Ask If Children's Aid Removed Girl Because 'Kin" Went over Heads," *Toronto Star*, 14 October 1950, 1 and 16.

79 Quoted in Beth Kaplan, "Lives Lived: Doris Margaret Michelin," *Globe and Mail*, 7 September 2000, A24.

80 Quoted in Biedema, *Mothering for the State*, 112.

81 Mrs. Mary Feldey quoted in Phyllis Harrison, *Home Children* (Winnipeg: Watson and Dwyer, 1979), 160.

82 Quoted in Bokma, "Families and Foster Care," 204.

83 Lisa Hepfner, "Beloved Foster Mother Dies," *Edmonton Journal*, 11 July 1998, B3. See a similar case of family traditions, Linda Goyette, "Good Citizen Award: A Recognition of Good Citizenship," *Edmonton Journal*, 11 February 1990, A7.

84 Quoted in William Speake, "Fostering Her Love; Gloucester Woman Honoured for Work with Developmentally Handicapped," *Ottawa Citizen*, 9 June 1993, B1.

85 Quoted in Vera Cline, "Our Three Years as Foster Parents," *United Church Observer* May 1961, 18.

86 Wright et al., *Summary Report*, 17.

87 See the reference to widows in Battel, *Children Shall Be First*, 106.

88 Quoted in Ina Swedler, "Mom's Mission: Home for Handicapped," *Ottawa Citizen*, 29 October 1989, D3.

89 Quoted in Sonja Drinkwater, "Foster Parents Honoured for Years of Service in Alberni," *Alberni Valley Times*, 20 December 2002, B11.

90 Harrison, "Foster Homefinding," 41.

91 Stephen Workman, "Lives Lived: Irene Revels Lydiard," *Globe and Mail*, 3 March 2000, A20.

92 For resistance, see Biedema, *Mothering for the State*, 45.

93 Ibid., 57.

94 Battel, *Children Shall Be First*, 106.

95 David Allen and Robert Purcell, "Adoption Inquiry, Timbrell Son, 21, Took Photos of Nude Girl, 14," *Toronto Star*, 7 November 1967, 1 and 2. See also "Foster Mother Fights for Girls," *Toronto Star*, 11 August 1967, 1; "Foster Mother Arrested Rather Than Give Up Girls," *Toronto Star*, 28 September 1967, 1; "Remanded 2 Weeks: Foster Mother Demands Trial," *Toronto Star*, 3 October 1967, 1.

96 "Adoption Problem: Timbrell Tug-of-War Left her Terrorized, Social Worker Says, *Toronto Star*, 27 October 1967, 1.

97 John Colebourn and Stuart Hunter, "Foster Kids Win Battle to Stay Together as a Family: Favourite Dinner, Gospel Singling Planned for Tonight," *The Province [Vancouver]*, 1 March 2002, A2.

98 See the claim for example in "Foster Parents Group Says Gov't Puts Kids in Jeopardy," *Kamloops Daily News*, 21 December 2000, A8. See also Steinhauer, *The Least Detrimental Alternative*, 160.

99 Murray, "Governing 'Unwed Mothers,'" 272.

100 Harrison, "Foster Homefinding," 9–10.

101 Swartz, "Mothering for the State," 581.

102 Evans, "Excellent Women and Troublesome Children," 139.

103 Ethel M. Chapman, "Could You Adopt a Baby?" *Maclean's*, December 1919, 116.

104 Anna G. Singleton, "Child Welfare Administration under Protection Acts in British Columbia: Its History and Development, 1901–1949" (MSW dissertation, University of British Columbia, 1950), 45.

105 Saunders, "Short Term Mothers," 16,

106 Ontario, Department of Public Welfare, *Annual Report* (1949–50), 19.

107 Biedema, *Mothering for the State*, 78.

108 "Court Gives Back Child to Mother Two Hearts Hurt," *Toronto Star*, 11 June 1926, 1.

109 "In Wartime, Need Grows for Good Foster Homes," *Saturday Night*, 19 September 1942, 4.

110 Mary Bowden quoted in *Globe and Mail*, 21 November 1983, in "Achieving the Vision of Deinstitutionalization: A Role for Foster Care?," ed. Carol Appathurai, Grant Lowery, and Terry Sullivan, *Child and Adolescent Social Work* 3, no. 1 (Spring 1986): 60.

111 R.L. Hegar, "Ch. 14 Kinship Foster Care," in Hegar and Scannagpieco, *Kinship Foster Care*, 230.

112 See Leo David, "Foster Fatherhood: the Untapped Resource," *The Family Coordinator* 20, no. 1 (January 1971): 49–54.

113 See Kim Bolan, "Judges Praises Courage of Abuse Victim," *Vancouver Sun*, 10 October 2007, B1 and B4.

114 Dingman, "An Unhappy Report on Foster Homes," 54–55.

115 "Adopted 4, Are Parents of the Year," *Toronto Star*, 9 January 1960, 8.

116 Battel, *Children Shall Be First*, 107.

117 Richard Clark, Letter in "The Mail," *Maclean's*, 16 August 2004, 8.

118 Bokma, "Families and Foster Care," 200.

119 Dingman, "An Unhappy Report on Foster Homes," 54

120 P.D. Steinhauer et al., "The Foster Care Research Project: Clinical Impressions," *American Journal of Orthopsychiatry* 59, no. 3 (July 1989): 461.

121 Cheryl Farris-Manning and Marietta Zandstra, *Children in Care in Canada: A Summary of Current Issues and Trends with Recommendations for Future Research* (Ottawa: Child Welfare League of Canada, 2003), 8.

122 Samantha quoted in Marvin Bernstein, *A Breach of Trust: An Investigation into Foster Home Overcrowding in the Saskatchewan Service Centre* (Saskatoon: Children's Advocate, February 2009), 50.

123 Steinhauer et al., "The Foster Care Research Project," 437.

124 Quoted in "Fostered 53, Never One Ill," *Toronto Star*, 10 January 1959, 3.

125 "Adopted 4, Are Parents of the Year," 8.

126 Lisa Hepfner, "Beloved Foster Mother Dies," *Edmonton Journal*, 11 July 1998, B.

127 Chris Thompson, "Foster Mom Lauded," *Windsor Star*, 24 May 2001, A3.

128 "Digby Foster Parents Win National Award, *Department of Community Services, Nova Scotia* (26 February 2001), Canadian Welfare League, http://www.gov.ns.ca/news/details.asp?id=20010226003.

129 "Governor General's Caring Canadian Award. David John Stewart," Office of the Governor General. http://archive.gg.ca/honours/search-recherche/honours-desc.asp?lang=e&TypeID=cca&id=4716.

130 Foster Parent-Bertolette Démosthène- nominated by Centre jeunesse de Montréal—institut universitaire," Canadian Welfare League, http://www.cwlc.ca/events/achievement-awards/2004.

131 Peter Clough, "Bounced around: An Investigation of the B.C. Foster Care System," *The Province [Vancouver]*, 29 August 2001, A6.

132 "About Us, " Foster Parent Society of Ontario, http://www.oacas.org/.

133 Mrs. A.I. Allen to Mr. W.D. McFarland, *Re: Youth Conference, 1967*, 17 May 1967, University of British Columbia, Koerner Library Vertical Files, xerox, 6.

134 Ibid., 1.

135 Biedema, *Mothering for the State*, 32.

136 Chris Wood, "Trouble on the Ranch," *Maclean's*, 12 April 1999, 27.

137 Peter Clough, "Foster Parents at War behind the Scenes," *The Province [Vancouver]*, 30 August 2001, A8.

138 See, for example, the description provided in Harrison, "Foster Homefinding" and "Foster Homes Needed," *United Church Observer*, 15 February 1966, 31. On the commonplace shortage in many jurisdictions, see Dalley, *Family Matters*, 235–45.

139 On this, see Joe Hudson, Richard Nutter, and Burt Galaway, "Contracting-Out and Program Evaluation: A Case Study," in *Carrots, Sticks and Sermons: Policy Instruments and Their Evaluation*, ed., Marie-Louise Bemelmans-Videc, Ray C. Rist, and Evert Vedunt (New Brunswick, NJ: Transaction Publishers, 2003), 165–84.

140 Leona Pedosuk and Elizabeth Ratcliffe, "Special Report: Using Foster Parents to Help Foster Parents: A Canadian Experiment," *Child Welfare* 58 (July/August 1979): 467.

141 *Treatment Foster Care: An Implementation Plan—Joining Science to Practice* (Richmond Hill, ON: Ontario Association of Residences Treating Youth, 22 October 2008. See also Yvonne Unrau, "Role Differentiation between Foster Parents and Treatment Foster Parents," in *Current Perspectives on Foster Family Care for Children and Youth*, ed. Brad McKenzie (Toronto and Dayton: Wall and Emerson, 1994), 112–23.

142 *Treatment Foster Care: An Implementation Plan*, 18.

143 Steinhauer, *The Least Detrimental Alternative*, 284–85.

144 See Nancy Hazel, *A Bridge to Independence: The Kent Family Placement Project* (Oxford: Basil Blackwell, 1981), 24–25.

145 See ibid., 35–36.

146 Steinhauer, *The Least Detrimental Alternative*, 291.

147 Ibid.,189.

148 Carol Appathurai, Grant Lowery, and Terry Sullivan, "Achieving the Vision of Deinstitutionalization: A Role for Foster Care?" *Child and Adolescent Social Work* 3, no. 1 (Spring 1986): 59.

149 Bernstein, *A Breach of Trust*, 3.

150 Ibid., 59.

Notes to Chapter 7

1   "An Open Letter Presented to the Government of Canada: Dear Mom and Dad,"
    Canada's Children (Fall 2000), 8, http://www.cwlc.ca/files/file/pubs/CCFa112000.pdf.

2   R. Flynn and C. Biro, "Comparing Developmental Outcomes for Children in Care with
    Those for Other Children in Canada," *Children and Society* 12 (1998): 228–33.

3   H. Philip Hepworth, *Foster Care and Adoption* (Ottawa: Canadian Council for Social
    Development, 1980); and Patrick Johnston, *Native Children and the Child Welfare Sys-
    tem* (Ottawa: Canadian Council for Social Development, 1983).

4   Hepworth, *Foster Care and Adoption in Canada*, 2–3 and 75.

5   Deborah Shapiro, "Fostering and Adoption: Converging Roles for Substitute Parents,"
    in *Adoption: Current Issues and Trends*, ed. Paul Sachdev (Toronto: Butterworth, 1984),
    269.

6   Evariste Thériault, "Introduction: Child Welfare Research and Development in a National
    Context," in *Child Welfare: Connecting Research, Policy, and Practice,* ed. Kathleen Kufeldt
    and Brad McKenzie (Waterloo: Wilfrid Laurier University Press, 2003), 1.

7   Raymond Lemay and Hayat Ghazal, *Looking after Children: A Practitioner's Guide* (Ottawa:
    University of Ottawa, 2007), 1.

8   Cheryl Farris-Manning and Marietta Zandstra, "Children in Care in Canada: A Sum-
    mary of Current Issues and Trends with Recommendations for Future Research," in *The
    Welfare of Canadian Children* (Ottawa: Child Welfare Council of Canada, 2007), 54–55.

9   "Anti-Oppression, Anti-Racism Policy" (Toronto: Children's Aid Society, 9 November
    2006), 1.

10 Patrick Johnston, *Native Children and the Child Welfare System*, 23; and Hepworth, *Fos-
    ter Care and Adoption*, 114.

11 Canada, Royal Commission on Aboriginal Peoples, *Report*, volume 3, 2.2, http://www
    .collectionscanada.gc.ca/webarchives/20071124125546/http://www.ainc-inac.gc.ca/
    ch/rcap/sg/sim2_e.html.

12 Nico Trocmé et al., *Understanding the Overrepresentation of First Nations Children in
    Canada's Child Welfare System: An Analysis of the Canadian Incidence Study of Reported Child
    Abuse and Neglect*, Doc. CIS-2003 (Toronto: Centre of Excellence for Child Welfare,
    2005), 16.

13 "Assembly of First Nations Signs Child Welfare Partnership Agreement and Launches
    Leadership Action Plan on First Nations Child Welfare," 21 November 2006, http://www
    .afn.ca/article.asp?id=3139.

14 Cheryl Farris-Manning and Marietta Zandstra, *Children in Care in Canada: A Summary
    of Current Issues and Trends with Recommendations for Future Research* (Ottawa: Child
    Welfare League of Canada, 2003), 6.

15 Michael Reid, "Understanding Children's Aid: Meaning and Practice in Ontario Chil-
    dren's Aid Societies, 1893–1912" (MA dissertation, Trent University, 2008), 97.

16 Farris-Manning and Zandstra, *Children in Care in Canada*, 3. See also Don Fuchs et al.,
    "Children with Disabilities Involved with the Child Welfare System in Manitoba: Cur-
    rent and Future Challenges," in *Putting a Human Face on Child Welfare: Voices from the
    Prairies*, ed. Ivan Brown et al. (Regina: Prairie Child Welfare Consortium, 2007), 127–45,
    http://www.cecw-cepb.ca/node/907.

17 Jason Brown, "Rewards of Fostering Children with Disabilities," *Journal of Family Social
    Work* 11, no. 1 (May 2008): 37.

18 W. James King, Morag MacKay, and Angela Sirnick, with the Canadian Shaken Baby Study Group, "Shaken Baby Syndrome in Canada: Clinical Characteristics and Outcomes of Hospital Cases," *Canadian Medical Association Journal* 168 (21 January 2003): 158.

19 Fuchs et al., "Children with Disabilities, 139 and 142.

20 J. Douglas Willms, "Socioeconomic Gradients for Childhood vulnerability," in *Vulnerable Children: Findings from Canada's National Longitudinal Survey of Children and Youth*, ed. J. Douglas Willms (Edmonton: University of Alberta Press, 2002), 77.

21 Shawn Bayes, "A Snowball's Chance: Children of Offenders and Canadian Social Policy," Elizabeth Fry Society of Greater Vancouver (Vancouver: Elizabeth Fry Society, 2003), http://www.elizabethfry.com/A_SNOWBALLS_CHANCE.pdf, 34.

22 Karen Dubinsky and Franca Iacovetta, "Murder, Womanly Virtue, and Motherhood: The Case of Angelina Napolitano, 1911–1922," *Canadian Historical Review* 57, no. 4 (1991): 305–31.

23 Alice Parizeau, *Protection de L'enfant: échec?* (Montreal: Les Presses de l'Université de Montreal, 1979), 174–75.

24 See, for example, the conclusion in Carolyne A. Gorlick, "Listening to Low-Income Children and Single Mothers: Policy Implications Related to Child Welfare," in *Child Welfare in Canada: Research and Policy Implications*, ed. Joe Hudson and Burt Galaway (Toronto: Thompson Educational Publishing, 1995), 288.

25 Joan Sangster, *Girl Trouble: Female Delinquency in English Canada* (Toronto: Between the Lines, 2002), 89.

26 Deborah Rutman et al., *When Youth Age Out of Care—Where to from There? Final Report Based on a Three Year Longitudinal Study* (Victoria: School of Social Work, University of Victoria, 2007), 32.

27 Joscelyn Dingman, "An Unhappy Report on Foster Homes," *Chatelaine*, December 1970, 55.

28 Paul Steinhauer, *The Least Detrimental Alternative: A Systematic Guide to Case Planning and Decision Making for Children* (Toronto: University of Toronto, 1991), 65.

29 "John," quoted in Cheryl Marlene Swidrovich, "Positive Experiences of First Nations Children in Non-Aboriginal Foster or Adoptive Care: De-Constructing the 'Sixties Scoop'" (MA dissertation, University of Saskatchewan, 2004), 57.

30 Gil Cardinal, Director, *Foster Child* (Ottawa: National Film Board, 1987).

31 Ontario, *Annual Report of the Superintendent of Neglected and Dependent Children*, Sessional Papers (1930), 12.

32 Lisa Fitterman, "Quebec Singer Known as Boule Noire Repeatedly Reinvented Himself," *Globe and Mail*, 5 July 2007, S9

33 Dorothy Howarth, "Ninety Children Need Homes," *Vancouver Sun*, 6 December, 1960, 2.

34 Cindy, quoted in Ellen Adelberg and Claudia Currie, "In Their Own Words," in *Too Few to Count: Canadian Women in Conflict with the Law*, ed. Ellen Adelberg and Claudia Currie (Vancouver: Press Gang Publishers, 1987), 85

35 Ibid., 86 and 88.

36 Reid, "Understanding Children's Aid," 142.

37 Ibid.

38 Sarah Davies, "Adoption Crisis: 10,000 Kids with No Place to Go," *Chatelaine*, December 1967, 30.

39 Donald E. Efron, "Strategic Therapy Interventions with Latency-Age Children," *Social Casework: The Journal of Contemporary Social Work*, 62, no. 9 (1981): 544.

40 Cardinal, *Foster Child*.

41 Harold Rich, Montreal Children's Hospital and Batshaw Youth and Family Centres, "The Effects of a Health Newsletter for Foster Parents on Their Perceptions of the Behavior and Development of Foster Children," *Child Abuse and Neglect* 20, no. 5 (May 1996): 437.

42 See Sparrow Lake Alliance, Children in Limbo Task Force, *Children in Limbo* (Scarborough, ON: Sparrow Lake Alliance, 1996).

43 Marvin Bernstein, *A Breach of Trust: An Investigation into Foster Home Overcrowding in the Saskatchewan Service Centre* (Saskatoon: Children's Advocate, February 2009), 76.

44 K.L.B. v British Columba, 2003 SCC 51, [2003] 2 S.C.R. 403 (Judgments of the Supreme Court of Canada), http://csc.lexum.umontreal.ca/en/2003/2003scc51/2003scc51.html.

45 Brian Raychaba, "'We Get a Life Sentence': Young People in Care Speak Out on Child Sexual Abuse," *Journal of Child and Youth Care,* Special Issue (1992): 129–39.

46 Bernstein, *A Breach of Trust,* 39–40.

47 Chandrakant P. Shah, "Psychiatric Consultations in a Child Welfare Agency: Some Facts and Figures," *Canadian Psychiatric Association Journal* 19, no. 4 (August 1974): 395.

48 Ibid., 394.

49 On the return to pessimism, see Sangster, *Girl Trouble*, 12 and passim.

50 Eleanor Stein et al., "Psychiatric Disorders of Children in Care: Methodology and Demographic Correlates," *Canadian Journal of Psychiatry* 39, no. 6 (August 1994): 341.

51 Charles W. Popper, "Child and Adolescent Psychopharmacology at the Turn of the Millennium," in *Practical Child and Adolescent Psychopharmacology*, ed. Stan Kutcher (Cambridge: Cambridge University Press, 2002), 7.

52 Margaret Philip, "Nearly Half of Children in Crown Care Are Medicated," *Globe and Mail*, 9 June 2007, A1. Treatment with psycho-pharmaceuticals began in the 1930s when it was reported that children "with behavior disorders" improved with amphetamine. See Popper, "Child and Adolescent Psychopharmacology," 1.

53 Clare C. Brant, "Native Ethics and Rules of Behaviour," *Canadian Journal of Psychiatry* 35, no. 6 (August 1990): 534.

54 Jane Grekul, Arvey Krahn, and David Odynak, "Sterilizing the 'Feeble-Minded': Eugenics in Alberta, Canada, 1929–1972," *Journal of Historical Sociology* 17, no. 4 (2004): 358–84. Natives were always overrepresented in terms of their share of the population, but they constituted only 6 percent of cases presented for sterilization (375).

55 See Sangster, *Girl Trouble*.

56 Peter Clough, "'I was what you call a high-needs foster kid,'" *The Province [Vancouver]*, 31 August 2001, A8.

57 Quoted in Wayne Mitic and Mary Lynne Rimer, "The Educational Attainment of Children in Care in British Columbia," *Child and Youth Care Forum* 31, no. 6 (December 2002): 409.

58 Michelle Molloy and regional facilitators, *Who Will Teach Me to Learn? Creating Positive School Experiences for Youth in Care* (Ottawa: National Youth in Care Network, 2001), 5–6.

59 Sangster, *Girl Trouble*, 95.

60 Percy White, quoted in Phyllis Harrison, *The Home Children* (Winnipeg: Watson and Dwyer, 1979), 108. See also Mrs. J. Breckenridge McGregor, *"Several Years After": An Analysis of the Histories of a Selected Group of Juvenile Immigrants brought to Canada in 1910*,

and in 1920, by British Emigration Societies (Ottawa: Canadian Council on Child Welfare, 1928).

61   See the case of James Wilde on an Ontario farm in Harrison, *Home Children*, 153.

62   Robert J. Flynn and Chantal Biro, "Comparing Developmental Outcomes for Children in Care with Those for Other Children in Canada," *Children and Society* 12 (1998): 232.

63   Molloy, *Who Will Teach Me to Learn?* 2.

64   Keith McPhee et al., "Educational Challenges for Children and Youth at Risk: Toward a Shared Responsibility," in *The Welfare of Canadian Children: It's Our Business* (Ottawa: Child Welfare Council of Canada, 2007), 135–36.

65   Janet Steffenhagen, "Kids in Government Care Drop Out at Shocking Rate, Report Says," *Vancouver Sun*, 30 May 2007, A3.

66   Rutman et al., *When Youth Age Out of Care*, 19.

67   Barbara A. Mitchell, *Family Matters: An Introduction to Family Sociology in Canada* (Toronto: Canadian Scholars' Press, 2009), 199.

68   Kathleen Kufeldt et al., "The Looking After Children in Canada Project: Educational Outcomes," in Kufeldt and McKenzie, *Child Welfare*, 188.

69   Rutman et al., *When Youth Age Out of Care*, 3.

70   Brian Raychaba, *Canadian Youth In Care: Leaving Care to Be on Our Own with No Direction from Home* (Ottawa: National Youth in Care Network, 1988). See also Andrée Cazabon, Director, *Wards of the Crown* (National Film Board of Canada, 2005). See also Fay E. Martin, "Tales of Transition: Leaving Public Care," in *Youth in Transition: Perspectives on Research and Policy*, ed. Burt Galaway and Joe Hudson (Toronto: Thompson Educational Publishing, 1996), 98–106.

71   Pat Kariel, *New Directions: Stepping Out of Street Life* (Calgary: Greenways Press, 1993), 1, 32, 43, and 51.

72   Farris-Manning and Zandstra, *Children in Care in Canada*, 12. See also on Toronto John Hagan and Bill McCarthy, *Mean Streets: Youth Crime and Homelessness* (Cambridge: Cambridge University Press, 1998), 23.

73   Pieta Woolley, "Neglected by the Province, Foster Care Is a Fast Track to the Streets," 13 December 2007, http://www.straight.com/article-124525/neglected-by-the-province -foster-care-is-a-fast-track-to-the-streets. See also Bruce Leslie and Francis Hare, "At Care's End: Child Welfare Grads and street Youth Services," in Kufeldt and McKenzie, *Child Welfare*, 239–47.

74   Asia Czapska, Annabel Webb, and Nura Taefi, *More Than Bricks and Mortar: A Rights-Based Strategy to Prevent Girl Homelessness in Canada* (Status of Women Canada, May 2008), 11, http://www.justiceforgirls.org. See also Office of Child and Family Service Advocacy, *Youth Running from Residential Care: "The Push" and "The Pull"* (Ontario, February 2006).

75   Excerpt from a letter to a Children's Aid Society from a youth in care, Ontario Advocate for Children and Youth, *Ninety Deaths, Ninety Voices Silenced*, 2007–8 report (Toronto: Office of the Ontario Advocate for Children and Youth, 2008), 12.

76   On this pattern, see Elizabeth Comack, *Women in Trouble* (Halifax: Fernwood Publishing, 1996), 60–61.

77   Dr. Don McCaskill, *Patterns of Native Criminality* (1974), as quoted in Bryan Loucks and Arnette Timothy, *Justice-Related Children and Family Services for Native People in Ontario: A Discussion Paper*, revised edition (Toronto: Ontario Native Council on Justice, 1981), 18.

78   For example, Parizeau, *Protection de L'enfant: échec?* 130.

79 Woolley, "Neglected by the Province." See also Leslie Hare, "At Care's End: Child Welfare Grads and Street Youth Services," in Kufeldt and McKenzie, *Child Welfare.*

80 Youth Voice, *Young People Say: Report from the Youth Consultation Initiative* (Ottawa: National Crime Prevention Council, 1997), 10. For the special vulnerability of those with psychiatric disorders, see also Eleanor Stein et al., "Psychiatric Disorders of Children 'In Care': Methodology and Demographic Correlates," *Canadian Journal of Psychiatry* 39, no. 6 (August 1994): 341–47.

81 See Phillip Buckner, *Canada and the British Empire* (Oxford: Oxford University Press, 2008), 168.

82 "Savannah Hall's Death in Foster Care Was Homicide, Inquest Rules," CBC News, 4 November 2007, http://www.cbc.ca/canada/british-columbia/story/2007/11/04/bc-verdict.html?ref=rss.

83 See Shana Ross and Nancy Health, "A Study of Self-Mutilation in Community Sample of Adolescents," *Journal of Youth and Adolescents* 31, no. 1 (February 2002): 67–77.

84 *Globe and Mail,* 23 February 2007, http://www.theglobeandmail.com. See the report of her family's history of alcoholism and sexual abuse in http://www.manitobacourts.mb.ca/pdf/tracia_owen.pdf.

85 "Annual Victims of Child Welfare Day," http://www.afterfostercare.ca/memorial.html.

86 Joy Parr, *Labouring Children: British Immigrant Apprentices to Canada, 1869–1924* (Toronto: University of Toronto Press, 1994), 75.

87 Marjory Harper, "Cossar's Colonists: Juvenile Migration to New Brunswick in the 1920s," *Acadiensis* 28, no. 1 (1998): 64.

88 McGregor, *"Several Years After,"* 21–23.

89 Miss Grace A. Towers, "Problems in Institutional Care," *Canadian Child and Family Welfare* 8, no. 2 (July 1932): 55.

90 Robert E. Mills, "The Placing of Children in Families," *Canadian Child and Family Welfare* 14, no. 1 (July 1938): 50.

91 Robert E. Mills, "The Child and the Institution," *Canadian Child and Family Welfare* 14, no. 3 (Sept. 1939): 45.

92 New Brunswick, Department of Health and Social Services, Social Services Branch, *Report of the Case of Westmorland County: Annual Report* (for the fiscal year ended 31 March 1957), 79.

93 June Rose, *For the Sake of the Children: Inside Dr. Barnardo's: 120 Years of Caring for Children* (London: Hodder and Stoughton, 1987), 96.

94 Cardinal, *Foster Child.*

95 Carol Dauphinais, *Living with Labels and Lies: A Life Story* (Vancouver: Carol Dauphais, 1997), 23.

96 Ibid., 19.

97 Manitoba Courts, "In the Matter of: the Fatality Inquiries Act and Tracia Owen (Deceased) D.O.D. August 24, 2005," Provincial Court of Manitoba, http://www.manitobacourts.mb.ca/pdf/tracia_owen.pdf.

98 Laura Curran "Longing to 'Belong': Foster Children in Mid-Century Philadelphia (1946–1963)," *Journal of Social History* 42, no. 2 (Winter 2008): 425–45.

99 See Swidrovich, "Positive Experiences of First Nations Children."

100 Quoted in the 1991 Community Panel, in Brian Wharf, "Organizing and Delivering Child Welfare Services: The Contributions of Research," in Hudson and Galaway, *Child Welfare in Canada,* 34.

NOTES TO CHAPTER SEVEN

101 Pat Kariel, *New Directions: Stepping Out of Street Life* (Calgary: Greenways Press, 1993),
     69. See also the conclusion in Ross A. Klein, Kathleen Kufeldt, and Scott Rideout,
     "Resilience Theory and Its Relevance for Child Welfare Practice," in *Promoting Resilience
     in Child Welfare*, ed. Robert John Flynn, Peter M. Dudding, and James G. Barber (Ottawa:
     University of Ottawa Press, 2005), 35.
102 See Elly Danica, *Don't: A Woman's Word* (Charlottetown: Gynergy Books, 1988).
103 Cardinal, *Foster Child*.
104 Unfortunately, their evolution and influence have yet to be precisely charted, but for a
     beginning, see Glenn E. Richardson, "The Metatheory of Resilience and Resiliency,"
     Journal of Clinical Psychology 53, no. 3 (March 2002): 307–21; and Louise Legault and
     Shaye Moffat, "Positive Life Experiences That Promote Resilience in Young People in
     Care," in Flynn, Dudding, and Barber, *Promoting Resilience in Child Welfare*, 173–90. See
     also the cases cited in Michael Ungar, "Contextual and Cultural Aspects of Resilience
     in Child Welfare Settings," in *Putting a Human Face on Child Welfare: Voices from the
     Prairies*, ed. Ivan Brown et al. (Regina: Prairie Child Welfare Consortium, 2007), 1–24;
     and Sharon McKay and Shelley Thomas Prokop, "Identity, Community, Resilience: The
     Transmission of Values Project," in Brown et al., *Putting a Human Face on Child Welfare*,
     25–58.
105 Legault and Moffat, "Positive Life Experiences That Promote Resilience in Young Peo-
     ple in Care," in Brown et al., *Putting a Human Face on Child Welfare*, 180–81 [exclama-
     tion in original].
106 See Lynn Abrams, *The Orphan Country: Children of Scotland's Broken Homes from 1845
     to the Present Day* Edinburgh: John Donald Publishers, 1998), 211, for her insightful dis-
     cussion of how Scottish youngsters have tried to negotiate their roles; and Cardinal,
     Foster Child.
107 Mary Wallace Black, in Harrison, *Home Children*, 117–19.
108 Earl Einerson, *The Moccasins* (Penticton, BC: Theytus Books, 2005).
109 Theytus Books, http://www.theytus.com/Book-List/The-Moccasins.
110 Swidrovich, "Positive Experiences of First Nations Children."
111 Peter Clough, "'I was what you call a high-needs foster kid,'" 8.
112 Radhika Panjwani, "People," *Mississauga News*, 24 October 2007, http://www.mississauga
     .com/article/7932.
113 Ontario Advocate for Children and Youth, *Ninety Deaths: Ninety Voices Silenced* 7.
114 See W.B. Carledge, in Harrison, *Home Children*, 173.
115 Dauphinais, *Living with Labels and Lies*, 63–4.
116 McGregor, "Several Years After," 12.
117 Beatrice Culleton Mosionier, *In Search of April Raintree* (Winnipeg: Portage and Main
     Press, 1999), 67.
118 "An Open Letter Presented to the Government of Canada," 8.
119 On the problem for sexual assault charges, see Robin F. Badgley, *Sexual Offences against
     Children: Report of the Committee on Sexual Offences against Children and Youths* (Ottawa:
     Minister of Justice and Attorney General of Canada and the Minister of National Health
     and Welfare, 1984), volume 1, chapter 14.
120 Flora Harrison, in Harrison, *Home Children*, 74.
121 Caroline Evans, "Excellent Women and Troublesome Children: State Foster Care in Tas-
     mania, 1896–1918," *Labour History* 83 (November 2002), http://www.historycooperative
     .org/journals/lab/83/evans.html, para. 44.

122 Cori Howard, "Stealing Home," *Vancouver Magazine*, October 2003, 60–64 and 66.
123 Yvonne Zacharaias, "Diane Gaudet: Our Sports Mom of the Year," *Vancouver Sun*, 9 May 2009, D2.
124 Ontario Advocate for Children and Youth, *Ninety Deaths, Ninety Voices Silenced*, 7.
125 Mrs. A.I. Allen to Mr. W.D McFarland, *Re: Youth Conference, 1967*, UBC Koerner Library Vertical Files, Xerox, 17 May 1967, 7–9.
126 See Bryan D. Palmer's valuable discussion of "Red Power," in *Canada's 1960s: The Ironies of Identity in a Rebellious Era* (Toronto: University of Toronto Press, 2009), chapter 10.
127 Marty Dunn, *Red on White: The Biography of Duke Redbird* (Toronto: New Press, 1971).
128 See John A. MacDonald, 'The Spallumcheen Indian Band By-Law and Its Potential Impact on Native Indian Child Welfare Policy in British Columbia,' *Canadian Journal of Family Law* 4 (July 1983): 75–95; and Christopher Walmsley, *Protecting Aboriginal Children* (Vancouver: UBC Press, 2006), 24–25.
129 Kathleen Kufeldt and Brad McKenzie, "Conclusions and Directions for the Future," in Kufeldt and McKenzie, *Child Welfare*, 431. See Evariste Thériault, "Introduction: Child Welfare Research and Development in a National Context," in Kufeldt and McKenzie, *Child Welfare*, 3 and passim. For the publications of the National Youth in Care Network, including *Speak the Truth in a Million Voices: It Is the Silence That Kills": Stories for Change* (2004) and *Broken Fairytales: Teenage Parenting and the Child Welfare System in Care: Stories for Support and Strength* (2004), see its website http://www.youthincare.ca/resources/tools.html.
130 See the website of Foster Care Council of Canada, http://www.afterfostercare.ca/index.html.
131 Ron Csillag, "Canada's First L'Arche Member Spread the Word," *Globe and Mail*, 9 May 2009, S16.

Notes to Conclusion

1 Dominique Marshall, "Reconstruction Politics, the Canadian Welfare State and the Formation of Children's Rights, 1940–1950," in *Family Matters: Papers in Post-Confederation Canadian Family History*, ed. Lori Chambers and Edgar-André Montigny (Toronto: Canadian Scholars' Press, 1998), 140.
2 Marilyn Callahan, "Feminist Approaches: Women Recreate Child Welfare," in *Rethinking Child Welfare in Canada*, ed. Brian Wharf (Toronto: McClelland and Stewart, 1993), 189. On the need to reinvigorate social work through feminist practice, see also Gale Wills, *A Marriage of Convenience: Business and Social Work in Toronto, 1918–1957* (Toronto: University of Toronto Press, 1995), especially the conclusions in chapter 7.
3 Olena Hankivsky, *Social Policy and the Ethic of Care* (Vancouver: UBC Press, 2004), 115.
4 H. Philip Hepworth, *Foster Care and Adoption in Canada* (Ottawa: Canadian Council on Social Development, 1980), 35.
5 See the call in Brian Wharf, *Community Work Approaches to Child Welfare* (Toronto: Broadview Press, 2002). See also the discussion in "The Tyranny of the Case," in Fay Weller and Brian Wharf, "Contradictions in Child Welfare," in *Too Small to See, Too Big to Ignore: Child Health and Well-being in British Columbia*, ed. Michael V. Hayes and Leslie T. Foster, Canadian Western Geographical Series no. 35, vol. 35 (Victoria: Department of Geography, University of Victoria, 2002), 151–53. See also the community

development projects in New Brunswick, Quebec, Manitoba, and Alberta described in Michèle Kérisit and Néré St.-Amand, "Taking Risks with Families at Risk: Some Alternative Approaches with Poor Families in Canada," in *Child Welfare in Canada: Research and Policy Implications*, ed. Joe Hudson and Burt Galaway (Toronto: Thompson Educational Publishing, 1995), 154–67.

6 Paul Kershaw, *Carefair: Rethinking the Responsibilities and Rights of Citizenship* (Vancouver: UBC Press, 2005), 7.

7 See Dominique Marshall's thoughtful "The Language of Children's Rights, the Formation of the Welfare State, and the Democratic Experience of Poor Families in Quebec, 1940–1955," *Canadian Historical Review* 78, no. 3 (September 1997): 409–41.

8 Ontario Advocate for Children and Youth, *Ninety Deaths, Ninety Voices Silenced*, 2007–8 report (Toronto: Office of the Ontario Advocate for Children and Youth, 2008).

9 Judge Ted Hughes, *BC Child and Youth: An Independent Review of B.C.'s Child Protection System* (Victoria: Minister of Children and Family Development, 2006), 78.

10 Marvin Bernstein, *A Breach of Trust: An Investigation into Foster Home Overcrowding in the Saskatchewan Service Centre* (Saskatoon: Children's Advocate, February 2009), 1, http://www.cecw-cepb.ca/publications/987.

11 Ibid., 2. See also David A. Tickell, *The Protection of Children: The Rights of Children: The Urgent Need to Improve a System in Crisis* (Saskatoon: Saskatchewan Ombudsman, 31 December 1986); Children's Advocate Office, *Child Death Review of Karen Rose Quill* (Saskatoon: Children's Advocate Office, 1998); Saskatchewan, Children's Advocate Office, *Children and Youth in Care Review: LISTEN to Their Voices* (Saskatoon: Children's Advocate Office, 2000).

12 Olena Hankivsky, *Social Policy and the Ethic of Care* (Vancouver: UBC Press, 2004), 135.

SELECTED BIBLIOGRAPHY

This volume draws on original and secondary sources examined over more than a decade. Where possible, all reports of provincial and territorial government departments responsible for child protection have been reviewed from the nineteenth century to the present. I have also searched out research reports, investigations, and royal commissions produced by voluntary societies, private agencies, state consultants and advisors, and participants in fostering. I have read representative newspapers from every region and entire runs of magazines such as *Chatelaine, Saturday Night, Maclean's,* and the *Star Weekly,* as well as professionally oriented journals such as the *Dominion Law Reports,* the *Canadian Medical Journal,* and *Canadian Welfare.* Such primary sources are referred to in detail in the chapter notes. What follows here is a list of the government and non-governmental reports, scholarly material, theses, and films that readers may find helpful to have grouped together as well as referred to separately.

Government and Non-Governmental Organization Reports

Aboriginal Children's Health: Leaving No Child Behind: Canadian Supplement to the State of the World's Children 2009. Toronto: Canadian UNICEF Committee, 2009.

Aboriginal Children's Survey: First Nations Children Living off Reserve. Ottawa: Statistics Canada, 2008.

Alberta. *In the Matter of the Child Welfare Act, 1965.* Hearings held before His Honour Judge H.S. Patterson, Chairman Frank J. Fleming, Esq., and Mrs. W.F Bowke, volume 3 at the Court House, Calgary, 9 and 10 March 1965.

Anderson, Leslie, et al. *Best Practice Approaches: Child Protection and Violence against Women.* Victoria: Ministry of Children and Family Development, May 2004.

Angus, Anne Margaret. *Children's Aid Society of Vancouver, B.C. 1901–1951.* Vancouver: Vancouver Children's Aid, 1951.

Anti-Oppression, Anti-Racism Policy. Children's Aid Society of Toronto, 9 November 2006.

Bagley, Christopher. *Child Sexual Abuse in Canada: Further Analysis of the 1983 National Survey.* Ottawa: Health and Welfare Canada, 1988.

Battel, Mildred E. *Children Shall Be First: Child Welfare Saskatchewan 1944–64.* Saskatoon, SK: Department of Children and Youth, Local History Program, 1980.

Bayes, Shawn. *A Snowball's Chance: Children of Offenders and Canadian Social Policy.* New Westminster, BC: Elizabeth Fry Society of Greater Vancouver, 2003.

Bernstein, Marvin. *A Breach of Trust: An Investigation into Foster Home Overcrowding in the Saskatchewan Service Centre.* Saskatoon: Children's Advocate, February 2009, http://www.cecw-cepb.ca/publications/987.

Broken Fairytales—Teenage Parenting and the Child Welfare System in Care: Stories for Support and Strength. Ottawa: National Youth in Care Network, 2004.

Bryce, Peter. *Report on the Indian Schools of Manitoba and the North-West Territories.* Ottawa: Queen's Printer, 1907.

Caldwell, George. *Child Welfare Services in New Brunswick: A Report to the Honourable W.R. Duffie, Minister of Welfare, Province of New Brunswick.* Ottawa: Canadian Welfare Council, October 1965.

Canada. Committee on Sexual Offences against Children and Youth. *Sexual Offences against Children: Report of the Committee on Sexual Offences against Children and Youth* (the Badgley Report), volumes 1 and 2. Ottawa: Department of Supply and Services, 1984.

———. *The Report of the Royal Commission on the Relations of Capital and Labour* (Ottawa: Queen's Printer, 1889).

———. *The Report of the Special Senate Committee on Poverty: Poverty in Canada* [Croll Report] (Ottawa: Senate of Canada, 1971).

———. Royal Commission on Aboriginal Peoples. *Public Policy and Aboriginal Peoples 1965–1992,* volume 3. Summaries of Reports by Provincial and Territorial Bodies and Other Organizations. Ottawa: Royal Commission on Aboriginal Peoples, 1994.

———. Senate. *Children: The Silenced Citizens: Final Report of the Standing Senate Committee on Human Rights.* Ottawa: Senate of Canada, 2007.

Cannings, K. *Bridging the Gap: Programs and Services to Facilitate Contact between Inmate Parents and Their Children.* Ottawa: Minister of the Solicitor General of Canada, 1991.

Changing the Landscape: Ending Violence—Achieving Equality. Ottawa: Ministry of Supply and Services, 1993.

Child and Youth Officer for British Columbia [Jane Morley]. *Heshook-ish Tsawalk: towards a State of Healthy Interdependence in the Child Welfare System.* Victoria: Child and Youth Officer for British Columbia, June 2006.

Couchman, Bob. "From Precious Resource to Societal Accessory: Canada's Children Six to Twelve Years of Age." National Children's Alliance, National Symposium, 22–24 March 2002.

Creese, Gillian, and Veronica Strong-Boag. *Still Waiting for Justice: Update 2009. Provincial Policies and Gender Inequality in BC*. Vancouver: BC Federation of Labour and the UBC Centre for Women's and Gender Studies, 8 March 2009.

Cunningham, Ron, and Ray D. Bollman. "Structure and Trends of Rural Employment: Canada in the Context of OECD Countries." *Statistics Canada, Agricultural and Rural Working Paper Series*, Doc. no. 28049 (1996), http://ideas.repec.org/p/ags/scarwp/28049.html#provider.

Czapska, Asia, Annabel Webb, and Nura Taefi. *More Than Bricks and Mortar: A Rights-Based Strategy to Prevent Girl Homelessness in Canada*. Status of Women Canada, May 2008.

Davidson, George F., IV. *Report on Public Welfare Services*, Royal Commission on Provincial Development and Rehabilitation. Halifax: King's Printer, 1944.

Elmore, Gene, Sharon Clark, and Sharon Dick. *A Survey of Adoption and Child Welfare Services to Indians of B.C*. Union of British Columbia Indian Chiefs, 18 February 1974.

Green, Norma. "Facts and Figures. Aboriginal Community Development in Corrections. Profile of an Aboriginal Woman Serving time in a Federal Institution." Correctional Service of Canada, http://www.csc-scc.gc.ca/text/prgrm/abinit/know/5-eng.shtml.

Henry, Frances, and Carol Tator. *Racial Profiling in Toronto: Discourses of Discrimination, Mediation, and Opposition*. Ottawa: Canadian Race Relations Foundation, September 2005.

Hughes, Colin. *Greater Trouble in Greater Toronto: Child Poverty in the GTA*. Toronto: Children's Aid Society, 2009.

Hughes, Judge Ted. *BC Child and Youth: An Independent Review of B.C.'s Child Protection System*. Victoria: Minister of Children and Family Development, 2006.

Indian Affairs and Northern Development. Program Evaluation Branch. *Child Care Task Force: A Report on B.C. Indian Child Care*. Department of Indian Affairs, May 1982.

Ivanova, Iglika. *BC's Growing Gap: Family Income Inequality, 1976–2006*. Vancouver: Canadian Centre for Policy Alternatives, March 2008.

Johnston, Patrick. *Native Children and the Child Welfare System*. Ottawa: Canadian Council on Social Development, 1983.

Kuptana, Rosemary. *No More Secrets: Acknowledging the Problem of Child Sexual Abuse in Inuit Communities: The First Step towards Healing*. Ottawa: Pauktuutit, 1991.

Law Commission of Canada, *Restoring Dignity: Responding to Child Abuse in Canadian Institutions*. Ottawa: Law Commission of Canada, 2000.

Laycock, Joseph E. *Survey of Ottawa's Child and Family Services: Final Draft Report for Planning and Policy Committee*. Ottawa: Welfare Council of Ottawa, 5 June 1953.

Leischner, Chris, et al. *Creating Solutions: Women Preventing FAS; Understanding Women's Substance Misuse*. Prince George, BC: Northern Family Health Society, 2001.

Lord, Margaret. *Final Report to the Minister of Social Services of the Panel to Review Adoption Legislation*. Victoria, BC: Ministry of Social Services, July 1994.

Loucks, Bryan, and Arnette Timothy. *Justice-Related Children and Family Services for Native People in Ontario: A Discussion Paper.* Revised edition. Toronto: Ontario Native Council on Justice, 1981.

McFarland, W.D. *Placement Resources Services: Children's Aid Society of Vancouver.* Vancouver: Children's Aid Society, November 1972.

McGregor, Mrs. J. Breckenridge. "Several Years After": An Analysis of the Histories of a Selected Group of Juvenile Immigrants Brought to Canada in 1910, and in 1920, by British Emigration Societies. Ottawa: Canadian Council on Child Welfare, 1928.

MacKay, Harry, and Catherine Austin. *Single Adolescent Mothers in Ontario: A Report of 87 Single Adolescent Mothers' Experiences, Their Situation, Needs, and Use of Community Services.* Ottawa: Canadian Council on Social Development, 1983.

MacLaurin, Bruce, and Megan McCormack. "Child Protection in Canada." In *The Welfare of Canadian Children: It's Our Business. A Collection of Resource Papers for a Healthy Future for Canadian Children and Families,* 73–82. Ottawa: Child Welfare Council of Canada, 2007.

MacLeod, Linda. *Battered but Not Beaten: Preventing Wife Battering in Canada.* Ottawa: Advisory Council on the Status of Women, 1987.

Mirchandani, Kiran, and Wendy Chan. *The Racialized Impact of Welfare Fraud Control in British Columbia and Ontario.* Ottawa: Canadian Race Relations Foundation, October 2005.

Nadjiwan, S., and C. Blackstock, *Caring across the Boundaries: Promoting Access to Voluntary Sector Resources for First Nations Children and Families.* Ottawa: First Nations Child and Family Caring Society of Canada, 2003.

National Report Card 2008: Inclusion of Canadians with Intellectual Disabilities. Canadian Association for Community Living, 2008.

Native Women's Association of Canada. *Claiming Our Way of Being: Matrimonial Real Property Solutions.* Ohsweken, ON: Native Women's Association of Canada, 2007.

Newfoundland and Labrador. Social Policy Advisory Committee. *Report of the Strategic Social Planning Public Dialogue,* volume 1: *What the People Said* (1997), http://www.gov.nl.ca/publicat/spac/volume1.htm#common.

Ninety Deaths, Ninety Voices Silenced. 2007–8 Report. Toronto: Office of the Ontario Advocate for Children and Youth, 2008.

Office of Child and Family Service Advocacy. *Youth Running from Residential Care: "The Push" and "The Pull.* Toronto, ON: Office of Child and Family Service Advocacy, February 2006.

"An Open Letter Presented to the Government of Canada: Dear Mom and Dad." In *Canada's Children.* National Youth in Care Network, 2000.

Pelletier, Gérard. *L'Histoire des enfants tristes.* Montreal: Action Sociale, 1950, http://orphelin.users2.50megs.com/triste01.html.

Public Health Agency of Canada. *Backgrounder on Government of Canada and FASD,* http://www.phac-aspc.gc.ca/fasd-etcaf/goc-bg-eng.php.

Public Health Agency of Canada. Working Group. "Joint Statement on Shaken Baby Syndrome," http://www.phac-aspc.gc.ca/dca-dea/publications/jointstatement_ web-eng.php.Raychaba, Brian. *Canadian Youth in Care: Leaving Care to Be on Our Own with No Direction from Home.* Ottawa: National Youth in Care Network, 1988.

Report Card on Child and Family Poverty in Canada (Campaign 2000 and 2009). Review Committee on Indian and Metis Adoptions and Placements. *Transcripts and Briefs.* Public Hearings, Special Hearings, Judge Edwin C. Kimelman. Chairman. Winnipeg: Manitoba Community Services, 1985.

Rosenthal, Carolyn J., and James Gladstone. *Grandparenthood in Canada.* Ottawa: Vanier Institute of the Family, 2000, http:// www.vifamily.ca.

Rural Women Making Change. *Rural Women: Employment Facts from ACTEW and Rural Woman Making Change Research Alliance* (2008), University of Guelph, http://www.rwmc.uoguelph.ca/page.php?p=1.

Saskatchewan. Children's Advocate Office. *Child Death Review Karen Rose Quill* Saskatoon: Children's Advocate Office, 1998.

———. Children's Advocate Office. *Children and Youth in Care Review: LISTEN to Their Voices.* Saskatoon: Children's Advocate Office, 2000.

Sparrow Lake Alliance. Children in Limbo Task Force, *Children in Limbo.* Scarborough, ON: Sparrow Lake Alliance, 1996.

Speak the Truth in a Million Voices: It Is the Silence That Kills: Stories for Change Ottawa: National Youth in Care Network, 2004.

"Study of Services to Unmarried Parents in Manitoba." Winnipeg: Welfare Council of Greater Winnipeg, 1 September 1960.

Tickell, David A. *The Protection of Children: The Rights of Children: The Urgent Need to Improve a System in Crisis.* Saskatoon: Saskatchewan Ombudsman, 31 December 1986.

UNICEF Canada, *What's Rights for Some 18@18: A Portrait of Canada's First Generation Growing Up under the UN Convention on the Rights of the Child.* Toronto: UNICEF Canada, 2007.

Valentine, Fraser. *Enabling Citizenship: Full Inclusion of Children with Disabilities and Their Parents.* Ottawa: Canadian Policy Research Networks, 2001.

Wachtel, Andy. "Child Welfare in Canada: Framework for Action." In *The Welfare of Canadian Children: It's Our Business. A Collection of Resource Papers for a Healthy Future for Canadian Children and Families,* 39–53. Ottawa: Child Welfare Council of Canada, 2007.

The Welfare of Canadian Children. Ottawa: Child Welfare Council of Canada, 2007.

Wright, Alexandra, et al. *Summary Report: Factors That Contribute to Positive Outcomes in the Awasis Pimicikamak Cree Nation Kinship Care Program.* Winnipeg: Centre of Excellence for Child Welfare and Health Canada, 2005.

Young People Say: Report from the Youth Consultation Initiative. Ottawa: National Crime Prevention Council, 1997.

Books, Anthologies, Book Chapters, Articles, and Conference Papers

Abrams, Lynn. *The Orphan Country: Children of Scotland's Broken Homes from 1845 to the Present Day*. Edinburgh: John Donald Publishers, 1998.

Adamoski, Robert. "Persistence and Privilege: Boarding and Single Fathers in the Practice of Child Rescue: 1901–1930." In *Child and Family Welfare in British Columbia: A History*, ed. Diane Purvey and Christopher Walmsley, 29–52. Calgary: Detselig Enterprises, 2005.

Adelberg, Ellen, and Claudie Currie. "In Their Own Words." In *Too Few to Count: Canadian Women in Conflict with the Law*, ed. Ellen Adelberg and Claudia Currie, 47–66. Vancouver: Pressgang Publishers, 1987.

Alaggia, Ramona, and Sarah Maiter. "Domestic Violence and Child Abuse: Issues for Immigrant and Refugee Women." In *Cruel but Not Unusual: Violence in Canadian Families*, ed. Ramona Maggia and Cathy Vine, 99–126. Waterloo: Wilfrid Laurier University Press, 2006.

Ambert, Anne-Marie. "Custodial Parents: Review and a Longitudinal Study." In *The One-Parent Family in the 1980s*, ed. Benjamin Schlesinger, 180–90. Toronto: University of Toronto Press, 1985.

Anderson, Doris. *Rebel Daughter: An Autobiography*. Toronto: Key Porter Books, 1996.

Anderson, Nancy F. "'Marriage with a Deceased Wife's Sister Bill' Controversy: Incest Anxiety and the Defense of the Family Purity in Victorian England." *Journal of British Studies* 21, 2 (Spring 1982): 67–86.

Angelides, Steven. "The Emergence of the Pedophile in the Late Twentieth Century." *Australia Historical Studies* 37 (October 2005): 272–95.

Anglin, James. "Staffed Group Homes for Youth: Toward a Framework for Understanding." In *Child Welfare: Connecting Research, Policy, and Practice*, ed. Kathleen Kufeldt and Brad McKenzie, 191–202. Waterloo: Wilfrid Laurier University Press, 2003.

Appathurai, Carol, Grant Lowery, and Terry Sullivan, "Achieving the Vision of Deinstitutionalization: A Role for Foster Care?" *Child and Adolescent Social Work* 3, no. 1 (Spring 1986): 50–67.

Appell, Annette R. "On Fixing 'Bad' Mothers and Saving Their Children." In *"Bad" Mothers: The Politics of Blame in Twentieth-Century America*, ed. Molly Ladd-Taylor and Lauri Umansky, 356–80. New York and London: New York University Press, 1998.

Armitage, Andrew. "Family and Child Welfare in First Nation Communities." In *Rethinking Child Welfare in Canada*, ed. Brian Wharf, 131–71. Ottawa: Canadian Council on Social Development, 1983.

———. "Lost Vision: Children and the Ministry for Children and Families." *BC Studies* 118 (Summer 1998): 93–122.

———. "The Policy and Legislative Context." In *Rethinking Child Welfare in Canada*, ed. Brian Wharf, 37–63. Toronto: McClelland and Stewart, 1993.

———, and Elaine Murray. "Thomas Gove: A Commission of Inquiry Puts Children First and Proposes Community Governance and Integration of Services." In

People, Politics, and Child Welfare in British Columbia, ed. Leslie T. Foster and Brian Wharf, 139–57. Vancouver: UBC Press, 2007.

Armitage, Winona. "The Unmarried Mother and Adoption." Proceedings of the Ninth Canadian Conference on Social Work, Winnipeg, June 1944.

Ayukawa, Midge Michiko, and Patricia E. Roy. "Japanese." In *Encyclopedia of Canada's Peoples,* ed. Paul Robert Magocsi, 842–60. Toronto: Multicultural History Society of Ontario and University of Toronto Press, 1999.

Backhouse, Constance. "Married Women's Property Law in Nineteenth-Century Canada," *Law and History Review* 6, no. 2 (1988): 211–57.

———. "Shifting Patterns in Nineteenth-Century Canadian Custody Law," In *Essays in Canadian Law,* ed. David Flaherty, vol. 1, 212–88. Toronto: University of Toronto Press, 1981.

Baillargeon, Denyse. *Making Do: Women, Family and Home in Montreal during the Great Depression.* Waterloo: Wilfrid Laurier University Press, 1999.

Baker, Maureen. *Restructuring Family Policies: Convergences and Divergences.* Toronto: University of Toronto Press, 2006.

Baines, Carol T. "The Children of Earlscourt, 1915–1948: All in the Same Boat: 'Except we were in a better boat.'" *Canadian Social Work Review* 11, no. 2 (Summer 1994): 184–200.

———, Patricia M. Evans, and Sheilia M. Neysmith "Women's Caring: Challenges for Practice and Policy." *Affilia* 7, no. 1 (Spring 1992): 21–44.

Balcolm, Karen. "'Phony Mothers' and Border-Crossing Adoptions: The Montreal-to-New York Black Market in Babies in the 1950s." *Journal of Women's History* 19, 1 (Spring 2007): 107–16.

———. "Scandal and Social Policy: The Ideal Maternity Home and the Evolution of Social Policy in Nova Scotia, 1940–51." *Acadiensis* 31, no. 2 (Spring 2002): 3–37.

Barer, B. "The 'Grands and Greats' of Very Old Black Grandmothers." *Journal of Aging Studies* 15, no. 1 (March 2001): 1–11.

Barker, Joanne. "Gender, Sovereignty, and the Discourse of Rights in Native Women's Activism." *Meridians: Feminism, Race, Transnationalism* 7, no. 1 (2006): 127–61.

———. "Gender, Sovereignty, Rights: Native Women's Activism against Social Inequality and Violence in Canada." *American Quarterly* 60, no. 2 (June 2008): 259–66.

Barman, Jean. *Growing Up British in British Columbia: Boys in Private School.* Vancouver: UBC Press, 1984.

———. "Separate and Unequal: Indian and White Girls at All Hallows School, 1884–1920," In *Indian Education in Canada: the Legacy,* ed. Jean Barman, Yvonne Hebert, and Don McCaskill, vol. 1, 110–31. Vancouver: UBC Press, 1986.

———. "Taming Aboriginal Sexuality: Gender, Power, and Race in British Columbia, 1850–1900." *BC Studies* 115/116 (Autumn/Winter 1997–98): 237–66.

Barter, Ken. "Working Conditions for Social Workers and Linkages to Client Outcomes in Child Welfare: A Literature Review." In *The Welfare of Canadian Children: It's Our Business. A Collection of Resource Papers for a Healthy Future for*

Canadian Children and Families, 152–58. Ottawa: Child Welfare League of Canada, 2007.

Baskin, Cindy. "Systemic Oppression, Violence and Healing in Aboriginal Families and Communities." In *Cruel but Not Unusual: Violence in Canadian Families*, ed. Ramona Maggia and Cathy Vine, 15–48. Waterloo: Wilfrid Laurier University Press, 2006.

Baunach, Phyllis Jo. *Mothers in Prison*. New Brunswick: Transaction Publishers, 1985.

Beise, Jan. *The Helping and the Helpful Grandmother: The Role of Maternal and Paternal Grandmothers in Child Mortality in the Seventeenth and Eighteenth Century Population of French Settlers in Quebec, Canada*. Max-Planck-Institute for Demographic Research, Working Paper no. 2004–004 (January 2004; revised September 2004).

Beito, David T. *From Mutual Aid to the Welfare State: Fraternal Societies and Social Services, 1890–1967*. Chapel Hill and London: University of North Carolina Press, 2000.

Bengtson, Vern L. "Beyond the Nuclear Family: The Increasing Importance of Multigenerational Bonds." *Journal of Marriage and the Family* 63, no. 11 (February 2001): 1–16.

Bernard, Candace, and Wanda Thomas Bernard. "Learning from the Past/Visions for the Future: The Black Community and Child Welfare in Nova Scotia." In *Community Work Approaches to Child Welfare*, ed. Brian Wharf, 116–30. Peterborough: Broadview Press, 2002.

Bernhard, Judith K., Patricia Landolt, and Luin Goldring. "Transnationalizing Families: Canadian Immigration Policy and the Spatial Fragmentation of Care-giving among Latin American Newcomers." *International Migration* 47, no. 2 (2008): 3–31.

Biedema, Baukje. *Mothering for the State: The Paradox of Fostering*. Halifax: Fernwood Publishing, 1999.

Bittman, Michael, et al. "Making the Invisible Visible: The Life and Time(s) of Informal Caregivers" In *Family Time: The Social Organization of Care*, ed. Nancy Folbre and Michael Bittman, 69–90. London: Routledge, 2004.

Blackford, Karen A. "Erasing Mothers with Disabilities through Canadian Family-Related Policy." *Disability, Handicap and Society* 8, no. 3 (1993): 281–94.

Blackstock, Cindy. "Aboriginal Children, Families and Communities." In *The Welfare of Canadian Children: It's Our Business. A Collection of Resource Papers for a Healthy Future for Canadian Children and Families*, 83–91. Ottawa: Child Welfare League of Canada, 2007.

———. "First Nations Child and Family Services: Restoring Peace and Harmony in First Nations Communities." In *Child Welfare: Connecting Research, Policy, and Practice*, ed. Kathleen Kufeldt and Brad McKenzie, 331–42. Waterloo: Wilfrid Laurier University Press, 2003.

———, Ivan Brown, and Marilyn Bennett. "Reconciliation: Rebuilding the Canadian Child Welfare System to Better Serve Aboriginal Children and Youth." In *Putting a Human Face on Child Welfare: Voices from the Prairies*, ed. Ivan Brown, et al., 59–87. Regina: Prairie Child Welfare Consortium, 2007.

Blake, Raymond B. "In the Children's Interest? Change and Continuity in a Century of Canadian Social Welfare Initiatives for Children." In *Social Fabric or Patchwork Quilt: The Development of Social Policy in Canada,* ed. Raymond B. Blake and Jeffrey A. Keshen, 221–36. Toronto: Broadview, 2006.

Blanchard, Brigitte. "Incarcerated Mothers and Their Children: A Complex Issue." *Forum on Corrections Research,* 16, no. 1 (2004): 45–46.

Blanchet, André. "The Impact of Normalization and Social Role Valorization in Canada." In *A Quarter-Century of Normalization and Social Role Valorization: Evolution and Impact,* ed. Robert J. Flynn and Raymond A. Lemay, 437–40. Ottawa: University of Ottawa Press, 1999.

Boris, Eileen. "On Cowboys and Welfare Queens: Independence, Dependence and Interdependence at Home and Abroad." *Journal of American Studies* 41 (2007): 599–621.

Boschma, Geertje. "A Family Point of View: Negotiating Asylum Care in Alberta, 1905–1930." *Canadian Bulletin of Medical History* 25, no. 2 (2008): 367–90.

Bouchard, Mary Alban. "Pioneers Forever: The Sisters of St. Joseph of Toronto and Their Ventures in Social Welfare and Health Care." In *Catholics at the "Gathering Place": Historical Essays on the Archdiocese of Toronto 1841–1991,* ed. Mark G. McGowan and Brian P. Clarke, 105–18. Toronto: Canadian Catholic Historical Association, 1993.

Boucher, Sophie, et al. "Consequences of an Institutionalized Childhood: The Case of the 'Duplessis Orphans.'" *Santé mentale au Québec* 33, no. 2 (Autumn 2008): 271–91.

Bourgeois, Ch.-E. *The Protection of Children in the Province of Quebec,* trans. Paul E. Marquis. Trois-Rivières: Bishop of Trois-Rivières, 1948.

Bowers, Bonita F., and Barbara J. Myers. "Grandmothers Providing Care for Grandchildren: Consequences of Various Levels of Caregiving." *Family Relations* 48, no. 3 (July 1999): 303–12.

Bowlby, John. *Maternal Care and Mental Health.* Geneva: World Health Organization, 1951.

Boyd, Susan C. *From Witches to Crack Moms: Women, Drug Law and Policy.* Durham, NC: Carolina Academic Press, 2004.

———. "The Journey to Compassionate Care: One Woman's Experience with Early Harm-Reduction Programs in BC." *Women's Health Network Magazine* 10, no. 1 (Fall/Winter 2007): 26–28.

———. "Women, Drug Regulation, and Maternal/State Conflicts." In *Women's Health in Canada: Critical Perspectives on Theory and Policy,* ed. Marina Morrow, Olena Hankivsky, and Colleen Varcoe, 327–54. Toronto: University of Toronto Press, 2007.

Bradbury, Bettina. "Canadian Children Who Lived with One Parent in 1901." In *Household Counts: Canadian Households and Families in 1901,* ed. Eric W. Sager and Peter Baskerville, 247–301. Toronto: University of Toronto Press, 2007.

———. "The Fragmented Family: Family Strategies in the Face of Death, Illness, and Poverty, Montreal, 1860–1885." In *Childhood and Family in Canadian History,* ed. J. Parr, 109–28. Toronto: McClelland and Stewart, 1982.

————. "Pigs, Cows and Boarders: Non-Wage Forms of Survival among Montreal Families, 1861–1891." *Labour/Le Travail* 14 (1984): 9–46.

Brand, Dionne. *No Burden to Carry: Narratives of Black Working Women in Ontario 1920s to 1950s.* Toronto: Women's Press, 1991.

Brandt, Gail Cuthbert, and Naomi Black. "'Il en faut un peu': Farm women and Feminism in Québec and France since 1945." *Journal of the Canadian Historical Association/ Revue de la Société historique du Canada* 1, no. 1 (1990): 73–96.

Brant, Clare C. "Native Ethics and Rules of Behaviour." *Canadian Journal of Psychiatry* 35, no. 6 (August 1990): 534–39.

Broder, Sheri. *Tramps, Unfit Mothers, and Neglected Children: Negotiating the Family in Late Nineteenth-Century Philadelphia.* Philadelphia: University of Pennsylvania Press, 2002.

Brown, Ivan, et al., eds. *Putting a Human Face on Child Welfare: Voices from the Prairies.* Regina: Prairie Child Welfare Consortium, 2007.

Brown, Jason. "Rewards of Fostering Children with Disabilities." *Journal of Family Social Work* 11, no. 1 (May 2008): 36–49.

Bryce, Peter. *The Story of a National Crime: Being a Record of the Health Conditions of the Indians of Canada from 1904 to 1921.* Ottawa: James Hope and Sons, 1922.

Buckner, Phillip. *Canada and the British Empire.* Oxford: Oxford University Press, 2008.

Buckworth, Kathy. *The Secret Life of Supermom.* Napierville, KY: Source Books, 2005.

Burke, D.A. "Transitions in Household and Family Structure: Canada in 1901 and 1991." In *Household Counts: Canadian Households and Families in 1901,* ed. Eric W. Sager and Peter Baskerville, 17–58. Toronto: University of Toronto Press, 2007.

Callahan, Marilyn. "The Administrative and Practice Context: Perspectives from the Front Line." In *Rethinking Child Welfare in Canada,* ed. Brian Wharf, 64–97. Toronto: McClelland and Stewart, 1993.

————. "Feminist Approaches: Women Recreate Child Welfare." In *Rethinking Child Welfare in Canada,* ed. Brian Wharf, 172–209. Toronto: McClelland and Stewart, 1993.

————, and Carolyn Attridge. *Women in Women's Work: Social Workers Talk about Their Work in Child Welfare,* Research Monograph no. 3. Victoria: University of Victoria, November 1990.

————, and Christopher Walmsley. "Rethinking Child Welfare Reform in British Columbia, 1900–60." In *People, Politics, and Child Welfare in British Columbia,* ed. Leslie T. Foster and Brian Wharf, 10–33. Vancouver: UBC Press, 2007.

————, and Karen Swift. "Great Expectations and Unintended Consequences: Risk Assessment in Child Welfare in British Columbia." In *People, Politics, and Child Welfare in British Columbia,* ed. Leslie T. Foster and Brian Wharf, 158–83. Vancouver: UBC Press, 2007.

————, and Karen Swift. "Victims and Villains: Scandals, the Press and Policy Making in Child Welfare." In *Child and Family Policies: Struggles, Strategies and Options,* ed. Jane Pulkingham and Gordon Ternowetsky, 40–57. Halifax: Fernwood Publishing, 1997.

———, et al. "Catch as Catch Can: Grandmothers Raising Their Grandchildren and Kinship Care Policies." *Canadian Review of Social Policy* 54 (Fall 2004): 58–78.

———, et al. "The Underground Child Welfare System: Grandmothers Raising Grandchildren." *Perspectives* 27, no. 5 (November 2005): 12–13.

Calloway, Colin G. *White People, Indians, and Highlanders: Tribal Peoples and Colonial Encounters in Scotland and America.* Oxford: Oxford University Press, 2008.

Camden, Elizabeth. *If He Comes Back He's Mine: A Mother's Story of Child Abuse.* Toronto: Women's Press, 1984.

Cameron, Gary. "Promoting Positive Child and Family Welfare." In *Child Welfare: Connecting Research, Policy, and Practice,* ed. Kathleen Kufeldt and Brad McKenzie, 79–100. Waterloo: Wilfrid Laurier University Press, 2003.

———. "The Nature and Effectiveness of Parent Mutual Aid Organizations in Child Welfare." In *Child Welfare in Canada: Research and Policy Implications,* ed. Joe Hudson and Burt Galaway, 66–81. Toronto: Thompson Educational Publishing, 1995.

Carbin, Clifton F. *Deaf Heritage in Canada; A Distinctive, Diverse, and Enduring Culture.* Toronto: McGraw-Hill Ryerson, 1996.

Carriere-Laboucane, Jeannine. "Kinship Care: A Community Alternative to Foster Care." *Native Social Work Journal* 1, no. 1 (1997): 43–53.

Carter, Sarah. *The Importance of Being Monogamous: Marriage and Nation Building in Western Canada to 1915.* Edmonton: University of Alberta Press, 2008.

Carty, Linda. "African Canadian Women and the State: 'Labour only, please.'" In *"We're rooted here and they can't pull us up": Essays in African Canadian Women's History,* ed. Peggy Bristow et al., 193–229. Toronto: University of Toronto Press, 1999.

Chambers, Lori. *Married Women and Property Law in Victorian Ontario.* Toronto: University of Toronto Press, 1997.

———. *Misconceptions: Unmarried Motherhood and the Ontario Children of Unmarried Parents Act, 1921 to 1969.* Toronto: University of Toronto Press, 2007.

Chan, Wendy, and Kiran Mirchandani. *Criminalizing Race, Criminalizing Poverty: Welfare Fraud Enforcement in Canada.* Halifax: Fernwood Books, 2007.

Chao, Ruth K., and J. Douglas Willms. "The Effects of Parenting Practices on Children's Outcomes." In *Vulnerable Children: Findings from Canada's National Longitudinal Survey of Children and Youth,* ed. J. Douglas Willms, 149–66. Edmonton: University of Alberta Press, 2002.

Chen, Anita Beltran. "Filipinos." In *Encyclopedia of Canada's Peoples,* ed. Paul Robert Magocsi, 501–13. Toronto: Multicultural History Society of Ontario and University of Toronto Press, 1999.

Chen, Xiaobei. "Constituting 'Dangerous Parents' through the Specter of Child Death: A Critique of Child Protection Restructuring in Ontario." In *Making Normal: Social Regulation in Canada,* ed. Deborah Brock, 209–34. Toronto: Nelson Thomson Learning, 2003.

————. *Tending the Gardens of Citizenship: Child Saving in Toronto 1880s–1920s*. Toronto: University of Toronto Press, 2005.

Chimbos, Peter D. "Greeks" In *Encyclopedia of Canada's Peoples,* ed. Paul Robert Magocsi, 615–26. Toronto: Multicultural History Society of Ontario and University of Toronto Press, 1999.

Christie, Nancy. *Engendering the State: Women, Work and Welfare in Canada*. Toronto: University of Toronto Press, 2000.

————. "Introduction." In *Mapping the Margins: The Family and Social Discipline in Canada, 1700–1975,* ed. Nancy Christie and Michael Gauvreau, 3–24. Montreal and Kingston: McGill-Queen's University Press, 2004.

————. "'A Painful Dependence': Female Begging Letters and the Familial Economy of Obligation." In *Mapping the Margins: The Family and Social Discipline in Canada, 1700–1975,* ed. Nancy Christie and Michael Gauvreau, 69–102. Montreal and Kingston: McGill-Queen's University Press, 2004.

Chupik, Jessa "'I know that I can handle him now': The Relationship between Families, Confined Children, and the Orillia Asylum, 1900–1935." Paper presented before the Canadian Historical Association, Toronto, May 2003.

Clarke, Brian P. *Piety and Nationalism: Lay Voluntary Associations and the Creation of an Irish-Catholic Community in Toronto, 1850–1895*. Montreal and Kingston: McGill-Queen's University Press, 1993.

Clarke, Mary Joplin. "Report of the Standing Committee on Neighbourhood Work." In *Saving the Canadian City: The First Phase 1880–1920,* ed. Paul Rutherford, 171–93. Toronto: University of Toronto Press, 1974.

Clarke, Nic. "'Sacred Daemons': Exploring British Columbian Society's Perceptions of 'Mentally Deficient' Children, 1870–1930." *BC Studies* 144 (Winter 2004–5): 61–89.

Cliché, Marie-Aimée. *Maltraiter ou punir? La violence envers les enfants dans les familles québécoises 1850–1969*. Montreal: Boréal, 2007.

Clio Collective. *Quebec Women: A History*. trans. Roger Gannon and Roslind Gill. Toronto: Women's Press, 1987.

Cohen-Schlanger, Miriam A., et al., "Housing as a Factor in Admissions of Children to Temporary Care: A Survey." *Child Welfare* 74, no. 3 (May–June 1995): 547-562.

Collin, Jean-Pierre. "Crise du logement et action catholique à Montréal, 1940–1960." *Revue d'histoire de l'Amérique française* 41, no. 2 (1987): 179–203.

Comacchio, Cynthia. *The Dominion of Youth: Adolescence and the Making of Modern Canada, 1920 to 1950*. Waterloo: Wilfrid Laurier University Press, 2006.

————. *Nations Are Built of Babies: Saving Ontario's Mothers and Children 1900–1940*. Montreal and Kingston: McGill-Queen's University Press, 1993.

Comack, Elizabeth. *Women in Trouble*. Halifax: Fernwood Publishing, 1996.

Connidis, Ingrid Arnet. "Sibling Ties across Time: The Middle and Later Years." In *The Cambridge Handbook of Age and Ageing,* ed. Malcolm L. Johnson, 429–36. Cambridge: Cambridge University Press, 2005.

Connors, Stompin' Tom. *Stompin' Tom: Before the Fame*. Toronto: Penguin, 1995.

Connors, Clare, and Kirsten Stalker. *The Experiences and Views of Disabled Children and Their Siblings: A Positive Outlook*. Philadelphia: Jessica Kingsley Publishers, 2003.

Corbett, Mary Jane. "Husband, Wife, and Sister: Making and Remaking the Early Victorian Family." *Victorian Literature and Culture* 31, no. 1 (2007): 1–19.

Courtwright, David T. "Drug Wars: Policy Hots and Historical Cools." *Bulletin of the History of Medicine* 78, no. 2 (Summer 2004): 440–50.

Creese, Gillian Isabel Dyck, and Arlene Tigar McLaren, "The 'Flexible' Immigrant: Household Strategies and the Labour Market." Working Paper no. 06–19, Research on Immigration and Integration in the Metropolis, Vancouver Centre of Excellence, December 2006.

Creighton, Helen. *A Life in Folklore*. Toronto: McGraw-Hill Ryerson, 1975.

Dallaire, Nichole, et al. "Social Prevention: A Study of Projects in an Urban Environment." In *Child Welfare in Canada: Research and Policy Implications*, ed. Joe Hudson and Burt Galaway, 123–39. Toronto: Thompson Educational Publishing, 1995.

Dalley, Bronwyn. *Family Matters: Child-Welfare in Twentieth-Century New Zealand*. Auckland: University Press and Historical Branch, Department of Internal Affairs, 1998.

Daly, Margaret. *The Revolution Game: The Short Unhappy Life of the Company of Young Canadians*. Toronto: New Press, 1970.

Danica, Elly. *Don't: A Woman's Word*. Charlottetown, PEI: Gynergy Books, 1988.

Danys, Milda. "Lithuanians." In *Encyclopedia of Canada's Peoples*, ed. Paul Robert Magocsi, 929–38. Toronto: Multicultural History Society of Ontario and University of Toronto Press, 1999.

Darroch, Gordon. "Families, Fostering, and Flying the Coop: Lessons in Liberal Cultural Formation." In *Household Counts: Canadian Households and Families in 1901*, ed. Eric W. Sager and Peter Baskerville, 197–246. Toronto: University of Toronto Press, 2007.

———. "Home and Away: Patterns of Residence, Schooling, and Work among Children and Never Married Young Adults, Canada, 1871 and 1901." *Journal of Family History* 26, no. 2 (April 2001): 220–50.

Dauphinais, Carol. *Living with Labels and Lies: A Life Story*. Vancouver: Carol Dauphais, 1997.

David, Leo. "Foster Fatherhood: The Untapped Resource." *Family Coordinator* 20, no. 1 (January 1971): 49–54.

Davies, Linda, et al. "Community Child Welfare: Examples from Quebec." In *Community Work Approaches to Child Welfare*, ed. Brian Wharf, 63–81. Peterborough: Broadview Press, 2002.

Dawson, Myrna. "Rethinking the Boundaries of Intimacy at the End of the Century: The role of Victim-Defendant Relationship in Criminal Justice Decision-Making over Time." *Law and Society Review* 38, no. 1 (2004): 105–38.

DeLiso, Michelle. *Godparents: A Celebration of Those Special People in Our Lives*. New York: McGraw-Hill, 2002.

Dhruvarajan,Vanaja. "Women of Colour in Canada." In *Gender, Race, and Nation: A Global Perspective*, ed. Vanaja Dhruvarajan and Jill Vickers, 99–122. Toronto: University of Toronto Press, 2002

Dillner, Luisa. *The Complete Book of Mothers-in-Law: A Celebration.* London: Faber, 2008.

Dillon, Lisa. *The Shady Side of Fifty: Age and Old Age in Late Victorian Canada and the United States.* Montreal and Kingston: McGill-Queen's University Press, 2008.

Dobrowolsky, Alexandra, ed. *Women and Public Policy in Canada: Neo-liberalism and After?* Toronto: Oxford University Press, 2009.

Dionne, André. "The Impact of Social Role Valorization on Government Policy in Quebec." In *A Quarter-Century of Normalization and Social Role Valorization: Evolution and Impact*, ed. Robert J. Flynn and Raymond A. Lemay, 463–71. Ottawa: University of Ottawa Press, 1999.

Dirks, Patricia. "Reinventing Christian Masculinity and Fatherhood: The Canadian Protestant Experience, 1900–1920." In *Households of Faith: Family, Gender and Community in Canada, 1760–1969*, ed. Nancy Christie, 290–316. Montreal and Kingston: McGill-Queen's University Press, 2002.

Dubinsky, Karen. *Babies without Borders: Adoption and Migration across the Americas.* Toronto: University of Toronto Press, 2010.

———. *Improper Advances: Rape and Heterosexual Conflict in Ontario, 1880–1929.* Chicago: University of Chicago Press, 1993.

———. "'We Adopted a Negro': Interracial Adoption and the Hybrid Baby in 1960s Canada." In *Creating Postwar Canada: Community, Diversity, and Dissent 1945–75*, ed. Magda Fahrni and Robert Rutherdale, 268–88. Vancouver: UBC Press, 2008.

———, and Franca Iacovetta. "Murder, Womanly Virtue, and Motherhood: The Case of Angelina Napolitano, 1911–1922." *Canadian Historical Association* 57, no. 4 (1991): 305–31.

Dufour, Rose, and Brigitte Garneau. *Naître rien: des orphelins de Duplessis, de la crèche à l'asile.* Ste-Foy, QC: Éditions multimondes, 2002.

Dumbrill, Gary C., "Parental Experience of Child Protection Intervention: A Qualitative Study." *Child Abuse and Neglect* 30, no. 1 (January 2006): 27–37.

Dunn, Marty. *Red on White: The Biography of Duke Redbird.* Toronto: New Press, 1971.

Dunn, Michel E., et al. "Moderators of Stress in Parents of Children with Autism." *Community Mental Health Journal* 31, no. 1 (February 2001): 39–52.

Durst, Douglas, Josephine McDonald, and Cecilia Rich. "Aboriginal Government of Child Child Welfare Services: Hobson's Choice?" *Child Welfare in Canada: Research and Policy Implications*, ed. Joe Hudson and Burt Galaway, 41–53. Toronto: Thompson Educational Publishing, 1995.

Eagle, Rita S. "The Separation Experience of Children in Long-Term Care: Theory, Research, and Implications for Practice." *American Journal of Orthopsychiatry* 64, no. 3 (July 1994): 421–34.

Efron, Donald E. "Strategic Therapy Interventions with Latency-Age Children." *Social Casework: The Journal of Contemporary Social Work* 62, no. 9 (1981): 543–50.

Elliott, Bruce S. *Irish Migrants in the Canada: A New Approach*. Montreal and Kingston: McGill-Queen's University Press, 2004.

Ethier, Louise S., et al. "Impact of a Multimesional Intervention Programme Applied to Families at Risk of Child Neglect." *Child Abuse Review* 9, no. 1 (2000): 19–36.

Evans, Caroline. "Excellent Women and Troublesome Children: State Foster Care in Tasmania, 1896–1918." *Labour History* 83 (November 2002): 131–48.

Evans, Patricia. "Eroding Canadian Social Welfare: The Mulroney Legacy, 1984–1993." In *Social Fabric or Patchwork Quilt: The Development of Social Policy in Canada*, ed. Raymond B. Blake and Jeffrey A. Keshen, 263–74. Toronto: Broadview Press, 2006.

Farris-Manning, Cheryl, and Marietta Zandstra. "Children in Care in Canada: A Summary of Current Issues and Trends with Recommendations for Future Research." In *The Welfare of Canadian Children: It's Our Business. A Collection of Resource Papers for a Healthy Future for Canadian Children and Families*, 54–72. Ottawa: Child Welfare Council of Canada, 2007.

Feldman, M.A., M. Leger, and N. Walton-Allen. "Stress in Mothers with Intellectual Disabilities." *Journal of Child and Family Studies* 6, no. 4 (December 1997): 471–85.

Felt, Pat, with Pam Walker. "My Life in L'Arche" In *Women with Intellectual Disabilities: Finding a Place in the World*, ed. Rannveig Traustadottir and Kelly Johnson, 217–28. London and Philadelphia: Jessica Kingsley Publisher, 2000.

Fewster, Gerry, and Thom Garfat. "Residential Child and Youth Care," In *Professional Child and Youth Care*, 2nd edition, ed. Roy V. Ferguson and Alan R. Pence, 15–43. Vancouver: UBC Press, 1993.

Fingerman, K. "The Good, the Bad and the Worrisome: Emotional Complexities in Grandparents' Experiences with Individual Grandchildren." *Family Relations* 47, no. 4 (1998): 403–14.

Finkel, Alvin. *Social Policy and Practice in Canada: A History*. Waterloo: Wilfrid Laurier University Press, 2006.

Fiske, Jo-Anne. "Child of the State, Mother of the Nation: Aboriginal Women and the Ideology of Motherhood." *Culture* 13, no. 1 (1993): 17–35.

———. "Gender and the Paradox of Residential Education in Carrier Society." In *Women of the First Nations: Power, Wisdom, and Strength*, ed. Christine Miller and Patricia Chuchryk, 167–82. Winnipeg: University of Manitoba Press, 1996.

Flint, Betty. *The Child and the Institution: A Study of Deprivation and Recovery*. Toronto: University of Toronto Press, 1967.

———, director. *Difference between Institutionally Reared and Home Reared Children*. National Film Board of Canada, 1967.

Flynn, R., and C. Biro. "Comparing Developmental Outcomes for Children in Care with Those for Other Children in Canada." *Children and Society* 12 (1998): 228–33.

———, and Tim D. Aubry. "Integration of Persons with Developmental or Psychiatric Disabilities: Conceptualization and Measurement." In *A Quarter-Century of Normalization and Social Role Valorization: Evolution and Impact*, ed. Robert J. Flynn and Raymond A. Lemay, 271–304. Ottawa: University of Ottawa Press, 1999.

Forrest, Colleen M. "Familial Poverty, Family Allowances, and the Normative Family Structure in Britain, 1917–1945." *Journal of Family History* 26, no. 4 (October 2001): 508–28.

Foster, Leslie T. "Trends in Child Welfare: What Do the Data Show?" In *People, Politics, and Child Welfare in British Columbia,* ed. Leslie T. Foster and Brian Wharf, 34–65. Vancouver: UBC Press, 2007.

———, and Wright, M. "Patterns and Trends in Children in the Care of the Province of British Columbia." In *Too Small to See, Too Big to Ignore: Child Health and Well-being in British Columbia,* ed. Michael V. Hayes and Leslie T. Foster, 103–40. Canadian Western Geographical Series vol. 35. Victoria: Department of Geography, University of Victoria, 2002.

Fournier, Julie J. "The Impact of Incarceration on the Mothering Role." *Forum on Corrections Research* 14, no. 1 (January 2002), http://www.csc-scc.gc.ca/text/pblct/forum/e141/e141ind-eng.shtml.

Francis, K.J., and D.A. Wolfe. "Cognitive and Emotional Differences between Abusive and Non-Abusive Fathers." *Child Abuse and Neglect: The International Journal,* 32 (2008): 1127–37.

Frank, David. "The Miner's Financier: Women in the Cape Breton Coal Towns, 1917." *Atlantis* 8, no. 2 (Spring 1983): 137–43.

Fraser, Sylvia. *In My Father's House: A Memoir of Incest and Healing.* Toronto: Doubleday, 1988.

Friendly, Martha, and Susan Prentice. *About Canada Childcare.* Halifax, NS: Fernwood Publishers, 2009.

Frost, Ginger Suzanne. "'The Black Lamb of the Black Sheep': Illegitimacy in the English Working Class, 1850–1939." *Journal of Social History* 37, no. 2 (Winter 2003): 293–322.

Fry, Alan. *How a People Die.* Toronto: Doubleday, 1970.

Fuchs, Don. "Preserving and Strengthening Families and Protecting Children: Social Network Intervention, A Balanced Approach to the Prevention of Child Maltreatment." In *Child Welfare in Canada: Research and Policy Implications,* ed. Joe Hudson and Burt Galaway, 113–22. Toronto: Thompson Educational Publishing, 1995.

———, et al. "Children with Disabilities Involved with the Child Welfare System in Manitoba: Current and Future Challenges." In *Putting a Human Face on Child Welfare: Voices from the Prairies,* ed. Ivan Brown et al., 127–45. Regina: Prairie Child Welfare Consortium, 2007.

Fuller-Thomson, Esme. "Grandparents Raising Grandchildren in Canada: A Profile of Skipped Generation Families." SEDAP Research Paper no. 132, McMaster University, October 2005.

Gabel, Katherine Denise Johnston. *Children of Incarcerated Parents.* Lanham, MD: Lexington Books, 1997.

Ganzevoort, PoHerman. "Dutch." In *Encyclopedia of Canada's Peoples,* ed. Paul Robert Magocsi, 435–50. Toronto: Multicultural History Society of Ontario and University of Toronto Press, 1999.

Gauvreau, Michael. *The Catholic Origins of Quebec's Quiet Revolution, 1931–1970.* Montreal and Kingston: McGill-Queen's University Press, 2007.

Geen, Rob, and Jill Duerr Berrick. "Kinship Care: An Evolving Service Delivery Option." *Children and Youth Services Review* 24, no. 1–2 (2002): 1–14.

Gerson, Carole, and Veronica Strong-Boag. "Championing the Native: E. Pauline Johnson Rejects the Squaw." In *Contact Zones: Aboriginal and Settler Women in Canada's Colonial Past,* ed. Katie Pickles and Myra Rutherdale, 47–66. Vancouver: UBC Press, 2005.

Gillis, John R. *A World of Their Own Making: Myth, Ritual, and the Quest for Family Values.* New York: Basic Books, 1996.

Gilroy, Joan. "Social Work and the Women's Movement." In *Social Work and Social Change in Canada,* ed. Brian Wharf, 52–78. Toronto: McClelland and Stewart, 1990.

Glavin, Terry, and Former Students of St. Mary's. *Amongst God's Own: The Enduring Legacy of St. Mary's Mission.* Mission, BC: Longhouse Publishing, 2002.

Gleason, Mona. *Normalizing the Ideal: Psychology, Schooling, and the Family in Postwar Canada.* Toronto: University of Toronto Press, 1999.

Golden, Janet. *Message in a Bottle: The Making of Fetal Alcohol Syndrome.* Cambridge, MA: Harvard University Press, 2005.

Gomez, Laura E. *Misconceiving Mothers: Legislators, Prosecutors, and the Politics of Prenatal Drug Exposure.* Philadelphia: Temple University Press, 1997.

Gordon, Linda. *Heroes of Their Own Lives: The Politics and History of Family Violence. Boston 1880–1960.* New York: Viking, 1988.

Gorlick, Carolyne A. "Listening to Low-Income Children and Single Mothers: Policy Implications Related to Child Welfare." In *Child Welfare in Canada: Research and Policy Implications,* ed. Joe Hudson and Burt Galaway, 286–97. Toronto: Thompson Educational Publishing, 1995.

Gouett, Paul M. "The Halifax Orphan House 1752–87." *Nova Scotia Historical Quarterly* 6, no. 3 (1976): 281–91.

Goyette, Martin, Céline Bellot, and Jean Panet-Raymond. *Le Project Solidarité Jeunesse: dynamiques partenariales et insertion des jeunes en difficulté.* Ste-Foy: Presses de l'Universié du Québec, 2006.

Graham, Elizabeth. *The Mush Hole. Life at Two Indian Residential Schools.* Waterloo, ON: Heffle Publishing, 1997.

———. "The Uses and Abuses of Power in Two Ontario Residential Schools: The Mohawk Institute and Mount Elgin," In *Earth, Water, Air and Fire: Studies in Canadian Ethnohistory,* ed. David McNab, 231–44. Waterloo: Wilfrid Laurier University Press, 1998.

Grayson, L.M., and J.M. Bliss, eds. *The Wretched of Canada: Letters to R.B. Bennett, 1930–35.* Toronto: University of Toronto Press, 1971.

Greenland, Cyril. *Preventing CAN Deaths: An International Study of Deaths Due to Child Abuse and Neglect.* London: Routledge Kegan and Paul, 1989.

Grekul, Jane, Arvey Krahn, and David Odynak. "Sterilizing the 'Feeble-minded': Eugenics in Alberta, Canada, 1929–1972." *Journal of Historical Sociology* 17, no. 4 (2004): 358–84.

Grizzle, Stanley, and John Cooper. *My Name's Not George: The Story of the Sleeping Car Porters*. Toronto: Umbrella Press, 1997.

Guildford, Janet. "The End of the Poor Law: Public Welfare Reform in Nova Scotia before the Canada Assistance Plan." In *Mothers of the Municipality: Women, Work, and Social Policy in Post-1945 Halifax*, ed. Judith Fingard and Janet Guildford, 49–75. Toronto: University of Toronto Press, 2005.

Hackler, James C. *The Prevention of Youthful Crime: The Great Stumble Forward*. Toronto: Methuen, 1973.

Hagan, John, and Bill McCarthy. *Mean Streets: Youth Crime and Homelessness*. Cambridge: Cambridge University Press, 1998.

Hamilton, Ian. *The Children's Crusade: The Story of the Company of Young Canadians*. Toronto: P. Martin, 1970.

Hammond, Wayne, and David Romney. "Treatment Revisited for Aboriginal Adolescent Solvent Abusers." In *Child Welfare: Connecting Research, Policy, and Practice*, ed. Kathleen Kufeldt and Brad McKenzie, 309–18. Waterloo: Wilfrid Laurier University Press, 2003.

Hankivsky, Olena. *Social Policy and the Ethic of Care*. Vancouver: UBC Press, 2004.

Hansen, Karen V. *Not-So-Nuclear Families: Class, Gender, and Networks of Care*. New Brunswick, NJ: Rutgers University Press, 2005.

Hare, Jan, and Jean Barman. *Good Intentions Gone Awry: Emma Crosby and the Methodist Mission on the Northwest Coast*. Vancouver: UBC Press, 2006.

Harper, Marjory. "Cossar's Colonists: Juvenile Migration to New Brunswick in the 1920s." *Acadiensis* 28, no. 1 (1998): 47–65.

Harris, Michael. *Unholy Orders: Tragedy at Mount Cashel*. Markham, ON: Viking, 1990.

Harrison, Phyllis. *Home Children*. Winnipeg: Watson and Dwyer, 1979.

Harvey, Kathryn. "Amazons and Victims: Resisting Wife-Abuse in Working-Class Montréal, 1869–1879." *Journal of the Canadian Historical Association* 2 (1991): 131–48.

Hatton, Mary Jane, Nicholas Bala, and Carole Curtis. "Representing Parents." In *Canadian Child Welfare Law: Children, Families and the State*, ed. Nicholas Bala et al., 2nd edition, 261–78. Toronto: Thompson Educational Publishing, 2004.

Hazel, Nancy. *A Bridge to Independence: The Kent Family Placement Project*. Oxford: Basil Blackwell, 1981.

Hegar, R.L. "Kinship Foster Care." In *Kinship Foster Care. Policy, Practice, and Research*, ed. Rebecca L. Hegar and Maria Scannagpieco, 225–40. New York: Oxford University Press, 1999.

Hepburn, Sharon A. Roger. *Crossing the Border: A Free Black Community in Canada*. Urbana and Chicago: University of Illinois Press, 2007.

Hepworth, H. Philip. *Foster Care and Adoption in Canada*. Ottawa: Canadian Council on Social Development, 1980.

Hertz, Rosanna. *Single by Chance, Mothers by Choice: How Women Are Choosing Parenthood without Marriage and Creating the New American Family*. Oxford and New York: Oxford University Press, 2006.

Hick, Steven. *Social Work in Canada: An Introduction.* Toronto: Thompson Educational Press, 2004.

———. *Social Welfare in Canada: Understanding Income Security.* Toronto: Thompson Educational Press, 2004.

Hogeveen, Bryan. "'The Evils with Which We Are Called to Grapple': Elite Reformers, Eugenicists, Environmental Psychologists, and the Construction of Toronto's Working Boy Problem, 1860–1930." *Labour/Le Travail* 55 (Spring 2005): 37–68.

———. "Toward 'Safer' and 'Better' Communities? Canada's Youth Criminal Justice Act, Aboriginal Youth and the Processes of Exclusion." *Critical Criminology* 13, no. 3 (January 2005): 287–305.

Holt, Simma. *Sex and the Teen-Age Revolution.* Toronto: McClelland and Stewart, 1967.

Homrighaus, Ruth Ellen. "Wolves in Women's Clothing: Baby-Farming and the *British Medical Journal,* 1860–1872." *Journal of Family History* 26, no. 3 (July 2001): 350–72.

House, Yvonne, and Harvey Stalwick. "Social Work and the First Nation Movement: 'Our Children, Our Culture.'" In *Social Work and Social Change in Canada,* ed. Brian Wharf, 79–113. Toronto: McClelland and Stewart, 1990.

Houston, Susan. "The 'Waifs and Strays' of a Late Victorian City: Juvenile Delinquents in Toronto." In *Childhood and Family in Canadian History,* ed. Joy Parr, 129–42. Toronto: McClelland and Stewart, 1982.

Howard-Bobiwash, Heather. "Women's Class Strategies as Activism in Native Community Building in Toronto, 1950–1975." *American Indian Quarterly* 27, no. 3 (2003): 566–82.

Howe, R. Brian, and Katherine Covell. "Children's Rights in Hard Times." In *The Welfare State in Canada:. Past, Present and Future,* ed. Raymond B. Blake, Penny E. Bryden, and J. Frank Strain, 230–45. Concord, ON: Irwin Publishing, 1997.

Hudson, Joe, Richard Nutter, and Burt Galaway. "Contracting-Out and Program Evaluation: A Case Study." In *Carrots, Sticks and Sermons: Policy Instruments and Their Evaluation,* ed. Marie-Louise Bemelmans-Videc, Ray C. Rist, and Evert Vedunt, 165–84. New Brunswick, NJ: Transaction Publishers, 2003.

Hudson, Peter, and Brad McKenzie. "Child Welfare and Native People: The Extension of Colonialism." *Le Travailleur social/The Social Worker* 49, no. 2 (Summer 1981): 63–88.

———, and Sharon Taylor-Heley. "First Nations Child and Family Services, 1982–1992." In *Social Fabric or Patchwork Quilt: The Development of Social Policy in Canada,* ed. Raymond B. Blake and Jeffrey A. Keshen, 251–62. Toronto: Broadview Press, 2006.

Humphrey, J. "Dependent-Care by Battered Women: Protecting Their Children." *Health Care for Women International* 16 (1995): 9–20.

Iacovetta, Franca. *Gatekeepers: Reshaping Immigrant Lives in Cold War Canada.* Toronto: Between the Lines, 2006.

———. "Gossip, Contest, and Power in the Making of Suburban Bad Girls: Toronto 1945–1960." *Canadian Historical Review* 80, no. 4 (December 1999): 585–623.

Irwin, I., S. Thorne, and C. Varcoe. "Strength in Adversity: Motherhood for Women Who Have Been Battered." *Canadian Journal of Nursing Research* 34, no. 4 (2002): 47–57.

Jaffe, Peter G., Nancy K.D. Lemon, and Samantha E. Poisson. *Child Custody and Domestic Violence: A Call for Safety and Accountability.* Thousand Oaks, CA: Sage Publications, 2002.

———, David Wolfe, and Susan K. Wilson. *Children of Battered Women.* Newbury Park, CA: Sage Publications, 1990.

James, Cathy. "Reforming Reform: Toronto's Settlement House Movement, 1900–20." *Canadian Historical Review* 82, no. 1 (March 2001): 55–90.

Joe, Rita. "The Honour Song of the Micmac: An Autobiography of Rita Joe." In *Keusultiek: Women's Voices of Atlantic Canada.* Halifax: Institute for the Study of Women, Mount St. Vincent University, 1993.

Johnson, Laura C., and Janice Dineen. *The Kin Trade: The Day Care Crisis in Canada.* Toronto: McGraw-Hill Ryerson, 1981.

Johnston, Patrick. *Native Children and the Child Welfare System.* Ottawa: Canadian Council for Social Development, 1983.

Jones, Andrew, and Leonard Rutman. *In the Children's Aid: J.J. Kelso and Child Welfare in Ontario.* Toronto: University of Toronto Press, 1981.

Jones, Kathy. "Listening to Hidden Voices: Power, Domination, Resistance and Pleasure within the Huronia Regional Centre." *Disability, Handicap and Society* 7, no. 4 (1992): 339–48.

Joyal, Renée. *Les Enfants, la société et l'état au Québec 1608–1989.* Montreal: Editions Hurtubise, 1999.

———. *L'évolution de la protection de l'enfance au Québec: des origins à nos jours.* Quebec City: Presses de l'Université du Québec, 2000.

Kalbach, Madeline A. "Ethnic Intermarriage in Canada." *Canadian Ethnic Studies* 34, no. 2 (2002): 25–69.

Kaprielian-Church, Isabel. "Armenians." In *Encyclopedia of Canada's Peoples,* ed. Paul Robert Magocsi, 215–31. Toronto: Multicultural History Society of Ontario and University of Toronto Press, 1999.

Kariel, Pat. *New Directions: Stepping Out of Street Life.* Calgary: Greenways Press, 1993.

Karsh, Yousuf. *In Search of Greatness: Reflections of Yousuf Karsh.* Toronto: University of Toronto Press, 1962.

Kelm, Mary-Ellen. "'A Scandalous Procession': Residential Schooling and the Re/Formation of Aboriginal Bodies, 1900–1950." *Native Studies Review* 11, no. 2 (1996): 51–88.

Kérisit, Michèle, and Néré St.-Amand. "Taking Risks with Families at Risk: Some Alternative Approaches with Poor Families in Canada." In *Child Welfare in Canada: Research and Policy Implications,* ed. Joe Hudson and Burt Galaway, 154–67. Toronto: Thompson Educational Publishing, 1995.

Kershaw, Paul. *Carefair: Rethinking the Responsibilities and Rights of Citizenship.* Vancouver: UBC Press, 2007.

————, Jane Pulkingham, and Sylvia Fuller. "Expanding the Subject: Violence, Care, and (In)Active Male Citizenship." *Social Politics: International Studies in Gender, State and Society* 15, no. 2 (Summer 2008): 182–206.

Kertzer, David, Heather Koball, and Michael J. White. "Growing Up as an Abandoned Child in Nineteenth-Century Italy." *History of the Family* 2, no. 3 (1997): 211–28.

King, James, Morag MacKay, and Angela Sirnick, with the Canadian Shaken Baby Study Group, "Shaken Baby Syndrome in Canada: Clinical Characteristics and Outcomes of Hospital Cases." *Canadian Medical Association Journal* 168, no. 2 (January 2003): 155–59.

Kitossa, Tamari. "Criticism, Reconstruction and African-Centred Feminist Historiography." In *Back to the Drawing Board: African Canadian Feminisms,* ed. Njoki Nathani Wane, Katerina Deliovsky, and Erica Lawson, 85–116. Toronto: Sumach Press, 2002.

Klein, Ross, A. Kathleen Kufeldt, and Scott Rideout. "Resilience Theory and Its Relevance for Child Welfare Practice." In *Promoting Resilience in Child Welfare,* ed. Robert John Flynn, Peter M. Dudding, and James G. Barber, 34–51. Ottawa: University of Ottawa Press, 2005.

Kline, Marlee. "Child Welfare Law: 'Best Interests of the Child' Ideology and First Nation." *Osgoode Hall Law Journal* 30, no. 2 (1992): 375–425.

————. "Complicating the Ideology of Motherhood: Child Welfare Law and First Nations Women." *Queen's Law Journal* 18, no. 2 (1993): 306–42.

Kramar, Kirsten Johnson. *Unwilling Mothers, Unwanted Babies: Infanticide in Canada.* Vancouver: UBC Press, 2005.

Krosenbrink-Gelissen, L.E. "Caring Is Indian Women's Business, but Who Takes Care of Them? Canadian Indian Women, the Renewed Indian Act and Its Implications for Women's Family Responsibilities, Roles and Rights." *Law and Anthropology* 7 (1992): 107–30.

Kufeldt, Kathleen. "Inclusive Care, Separation, and Role Clarity in Foster Care: The Development of Theoretical Constructs." In *Child Welfare in Canada: Research and Policy Implications,* ed. Joe Hudson and Burt Galaway, 337–50. Toronto: Thompson Educational Publishing, 1995.

————, J. Armstrong, and M. Dorosh. "How Children in Care View Their Own and Their Foster Families: A Research Study." *Child Welfare* 74, no. 3 (May–June 1995): 695–718.

————, and Brad McKenzie. "Conclusions and Directions for the Future." In *Child Welfare: Connecting Research, Policy, and Practice,* ed. Kathleen Kufeldt and Brad McKenzie, 429–474. Waterloo: Wilfrid Laurier University Press, 2003.

————, et al. "The Looking after Children in Canada Project: Educational Outcomes." In *Child Welfare: Connecting Research, Policy, and Practice,* ed. Kathleen Kufeldt and Brad McKenzie, 177–90. Waterloo: Wilfrid Laurier University Press, 2003.

Lacharité, Carl, Louise Ethier, and Germain Courture. "The Influence of Partners on Parental Stress of Neglectful Mothers." *Child Abuse Review* 5, no. 1 (1996): 18–33.

Langton, Anne. *The Story of Our Family.* Manchester: Thos Sowler and Company, 1881.

Laporte, Lise. "Un défi de taille pour les centres jeunesse. Intervenir auprès des parents ayant un trouble de personnalité limite." *Santé mentale au Québec* 32, no. 2 (2007): 97–114.

Laroque, Emma. "Culturally Appropriate Models in Criminal Justice Applications." In *Aboriginal and Treaty Rights in Canada,* ed. Michael Asch, 75–96. Vancouver: UBC Press, 1998.

Lavell-Harvard, D. Memee, and Jeannette Corbiere Lavell, eds. *'Until Our Hearts Are on the Ground': Aboriginal Mothering, Oppression, Resistance and Rebirth.* Toronto: Demeter Press, 2006.

Legault, Louise, and Shaye Moffat. "Positive Life Experiences That Promote Resilience in Young People in Care." In *Promoting Resilience in Child Welfare,* ed. Robert John Flynn, Peter M. Dudding, and James G. Barber, 173–90. Ottawa: University of Ottawa Press, 2005.

Lemay, Raymond, and Hayat Chazal. *Looking after Children: A Practitioner's Guide.* Ottawa: University of Ottawa Press, 2007.

Leslie, Bruce, and Francis Hare. "At Care's End: Child Welfare Grads and Street Youth Services." In *Child Welfare: Connecting Research, Policy, and Practice,* ed. Kathleen Kufeldt and Brad McKenzie, 239–47. Waterloo: Wilfrid Laurier University Press, 2003.

Lévesque, Andrée. *Making and Breaking the Rules: Women in Quebec, 1919–1939.* trans. Yvonne M. Klein. Toronto: McClelland and Stewart, 1994.

Lindsey, Duncan. "Factors Affecting the Foster Care Placement Decision: An Analysis of National Survey Data." *American Journal of Orthopsychiatry* 61, no. 2 (April 1991): 272–81.

Little, Margaret. *"No Car, No Radio, No Liquor Permit": The Moral Regulation of Single Mothers in Ontario, 1920–1997.* Toronto: University of Toronto Press, 1998.

McClung, Nellie L. *In Times Like These.* Toronto: McLeod and Allen, 1915.

McCuaig, K. *The Weariness, the Fever, and the Fret: The Campaign against Tuberculosis in Canada, 1900–1950.* Montreal and Kingston: McGill-Queen's University Press, 1999.

McDaniel, Susan, and Robert Lewis. "Did They or Didn't They? Intergenerational Supports in Families Past: A Case Study of Brigus, Newfoundland, 1920–1945." In *Family Matters: Papers in Post-Confederation Canadian Family History,* ed. Lori Chambers and Edgar-André Montigny, 475–98. Toronto: Canadian Scholars' Press, 1998.

Macdonald, Heidi. "Doing More with Less: The Sisters of St. Martha (PEI) Diminish the Impact of the Great Depression." *Acadiensis* 33, no. 1 (Fall 2003): 21–46.

Macdonald, Helen J. "Boarding-Out and the Scottish Poor Law, 1845–1914." *Scottish Historical Review* 75, no. 2 (1996): 197–220.

MacDonald, John A. "The Spallumcheen Indian Band By-Law and Its Potential Impact on Native Indian Child Welfare Policy in British Columbia." *Canadian Journal Family Law* 4 (July 1983): 75–95.

McDonald, Katrina Bell, and Elizabeth M. Armstrong. "De-Romanticizing Black Inter-generational Support: The Questionable Expectations of Welfare Reform." *Journal of Marriage and the Family* 63, no. 1 (February 2001): 213–23.

MacDonald, Kelly A. *The Road to Aboriginal Authority over Child and Family Services: Considerations for an Effective Transition.* Vancouver: Centre for Native Policy and Research and Canadian Centre for Policy Alternatives, 2008.

MacDonald, Nancy, Joan Glode, and Fred Wien. "Respecting Aboriginal Families: Pathways to Resilience in Custom Adoption and Family Group Conferencing." In *Handbook for Working with Children and Youth: Pathways to Resilience across Cultures and Contexts,* ed. Michael Ungar, 357–70. Thousand Oaks, London, and New Delhi: Sage Publications, 2005.

McGillivray, Ann. "Transracial Adoption and the Status Indian Child." *Canadian Journal of Family Law* 4 (1985): 437–69.

McGregor, Mrs. J.B. "The Care of the Child Who Is Different." Proceedings of the Sixth Canadian Conference on Child Welfare. Ottawa: Canadian Council on Child Welfare, 1928.

McIntosh, Mary. "Social Anxieties about Lone Motherhood and Ideologies of the Family: Two Sides of the Same Coin." In *Good Enough Mothering? Feminist Perspectives on Lone ,Motherhood,* ed. Elizabeth B. Silva, 148–56. London and New York: Routledge, 1996.

McIntosh, Robert G. *Boys in the Pits: Child Labour in Coal Mining.* Montreal and Kingston: McGill-Queen's University Press, 2000.

McIntyre, Sheila. "Feminist Movement in Law: Beyond Privileged and Privileging Theory." In *Women's Legal Strategies in Canada,* ed. Radha Jhappan, 42–98. Toronto: University of Toronto Press, 2002.

McIvor, Sharon D. "Self-Government and Aboriginal Women," In *Feminisms and Womanisms: A Women's Studies Reader,* ed. Althea Prince and Susan Silva-Wayne, 25–42. Toronto: Women's Press, 2004.

McKay, Sharon, and Shelley Thomas Prokop, "Identity, Community, Resilience: The Transmission of Values Project." In *Putting a Human Face on Child Welfare: Voices from the Prairies,* ed. Ivan Brown et al., 25–58. Regina: Prairie Child Welfare Consortium, 2007.

McKenzie, Brad. "The Development of Foster Family Care." In *Current Perspectives on Foster Family Care for Children and Youth,* ed. Brad McKenzie, 59–73. Toronto and Dayton: Wall and Emerson, 1994.

———, Sally Palmer, and Wanda Thomas Barnard. "Views from Other Provinces." In *People, Politics, and Child Welfare in British Columbia,* ed. Leslie T. Foster and Brian Wharf, 217–25. Vancouver: UBC Press, 2007.

———, Esther Seidl, and Norman Bone. "Child Welfare Standards in First Nations: A Community-Based Study." In *Child Welfare in Canada: Research and Policy Implications,* ed. Joe Hudson and Burt Galaway, 54–65. Toronto: Thompson Educational Publishing, 1995.

McKie, Craig. "An Overview of Lone Parenthood in Canada." In *Single Parent Families: Perspectives on Research and Policy,* ed. Joe Hudson and Burt Galaway, 53–72. Toronto: Butterworth Publishing, 1993.

MacLaurin, Bruce Nico Trocmé, and Barbara Fallon. "Characteristics of Investigated Children and Families Referred for Out-of-Home Placement." In *Child Welfare: Connecting Research, Policy, and Practice,* ed. Kathleen Kufeldt and Brad McKenzie, 27–40. Waterloo: Wilfrid Laurier University Press, 2003.

McPhee, Keith, et al. "Educational Challenges for Children and Youth at Risk: Toward a Shared Responsibility." In *The Welfare of Canadian Children: It's Our Business.* 133–41. Ottawa: Child Welfare Council of Canada, 2007.

Maguire, Constance A. "Kate Simpson Hayes, Agnes Agatha Hammell, and 'the Slur of Illegitimacy.'" *Saskatchewan History* 50, no. 2 (Fall 1998): 7–23.

Malacrida, Claudia. "Performing Motherhood in a Disablist World: Dilemmas of Motherhood, Femininity and Disability." *Journal of Qualitative Studies in Education* 22, no. 1 (2009): 99–117.

———. "Negotiating the Dependency/Nurturing Tightrope: Dilemmas of Motherhood and Disability." *Canadian Review of Sociology and Anthropology* (1 November 2007), http://www.accessmylibrary.com/coms2/summary_0286–33832059_ITM.

Malarek, Victor. *Hey Malarek!* Halifax: Formac Publishing Company, 1984.

Maltais-Valois, B. "The Right to a Quality Life." *Entourage* 6, no. 2 (1991): 12–13.

Mann, W.E. "The Social System of a Slum: The Lower Ward, Toronto." In *The Community in Canada. Rural and Urban,* ed. Satadal Dasgupta, 294–310. Lanham, MD: University Press of America, 1996.

Maracle, Lee. *Daughters Are Forever.* Vancouver: Raincoast Books, 2002.

Marino, Mary C. "Aboriginals: Siouans." In *Encyclopedia of Canada's Peoples,* ed. Paul Robert Magocsi, 93–98. Toronto: Multicultural History Society of Ontario and University of Toronto Press, 1999.

Marmor , Theodore R., Jerry L. Mashaw, and Philip L. Harvey. *America's Misunderstood Welfare State: Persistent Myths, Enduring Realities.* New York: Basic Books, 1992.

Marshall, Dominique. "The Language of Children's Rights, the Formation of the Welfare State, and the Democratic Experience of Poor Families in Quebec, 1940–1955." *Canadian Historical Review* 78, no. 3 (September 1997): 409–41.

———. "Reconstruction Politics, the Canadian Welfare State and the Formation of Children's Rights, 1940–1950." In *Family Matters: Papers in Post-Confederation Canadian Family History,* ed. Lori Chambers and Edgar-André Montigny, 135–56. Toronto: Canadian Scholars' Press, 1998.

———. *Social Origins of the Welfare State: Quebec Families, Compulsory Education, and Family Allowances, 1940–1955,* trans. Nicola Doone Danby. Waterloo: Wilfrid Laurier University Press, 2006.

Martin, Fay E. "Tales of Transition: Leaving Public Care." In *Youth in Transition: Perspectives on Research and Policy,* ed. Burt Galaway and Joe Hudson, 98–106. Toronto: Thompson Educational Publishing, 1996.

Matthews, Hugh, et al. "Growing-up in the Countryside: Children and the Rural Idyll." *Journal of Rural Studies* 16, no. 2 (April 2000): 141–267.

Maunders, David. "Awakening from the Dream: The Experience of Childhood in Protestant Orphan Homes in Australia, Canada and the United States." *Child and Youth Care Forum* 23, no. 6 (December 1994): 393–412.

Mennill, Sally, and Veronica Strong-Boag. "Identifying Victims: Child Abuse and Death in Families." *Canadian Bulletin of Medical History* 25, no. 2 (2008): 11–33.

Miller, James R. *Shingwauk's Vision: A History of Native Residential Schools.* Toronto: University of Toronto Press, 1995.

Milloy, John. *"A National Crime": The Canadian Government and the Residential School System, 1879 to 1986.* Winnipeg: University of Manitoba Press, 1999.

Mitchell, Barbara A. *Family Matters: An Introduction to Family Sociology in Canada.* Toronto: Canadian Scholars' Press, 2009.

Mitchell, Shirley. "These Pictures Are Dear to My Heart." In *Keusultiek: Women's Voices of Atlantic Canada.* Halifax: Institute for the Study of Women, Mount St. Vincent University, 1993.

Mitic, Wayne, and Mary Lynne Rimer. "The Educational Attainment of Children in Care in British Columbia." *Child and Youth Care Forum* 31, no. 6 (December 2002): 397–414.

Moody, David. *Scottish Family History.* Baltimore: Genealogical Publishing, 1994.

Moore, Marianne. "Social Control or Protection of the Child? The Debates on the Industrial Schools Acts 1857–1894." *Journal of Family History* 33, no. 4 (October 2008): 359–87.

Moran, Bridget. *A Little Rebellion.* Vancouver: Arsenal Pulp Press, 1992.

———, and Mary John. *Stoney Creek Woman: The Story of Mary John.* Vancouver: Arsenal Pulp Press, 1989.

Morin, Claude. "Beyond Kinship and Households: Godparents and Orphans: An Introduction." *The History of the Family* 5, no. 3 (November 2000): 255–57.

Morton, Suzanne. *Ideal Surroundings: Domestic Life in a Working-Class Suburb.* Toronto: University of Toronto Press, 1995.

———"From Infant Homes to Daycare: Child Care in Halifax." In *Mothers of the Municipality: Women, Work and Social Policy in Post-1945 Halifax,* ed. Judith Fingard and Janet Guildford, 169–88. Toronto: University of Toronto Press, 2004.

———. "Nova Scotia and Its Unmarried Mothers, 1945–1975." In *Mapping the Margins: The Family and Social Discipline in Canada, 1700–1975,* ed. Nancy Christie and Michael Gauvreau, 327–48. Montreal and Kingston: McGill-Queen's University Press, 2004.

Mosionier, Beatrice Culleton. *In Search of April Raintree.* Winnipeg: Portage and Main Press, 1999.

Mossman, Mary Jane. *Families and the Law in Canada.* Toronto: Emond Montgomery Publications, 2004.

Mossop, Judith, and Kim James. "Motherhood, Madness, and the Law." *University of Toronto Law Journal* 45, no. 2 (Spring 1995): 107–42.

Murdoch, Lydia D. "From Barrack Schools to Family Cottages: Creating Domestic Space for Late Victorian Poor Children." In *Child Welfare and Social Action,* ed. Jon Lawrence and Pat Starkey, 147–73. Liverpool: Liverpool University Press, 2001.

Murphy, H.B.M. "Foster Home Variables and Adult Outcomes." *Mental Hygiene* 48, no. 4 (October 1964): 587–99.

Murray, Karen Bridget. "Governing 'Unwed Mothers' in Toronto at the Turn of the Twentieth Century." *Canadian Historical Review* 85, no. 2 (2004): 253–76.

Myers, Tamara. *Caught: Montreal's Modern Girls and the Law 1969–1945.* Toronto: University of Toronto Press, 2006.

Neff, Charlotte. "The Education of Destitute Homeless Children in Nineteenth-Century Ontario." *Journal of Family History* 29, no. 1 (January 2004): 3–46.

———. "Government Approaches to Child Neglect and Mistreatment in Nineteenth-Century Ontario." *Histoire sociale/Social History* 41, no. 81 (May 2008): 165–214.

———. "The Use of Apprenticeship and Adoption by the Protestant Orphans' Home 1853–1869." *Histoire sociale/Social History* 30, no. 60 (November 1997), 333–85.

———. "Youth in Canada West: A Case Study of Red Hill Farm School Emigrants, 1854–68." *Journal of Family History,* 25, no. 4 (October 2000), 432–91.

Nelson, Jennifer J. *Razing Africville: A Geography of Racism.* Toronto: University of Toronto Press, 2008.

Neysmith, Sheila M. "Women's Caring: Challenges for Practice and Policy." *Affilia* 7, no. 1 (Spring 1992): 21–44.

Noel, Françoise. *Family Life and Sociability in Upper and Lower Canada, 1780–1870: A View from Diaries and Family Correspondence.* Montreal and Kingston: McGill-Queen's University Press, 2003.

Nootens, Thierry. "'For Years We Have Never Had a Happy Home': Madness and Families in Century Montreal." In *Mental Health and Canadian Society: Historical Perspectives,* ed. James E. Moran and David Wright, 49–68. Montreal and Kingston: McGill-Queen's University Press, 2006.

Oberman, Michelle. "Mothers Who Kill: Cross-Cultural Patterns in and Perspectives on Contemporary Maternal Filicide." *International Journal of Law and Psychiatry* 26 (2003): 493–514.

Palmer, Bryan D. *Canada's 1960s: The Ironies of Identity in a Rebellious Era.* Toronto: University of Toronto Press, 2009.

Parazelli, Michel. *La Rue attractive: parcours et partiques identitaires des jeunes de la rue.* Ste-Foy: Presses de l'Université du Québec, 2002.

Parizeau, Alice. *Protection de L'enfant: échec?* Montreal: Les Presses de l'Université de Montreal, 1978.

Parr, Joy. *The Gender of Breadwinners: Women, Men, and Change in Two Industrial Towns, 1880–1950.* Toronto: University of Toronto Press, 1990.

———. *Labouring Children. British Immigrant Apprentices to Canada, 1869–1924.* Toronto: University of Toronto Press, 1994.

Peers, Laura, and Jennifer Brown. "'There is no end to relationships among the Indians': Ojibwa Families and Kinship in Historical Perspective." *History of the Family* 4, no. 4 (1999): 529–55.

Pepler, Debra J., and Kenneth H. Rubin, eds., *The Development and Treatment of Childhood Aggression.* Hillside, NJ: Lawrence Erlbaurn Associates, 1991.

Petrie, Anne. *Gone to an Aunt's.* Toronto: McClelland and Stewart, 1998.

Phoenix, Ann. "Social Constructions of Lone Motherhood: A Case of Competing Discourses." In *Good Enough Mothering? Feminist Perspectives on Lone Motherhood,* ed. Elizabeth B. Silva, 175–90. London and New York: Routledge, 1996.

Pineo, Peter C. 18. "The Extended Family in a Working-Class Area of Hamilton." In *The Community in Canada. Rural and Urban,* ed. Satadal Dasgupta, 328–38. Lanham, MD: University Press of America, 1996.

Popper, Charles W. "Child and Adolescent Psychopharmacology at the Turn of the Millennium." In *Practical Child and Adolescent Psychopharmacology,* ed. Stan Kutcher, 1–37. Cambridge: Cambridge University Press, 2002.

Posen, Sara. "Examining Policy from the 'Bottom up': The Relationship between Parents, Children and Managers at the Toronto Boys' Home, 1859–1920." In *Family Matters: Papers in Post-Confederation Canadian Family History,* ed. Lori Chambers and Edgar-André Montigny, 3–18. Toronto: Canadian Scholars' Press, 1998.

Poutanen, Mary Anne. "Bonds of Friendship, Kinship, and Community: Gender, Homelessness, and Mutual Aid in Early-Nineteenth-Century Montreal." In *Negotiating Identities in Nineteenth- and Twentieth-Century Montreal,* ed. Bettina Bradbury and Tamara Myers, 25–48. Vancouver: UBC Press, 2005.

Pratt, Geraldine. "'Is This Canada?': Domestic Workers' Experience in Vancouver, BC." In *Gender, Migration and Domestic Service,* ed. J.H. Momsen, 23–42. London and New York: Routledge, 1999.

Prentice, Susan, ed. *Changing Child Care: Five Decades of Child Care Advocacy and Policy in Canada.* Halifax, NS: Fernwood Publishing Company, 2001.

Purdy, Sean. "'It was tough on everybody': Low-Income Families and Housing Hardship in Post–World War II Toronto." *Journal of Social History* 37, no. 2 (Winter 2003): 457–82.

Purvey, Diane. "Alexandra Orphanage and Families in Crisis in Vancouver, 1892–1938." In *Dimensions of Childhood: Essays on the History of Children and Youth in Canada,* ed. Russell Smandych, Gordon Dodds, and Alvin Esau, 107–33. Winnipeg: Legal Research Institute of the University of Manitoba, 1991.

Rains, Prue, and E. Teram. *Normal Bad Boys. Public Policies, Institutions, and the Politics of Client Recruitment.* Montreal and Kingston: McGill Queen's University Press, 1992.

Raychaba, Brian "'We Get a Life Sentence': Young People in Care Speak Out on Child Sexual Abuse," *Journal of Child and Youth Care,* Special Issue (1992): 129–39.

Raymond, Jean Panet, and Robert Mayer. "The History of Community Development in Quebec." In *Community Organizing: Canadian Experiences,* ed. Brian Wharf and Michael Clague. 29–61. Toronto: Oxford University Press, 1997.

Reaume, Geoffrey. "Mental Hospital Patients and Family Relations in Southern Ontario." In *Family Matters: Papers in Post-Confederation Canadian Family History*, ed. Lori Chambers and Edgar-André Montigny, 271–88. Toronto: Canadian Scholars' Press, 1998.

Rich, Harold, Montreal Children's Hospital, and Batshaw Youth and Family Centres. "The Effects of a Health Newsletter for Foster Parents on Their Perceptions of the Behavior and Development of Foster Children." *Child Abuse and Neglect* 20, no. 5 (May 1996): 437–46.

Richardson, Glenn E. "The Metatheory of Resilience and Resiliency." *Journal of Clinical Psychology* 53, no. 3 (March 2002): 307–21.

Robinson, G.C., R.F. Conroy, and J.L. Conroy, *The Canim Lake Survey of Special Needs Children*. Vancouver: University of British Columbia, March 1985.

Robson, Krista. "'Canada's Most Notorious Bad Mother': The Newspaper Coverage of the Jordan Heikamp Inquest." *Canadian Review of Sociology and Anthropology* 42, no. 2 (2003): 217–32.

Rodger, Susan, Anne Cummings, and Alan W. Leschied. "Who Is Caring for Our Most Vulnerable Children? The Motivation to Foster in Child Welfare." *Child Abuse and Neglect* 30, no. 10 (October 2006): 1129–42.

Rooke, Patricia T., and R. L. Schnell. "Child Welfare in English Canada, 1920–1948." *Social Science Review* 55, no. 3 (1981): 484–506.

———. *Discarding the Asylum: From Child Rescue to the Welfare State in English Canada*. Landham, MD: University Press of America, 1983.

Rose, June. *For the Sake of the Children: Inside Dr. Barnardo's 120 Years of Caring for Children*. London: Hodder and Stoughton, 1987.

Ross, Shana, and Nancy Health. "A Study of Self-Mutilation in Community Sample of Adolescents." *Journal of Youth and Adolescents* 31, no. 1 (February 2002): 67–77.

Rotskoff, Lori. *Love on the Rocks: Men, Women, and Alcohol in Post–World War II America*. Chapel Hill, NC: University of North Carolina Press, 2002.

Rutman, Deborah et al. *When Youth Age Out of Care—Where to from There? Final Report Based on a Three-Year Longitudinal Study*. Victoria: School of Social Work, University of Victoria, 2007.

Sachdev, Paul. *Unlocking the Adoption File*. Lexington, KY: Lexington Books, 1989.

Saint-Pierre, Arthur. *Témoignages sur nos Orphelinats: Recueillis et commentés*. Montreal: Fides, 1946.

Sangster, Joan. *Girl Trouble: Female Delinquency in English Canada*. Toronto: Between the Lines, 2002.

———. "Masking and UnMasking the Sexual Abuse of Children: Perceptions of Violence against Children in 'The Badlands' of Ontario, 1916–1930." *Journal of Family History*, 25, no. 4 (October 2000): 504–26.

———. *Regulating Girls and Women: Sexuality, Family and the Law in Ontario, 1920–1960*. Toronto: Oxford University Press, 2001.

Satzewich, Vic, and Terry Wotherspoon. *First Nations: Race, Class, and Gender Relations*. Regina: Canadian Plains Research Center, 2000.

Savage, Leslie. "Perspectives on Illegitimacy: The Changing Role of the Sisters of Misericordia in Edmonton, 1900–1906." In *Studies in Childhood History: A Canadian Perspective*, ed. Patricia T. Rooke and R.L. Schnell, 105–33. Calgary: Detselig Enterprises, 1982.

Scannagpieco, Maria, and Rebecca L. Hegar. "Kinship Foster Care in Context." In *Kinship Foster Care: Policy, Practice, and Research*, ed. Rebecca L. Hegar and Maria Scannagpieco, 1–16. New York: Oxford University Press, 1999.

Scarth, Sandra, and Richard Sullivan. "Child Welfare in the 1980s: A Time of Turbulence and Change." In *People, Politics, and Child Welfare in British Columbia*, ed. Leslie T. Foster and Brian Wharf, 83–96. Vancouver: UBC Press, 2007.

Schlesinger, Benjamin. *The One-Parent Family in the 1980s: Perspectives and Annotated Bibliography 1978–1984*. Toronto: University of Toronto Press, 1985.

Scott, Dorothy, and Shurlee Swain. *Confronting Cruelty: Historical Perspectives of Child Abuse*. Melbourne: Melbourne University Press, 2002.

Shalay, Nancy, and Keith Brownlee. "Narrative Family Therapy with Blended Families." *Journal of Family Psychotherapy* 18, no. 2 (2007): 17–30.

Shapiro, Deborah. "Fostering and Adoption: Converging Roles for Substitute Parents." In *Adoption: Current Issues and Trends*, ed. Paul Sachdev, 267–86. Toronto: Butterworth, 1984.

Shorkey, Deena, and Barbara Mitchell. "Grandparents Raising their Grandchildren." In *Child Welfare: Connecting Research, Policy, and Practice*, ed. Kathleen Kufeldt and Brad McKenzie, 147–56. Waterloo: Wilfrid Laurier University Press, 2003.

Silman, Janet, editor. *Enough Is Enough: Aboriginal Women Speak Out*. Toronto: Women's Press, 1987.

Silva-Wayne, Susan. "Contributions to Resilience in Children and Youth: What Successful Child Welfare Graduates Say." In *Child Welfare in Canada: Research and Policy Implications*, ed. Joe Hudson and Burt Galaway, 308–23. Toronto: Thompson Educational Publishing, 1995.

Silverman, Peter. *Who Speaks for the Children? Giving Voice to a Forgotten Generation*. Toronto: Stoddart, 1989.

Silverman, Robert, and Leslie Kennedy. *Deadly Deeds: Murder in Canada*. Toronto: Nelson Canada, 1993.

Slaughter, Olivia, and Jean Kubelun. *Life as a Mother-in-Law: Roles, Challenges, Solutions*. Indianapolis, IN: Dog Ear Publishing, 2008.

Slonim, Reuben. *Great to Be an Orphan*. Toronto: Clarke, Irwin and Company, 1983.

Solanger, Ricki. *Wake Up Little Susie: Single Pregnancy and Race before Roe v. Wade*. New York: Routledge, 2000.

Sproule-Jones, Megan. "Crusading for the Forgotten: Dr. Peter Bryce, Public Health, and Prairie Native Residential Schools." *Canadian Bulletin of Medical History*, 13, no. 2 (1996): 199–224.

Stein, Eleanor, et al. "Psychiatric Disorders of Children in Care: Methodology and Demographic Correlates." *Canadian Journal of Psychiatry* 39, no. 6 (August 1994): 341–47.

Steinhauer, P.D., et al. "The Foster Care Research Project: Clinical Impressions." *American Journal of Orthopsychiatry* 59, no. 3 (July 1989): 430–41.

———. *The Least Detrimental Alternative: A Systematic Guide to Case Planning and Decision Making for Children in Care.* Toronto: University of Toronto Press, 1991.

———. "The Management of Children Admitted to Child Welfare Services in Ontario: A Review and Discussion of Current Problems and Practices." *Canadian Journal of Psychiatry* 29, no. 6 (October 1984): 473–84.

———. "The Preventive Utilization of Foster Care." *Canadian Journal of Psychiatry* 33, no. 6 (August 1988): 459–67.

Strawbridge, J., et al. "New Burdens. More of the Same? Comparing Grandparent, Spouse, and Adult-Child Caregivers." *The Gerontologist,* 37, no. 4 (1997): 505–10.

Strega, Susan. "Failure to Protect: Child Welfare Interventions When Men Beat Mothers." In *Cruel but Not Unusual: Violence in Canadian Families,* ed. Ramona Maggia and Cathy Vine, 237–66. Waterloo: Wilfrid Laurier University Press, 2006.

———, et al. "Connecting Father Absence and Mother Blame in Child Welfare Policies and Practice." *Children and Youth Services Review* 30, no. 7 (July 2008): 705–16.

Strong-Boag, Veronica. "Casual Fornicators, Young Lovers, Deadbeat Dads, and Family Champions: Men in Canadian Adoption Circles in the 20th Century." In *Science, Polity, and Society in Canada: Essays in Honour of Michael Bliss,* ed. Elsbeth Heaman and Alison Li, 211–37. Toronto: University of Toronto Press, 2008.

———. "Children of Adversity": Disabilities and Child Welfare in Canada from the Nineteenth Century to the Twenty-First." *Journal of Family History* 32, no. 4 (2007): 413–32.

———. *Finding Families, Finding Ourselves: English Canada Confronts Adoption from the Nineteenth Century to the 1990.* Toronto: Oxford University Press, 2006.

———. "'A People Akin to Mine': Indians and Highlanders within the British Empire." *Native Studies Review* 14, no. 1 (2001): 27–53.

———. "Sisters Are Doing It for Themselves, or Not: Aunts and Caregiving in Canada." *Journal of Comparative Family Studies* 40, no. 5 (Autumn 2009): 791–807.

Struthers, James. "In the Interests of the Children': Mothers' Allowances and the Origins of Social Security in Ontario, 1917–1930." In *Social Fabric or Patchwork Quilt: The Development of Social Policy in Canada,* ed. Raymond B. Blake and Jeffrey A. Keshen, 59–87. Toronto: University of Toronto Press, 2006.

———. *The Limits of Affluence: Welfare in Ontario, 1920–1970.* Toronto: University of Toronto Press, 1994.

———. "A Profession in Crisis: Charlotte Whitton and Canadian Social Work in the 1930s," *Canadian Historical Review* 62, no. 2 (March 1981): 169–85.

Sturino, Franc. "Italians." In *Encyclopedia of Canada's Peoples,* ed. Paul Robert Magocsi, 787–832. Toronto: Multicultural History Society of Ontario and University of Toronto Press, 1999.

Sutherland, Neil. *Children in English-Canadian Society.* Waterloo: Wilfrid Laurier University Press, 2000.

Swain, Shurlee. "Sweet Childhood Lost: Idealized Images of Childhood in the British Child Rescue Literature." *Journal of the History of Childhood and Youth* 2, no. 2 (Spring 2009): 198–214.

———, with Renate Howe. *Single Mothers and Their Children: Disposal, Punishment and Survival in Australia.* New York: Cambridge University Press, 1995.

Swanson, Jean. *Poor-Bashing: The Politics of Exclusion.* Toronto: Between the Lines, 2001.

Swartz, Teresa Toguchi. "Mothering for the State: Foster Parenting and the Challenges of Government-Contracted Carework." *Gender and Society* 18, no. 5 (October 2004): 567–87.

Swift, Karen. "Contradictions in Child Welfare: Neglect and Responsibility." In *Women's Caring: Feminist Perspectives on Social Welfare,* ed. Carol T. Baines, Patricia M. Evans, and Sheila M. Neysmith, 160–87. Toronto: Oxford University Press, 1998.

———. *Manufacturing "Bad Mothers": A Critical Perspective on Child Neglect.* Toronto: University of Toronto Press, 1995.

———, and Marilyn Callagan, *At Risk: Social Justice in Child Welfare and Other Social Services.* Toronto: University of Toronto Press, 2009.

Tait, Caroline L. "Disruptions in Nature, Disruptions in Society: Aboriginal Peoples of Canada and the 'Making' of Fetal Alcohol Syndrome." In *Healing Traditions: The Mental Health of Aboriginal Peoples in Canada,* ed. Laurence J. Kirmayer and Fail Guthrie Valaskakis, 196–220. Vancouver: UBC Press, 2009.

Tanner, J.L., and American Academy of Pediatrics. Committee on Psychosocial Aspects of Child and Family Health Pediatrics. "Parental Separation and Divorce: Can We Provide an Ounce of Prevention? Commentary." *Pediatrics* 110, no. 5 (November 2002): 1007–9.

Thakkar, Rasesh. "Gujaratis." In *Encyclopedia of Canada's Peoples,* ed. Paul Robert Magocsi, 630–38. Toronto: Multicultural History Society of Ontario and University of Toronto Press, 1999.

Thériault, Evariste. "Introduction: Child Welfare Research and Development in a National Context." In *Child Welfare: Connecting Research, Policy, and Practice,* ed. Kathleen Kufeldt and Brad McKenzie, 1–10. Waterloo: Wilfrid Laurier University Press, 2003.

Thorpe, M.B., and G.T. Swart. "Risk and Protective Factors Affecting Children in Foster Care: A Pilot Study of the Role of Siblings." *Canadian Journal of Psychiatry* 37, no. 9 (November 1992): 616–22.

Tinney, Mary-Anne. "Special Report: Role Perceptions in Foster Parent Associations in British Columbia." *Child Welfare* 64, no. 1 (1985): 73–79.

Titterington, Lee. "Foster Care Training: A Comprehensive Approach." *Welfare* 69, no. 2 (March/April 1990): 157–65.

Todd, Sarah, and Colleen Lundy. "Framing Woman Abuse: A Structural Perspective." In *Cruel but Not Unusual: Violence in Canadian Families,* ed. Ramona Maggia and Cathy Vine, 327–70. Waterloo: Wilfrid Laurier University Press, 2006.

Tone, Andrea. "Listening to the Past: History, Psychiatry, and Anxiety." *Canadian Journal of Psychiatry* 50 (2005): 373–80.

Trocmé, Nico, et al. "The Canadian Incidence Study of Reported Child Abuse and Neglect: Methodology and Major Findings." In *Child Welfare in Canada: Research and Policy Implications,* ed. Joe Hudson and Burt Galaway, 13–26. Toronto: Thompson Educational Publishing, 1995.

Unrau, Yvonne. "Role Differentiation between Foster Parents and Treatment Foster Parents." In *Current Perspectives on Foster Family Care for Children and Youth,* ed. Brad McKenzie. 112–23. Toronto and Dayton: Wall and Emerson, 1994.

Valentine, Gill. "A Safe Place to Grow Up? Parenting, Perceptions of Children's Safety and the Rural Idyll." *Journal of Rural Studies* 13, no. 2 (April 1997): 137–48.

Valverde, Mariana. *The Age of Light, Soap, and Water: Moral Reform in English Canada, 1885–1925.* Toronto: McClelland and Stewart, 1991.

Van Allen, Charlotte. *Daddy's Girl.* Toronto: McClelland and Stewart, 1980.

Van den Brink, J.H. *The Haida Indians: Cultural Change Mainly between 1876–1970.* Leiden: E.J. Brill, 1974.

Van Krieken, Robert. *Children and the State: Social Control and the Formation of Australian Child Welfare.* North Sydney, Australia: Allen and Unwin, 1991.

Varcoe, Colleen, and Gweneth Hartrick Doane. "Mothering and Women's Health." In *Women's Health in Canada: Critical Perspectives on Theory and Policy,* ed. Marina Morrow, Olena Hankivsky, and Colleen Varcoe, 297–323. Toronto: University of Toronto Press, 2007.

———, and L. Irwin. "'If I killed you, I'd get the kids': Women's Survival and Protection Work with Child Custody and Access in the Context of Woman Abuse." *Qualitative Sociology* 27, no. 1 (2004): 77–99.

Villeneuve, J.-M. Rodrigues Cardinal, O.M.I. Preface to *Témoignages sur nos Orphelinats: Recueillis et Commentés* by Arthur Saint-Pierre. Montreal: Fides, 1946.

Von Gernet, Alexander. "Aboriginals: Iroquoians." In *Encyclopedia of Canada's Peoples,* ed. Paul Robert Magocsi, 56–64. Toronto: Multicultural History Society of Ontario and University of Toronto Press, 1999.

Wadden, Marie. *Where the Pavement Ends: Canada's Aboriginal Recovery Movement and the Urgent Need for Reconciliation.* Vancouver: Douglas and McIntyre, 2008.

Wade, Jill. *Houses for All: The Struggle for Social Housing in Vancouver, 1919–1950.* Vancouver: UBC Press, 1994.

Wagamese, Richard. *Keeper'n Me.* Toronto: Doubleday Canada, 1994.

Wall, Sharon. *The Nurture of Nature: Childhood, Anti-Modernism, and Ontario Summer Camps, 1920–55.* Vancouver: UBC Press, 2009.

Walmsley, Christopher. *Protecting Aboriginal Children.* Vancouver: UBC Press, 2006.

Ward, Peter. "Unwed Motherhood in Nineteenth-Century English Canada." *Historical Papers.* Canadian Historical Association 60 (1981): 34–56.

Warsh, Cheryl K. *Prescribed Norms: Women and Health in Canada and the United States since 1800.* Toronto: University of Toronto Press, 2010.

Watson, Lisa. "In the Best Interest of the Child: The Mother–Child Program." *Forum on Corrections* Research 7, no. 2 (May 1995), http://www.csc-scc.gc.ca/text/pblct/forum/e072/e072h-eng.shtml.

Wearing, Betsy M., and Christine G. Wearing. "Women Breaking Out: Changing Discourses on Grandmotherhood?" *Journal of Family Studies* 2, no. 2 (October 1996): 165–78.

Weller, Fay, and Brian Wharf. "Contradictions in Child Welfare." In *Too Small to See, Too Big to Ignore: Child Health and Well-being in British Columbia,* ed. Michael V. Hayes and Leslie T. Foster, 141–59. Canadian Western Geographical Series no. 35. Victoria: Department of Geography, University of Victoria, 2002.

Wharf, Brian. "Addressing Public Issues in Child Welfare." In *Child Welfare: Connecting Research, Policy, and Practice,* ed. Kathleen Kufeldt and Brad McKenzie, 421–28. Waterloo: Wilfrid Laurier University Press, 2003.

———. *Community Work Approaches to Child Welfare.* Toronto: Broadview Press, 2002.

———. "The Constituency/Community Context." In *Rethinking Child Welfare in Canada,* ed. Brian Wharf, 98–127. Toronto: McClelland and Stewart, 1993.

———. "Introduction." In *People, Politics, and Child Welfare in British Columbia,* ed. Leslie T. Foster and Brian Wharf, 1–9. Vancouver: UBC Press, 2007.

———. "Organizing and Delivering Child Welfare Services: The Contributions of Research." In *Child Welfare in Canada: Research and Policy Implications,* ed. Joe Hudson and Burt Galaway, 2–12. Toronto: Thompson Educational Publishing, 1995.

Wheatley, Thelma. *My Sad Is All Gone: A Family's Triumph over Violent Autism.* Lancaster, OH: Lucky Press, 2004.

White, Deena. "Contradictory Participation: Reflections on Community Action in Quebec." In *Community Organizing: Canadian Experiences,* ed. Brian Wharf and Michael Clague. 62–90. Toronto: Oxford University Press, 1997

Whittington, Barb, et al. *Supporting Grandparents Raising Grandchildren: Resource Booklet,* 2nd edition. Victoria: University of Victoria, January 2007.

Wicks, Ben. *Yesterday They Took My Baby: True Stories of Adoption.* Toronto: Stoddart, 1993.

Williams, Bill. Foreword to *Amongst God's Own: The Enduring Legacy of St. Mary's Mission* by Glavin and Former Students of St. Mary's. Mission, BC: Longhouse Publishing, 2002.

Williams, Charmaine C. "Race (and Gender and Class) and Child Custody: Theorizing Intersections in Two Canadian Custody Cases." *National Women's Studies Association Journal* 16, no. 2 (Summer 2004): 46–69.

Willms, J. Douglas. "Socioeconomic Gradients for Childhood Vulnerability." In *Vulnerable Children: Findings from Canada's National Longitudinal Survey of Children and Youth,* ed. J. Douglas Willms, 71–102. Edmonton: University of Alberta Press, 2002.

Wills, Gale. *A Marriage of Convenience: Business and Social Work in Toronto, 1918–1957.* Toronto: University of Toronto Press, 1995.

Winks, Robin W. *The Blacks in Canada,* 2nd edition. Montreal and Kingston: McGill-Queen's University Press, 1997.

Winzer, Margaret A. *The History of Special Education.* Washington: Gallaudet University Press, 1993.

Wolfensberger, Wolf. "A Contribution to the History of Normalization, with Primary Emphasis on the Establishment of Normalization in North America between 1967–1975." In *A Quarter-Century of Normalization and Social Role Valorization: Evolution and Impact*, ed. Robert J. Flynn and Raymond A. Lemay, 51–116. Ottawa: University of Ottawa Press, 1999.

——. *The Principle of Normalization*. Toronto: National Institute on Mental Retardation, 1972.

Woodsworth, James Shaver. *My Neighbour*. Toronto: University of Toronto Press, 1911; reprinted 1972.

Wright, Donald. *The Professionalization of History in English Canada*. Toronto: University of Toronto Press, 2005.

Wright, Mary Ellen. "Unnatural Mothers: Infanticide in Halifax, 1850–1975." *Nova Scotia Historical Review* 7, no. 2 (1987): 16.

Young, Leontine. *Out of Wedlock*. New York: McGraw-Hill, 1959.

Zmora, Nurth. *Orphanages Reconsidered: Child Care Institutions in Progressive Era Baltimore*. Philadelphia: Temple University Press, 1994.

Unpublished Theses

Albujar, Yolanda Hernandez. "Transferred Motherhood: Life Experiences of Latin American Mothers in Italy." MA dissertation, University of Florida, 2004.

Baines, Carol T. "From Women's Benevolence to Professional Social Work: The Care of the Wimodausis Club and the Earlscourt Children's Home, 1902–1971." PhD dissertation, University of Toronto, 1990.

Balcom, Karen. "The Traffic in Babies: Cross-Border Adoption, Baby-Selling the Development of Child Welfare Systems in the United States and Canada, 1930–1960." PhD dissertation, Rutgers University, 2002.

Barker, Jayne. "Out-of-Home Care for Children and Youth with Serious Emotional Disturbances." MA dissertation, Royal Roads University, 2000.

Burban, Christell. "Les origines institutionnelles de la protection de l'enfance au Québec: l'école d'industrie de Notre-Dame de Monfort (1883–1913)." Mémoire en histoire, Université de Rennes, 1997.

Chupik-Hall, Jessa. "'Good Families Do Not Just Happen': Indigenous People and Child Welfare Services in Canada, 1950–1965." PhD dissertation, Trent University, 2001.

Cote, Maurice N. "The Children's Aid Society of the Catholic Archdiocese of Vancouver: Its Origins and Development, 1905–1953." MSW dissertation, University of British Columbia, 1953.

Cox, Bruce. "Alternatives to Apprehending Native Children in Urban Settings: A Case Study." University of Victoria, School of Social Work, Social Work 304 Practicum, 29 April 1988.

Dale, Gilbert. Dynamiques de l'institutionnalisatin de l'enfance délinquante et en besoin de protection: le cas des écoles de réforme et d'industrie de l'hospice Saint-Charles de Québec, 1870–1950." MA dissertation, Université Laval, 2006.

Harrison, Constance M. "Foster Homefinding: A Study of Effective Ways of Increasing the Number of Foster Homes Available for Children." MSW dissertation, University of Toronto, 1948.

Jose, Maria Christina, "Women Doing Life Sentences: A Phenomenological Study." PhD dissertation, University of Michigan, 1985.

Lepp, Annalee. "Dismembering the Family: Marital Breakdown, Domestic Conflict, and Family Violence in Ontario, 1830–1920." PhD dissertation, Queen's University, 2001.

Panitch, Melanie R. "Accidental Activists: Mothers, Organization and Disability." PhD dissertation, City University of New York, 2006.

Rand, Mary E. "Implications When Grandmothers Assume Responsibility for the Care of Children Whose Mothers Are Working for Pay." MSW dissertation, Maritime School of Social Work, May 1956.

Reid, Michael. "Understanding Children's Aid: Means and Practice in Ontario Children's Aid Societies, 1893–1912." MA dissertation, Trent University, 2009.

Rutty, Christopher. "'Do something! … Do anything!' Poliomyelitis in Canada 1927–1962." PhD dissertation, University of Toronto, 1995.

Singleton, Anna G. "Child Welfare Administration under Protection Acts in British Columbia: Its History and Development, 1901–1949." MSW dissertation, University of British Columbia, 1950.

Swidrovich, Cheryl Marlene. "Positive Experiences of First Nations Children in Non-Aboriginal Foster or Adoptive Care: De-Constructing the 'Sixties Scoop.'" MA dissertation, University of Saskatchewan, 2004.

Timpson, Joyce. "Four Decades of Child Welfare Services to Native Indians in Ontario: A Contemporary Attempt to Understand the 'Sixties Scoop' in Historical, Socioeconomic and Political Perspective." PhD dissertation, Wilfrid Laurier University, 1993.

Whiteford, Heather J. "Special Needs Adoption: Perspectives on Policy and Practice." MSW dissertation, University of British Columbia, 1988.

Films

Abomsawin, Alanis, director. *Richard Cardinal: Cry from a Diary of a Metis Child*. Ottawa: National Film Board of Canada, 1986.

Cardinal, Gil, director. *David with F.A.S.* Ottawa: National Film Board of Canada, 1997.

——, director. *Foster Child*. Ottawa: National Film Board of Canada, 1987.

Cazabon, Andrée, director. *Wards of the Crown*. Ottawa: National Film Board of Canada, 2005.

Hamilton, Sylvia D., director. *Black Mother, Black Daughter*. Ottawa: National Film Board of Canada, 1989.

Prieto, Claire, director. *Older, Stronger, Wiser*. Ottawa: National Film Board of Canada, 1989.

INDEX

Aboriginal children. *See* First Nations
abuse, 91–92, 96, 97–100, 108; of alcohol
and drugs, 132–33; battered and
shaken babies, 97–98, 176; child
sexual abuse, 98, 99, 130, 177; fetal
alcohol spectrum disorder (FASD),
98–99; fetal alcohol syndrome (FAS),
176; from foster parents, 149, 165;
increase in complaints, 99–100; in
institutions, 61, 105; from kin, 156;
uncertainty of findings, 99; witnessing
domestic violence, 99, 129, 130. *See
also* violence
adoption: breadwinner fathers expected,
82; cost-saving before benefit to child,
83; increased regulation, 81, 82; and
national values, 2, 81; often a good-
news story, 3, 80; preferred method
(1920s–60s), 66–67, 75, 80–83; shortages, 87–88
African Canadians, 20, 25, 30, 32,
119–20, 126, 129
age of children in care, 178
Akenson, Donald, 20
Alexandra Orphanage (Vancouver),
45–46
All Hallows Anglican School (BC), 36

Anderson, Doris, 28
Anne of Green Gables, 13
apprenticeship, 12, 20, 37, 41
Armitage, Andrew, 94
aunts, 18, 22, 25–27, 109, 155

baby farmers, 57–58
Bagley, Christopher, 98
Baillargeon, Denyse, 26
Baines, Carol T., 36, 69
Barnardo children, 116, 149, 178, 188,
193
Beck, Sharon, 145
Bedard Commission, 106
behaviour problems, 182–83
Berton, Frank, 46
best interest of child: belief emerging, 43,
100; family or child, 92; fostering
problems, 91–92; frequent failure to
promote, 202. *See also* rights of
children
Biedema, Baukje, 162
birth families. *See* first families
Black Mother, Black Daughter (film), 126
Bowlby, John, 61
Boyd, Susan C., 132
Bradbury, Bettina, 117, 146